A Landmark Study of CEOs from 28 Countries

GLOBAL LITERACIES

Lessons on Business Leadership and National Cultures

ROBERT ROSEN

PATRICIA DIGH, MARSHALL SINGER, and CARL PHILLIPS

SIMON & SCHUSTER

NEW YORK LONDON SYDNEY SINGAPORE

SIMON & SCHUSTER
Rockefeller Center
1230 Avenue of the Americas
New York, NY 10020

Manufactured in the United States of America

10 9 8 7 6 5 4 3 2 1

Library of Congress Cataloging-in-Publication Data

Global literacies : lessons on business leadership and national cultures : a landmark study of CEOs from 28 countries / Robert Rosen . . . [et al.].
p. cm.
Includes bibliographical references and index.
1. Chief executive officers. 2. Leadership.
I. Rosen, Robert, date.
HD38.2.G58 2000
658.4'092—dc21 99-054914

ISBN 0-684-85902-5

To leaders courageous enough to learn
from the rest of the world

CONTENTS

TO THE READER

As a psychologist and businessman, I have spent the last twenty years studying and advising executives and their organizations. I have written three books on leadership and, as CEO of Healthy Companies International, have consulted with dozens of Global 1000 corporations, governments, and entrepreneurial growth companies around the world. But when it came to writing *Global Literacies*, I needed help.

In 1997, I discovered that Watson Wyatt Worldwide, an international consulting firm, was interested in the same topic. So we created a joint project with unprecedented reach and scope. Our goal was simple: We would conduct a worldwide search for leaders who are globally literate and whose companies are winning in the global marketplace. We would go to them, on six continents, and sit face-to-face with them to hear their stories in their own words. Then we would tell their stories—and extract the lessons of global leadership. The results of this qualitative and quantitative study serve as the cornerstone for this book.

Global Literacies is a living example of collaborative individualism at work—four strong, independent people working together. I was truly blessed to work with three of the finest colleagues. Patricia Digh is a business analyst focused on emerging issues and was formerly vice president of international and diversity programs for the Society for Human Resource Management. Marshall Singer is professor emeritus of international and intercultural affairs at the University of Pittsburgh and a leading expert in intercultural management. Carl Phillips is one of the leading consultants in executive development and formerly worldwide director of organization effectiveness at Watson Wyatt Worldwide. Collectively, we have more than 120 years of work experience and have lived or worked in more than 120 countries.

As leaders in global business, each person brought something special to the table. But the real challenge was to tap our collective intelligence. We needed to learn how to express our wisdom, acknowledge our prejudices, and argue our points of view. Rest assured that each of us was sufficiently challenged along the way, and the book is better for it. With time, our thinking became strengthened and magnified by this unique partnership. We each walk away wiser for it.

We are all reflections of our past. Nowhere is this truer than writing and reading a book. Each of us sees through our own unique cultural lens. Ours is a North American lens, with a particular slant toward the United States. We come from a future-focused, short-term, action-oriented society in a culture of liberty and freedom. We are direct, verbal problem solvers committed to learning. This lens influences how we see the world. But not all people and countries see the world the way we do. Nor should they.

Some would argue that for the first time in modern history, the United States is the only world superpower. Its influence—military, political, economic, and cultural—is having a major impact on the nations of the world. Many are comfortable with the U.S. position; they aspire to be like us or like being taken care of. But there are others who resent American omnipresence—now more than ever—and have a very different definition of how a successful society should look. Undoubtedly, this will influence their reactions to this book.

In the United States, we are experiencing a renewed sense of national pride and success. Many believe that our booming free market economy is leading the world and our democratic government is a model for all. Despite these successes, our greatest danger is arrogance. If we are not careful we will become too smug and ethnocentric. We will overestimate our abilities and underestimate what we can learn from others. This too will influence how this book is read.

Any study attempting to characterize a given culture is complicated and risky. No one is simply a product of his or her culture, and we all justifiably resent being culturally typecast. Our examination of culture was undertaken with the specific goal of understanding the "commercial ethos" of a country—how business is conceived, organized, and conducted in different cultures. We know that this kind of understanding will be increasingly important in a marketplace in which each nation has the world at its borders.

As a team, we were commited to overcoming these blind spots as much as possible. We wanted to be objective, honest, and fair when writing about the world. That is why we spent so much time conducting research, visiting leaders in their home countries, contacting embassies, reading national publications, and questioning ourselves. You will be the best judge of whether we were successful.

As the lead author of this book, I am no stranger to business leadership. I had conducted a six-year research effort on American leadership and healthy organizations, funded by the John D. and Catherine T. MacArthur Foundation. In that project I looked for examples inside the United States, and wondered how U.S. principles would translate around the world and what lessons we could learn from other countries.

Global Literacies presents a fresh, dynamic approach to leading global business in the twenty-first century that is relevant to all leaders at all levels in all regions of the world. Told through the real-life stories of seventy-five

CEOs from twenty-eight countries and a survey of 1,200 executives worldwide, we hope the book will be useful to a wide international audience.

Our philosophy is a positive one. We focus on strengths and contributions: the leaders' best thinking, the companies' best practices, the countries' best contributions. While we believe that people learn best from positive stories that tell the truth, we also recognize that leaders, companies, and countries have shortcomings, prejudices, and blind spots. We simply want to learn from their best.

Inevitably, we make broad generalizations throughout the book, and there will always be exceptions to our statements. As we highlight these general differences, it is important to know that we have no desire to offend anyone. Our commitment is simply to present what we see and do so honestly.

We also want to acknowledge that at any point in time, the companies listed in this book may be performing well—or not so well—in the marketplace. This doesn't concern us too much. Inevitably, good companies go through both profitable and difficult periods. It is their sustaining lessons of leadership that matter.

Finally, let me share a few thoughts about my experience of traveling. Over a two-year period I visited thirty countries. I traveled 250,000 miles, equivalent to ten times around the globe. From the rain forests of Brazil to the Great Buddha of China, from the fjords of Norway to the cape of South Africa, from Sydney Harbor to the skyscrapers of New York City, I walked the streets and met the local people. When you travel to so many diverse cultures in such a concentrated period of time, you can't help but see the world's similarities and differences. The regions of the world, including the Americas, Europe, Asia and Australia, the Middle East, and Africa, are clearly coming together into one world humanity. Yet there are thousands of colorful threads that create the fabric of the richly diverse peoples of the world.

Along the way, I discovered what anthropologists have known for years: that when you travel, you learn as much about your own culture as you do about others. Today, I'm still a proud citizen of the United States. Yet something happened inside me. In a mysterious, almost unconscious way, I became a global citizen. And there's no turning back. I will forever be a citizen of the world.

I hope you enjoy the book.

R.R.

September 1999

PART ONE

THE SEARCH FOR GLOBAL COMPETITIVENESS

CHAPTER ONE

THE NEW BUSINESS REALITY

I STILL REMEMBER my first trip to Japan. Surrounded by the signs and sounds of Japanese, I felt utterly lost. Unable to decipher even the most basic information in restaurants and on city streets, I retreated into myself. It was hard to stretch into unfamiliar territory. When I asked questions, people reacted in ways I couldn't quite understand. I simply couldn't read their psychology.

In an instant, I understood what it means to be illiterate. Only when I got home, relieved to be back in the United States, did I fully recognize the personal cost of global illiteracy. Like adults who can't read, I had hidden the fact that I couldn't understand the verbal and nonverbal cues around me. Although intrigued by the differences, I spent a lot of energy protecting myself for fear of appearing foolish. I felt defensive, making it difficult to fully experience the world of Japan.

Being illiterate, even for that short period of time, taught me a lot about the power of literacy in our lives. Many of us take literacy for granted. We can't imagine—or remember—a world in which we were not able to read. But all of us were there at one time.

Watching a child learn to read is like witnessing a miraculous process unfold. A whole world suddenly opens up to him or her, enriching life beyond measure, adding depth and feeling to every experience.

We urge children to read at such an early age, and we worry when they don't proceed at the right pace. We do everything we can—buy them books, take them to libraries, show them flash cards—to ensure they master this new language, these strange, black hieroglyphics.

Once children have mastered basic words, we urge them toward greater complexity of ideas. One-syllable words give way to three-syllable ones, complex descriptions paint a picture richer than simple picture books, and dialogues become multilayered and more subtle.

But literacy doesn't matter just to children. In the new global world of business, we're all beginning readers. Like children, we must learn to read the world's new language by deciphering the handwriting, engaging in dialogues, and sharing ourselves in the process.

Literacy matters. And the worst thing for adults in the twenty-first century is being unable to read the world. Being able to read this emerging world allows us to witness an unfolding, an opening up of new possibilities. To fully participate in the global society, we need a common vocabulary, syntax, and grammar, and a rich base of knowledge. We need to move beyond comprehension of letters and language to a deeper understanding of ourselves, our customers, our markets, and the cultures of the world.

Global literacy is our new language for the twenty-first century.

The Twenty-first-Century Marketplace

We stand on a precipice, stepping into a new era, a time of enormous change and uncertainty characterized by the emergence of the first truly borderless, interconnected global economy. It's the world's youngest economy, fueled by the spread of free markets and democracy around the world.

Walls are crumbling among markets, organizations, and nations. People, information, labor, and capital move freely as never before. Global media, international travel, and communications have eroded distance and borders, linking us instantly to one another from Prague to Shanghai, from Lima to London. A tightly woven fabric of distant encounters and instant connections knits our diverse world together.

Ours is a unique place in history. Not since the Industrial Revolution have we faced such forces in two fundamental areas of world society: the electronic information revolution and global economic interdependence. This isn't just a change in degree, but a fundamental change in kind. Globalization is a new international system that is shaping domestic and international politics and changing the rules of trade. A dynamic and ongoing process, globalization involves the integration of markets and nation-states, enabling individuals, corporations, and countries to reach the world farther, faster, deeper, and cheaper.

We live in a networked, interconnected world with computer devices embedded in telephones, cars, televisions, and household appliances. The Internet and electronic commerce are dramatically changing how we do business. Our relationships with customers and suppliers have forever been altered, and employees have access to information never dreamed of ten years ago. Everyone is talking to everyone else in real time.

Add to that the fact that all business is global and all markets are local. World markets rise and fall together. Currency traders in Shanghai, Toronto, and London interact at a moment's notice. Global mergers and acquisitions have created megabusinesses with social and political ramifications we couldn't have planned for. The sheer number of competitors around the world continues to increase exponentially, and we're now racing to serve global customers, not just local ones.

In the twenty-first century, competition comes from all corners. Not only does the United States compete with Taiwan and Switzerland for jobs and customers, but businesses in Chicago must also compete locally with companies from Canada and Sweden.

Furthermore, businesses in various countries are infiltrating one another's territories as never before. For example, European firms own large portions of the American publishing industry, while the United States owns much of the Brazilian banking system. Japan owns a large portion of the world's automobile market, while Scandinavian companies provide a majority of the world's mobile telephones. India produces the world's tractors, France is the largest producer of glass, Chile is the leading supplier of copper, and China produces many of the world's apples.

Global brands bring us together, linking people in Cape Town to unlikely partners in the West Bank. Global consumerism has skyrocketed, creating a proliferation of global brands while homogenizing consumer tastes. People in the most remote regions of our world recognize the red Coke can, McDonald's golden arches, and the silver medallion of Mercedes-Benz.

International trade is burgeoning, as evidenced by explosions of foreign direct investment, export expansion, and the growth of multinational corporations. Globally connected capital markets are producing open, transparent exchanges where investment flows seamlessly among trading floors worldwide.

Even within companies, cubicles are disappearing in favor of virtual teams. Companies seek suppliers, customers, and employees globally. Sharing techniques among industries and across national borders, they develop network organizations that are fast, flat, flexible knowledge companies. Their corporate cultures are characterized by less bureaucracy, more teamwork, and infectious entrepreneurship. In this competitive marketplace of winners and losers, there is a race for brainpower, creating whole new knowledge-generating industries.

Government's role is also diminishing as the world moves from state control to market economies and the privatization of business. Increasing pluralism and democracy accelerate the creation of one global community with common interests and concerns.

But not all is good news and global harmony. New threats proliferate. Chemical and biological warfare, urban terrorism, and digital espionage represent only a portion of our global minefield. And threats of nationalism are lurking just under the surface.

Still, there's no turning back. These trends toward a truly integrated, borderless, global economy will continue and accelerate. The overarching

GLOBAL TRENDS

- **Globalizing Growth:** The globalization of companies and brands makes it difficult, if not impossible, to determine the "home country" of many corporations.
- **International Megamergers:** Global mergers create giant multinational corporations that are larger, richer, and more powerful than many countries.
- **Regional Economic Power:** Strong regional trade associations, such as the European Union, NAFTA, ASEAN, and Mercosur, will enhance geographic economic bases around the world.
- **Economic Interdependence:** Strong global monetary and regulatory agencies will be required to handle severe volatility in the international financial system.
- **Privatizing Power:** The privatization of state-run enterprises and the diminished economic decision-making power of nation-states will continue if there is no major worldwide depression.
- **Identity Problems:** In an increasingly interconnected world, people will be torn between being global cosmopolitans, regional traders, national cheerleaders, ethnic personalities, and local citizens.
- **American Backlash:** Defensiveness against ubiquitous American culture, democracy, military might, and free-market capitalism will counter the continuing strength of the United States as the primary world power.
- **European Integration:** The economic integration of Europe and its euro, with the seemingly inevitable political integration to follow, will further solidify that continent's influence on the world stage.
- **Asian Rebound:** The hardworking nature of Asians and their social and family networks, combined with their commitment to education, form a strong foundation for their economies to rebound—and sooner rather than later.
- **China, Inc.:** If China holds together as one nation and if its economic development continues, this will become the largest, most important market in the world.
- **Haves and Have-Nots:** The gap between the haves and have-nots, both within and among countries, will continue to widen unless more developed countries make a stronger commitment to wealth creation and wealth distribution in less developed nations.
- **Ethnic Conflicts:** The number and intensity of ethnic conflicts will increase worldwide, as will "terrorism" driven by these ethnic and religious differences.
- **Economics Versus Environmentalism:** As economic development expands globally, pollution and global warming will accelerate, creating political and economic conflicts in all countries, with all parties culpable.
- **Demographic Dilemmas:** The swelling population of young people in the developing world and the need to create jobs for them—combined with the growth of the elderly population in the developed world and the need to take care of them—will create economic and political challenges for all.

market in the twenty-first century *is* the global market, an interconnected and complex system we must understand. Globalization is the tidal wave—our worldwide tsunami—of the twenty-first century. As Peter Bonfield, CEO of British Telecommunications, put it, "I can't promise anyone a smooth ride over the next few years, but I think that's good news, because great turbulence also means great opportunities."

Traveling Around the World

To fully understand this new twenty-first century marketplace, we need to go out into the world and experience it.

This book will take you on such a journey through the world's major regions—Europe, the Americas, Asia, Africa, and beyond—each with its own unique personality, economy, and geography, and each with its own distinctive leaders.

North America is the land of shareholder capitalism, individualism, and economic triumph. Home of the primary world superpower, North America thrives on venture capital, Hollywood, and the technological revolution. The land of opportunity, the United States is also a nation of the middle class, yet with great disparities among social and economic classes and violence, drug use, and broken families. The North American Free Trade Agreement links the United States with both Canada, home of multiculturalism and tolerance, and Mexico, a nation of survivalists and relationship builders. With the economic convergence of "Euroland," North America will need to learn to function better as a partner, not a superpower.

North America is also home to Doug Ivester, CEO of the Coca-Cola Company. Ivester is a strong and restless leader who, like American frontiersmen before him, has a destination in mind. He is driven to create value, to communicate aggressively, and to teach others how to reach their goals.

Latin America is a region of paradox. Vulnerable to external shocks, like the recent global financial turmoil that began in Asia, this region also demonstrates a growing resilience and capacity for response. Home of capital flight, collapsing trade, and lower commodity prices, Latin America is also a land with a rich cultural and intellectual history and home of some of the world's greatest writers and artists. In an increasingly chaotic global environment, its trials by fire may prepare it best for what's ahead.

Gustavo Cisneros knows the strengths and shortcomings of this part of the world. A powerful media king, Cisneros and his Caracas-based Cisneros Group of Companies is committed to bringing the world to Latin America and bringing Latin America to the world. A man intent on creating networks of partners, Cisneros personifies the cultural norm of relationship building that defines Latin America.

Europe is a continent in transition, a land of unprecedented economic and political convergence. A culture of intellectualism and social responsibility, the European Union is just beginning to realize its aggregate power. With a healthy respect for tradition, Europe is also learning how to embrace the future. The cultural differences among Europeans have narrowed over the past few decades, though economic conditions in the EU nations vary widely. The role of business is also changing, becoming more focused on shareholder value than ever and driven in part by the fact that 35 percent of stock on the French stock exchange is foreign-owned; in Germany, 25 percent; in Spain, 35 percent; and in the Netherlands, 40 percent.

No one tracks these changes more closely than Helen Alexander, CEO of the Economist Group in Great Britain. Her job is to provide other business leaders with the latest global news and a point of view. *The Economist* is global to its bones, delivering the news with intellect and insight. "We teach international perspective and communicate context," she says. To do that, she must be able to move fluidly across the world's cultures herself.

Asia brings us traditions of diversity and collectivism. A region with an emerging middle class despite its economic crisis, it is shifting from being labor-intensive and agricultural to developing high-tech manufacturing and service-oriented economies. Asians value education, hard work, relationships, and collective mindsets. They are masters at understanding paradox and creating mutually dependent networks of customers, suppliers, and companies. Coping with the changing role of women and youth, Asian businesses are shifting from hierarchical to participative management and from seniority-based to performance-based reward systems.

At more than 80 years of age, Canon's honorary chairman, Ryuzaburo Kaku, exemplifies both the old and the new Asia. A visionary leader, Kaku works to ensure that the world's business leaders know about the concept of *kyosei*—living and working for the common good. It's a philosophy that allows Kaku to seek innovative ways for Canon to do good while making money, and to be a powerful force for social, political, and economic transformation.

This is just a taste of our journey around the world. Yet the idea of hopping from one region to another is itself antiquated. Even this viewpoint is changing as regions compete and cooperate, changing identities and personalities, developing new strengths and shortcomings, and bumping up against one another in a borderless, multicultural world.

The Borderless Economy in a Multicultural World

Beware. And be ready.

This new, borderless economy is changing faster than our ability to manage it. For companies to thrive, they must learn to excel in a multicul-

THE MOST INTERNATIONAL COMPANIES

Our survey of over 1,000 CEOs around the world shows:

International Customers

(Percentage of companies with customers in six or more countries)

- Europe: 83%
- Australia/New Zealand: 75%
- Asia: 68%
- Latin America: 62%
- North America: 57%

International Suppliers

(Percentage of companies with suppliers in six or more countries)

- Europe: 76%
- Australia/New Zealand: 75%
- Asia: 69%
- Latin America: 55%
- North America: 50%

International Employees

(Percentage of companies with employees in six or more countries)

- Europe: 67%
- Australia/New Zealand: 64%
- Asia: 56%
- North America: 43%
- Latin America: 33%

tural world. They must also learn how to cross the new invisible borders of national culture. But as Doug Ivester, CEO of Coca-Cola, discovered after the 1999 "Coke scare" in Belgium and France, it's easy to be fooled by the transparency of such borders: "As economic borders come down, cultural barriers go up, presenting new challenges and opportunities in business."

All this turbulence and confusion make us nervous and defensive. Our sensitivities are heightened as competitors and collaborators emerge from unlikely places. We may respond by pulling in, becoming more ethnocentric and nationalistic. There is a backlash to globalization, one born of our lack of knowledge and readiness and exacerbated by the economic pinches we feel. Not everyone is equipped to run fast, but some are—and they respond by opening up, soaking up cultural differences in order to maximize their own awareness and learning.

This porous economy will not bring an end to national history, politics, identity, and nationalism. In fact, the values and identities of culture are being challenged—and enhanced—as never before. We must leap at the opportunity to learn from our differences and leverage that learning for competitive advantage, rather than hide, ridicule, or ignore them.

The world is at once borderless, multicultural, and a burgeoning hybrid of cultures. Expanded tourism, the dissemination of pop culture, global migration, Internet communities—all these have led to unprecedented worldwide connectedness. Traditional boundaries between politics, culture, technology, finance, national security, and ecology are disappearing. There are ecological connections between the Hong Kong flu and the Chernobyl nuclear reactor disaster, political connections between NATO and the war in Kosovo, and economic connections such as those we saw played out during the Asian financial crisis. The media—TV, newspapers, and film—bring us closer to others simultaneously. Business leaders must be capitalists, psychologists, technologists, and culturalists: they must understand the seamless interaction of all these dimensions, the interconnectedness of which creates our twenty-first-century culture.

But this seeming dissolution of national borders triggers the "immune system," moving people and countries into self-protection mode, resulting in increased nationalistic fervor, higher import barriers, hostility to foreign control and ownership, clashes among countries and multinationals, and a backlash against American culture.

As Russia's economy crumbled, the Russians wanted to turn from their new free marketplace back to their old controlled economy. As Malaysia's economy faltered, the government closed its doors to foreign investment, believing that "outsider" money had held the country hostage. And the United States and Europe continue to have trade spats about bananas and beef while the world's DaimlerChryslers and Deutsche Banks create massive transglobal mergers.

As a result of these cultural clashes, we resent the "others," fearful of the jobs they'll take and the market share they'll gain. Economic collapse in Asia—once so far removed from us—has hit everyone's bottom line, and we have reverted to an "us-versus-them" mentality. People's raw selves surface more easily. And as chronically turbulent times become more commonplace, more, not fewer, cross-cultural barriers will confront us. How will we navigate?

We feel threatened and defensive for reasons both simple and complex: while our world has changed dramatically, our models of how to see, think, act, and mobilize in that world have not changed. Much of the world still thinks in absolute dichotomies—black/white, good/bad, win/lose, have/take—which leads us to this defensive posture against "difference."

Simply put, we don't have the mental software—the operating system—to fully grasp what our new world means. We're using old minds to grapple with new rules. But it's not just our mental models that aren't sufficient; we don't have the systems in place to deal with globalization, either.

HOW GLOBAL ARE YOU?

Whether a domestic or a global enterprise, every company is grappling with the same fundamental questions: Should we seek local or international customers, domestic or foreign employees, local or nonlocal suppliers, domestic or foreign investors? Not all companies should go global, but all need to be aware of best practices from around the world to be successful at home and abroad. There are five stages of globalization:

- **Domestic enterprises** operate solely in a domestic marketplace.
- **Exporters** produce primarily in the home country but sell in other countries as well.
- **International enterprises** conduct production and sales activities in the home country and abroad, but are managed primarily by the home-country headquarters.
- **Multinational enterprises** have production and sales operations in multiple countries that are operated as local entities.
- **Global enterprises** have production and sales operations in multiple countries coordinated as a large, integrated global entity.

Source: *Adapted from Terence Brake, Kim Sullivan, and Danielle Walker,* Doing Business Internationally: The Cross-Cultural Challenges *(Princeton, N.J.: Princeton Training Press, A Division of Training Management Corporation, 1992).*

Our survey of business executives reveals how global their companies are:

- Domestic: 25%
- Export: 13%
- International: 21%
- Multinational: 21%
- Global: 20%

Hesitant to pass judgment in an environment of political correctness, we try to ignore the fact that cultural differences exist, or we paint them as obstacles to overcome. Instead, they are resources we must learn from, opportunities we must exploit, and differences we must manage.

The New Global Assets

Companies used to live or die primarily by the availability of materials—steel, plastic, and pig iron—from which they manufactured their products. They were in the business of moving molecules: objects and manufactured goods. But now those commodities have changed somewhat. Steel has given way to brain cells, and we don't just move molecules anymore, we move knowledge. Because globalization and technology have leveled the playing field, and since we've reached a high level of sophistication in our systems and processes, our people provide our only remaining competitive advantage.

Companies such as Toyota, Vivendi, and Motorola understand this. They mobilize three key global assets: people, relationships, and culture. They work hard to develop cultures of "globally literate" leaders at all levels: leaders who develop their own potential and that of others, who cultivate collaborative relationships, and who manage their own culture and the cultures of others.

To understand how this focus evolved, it's important to look back at the management revolutions of the past twenty years. From quality and customer service in the 1980s through reengineering, renewal, and growth in the 1990s, we have witnessed a steady increase in the importance of people to the bottom line. Our new focus on global leadership and world-class companies is a natural outgrowth of these management revolutions. Driven by globalization, the integration of the soft and hard issues of business is becoming a twenty-first century leadership imperative.

- *People.* Increasingly, people are the new corporate resource. Businesses fight to attract, retain, develop, and motivate the best and brightest, seeking new ways to measure and enhance the value of their human capital. People's knowledge, skills, experience, and capabilities are seen as the new corporate assets. And as the value of people becomes more obvious, companies create organizational practices, processes, and systems that leverage human capital to create value for their customers.
- *Relationships.* People work not in isolation but in close interaction with others, both inside and outside their companies. Companies must cultivate strong, healthy internal and external relationships to enhance value through teams, networks, suppliers, and even alliances and joint ventures with competitors. In some cases, virtual teams work together indefinitely without meeting, linked by technology that erases boundaries of time and place.
- *Culture.* The third key asset is cultural wisdom—our deep understanding of our own culture and those of others—which enables companies to mobilize diverse peoples, serve diverse customers, and operate around the world.

These three assets are inextricably linked. Each is indelibly influenced by the electronic technology revolution and global interdependence. And when they are mobilized, they create value and wealth for the organization. "It's one thing to be successful in the borderless economy, it's another thing altogether to thrive in a multicultural world," says Daniel Vasella, chairman and CEO of Switzerland-based Novartis, one of the world's leading pharmaceutical companies. Leaders who leverage employees' intellectual capital, collaborative relationships, and cultures will thrive in the new millennium.

A New Approach to Leadership

"Leadership is taking an organization to a place it could not have otherwise gone and doing it in a way that gives people a sense of optimism and confidence in the future." George Fisher, retired CEO of Kodak, in the United States, knows that the next century's challenges will be human ones.

By making the most of their global assets today, world-class companies such as Kodak are positioning themselves to be the business leaders of the twenty-first century. All of this requires a new approach to leadership.

Yet we're in a leadership dilemma. We need global leaders at a time when markets and companies are changing faster than the ability of leaders to reinvent themselves. We have a shortage of global leaders at a time when international exposure and experience are vital to business success. And we need internationally minded, globally literate leaders at a time when leadership styles are in transition around the world.

Good leadership is a major catalyst for growth; bad leadership can be the primary cause of business failure. Leading people through change is leaders' most important challenge; overcoming resistance to that change is the toughest obstacle of all. Culture and traditions are our greatest roadblocks. To maneuver around them, we need a new cadre of globally literate leaders who understand both themselves and others. We need leaders who are comfortable working across and around the many cultural barriers that threaten to divide us.

The world of today's leaders is full of paradoxes and contradictions. Leaders negotiate through minefields every day: balancing the needs of stakeholders, choosing between cutting costs and developing people, managing in both the short and long term, deciding whether to centralize or decentralize operations, and simultaneously leading global and local lives.

Leaders are kept awake at night by hard business realities: the need to generate profitable growth, reach markets quickly, protect their reputation, and anticipate the unexpected.

But their deeper sleeplessness comes from the human challenges: How can they acquire and retain the best talent to lead their companies through change? How can they promote teamwork across boundaries and borders? How can they develop executives to lead in the world? "Our scarcest resource is globally literate leaders," warns Alfred Zeien, chairman and CEO of Gillette, one of the United States' most global companies.

So who are these new, globally literate leaders? They include people such as Ogilvy & Mather CEO Shelly Lazarus in the United States, Toyota CEO Hiroshi Okuda in Japan, China Resources CEO Madame Zhu Youlan in Hong Kong; and British Telecommunications CEO Sir Peter Bonfield in London. Singapore Airlines CEO Cheong Choong Kong and Ericsson chairman Lars Ramqvist in Sweden are also globally literate.

These men and women have spent their lives operating in the global business environment. They are exemplars of the kind of leaders we will need in the twenty-first century. Emotionally intelligent and business-savvy, they apply their cultural wisdom to teach the world about the import of global literacy. They see the world through a new lens and build new kinds of companies. Because they value the power of human assets, they work hard to create environments that liberate people's passions and unleash their talents. Building a globally literate workforce is their key to world-class excellence.

A Landmark Study of CEOs

Global Literacies is based on a landmark four-year study of global leadership and world-class companies.

Our objective was to create a fresh, practical, and teachable framework that could be used by business leaders throughout the world. By identifying common characteristics of leading CEOs and their world-class companies, and by defining the factors most likely to predict business success, we wanted to demonstrate how leaders must think, act, and mobilize people to succeed in the twenty-first century.

Our three-part strategy included face-to-face CEO interviews, a global CEO survey, and research into national cultures around the world. And we went straight to the source: the CEOs themselves.

We first met with seventy-five leading CEOs of multinational companies from twenty-eight countries. Through in-depth, face-to-face interviews coupled with extensive corporate background research, we explored the origins, character, and effectiveness of business leadership. We also sought to understand how national culture influences leadership and corporate competitiveness. We asked: How are you leading in the global environment? What kinds of business challenges are you facing? What is your leadership philosophy? How are you building a world-class company? How are you developing a culture of leaders? And what are the unique contributions that your country makes to our understanding of global leadership? Their answers shed new light on the universal qualities of leadership and how leadership varies around the world.

Part two was designed to reach well beyond these interviews. We conducted a quantitative survey of more than a thousand CEOs in eighteen countries. As you will see later in the book, we created a "Global Quotient" based on these survey findings to assess how well prepared CEOs from different countries are for these new, global challenges.

Finally, fascinated by the role of national culture, we conducted a series of in-depth studies of national cultures, examining the impact of history, ge-

About the Leaders

- Number of CEOs interviewed: 75
- Number of countries represented: 28
- Total annual sales: US$725 billion
- Total number of employees: 3.5 million
- Total number of countries with company operations: 200

About the Survey

- There were 1058 respondents in 18 countries.
- The respondents were CEOs, presidents, managing directors, or chairmen.
- The average number of employees per company was 24,748.
- Respondents had been an average of 15 years in their current organization. .
- Respondents had been an average of 6.4 years in their current position.
- 60% of respondents had been promoted from within.
- 85% of companies had been in existence more than 20 years.
- 83% of respondents were natives of the country where they are based.
- 19% of their company boards of directors are noncitizens of the company's home country.
- The respondents spoke an average of two languages.
- 65% of the companies have customers in 6 or more countries
- 58% of the companies have suppliers in 6 or more countries
- 48% of the companies have employees in 6 or more countries

ography, economics, politics, and culture on leadership and business success in twenty-eight countries.

This three-part strategy—qualitative interviews, quantitative surveys, and country research—enabled us to produce an intellectually well grounded, real-world picture of leadership in the twenty-first century. Our list of global literacies emerged from our listening to people around the world.

How to Read This Book

"Jet-setters" aren't the only ones with international portfolios anymore. Whether you're in the executive suite of a Global 1000 corporation, seeking career advancement in a government agency, or answering phones in the customer service center of a nonprofit organization, you're faced with a barrage of global issues every day.

All of us, not just CEOs, are citizens of and traders in the global economy. When we get up in the morning, we may brew coffee in a pot from Germany, shave with a razor made in Taiwan, eat butter shipped from New Zealand, and drive a car made in Japan. While images of the conflict in Kosovo invade our living rooms at night, we may be eating a Chinese dinner with chopsticks made in Mexico. We e-mail friends and associates in Israel on computers made in Malaysia.

Global Literacies provides a new approach to leadership to help you navigate this world terrain. It's written for all people at all levels in all regions of the world. It outlines a new language for mobilizing people in a globalized world, even if we never leave our home country. And it centers on the lessons we can learn from the stories of extraordinary leaders and their national cultures to be globally literate ourselves.

This isn't a book about cross-cultural etiquette. It's not an encyclopedia of facts and figures. We don't describe theory or unattainable ideals. Nor is it a book of quick fixes.

Rather, *Global Literacies* is a blueprint for learning. As with learning the rules of grammar learning these literacies is not the same as being able to speak or sing, but with time and practice, doing so will make for fluent leading. That's why we call them "global literacies."

This book will show you how to survive and thrive in the borderless, multicultural marketplace. You'll learn how to develop your own global leadership philosophy and turn that philosophy into leadership practice by hardwiring your organization with the beliefs and behaviors necessary for success.

By learning about lessons and innovations from around the world, you'll also learn more about your own culture—and how both your own culture and those of others influence the way you do business. By successfully traversing the new invisible borders of culture, we'll help you use culture as a tool for competitive advantage. Whether you work for a multinational in Germany, a regional supermarket in Japan, or a local bank in the United States, every leader must become globally literate to compete at home and abroad.

The book is organized into four parts:

Part I: The Search for Global Competitiveness

Today's leaders are bombarded with the complexity of our borderless, multicultural world. Part I will uncover the new global assets of successful business—people, relationships, and culture—and show why we need global leadership to make sense of this new world. We'll explore the universals for twenty-first-century business: the world drivers, national realities, business questions, and leadership literacies critical for success in business.

Part II: The Four Global Literacies

What's needed in this new, increasingly complex world is a new language of global business, a language where leaders see the world's business challenges as opportunities, think with an international mindset, act with fresh global-centric leadership behaviors, and mobilize world-class companies. The four global literacies outlined in Part II will explain the new language that leaders must learn to speak and understand:

Personal literacy: Understanding and valuing yourself

Social literacy: Engaging and challenging others

Business literacy: Focusing and mobilizing your organization

Cultural literacy: Valuing and leveraging cultural difference

Through profiles of CEOs and their world-class companies, we'll see clearly what these literacies require and how they apply to business situations.

Part III: The Global Literacies at Work

Theory is one thing; practice is another. The bottom line is that the four global literacies must be implemented inside your own company. These literacies help you solve the five universal business questions that all organizations, regardless of industry, size, or country must answer:

Purpose: Where are we going?

Plan: How do we get there?

Networks: How do we work together?

Tools: What resources do we need?

Results: How do we measure success?

The CEOs themselves will be your guide through each of these questions. Through their stories, you'll get real-life examples of how leaders and their businesses are answering these universal questions in culturally unique ways.

Part IV: Becoming a Globally Literate Leader

To become a globally literate leader, you'll have to accept the challenge and plot your own learning plan for literacy. Like learning a foreign language, this takes continual, daily practice and dialogue with others who are fluent in the same language. We'll close with your leadership challenge for global literacy.

THE GLOBAL LEADERS INTERVIEWED, AND THEIR WORLD-CLASS COMPANIES

Face-to-face interviews conducted in their home countries

Australia
Dennis Eck, Managing Director and CEO, Coles Myer Ltd.
E. T. "Ted" Kunkel, President and CEO, Foster's Brewing Group
John McFarlane, CEO, Australia and New Zealand Banking Group

Bangladesh
Muhammad Yunus, Founder and Managing Director, Grameen Bank

Belgium
Baron Philippe Bodson, CEO, Tractebel

Brazil
Paulo Cunha, Chairman and CEO, Ultrapar Participações
Luiz Kaufmann, Former President, Aracruz Celulose, SA

Canada
Robert Atkinson, Chairman and CEO, Lumonics
James Stanford, President and CEO, Petro-Canada

Chile
Guillermo Luksic, CEO, The Luksic Group

China
Peter Ma, President and CEO, Ping An Insurance Company
Manuel V. Pangilinan, Managing Director, First Pacific Company
Blair Pickerell, President, Jardine Pacific
Zhu Youlan, CEO, China Resources

Denmark
Mads Øvlisen, President and CEO, Novo Nordisk A/S

France
Jean-Louis Beffa, President and Director-General, Isover Saint-Gobain
Jean-Marie Messier, Chairman and CEO, Vivendi
Anne-Marie Taittinger-Bonnemaison, Chairman and CEO, Société du Louvre

Germany
Rolf-Ernst Breuer, Chairman, Deutsche Bank AG
Friedrich Schock, Chairman, Schock Holdings
Frank Straub, President, Blanco GmbH

India
Keshub Mahindra, Chairman, Mahindra & Mahindra, Ltd.
Kumar Mangalan Birla, CEO and Group Chairman, The Birla Group

Indonesia
Suyanto Gondokusumo, Chairman and Director, Dharmala Sakti Sejantera, PT

Italy
Guglielmo Moscato, Chairman, ENI S.p.A.
Francesco Trapani, CEO, Bulgari S.p.A.

Japan
Ryuzaburo Kaku, Honorary Chairman of the Board, Canon
Nobuyuki Masuda, CEO, Mitsubishi Heavy Industries
Hiroshi Okuda, President, Toyota Motor Corporation

Netherlands
Aad Jacobs, Chairman, retired, ING Groep N.V.
Leo van Wijk, President and CEO, KLM Royal Dutch Airlines

New Zealand
Warren Larsen, CEO, The New Zealand Dairy Board

Philippines
Andres Soriano III, Former Chairman and CEO, San Miguel Corporation

Singapore
Cheong Choong Kong, Deputy Chairman and CEO, Singapore Airlines

South Africa
Warren Clewlow, Managing Director, Barlow Rand Ltd.
Graham Mackay, Managing Director, South African Breweries
Eric Molobi, CEO, Kagiso Investment Trust

South Korea
Lee Kun-Hee, Chairman, Samsung Electronics

Sweden
Lars-Eric Petersson, President and CEO, Skandia Insurance
Lars Ramqvist, Chairman and CEO, LM Ericsson
Michael Treschow, President and CEO, AB Electrolux

Switzerland
Daniel Vasella, President and CEO, Novartis AG

Taiwan
Stan Shih, CEO, Acer Group

Turkey
Sakip Sabanci, Chairman, Sabanci Holdings

United Kingdom
Helen Alexander, Managing Director, The Economist Group
Sir Peter Bonfield, CEO, British Telecommunications
John Donaldson, Managing Director, The Thomas Cook Group

United States
Ray Anderson, Chairman and CEO, Interface, Inc.
Juergen Bartels, Chairman and CEO, Westin Hotels & Resorts
Philip Condit, Chairman and CEO, Boeing Company
Amy DiGeso, Former President and CEO, Mary Kay Cosmetics
George M.C. Fisher, Chairman and CEO (retired), The Eastman Kodak Company
Robert W. Galvin, Chairman of the Executive Committee, Motorola, Inc.
Mary Kay Haben, Executive Vice President, Kraft Foods International
John Hendricks, CEO, Discovery Communications, Inc.
M. Douglas Ivester, Chairman and CEO, The Coca-Cola Company
Robert H. Jenkins, CEO and Chairman, Sundstrand Corporation
Shelly Lazarus, CEO, Ogilvy & Mather Worldwide
Dana G. Mead, Chairman and CEO, Tenneco, Inc.
Alfred M. Zeien, Chairman and CEO (retired), The Gillette Company

Venezuela
Gustavo A. Cisneros, Chairman and CEO, The Cisneros Group of Companies

CHAPTER TWO

THE CULTURES OF TWENTY-FIRST-CENTURY BUSINESS

TODAY, 90 PERCENT OF THE INFORMATION collected by companies is about what's going on *inside* the business. That's changing, and quickly. In the future, companies will require essentially new information about the *outside* world: customers, markets, technologies, competitors, and national cultures. As Peter Drucker warns, "Tomorrow's business challenges are less technical than they are cultural. Culture must be managed just like any other business phenomenon."

This rich context in which companies find themselves is complex. Understanding requires us to think on multiple levels simultaneously, sometimes holding conflicting thoughts and facts in our heads at the same time. Leading in this external world and across these cultures will become the most critical skill as we move into the twenty-first century.

Why is culture so important in a borderless world? Shouldn't it matter less, not more?

Hardly. As our national borders dissolve, we assert our cultural ones more fiercely. Every night as we watch the evening news, we witness cultures bouncing up against one another: Croats versus Serbs, accountants versus marketers, Gen Xers versus baby boomers, blacks versus whites, natives versus immigrants, the European Union versus NAFTA, Mac versus PC.

Technology links cultures instantaneously, creating astounding transparency and opportunities for connection and collaboration—or for conflicts and misunderstandings. We meet one another with considerable baggage from our own cultural programming, much of it unchecked and unrealized.

Culture has invisible borders, so porous that we sometimes don't even know we're crossing them. Culture is the context in which we live, the windows through which we experience the world: our attitudes (judgments about people, places, and cultures), our values (desires, wants, and needs), and our identities (who we are and who they are). All are part of the many layers of culture, whether national, linguistic, corporate, ethnic, racial, or individual.

As the underlying foundation that frames reality for people, culture defines acceptable and unacceptable behaviors, influencing our biases and prejudices. It's so much a part of our lives that it's difficult to step back far enough to see it clearly; in fact, it's far easier to read—or misread—another culture from a distance.

Culture roots and anchors us; it identifies and locates us in the world, providing what Thomas Friedman, author of *The Lexus and the Olive Tree*, calls our "olive tree," or sense of belonging. Yet, we strive toward improvement and prosperity—the "Lexus" in Friedman's equation—and we must find a healthy balance between preserving our sense of identity and doing what it takes to survive and thrive within a globalized system. If participation comes at the price of our identity and culture, we rebel.

While we hear a lot about cultural difference, in fact we're as much alike as we are different. Our global world abounds with universals—common human desires, business challenges, and national realities—that link people, organizations, and nations into one humanity.

Yet while we are the same, each of us is motivated differently; each company has its own challenges, and each country grapples with its own worldview. What is similar and different among us, how those similarities and differences influence business performance, and how we can learn from and leverage them are the heart of this book.

To use these differences, we must learn to read culture, like looking below the surface of an iceberg to see the deposits of experiences and history. And we must not underestimate its influence.

Tomorrow's leaders strive to be culturally wise. They appreciate similarities and differences between people, companies, and countries, and they know well that superficial understanding has tremendous negative impact on business. They understand the impact of culture on management strategy and style, and they know how to bring diverse people from different cultures together.

They ask questions such as:

- What leadership qualities and business practices are fundamental to my own national culture?
- How can I create business cultures that mobilize diverse people in a multicultural world?
- How do businesses in different countries operate in culturally unique ways?
- What are the lessons and innovations to be learned around the world?

To these leaders, three points are critical. First is the importance of context: understanding the external business environment and all its ramifications. Second is understanding culture at many different levels: the worldview, the national perspective, the business environment, and the eye of the leader. And last is understanding that each culture has two levels of analysis: what is universal to all people, businesses, and countries, and what is unique to each. Understanding universals and uniquenesses is a core competency for the globally literate leader.

The Layers of Culture

In our jobs, each of us is dealt a deck of cards that we must leverage for competitive advantage. To help you understand the hand you're dealt, our twenty-first-century model of culture introduces you to the four levels of culture: world culture, national culture, business culture, and leadership culture (see Figure 1). All four cultures are vital, each interacting with the others—and we must learn from all of them to play our hand.

Figure 1. The Cultures Of Twenty-first-Century Business

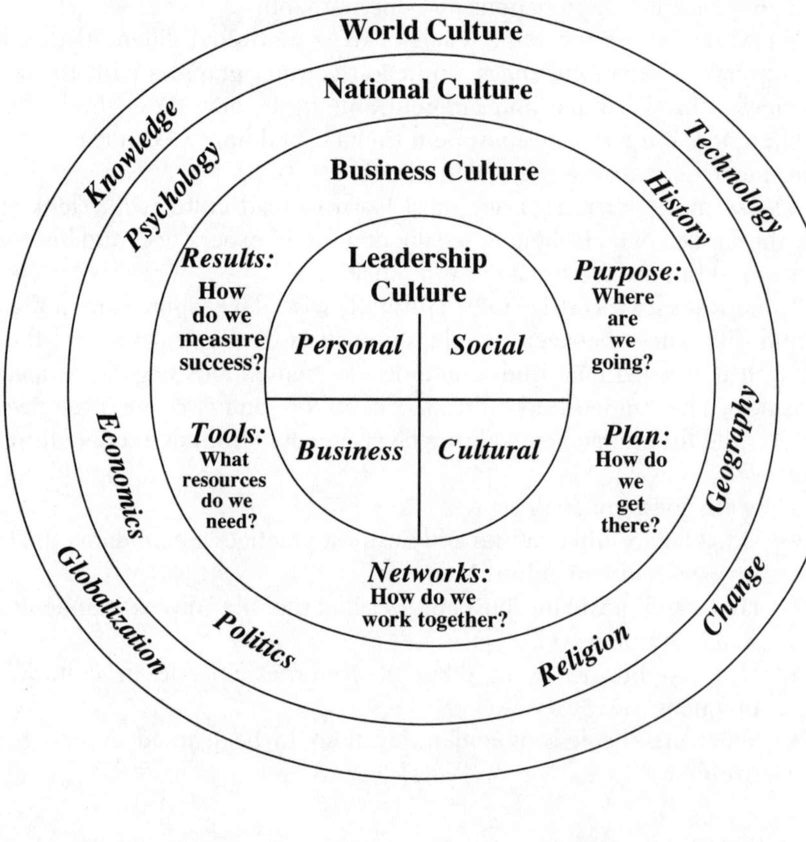

The leaders whose stories you will read understand that all four layers of culture matter. They use these cultures like any other business asset, as tools for business success, turning them into strengths instead of liabilities.

Over the next several pages, we will introduce you to each of the four layers of culture, showing their component parts and the intricate interplay among them.

World Culture

World culture sets the stage for doing business in the twenty-first century. Shaped by four dynamic forces—knowledge, technology, change, and globalization—world culture influences us, regardless of our country, industry, or size of business.

The Knowledge Explosion

We are inundated with information, almost buried by the weight of it, struggling to decipher what's important. We're creating whole new industries just to manage information—and to distill knowledge from it. The proliferation and access to information—through satellites, the Internet, and cable television—create lower barriers to entry and faster speed to market. Corporate balance sheets are being fundamentally re-created to account for a whole new asset: the brains of the people in our companies. This knowledge explosion requires a new kind of understanding grounded in transparency and authenticity. Consider the following facts:

- More information was produced in the last thirty years than in the previous five thousand years; our information supply doubles every five years.
- Annually, more than 50,000 books are published in the United States alone, and 400,000 journals are published globally, reports *The Washington Post.*
- *Time* magazine reports that three quarters of the world's mail is currently written in English, as is 80 percent of e-mail.
- According to the U.S. Department of Labor, at least 44 percent of all workers are in data services—gathering, processing, retrieving, or analyzing information.

The Technology Revolution

Technology is connecting us in ways we could hardly imagine just ten years ago. Networks of technology enable increasing numbers of people to reach farther and faster, exchanging information, knowledge, and money like never before. With the World Wide Web, it's a revolution that demands new kinds of relationships driven by speed and collaboration. Consider these statistics:

- Dataquest reports that by the end of 2001, approximately 268 million personal computers will be connected to one another.
- *Business Week* notes that it took radio more than thirty years to reach 60 million people and television 15 years to reach the same number. It has taken just three years for the Internet to reach more than 90 million people.
- The cost of computing power drops roughly 30 percent each year, and microchips are doubling in performance power every eighteen months.
- Forrester Research reports that business-to-business transactions over the Internet among U.S. businesses will grow to $326 billion in 2002.

Unrelenting Change

The pace of change—hardly discernible in the past—has turned from a glacier into an avalanche. We are forced into new and sometimes frightening levels of chaos and ambiguity. Our organizations are merging and altering form so quickly that we race to keep up. The only preparation we have is the knowledge that what we know will constantly change. Consider these facts:

- *The Economist* reports that from 1990 to 1998, the number of merger and acquisition deals worldwide increased from 11,300 to 26,200, bumping corporate and national cultures up against one another with increasing rapidity.
- More than 20,000 strategic alliances have been formed within the last two years alone, notes *Foreign Policy.*
- In 1940, there were only 75 independent countries in the world; today there are 176.
- In 1977, a secure telex from a bank in New York to one in Hong Kong cost $15. Now it costs about 30 cents, according to *Business Week.*

Irreversible Globalization

Driven by knowledge, technology, and change, the world is linked in new ways; even the corner store has gone global. We have to develop new ways of thinking and acting globally and locally simultaneously. Globalization has driven multiculturalism, and our national and regional cultures are connecting as never before. Consider these facts:

- In 1999, the world's business giants expect to spend a record $440 billion expanding their overseas operations, says a report by the U.N. Conference on Trade and Development.
- The *National Post* reports that more than US$1.5 trillion moves around the world every day in foreign exchange markets.
- In the previous decade, the number of non-U.S. listings on the U.S. Stock Exchange increased by 300 percent, according to a World Economic Forum study.
- Standard and Poor's notes that, by 2005, world exports of goods and services will reach $11.4 trillion, or 28 percent of world gross domestic product, nearly double 1998's $6.5 trillion.
- International joint ventures have grown 25 percent in the last five years alone.
- In 1955, 75 of the 100 largest industrial businesses in the world were American; by 1996, that number had dropped to 24. Only eight U.S. industrials are likely to be in the top 100 by the year 2037, says the *Harvard Business Review.*
- According to a recent Deloitte & Touche study of 1,600 institutional investors, the proportion of total U.S. pension fund assets invested in international equities rose from 6.4 percent in 1993 to 10.7 percent ($431 billion) in 1997 and is expected to surpass 12 percent ($611 billion) by 2000.

Everyone is grappling with these universal drivers. But each of us experiences them through our own lens, interpreting and managing them differently from Sweden to Bangladesh, from Ericsson to Grameen Bank, and from Lars Ramqvist to Muhammad Yunus.

We're not just *reacting* to these drivers, we're *interacting* with them. They are actually changing people, companies, and countries, with positive and negative consequences. They are creating an entirely new level of complexity for leaders. To fully understand world culture, we must see it in relation to the other three layers of culture—national, business, and leadership.

National Cultures

The world may be global, but our lives are local.

While we increasingly live as global citizens, our respective journeys must originate somewhere. We have a passport—and a mindset—that shows our starting point.

Understanding national culture will be critical. To be successful, we must understand history, geography, economics, politics, religion, and psychology. From its inception, management science was created to link these disciplines and help us manage our organizations more effectively. In the new marketplace, globally literate leaders must rely on these disciplines once again. But this time, they use them to understand the national dynamics of local markets around the world.

Nations are both builders and sustainers of culture. Each nation enters the global marketplace with its own cultural mindset—its own political and economic history, national interests, and everyday realities. Each country has both good and bad aspects; each has its own strengths and shortcomings. Because of this, they differ dramatically in how they see the world.

Yet every country grapples with the same universal concerns: achieving economic success, protecting national security, celebrating customs, and promoting the quality of life for its citizens. Each responds to these concerns in its own way.

History

Historian Arthur Schlesinger has said, "The only antidote to a shallow knowledge of history is a deeper knowledge, the knowledge which produces not dogmatic certitude, but diagnostic skill, not clairvoyance, but insight."

History matters. Wars, social movements, empires, heroes, and catastrophes—all these bits and pieces of any nation's history aren't just fodder for textbooks but part of each country's living world. History influences all nations, all citizenries, and the industries, companies, and leaders that arise within them.

Globally literate leaders know this.

They know they cannot understand Japanese business today without understanding its history of farming and isolation. They can't understand the splintering of Germany's enormous industries unless they understand the role of those industries in World War II. They know that being aware of the sea trading and invasions that shaped the Netherlands will help them understand the Dutch today. And the 4,500-year difference in age between the United States and China helps explain some of the challenges those two nations face in their complex relationship.

In affecting the culture and people of a country, history also influences the cultures of its industries and companies. But history need not be a straitjacket. For example, Deutsche Bank has acknowledged its part in the dark days of Auschwitz and has used that knowledge to learn about its past and move on.

Geography

Tall mountains and wide oceans no longer slow us down, let alone separate us. As a result, we tend to minimize or underestimate the impact of geography even as it continues to shape our national cultures. Every nation's land, water, neighbors, topography, size, natural resources, and climate are integral to the character of its culture, industries, countries, and leaders.

New Zealand is a small island nation. Despite its isolation in the middle of the Pacific Ocean, it has finely developed its international skills—it had to in order to survive. The Swedes are leaders in measuring intellectual capital because its people are Sweden's foremost natural resource. Brazil and Indonesia are very successful paper and pulp producers because of a natural advantage: trees grow three times faster in their warm climates than elsewhere in the world.

For some nations, a wealth of natural resources has proved to be a disadvantage. For example, most American businesses failed to think globally for the first half of the twentieth century because they operated in a nation that spanned a full continent and enjoyed an extraordinary wealth of natural resources and a large and relatively affluent population. Thus a wealth of domestic opportunities isolated the United States from the rest of the world. On the other hand, the small size of Switzerland, Denmark, and Singapore forced these countries to think internationally—it was their only hope for survival, let alone growth. They became world-renowned traders as a result.

Religion

Religion influences the values of people in a culture. Over time, it becomes part of the relationships and institutions of that culture. An integral part of the world, religion leads many of the crucial developments in human history and guides how people live their lives.

Here is a list of the world's major religions. These admittedly superficial descriptions don't capture their rich heritage and doctrine, nor do they reflect the divergent practices and beliefs within each. Yet we offer them as a starting point for understanding this important facet of national culture:

HINDUISM. Founded in India, Hinduism is based on the world's oldest religious text, the Rig-Veda. With many different sects and practices, it is the third most widely practiced religion in the world today. Hinduism encourages the practice of the Seven Duties (honesty, courage, service, faith, self-control, purity, and nonviolence); respect for all since everything is considered sacred; and development of one's internal power through yoga and meditation. Hinduism inspires leaders to serve everyone by embracing these practices in their daily lives.

BUDDHISM. Siddhartha Gautama ("Buddha") lived in northern India and founded Buddhism. Practiced by many sects throughout Asia, it is also becoming popular in the West. The beliefs of Buddhism are centered on the Four Noble Truths: that life is suffering; that suffering is caused by desire; that desires can be broken; and that the way to break the chain is by following the Eightfold Path to Nirvana through training in concentration and meditation. Buddhism serves as a model for leaders to be democratic in their relationships.

CONFUCIANISM. Confucianism is a doctrine of beliefs, morals, and behaviors founded on the teachings of Confucius, one of China's most influential thinkers. Confucius combined a theory of human nature with a political theory to produce a specific doctrine *(dao)* on how to act in the world. As a religion and philosophy, it is practiced today mainly in China, but also in Japan, Korea, and other parts of Asia. Practices of Confucianism include respecting ancestors and elderly citizens, meditating, and treating all people with respect.

TAOISM. Taoism is a religion and philosophy based on the teachings of Lao-tzu, who lived in China in the sixth century B.C.E. Taoism is practiced today in China, Japan, and other parts of Asia. The central tenets of Taoism are: that there is a Oneness *(tao)* that underlies the universe; that everything is related and part of everything else; and that happiness is achieved by allowing the *tao* to flow freely, without human intervention. The goal of man is to achieve a combination of suppleness, simplicity, and freedom by "being" rather than "doing." The Taoist leader leads in such a way that no one knows he's leading.

JUDAISM. Judaism is the oldest Western religion, based on the Old Testament of the Hebrew Bible. Its followers are primarily in Israel and the United States. Its central beliefs include: that there is one God who is the creator and ruler of the universe; that God is a caring and just God who created humans and gave them the ability to choose between good and evil; and that God has provided a divine law, the Torah. Judaism's contributions have included a passion for learning and meaning; the importance of suffering in learning life's lessons; and hope as a central way of dealing with challenge.

CHRISTIANITY. Christianity is founded on the life of Jesus, whose teachings are presented in the New Testament of the Holy Bible. The largest and most widely practiced religion in the world, its principal beliefs are: that there is one God consisting of three divinities; that Jesus was God incarnated in human form when he lived on Earth; that man is born with original sin; and that man can redeem himself and achieve life after death. Christianity emphasizes the spiritual connectedness of all things; faith and hope; love and fairness toward one's fellowman; and spreading one's beliefs around the world.

ISLAM. Islam is the second largest religion in the world, with followers mainly in the Middle East, Central and Southeast Asia, and Africa. It was founded on the life and teachings of Mohammed, the principal prophet of Allah, which are revealed in the Koran. Its principal beliefs and practices include: belief in one God and practice of the Five Pillars: confessing one's faith in God, praying daily, giving alms to the needy, observing Ramadan with fasting, and making at least one pilgrimage to Mecca during one's lifetime. Islam emphasizes strict discipline, the realization of one's potential, respect for others, and the equality of all races.

IS PERSONAL LEADERSHIP RELATED TO FAITH?

Countries whose leaders attribute personal leadership to religious and spiritual beliefs:

- *Most:* Japan, United States, China
- *Least:* Hong Kong, Sweden, South Korea

Economics

Obviously, business leaders need to know about the economic conditions of the world. The interconnectedness of our national economies is what will be different in the twenty-first century. All leaders must be students in global economics. By making the private sector the primary engine of economic growth, privatizing industry, and deregulating markets and economies, we've grown economies and shrunk politics around the world.

According to the World Economic Forum, international competitiveness is the ability of a nation's economy to make rapid and sustained gains in living standards. They rate national economies according to eight quantitative and qualitative factors of competitiveness:

- *Openness:* Is the economy open to international trade and finance?
- *Finance:* How well developed are the financial markets?
- *Technology:* What is the quality of the technological infrastructure?
- *Labor:* Is the labor market efficient and flexible?
- *Government:* What is the level of government regulation of the economy?
- *Infrastructure:* What is the quality of the physical infrastructure (e.g., transportation and utilities)?
- *Management:* Is the business management trained in modern techniques?
- *Institutions:* How impartial and stable are the judicial and political institutions?

Every country has a set of both assets and liabilities, such as the rich agribusiness and high unemployment of Argentina or the sophisticated financial sector and high business tax rates of Australia. Brazil's assets are its

THE ECONOMIC MINDSET OF COUNTRIES

As countries expand their trading in the global marketplace, we begin to see commonalities among them. New configurations arise that go beyond national identity and regional interest. Below is a list of countries grouped by these new "economic mindsets":

- **Entrepôt:** Small, open economies that specialize in providing trade and financial services to the rest of the world, such as Hong Kong, Luxembourg, Singapore, and Switzerland
- **Anglo-Saxon:** Ireland, the United Kingdom, Australia, Canada, New Zealand, and the United States
- **European Union:** The continental western European countries, except for Luxembourg, Switzerland, Norway, and some small principalities
- **Asian manufacturing:** China, Indonesia, Japan, Korea, Taiwan, Malaysia, Thailand, and Philippines
- **Transition:** Czech Republic, Hungary, Poland, Russia, Slovakia, Ukraine, and Vietnam
- **Latin American:** Argentina, Brazil, Chile, Colombia, Mexico, Peru, and Venezuela
- **Other:** Countries that don't fit into the other classifications, including Bangladesh, Egypt, Iceland, India, Israel, Jordan, Norway, South Africa, Turkey, and Zimbabwe

Source: *World Economic Forum.*

THE COMPETITIVENESS OF NATIONS

World Economic Forum 1999 Ranking of Fifty-nine Nations on the Eight Criteria for Global Competitiveness

1. Singapore	21. Chile	41. Greece
2. United States	22. Korea	42. Argentina
3. Hong Kong	23. France	43. Poland
4. Taiwan	24. Belgium	44. Turkey
5. Canada	25. Germany	45. Slovak Republic
6. Switzerland	26. Spain	46. El Salvador
7. Luxembourg	27. Portugal	47. South Africa
8. United Kingdom	28. Israel	48. Vietnam
9. Netherlands	29. Mauritius	49. Egypt
10. Ireland	30. Thailand	50. Venezuela
11. Finland	31. Mexico	51. Brazil
12. Australia	32. China	52. India
13. New Zealand	33. Philippines	53. Ecuador
14. Japan	34. Costa Rica	54. Colombia
15. Norway	35. Italy	55. Bolivia
16. Malaysia	36. Peru	56. Bulgaria
17. Denmark	37. Indonesia	57. Zimbabwe
18. Iceland	38. Hungary	58. Ukraine
19. Sweden	39. Czech Republic	59. Russia
20. Austria	40. Jordan	

immense natural resources; its liabilities include its poor infrastructure. Germany boasts a highly educated workforce that is offset by its costly welfare system. Each country around the world has a complex set of counterbalancing pluses and minuses—and it's the job of globally literate leaders to know how the math works.

As we enter the twenty-first century, there are three ways of considering countries and their national realities.

The first is by geography—the countries themselves. The second is as partners in such trading blocs as NAFTA (the United States, Canada, and Mexico), the European Union, ASEAN (Asian nations), and Mercosur (South America). The third is from the perspective of each country's economic mindset, the way each positions itself in the world economy: Entrepôt, Anglo-Saxon, European Union, Asian Manufacturing, Transition, Latin American, and so forth.

Politics

"Knowledge of human nature is the beginning and end of political education," wrote philosopher Henry Adams. He intuitively knew what we're coming to realize more fully today—that people, politics, culture, and business are inseparable.

As we enter the twenty-first century, economic prosperity demands political legitimacy, and reinventing government lies at the heart of economic growth. As the role of governments changes and their margin to maneuver shrinks before the overwhelming power of financial markets, they must strive harder to create the best environment for economic activity. They must educate workers, create appropriate legal and corporate governance systems, and equip citizens with the skills and expertise needed to succeed in the global world. Governments will increasingly be judged on their ability to address the social repercussions of globalization.

Claude Smadja, managing director of the World Economic Forum, knows that politics plays a pivotal role in the new global economy: "We must get rid of the fallacy that globalization somehow means the end or the shrinking of the role of governments. Instead, it forces a substantial transformation of that role. The penalty for failing to adapt will be social instability and political backlash as people come to rely on nongovernmental channels to express their fears and aspirations."

As Thomas Friedman, foreign correspondent for the *New York Times*, warns, globalization doesn't end geopolitics; instead, it raises the costs of using war to pursue honor and self-interest. Nations must ask themselves a whole new set of questions: How wired and how fast is our country? Are we harvesting knowledge? Are we open and agile? How good is our country's "brand"?

Around the globe, we're experiencing a new common vision of world democracy and free-market capitalism. And we're moving toward more empowered governments, more responsible institutions, and a stronger civil society.

As World Bank president Jim Wolfensohn warns, "All nations need good government systems, justice systems, financial systems, and social systems. The efficiency of those systems is critical to the competitiveness of nations."

Psychology

Every one of us has his or her own unique personal psychology. As citizens of a nation, we bring together our respective psychologies in the creation of a national mindset that reflects our character as a people and influences the philosophy of our leaders and the cultures of our institutions. To understand this, it's important to focus on the key elements of national psychology.

Time

While most of us measure time with clocks and watches, our experience of that time can be radically different depending on where we are in the world. Is time a commodity that can be planned for and harnessed, or is it beyond our control? Punctuality, deadlines, whether we focus on the past, present, or future—all these are culturally influenced. There are three key aspects to time that we must understand about national cultures:

- *Time perspective: past, present, future:* Do we place high value on tradition and heritage, on current reality, or on future advancement and progress?
- *Timeline: short-term versus long-term:* Are we focused on quarterly reports or fifty-year plans?
- *Time style: monochronic versus polychronic:* Is time divided into neat, linear compartments, or is it a way of measuring in which many things can be done simultaneously?

Relationships

The way we interact with others is also a cultural yardstick. Whether we communicate in words or gestures, rely on explicit or implicit meaning, or see the world through the lens of ourselves as individuals or as part of a group all create another level of complexity in our national psychology.

- *Relationship strategy: implicit versus explicit:* Are things understood without being explicitly stated, or is the exchange of facts and information stressed?
- *Relationship skill: verbal versus nonverbal:* Do we rely on words to communicate meaning, or do we mainly communicate through gestures and hidden meaning?
- *Relationship style: individual versus group:* Does the "I" predominate over the "we," or the other way around?
- *Relationship structure: hierarchical versus egalitarian:* Do we value power differences between individuals and groups, or do we value equality, collaboration, and shared power?
- *Relationship status: achieved versus ascribed:* Do we believe that what you know and how you perform determines business success, or is it more important to have access to important people through family, school, and other connections?

Activity

How we interact with our environment is another component of our national psychology. Do we take charge and assume control over the outside world, or are we more fatalistic, believing it's not possible to influence the natural course of events?

- *Activity orientation: doing, being, becoming:* Are we task-, relationship-, or possibility-centered?
- *Activity approach: linear versus circular:* Do we break problems into small, logical chunks, or do we prefer holistic thinking that focuses on the interrelationships between components?
- *Activity strategy: universal versus situational:* Are we the same in all circumstances, or do situations influence our behavior?
- *Activity agenda: change versus status quo:* Do we accept ambiguity and change as an integral part of life, or do we have an emotional need for rules and stability?

HOW SOUTH AFRICAN BREWERIES MANAGES ITS NATIONAL REALITIES

Business: *Africa's largest and the world's fourth-largest brewery in the world, SAB is a holding company with four divisions: beer (70 percent of business) and other beverages, retailing, hotels, and manufacturing.*
Employees: *81,000. Blacks now make up 52 percent of the beer division's salaried employees, 32 percent of management, and 13 percent of executives.*

In 1991, South Africa reentered the world stage in a hurry. Long isolated from the world and hampered by long-standing tensions between business and government, companies there found themselves literally running to catch up.

Businesses in South Africa received little warning of the changes that awaited them. "We've had to do things quickly," says Graham Mackay, CEO of South African Breweries (SAB). "We're immersed in the country's transition and facing substantial realignment problems." In the face of extraordinary challenges, SAB is working hard to play with the deck of cards it has been dealt. And it's succeeding.

What are the national realities that SAB was dealt?

Politically, the government's funding of apartheid resulted in tensions between government and business, resulting in tariffs and trade barriers that are just now being dismantled. Historically, South Africa's legacy of institutionalized racism created an unskilled labor force and a global public relations problem that had an adverse impact on this resource-rich nation. Organizationally, SAB is in the beer business in a country known for mineral wealth, not for hops. Culturally, South Africa still struggles with racial and gender issues at all levels of society.

This white-managed company has long known that it must be a progressive employer. It couldn't let national baggage hamper its global strategy, and it had to acknowledge that it was a consumer- and labor-intensive company in a country with limited skills.

As a result, SAB developed a strong people strategy. It launched massive training and equal opportunity programs—as well as an external customer growth strategy. It recognized that by developing internal diversity, it could enhance external sales. "We were the first large company to look purposefully at equal employment in the 1980s," Mackay says. "We did the best we could within the political confines of the day. It wasn't perfect, it's not perfect now, but we made a lot more effort much earlier than others. We don't allow tokenism. We maintain high standards and fire people when they're not performing, black or white."

With this unwavering commitment, it would be easy to put SAB on a pedestal. "Don't," says Mackay. SAB became a model of social progressiveness out of enlightened self-interest: "Of all the big companies in South Africa, we're by far the most mass consumer-oriented. We needed to be progressive, politically acceptable, and sympathetic to all consumers in South Africa."

While focusing on South African challenges, SAB is also building a global strategy that depends on local breweries and local brands. SAB recently registered on the London Stock Exchange for international financing, along with other South African companies seeking to escape exchange controls at home. "We're scrambling to spread ourselves internationally," notes Mackay.

Mackay knows that if SAB wants something done, it will have to do it itself: "We can't rely on the system in South Africa because it often falls down, so we do things ourselves in a resourceful, self-reliant way." That's one reason SAB invests in education—and why other companies poach its well-trained employees. "Our beer division," says Mackay, "is the biggest, best-equipped, and most ambitious private training establishment in the booming world. We're a long way from the centers of learning in Europe and the U.S., but we expect the same standards of performance from this company as the best over there."

That's the point: SAB is isolated and operating in a difficult and unsophisticated business environment, but it must perform as an equal on the world stage. That's Mackay's primary challenge—and his greatest paradox: "Our attempt to be globally competitive bumps us up against the real challenge in South Africa, which is to create jobs.

"When I took over our big packaging lines, we used forty-two workers to package seven hundred bottles a minute. That number's now ten or eleven workers, with higher efficiency and quality. But unless you have an economic climate that absorbs those jobs, you're essentially putting consumers out of work.

"I admire how big American multinationals go global. They just move straight ahead and pour resources out to make it work. But that won't work for us. We don't have a money or resource problem, we have a competency problem."

In various ways, these national realities have influenced all the leaders whose stories you'll read. We have tried to tell their stories and describe their best practices by showing how their history, geography, religion, politics, economics, and psychology have influenced them as leaders, helped shape their companies, and reflect their national cultures.

THE MOST DOMESTIC AND MOST GLOBAL COMPANIES

Countries with the Largest Percentage of Domestic Companies

- Philippines
- United States
- Japan
- Australia
- Brazil

Countries with the Largest Percentage of Global Companies

- Sweden
- Netherlands
- Singapore
- Germany
- New Zealand

Business Cultures

Like South African Breweries, most businesses pursue the same goals: to delight customers, grow the business, and make a profit for its owners. Each business serves the same kinds of stakeholders, too: shareholders, customers, suppliers, employees, and the community.

Yet for all these similarities, every company pursues its goals and serves its stakeholders in a way unique to itself and its country of origin. For example, U.S. businesses tend to focus on shareholder return, while their European counterparts put greater emphasis on employee morale and Asian businesses focus on harmony within their communities. Clearly, across all these differences, there is a global movement toward a model of business that focuses on shareholder capitalism. Companies also tend to specialize in whatever the country does best, as a reflection of their national origin, unique resources, and core competencies.

Furthermore, every company has a culture of its own, shaped by its history and industry, the unique realities it faces, and its leader's personality.

High-tech firms, for example, are different from steel companies. Toyota's corporate culture is different from those of Ford, Fiat, and DaimlerChrysler.

What becomes most clear by talking to CEOs around the world is that every business—regardless of size, industry, or region—must answer the same five questions to succeed:

PURPOSE: *Where Are We Going?*
Companies must create a compelling purpose, a vision and ideology that inspire their people to believe in something that matters. By defining what they stand for, companies create a unity of purpose and a common direction. People then tailor this purpose to their local situation.

PLAN: *How Do We Get There?*
Companies must create a road map for the future, one that clarifies strategies and priorities, yet evolves with changing realities. In the fast, flexible twenty-first-century organizations, structures, processes, and people must work together to serve the business goals. The challenge is to distinguish global from local.

NETWORKS: *How Do We Work Together?*
Companies must build relationships in a climate of trust and teamwork. By developing companywide networks and actively managing knowledge, they link people, information, and technology. Building external alliances connects them with the world—across cultures.

TOOLS: *What Resources Do We Need?*
Companies must create the right tools and resources for people to succeed. The twenty-first-century tools are challenging jobs, learning opportunities, cross-cultural experiences, and a share in the business. By investing in human capital, companies develop leaders who excel across national cultures.

RESULTS: *How Do We Measure Success?*
Companies must build value-creating organizations for all their stakeholders. By painting a picture of success, leveraging new kinds of capital, and valuing their intangible assets, companies institutionalize a bias for action and create a culture of results. They give something back to global society.

In Part III of the book, we will examine these five business questions and show how leaders from companies around the world are creatively solving these universal business questions in their own culturally unique way.

Leadership Cultures

As with countries and companies, people are the same and people are different. Whether in Shanghai, China; Rockford, Illinois; Bergen, Norway; or Buenos Aires, Argentina, people have the same basic drives: a desire for a life purpose and meaning; a need for self-esteem; and a desire to be connected with others who matter, whether in a family, community, or tribe. Yet all of us express these human drives in our own unique way through our personality, motivations, and strengths and shortcomings.

Leaders are people, too. Around the world, they are both the same and different. While concepts of leadership are universal, with a long history across different eras and civilizations, they play out differently in different areas of the world. We all seek leaders, but we seek them for different reasons and in different ways, depending on our cultural background. The most successful business leaders exhibit universal leadership qualities that we call "global literacies":

- *Personal literacy* involves understanding and valuing yourself. In a world exploding with information, companies are forced to be more transparent. Leaders must be self-aware, open, honest, and committed to their own learning. Motivated by strongly held principles and beliefs, personally literate leaders face change with confidence and are passionate about excellence and success.
- *Social literacy* is about challenging and engaging others. The technological revolution has created a global world of speed and complexity that requires collaborative leaders who can build productive relationships and networks around the world. By communicating deeply, teaching and coaching, and transforming conflict into creative action, socially literate leaders inspire others to action and greatness.
- *Business literacy* is about focusing and mobilizing your organization. Unrelenting change forces companies to be fast and flexible as they navigate through chaos to create value for customers. By creating environments that bring out the best in people and by teaching them how the business works, business-literate leaders build cultures of learning and innovation. Liberating leaders at all levels is their secret of success.
- *Cultural literacy*, knowing about and leveraging cultural differences, is the fourth global literacy. While all business is global, all markets are local. Our globalized, multicultural world requires leaders with a keen understanding of national cultures. By learning from other countries, culturally literate leaders build cultural bridges, enabling them to leverage culture as a tool for competitive advantage.

These are the four global literacies. They are the leadership universals for the twenty-first century, relevant to all business leaders. Naturally, each of us will put our own personal stamp on them, depending on where we live, work, or conduct business.

Managing the Four Cultures

These four cultures—world, national, business, and leadership—each has universal realities and unique responses. We live simultaneously in all four levels, moving into and out of the different circles. Daily we are bombarded with the world culture drivers, influenced consciously and unconsciously by the realities of national culture, presented with daily challenges in business culture, and required to experience leadership culture every day on the job. We must understand how they interact and influence one another.

The cultures of countries shape the character and competencies of their peoples and, in turn, the national values that inform the selection of leaders. The leaders, in turn, shape the culture and competencies of institutions, which shape and alter the country's history and culture.

Take the United States, for example. The United States grows strong, entrepreneurial, and individualistic leaders such as Doug Ivester, CEO of Coca-Cola. The energy and boldness with which Ivester operates have become part of the culture of Coca-Cola and the United States. The American culture and Coca-Cola then cultivate the development of these leadership behaviors in others, in an endless cycle of reinforcement. Similarly, this process has occured with the creative, affable energy of Francesco Trapani, CEO of Bulgari in Italy, or the respectful relationship building of Peter Ma, CEO of Ping An in China.

To simplify these complex interrelationships, we've organized *Global Literacies* to show how business leaders personify the four global literacies, solve the five business challenges, and grapple with their national realities in culturally unique ways.

Lessons from Around the World

We need to learn from everywhere. Yet people from different parts of the world teach us different things. Each country has a unique story to tell. And over time each country develops a unique management competency, based on its national character and culture. Respecting these distinctions, and celebrating and learning from them, is key. (See Figure 2, on the next page.)

Western management thinking since World War II has greatly influenced much of the world. The destruction of Europe and Japan after the war, the expansion of U.S. companies and culture, and the Western education of children of wealthy families from around the world led to a Western-focused business culture.

FIGURE 2.

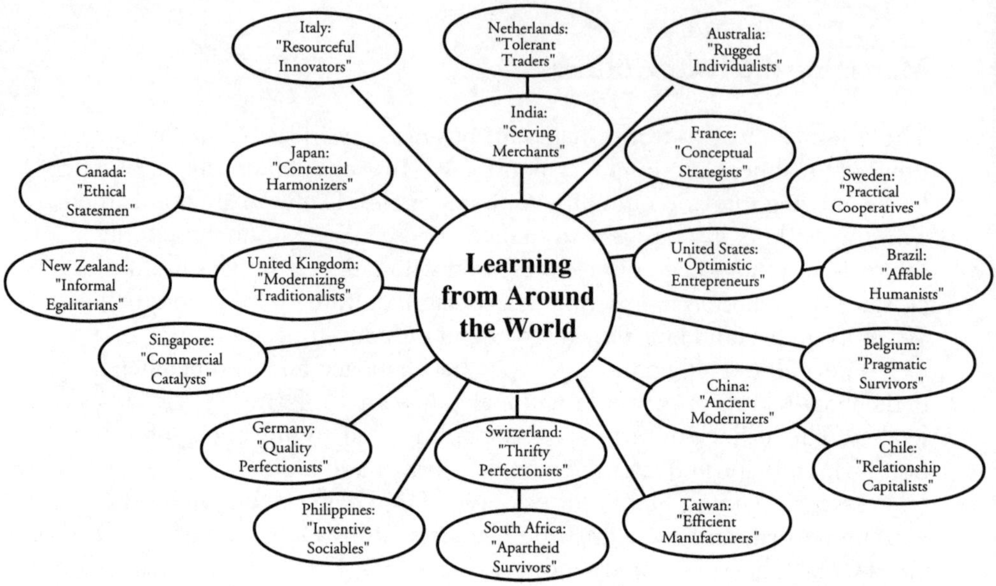

© Robert H. Rosen 1999

But the world is changing. Many of the world's children have returned home from their Western education to run businesses; many non-Western countries have entered the global marketplace, found a niche, and grown considerably. They have built large enterprises, enhanced their self-esteem, and cultivated a unique management philosophy and style. These companies are accessing global financial markets, gaining power, appreciating their roots, and celebrating their unique contributions to our thinking about business. Other countries never bought into the American dream in the first place and never lost faith in their heritage and their contribution.

Today, special leadership contributions are being made by all the nations of the world. It's not a matter of superiority, but of difference. Each country does a number of things well, and each does a few things better than others.

We're talking not about stereotypes of national culture but about prevailing national tendencies. There's a difference between cultural stereotyping and cultural profiling, between cultural prejudice and cultural contribution. Naturally, not all leaders or companies in a culture personify their country's natural tendency. But many do. From the efficient manufacturing mindset of the Taiwanese to the tolerant traders of the Netherlands to the optimistic entrepreneurs of the United States, there are lessons to be learned from all. The challenge is to acknowledge and own your country's

HOW GLOBALLY SUCCESSFUL IS YOUR COUNTRY?

In our global survey of business executives, we created a "Global Success Quotient" to identify the most globally active, financially successful companies in our sample. The quotient is based on two factors:

- **International activities:** Percentage of international revenues, customers, employees, and suppliers; whether the company is domestic, exporter, international, multinational, or global; the degree of global expansion activities during the last two years and projections for the next five years.
- **Financial performance:** Overall financial performance relative to the performance of other firms in their industry over the last two years; shareholder investment, growth in market share and net income, and return on sales.

To determine which countries had the highest percentage of "globally successful" companies, we examined the survey results by country. Here are our rankings, from most globally successful to least:

- France
- Netherlands
- New Zealand
- Sweden
- Germany
- Mexico
- United Kingdom
- Singapore
- China/Hong Kong
- Argentina
- South Korea
- Canada
- Australia
- United States
- Brazil
- Philippines
- Japan

unique contribution, enrich its management and learning style, and assimilate differences from other countries without being overwhelmed by them.

As you continue reading, we will introduce you to countries around the world and share the lessons of their leaders.

PART TWO

THE FOUR GLOBAL LITERACIES

Creating a New Language of Business

Language is the expression of culture, enabling us to communicate through the ages with people who share our history and identity. We rely on words to express ourselves, solve problems, and forge links with others.

But language can be both an enabler and a jailer. By its very nature, a language creates both insiders and outsiders—people who speak and understand it and people who don't. And spoken language is just the tip of an iceberg rooted in nonverbal communication and hidden messages. In the twenty-first century, as people live and work across cultures, common language will become increasingly critical to success.

Today's common business language is English. It is the language of globalization, with increasing numbers of companies making its competency a prerequisite for promotions. English is the official language of the European Central Bank and of cyberspace; its spread of English as the world business language has been both a consequence of and contributor to globalization. Yet there are more than 1,200 standardized languages today—and globalization requires speakers and readers of local languages to be multilingual, often with English as their second language.

To be successful in the twenty-first century, we must go beyond English to develop a richer, more universal language that deepens our perspective and broadens our horizons. The new world of business requires a fresh language, one that releases our thinking, catalyzes our connections, and facilitates global understanding. We need a new human language that transcends traditional cultural borders.

Global literacy is a state of *seeing, thinking, acting, and mobilizing* in culturally mindful ways. It is the new twenty-first-century leadership competency—to be world-class, at home and abroad. And it depends on four separate competencies: personal, social, business, and cultural. These are the leadership universals.

Interrelated and interdependent, each of the four global literacies forms the foundation for the next. By understanding and valuing yourself, you are able to fully engage and challenge people, enabling you to focus and mobilize your organization, ultimately leveraging culture as a tool for competitive advantage.

Your four literacies will constantly evolve and deepen as you interact in the world. And as leaders get new information from changing business circumstances and cultures, the literacies are sharpened.

One way to understand the global literacies is to imagine that each of us sees the world through a prism, with inputs such as world drivers, national realities, business challenges, and our own personal issues. Millions of these bits of data bombard us everyday, and we must open the lens of our mind to allow the information to come in. Only through a process of filtering—of perceiving, analyzing, and synthesizing—can we make sense of the world.

Many of us have a lens that is blurry, lacking depth and focus. But that won't work in the twenty-first century. Instead, we must clean our lens so we can see the world more clearly. The four global literacies act as a filter and translator that interpret and analyze all this information. These filters help us understand the world, moving from seeing the world in black and white to seeing it in color.

When you become proficient in the four global literacies, you begin to:

- *See* the world's challenges and opportunities—which expands your horizons, illuminating your perceptions of the world
- *Think* with an international mindset—which helps you develop a global mindset with beliefs and attitudes that enable you to think internationally
- *Act* with fresh global-centric leadership behaviors—which teaches new relationship skills that help you navigate through the global marketplace
- *Mobilize* a world-class company—which helps you inspire and mobilize people across national cultures

When we successfully employ our global literacies, we learn to lead with a worldview and a fresh global approach to work. By living the four global literacies, you will live a more personally fulfilling, productive, and profitable life.

Every leader whose company is preparing for the new millennium has a story and a vision like that of Phil Condit of Boeing (see opposite page). Their stories reveal the requirements for success for *all* managers moving into the new century. These leaders are globally literate. They're asking the right questions. They're creating their own languages. And they're winning because of it.

Each of the four literacies is presented in the chapters that follow. Along the way, you will meet business leaders from around the world who illustrate them in thought and action.

THE TWENTY-FIRST-CENTURY SUCCESS

Personal literacy + Social literacy + Business literacy + Cultural literacy
=
Global literacy = world-class excellence

Culture in the Cockpit

Philip Condit knows that global literacy matters. It may even be the difference between life and death.

As chairman and CEO of the Boeing Company, Condit paid close attention when a Korean Airlines Boeing jet crashed in Guam in 1997, killing 228 people. When *The Washington Post* reported a theory that Korean traditions of respecting authority and saving face had played a role in the crash, Condit took the initiative to educate employees and customers about collaboration in the cockpit and the company. Presumed stuck in his own cultural mindset, the junior officer aboard that ill-fated flight wouldn't have confronted the senior officer with information that might have averted the disaster. Culture, we learn daily, is playing an increasingly important role in our lives and work.

Condit knows that Boeing's twenty-first-century success depends on creating a new breed of globally literate leaders in the cockpit and beyond. The world's largest commercial and military aircraft manufacturer, Boeing serves customers in 145 countries, employs more than 231,000 people worldwide, and has a reputation as producer of the most technologically advanced and reliable planes in the world. In 1998, revenues topped $56 billion. With numbers like these, Condit knows that it's vital to have global leaders at *all* levels of his business, in *all* regions of the world. While Boeing has had challenges—from integrating McDonnell Douglas and Rockwell to surviving stock fluctuations—Condit has stayed true to that vision.

"I need leaders who are global traders with a different way of thinking, acting, and mobilizing people in the world," says Condit.

Boeing's "Vision 2016," says Condit, is the blueprint: "People working together as one global company for aerospace leadership. Vision 2016 promotes four important leadership qualities:

First, global leaders must know their culture and the cultures of others, the conscious and subconscious environment in which we all live. "The best managers will combine the wisdom of American, Asian, and European thinking," says Condit.

Second, they have to be able to think differently about themselves and others. In order to succeed in the world economy, you have to know yourself as well as you know others. "Global managers must be self-aware, humble, and willing to learn and reinvent themselves for the future. Why? The only constant is change," Condit reminds us.

Third, they have to learn to work together. "None of us is as smart as all of us," Condit notes. "Yet if you look at the task we're trying to accomplish—flying an airplane or space station—there's no human being who can do it alone. One person can't even come close." The workers at Boeing know that making a plane, just like flying one, is a collaborative effort from the top down.

Finally, they must understand the business—how the business works, how the company makes money, how capital flows around the world. "I need people who understand the global marketplace with a real sense of urgency," says Condit. As international competition mounts against Boeing from companies such as Airbus Industrie and as mergers between giants such as Boeing and McDonnell Douglas become the norm, businesses must make swift decisions to hold their place in the market.

Boeing is calling on its managers to implement not one but all four of these leadership skills. "One . . . is simply not enough," stresses Condit.

WHO SPEAKS THE MOST LANGUAGES?

(Average number of languages spoken by business executives)

- Netherlands: 3.9
- Sweden: 3.4
- Brazil: 2.9
- Germany: 2.7
- Philippines: 2.7
- France: 2.7
- Singapore: 2.6
- Japan: 2.6
- Mexico: 2.5
- South Korea: 2.5
- Hong Kong: 2.3
- Canada: 1.8
- New Zealand: 1.6
- United Kingdom: 1.5
- United States: 1.5
- Australia: 1.4

CHAPTER THREE

PERSONAL LITERACY

Understanding and Valuing Yourself

In a world exploding with information, companies must be transparent. Their leaders must be open, honest, and committed to learning. Motivated by principles, they must face change with passion and confidence.

PERSONAL LITERACY is the first building block of global literacy.

The foundations of personal literacy are: self-awareness—understanding yourself; self-development—renewing yourself; and self-esteem—valuing yourself.

Personally literate leaders must master these key behaviors:

- Aggressive insight
- Confident humility
- Authentic flexibility
- Reflective decisiveness
- Realistic optimism

On the surface, these paired behaviors may seem contradictory; their juxtaposition may jar you. You may feel drawn to one or the other end of the continuum, thinking that you can be either reflective or decisive, but rarely both at the same time. You feel you can be realistic or optimistic, but not both concurrently. But while that kind of "either-or" thinking might have worked in the past, our complex global world has outgrown that mindset.

Instead, we need to grow the capacity to think in "both-and" rather than "either-or" terms, as our Asian colleagues have successfully done for generations. As personally literate leaders, we must see qualities we assume to be opposites as part of the same continuum—and interdependent—rather than as polar opposites.

Our challenge is to hold and process seemingly contradictory concepts such as these inside our head simultaneously. Leadership solutions lie in resolving and balancing the creative tensions among them, in understanding deeply how to both be confident and humble, authentic and flexible, aggressive and insightful.

Achieving personal literacy is easier said than done. Each of us leans naturally toward one end of the continuum of these behaviors—or the other. Learning humility may be a lifelong challenge for the arrogant leader, and humble leaders may find it difficult to make bold decisions, take risks, and stand up for themselves. Some leaders take pride in having strong values but are inflexible and moralistic. Others are so flexible that they never develop a clear sense of right and wrong. Some leaders reflect too long without acting, while others act without thinking. The challenge is to know where you stand on the continuum of each personal literacy behavior—and to be open to developing skills at the other end. Having access to the tools at both ends is where the real competitive advantage lies.

Each of these behaviors that comprise personal literacy requires exploration: What do these concepts mean to you? How do they interact and balance? What do they look like in practice? How does culture influence them?

Aggressive Insight

During a speech in Frankfurt, Germany, Lee Kun-Hee announced that change begins with him. To effect change in groups, he said, "we must initiate change within ourselves." The chairman of Korea's Samsung Electronics, Lee knows that change must come from the inside out. "You have to know yourself well," he says, "your habits, strengths, and shortcomings. Questioning yourself thoroughly is the beginning of change."

Lee models the first step toward global literacy—committing to a continuous and intentional process of self-awareness and renewal. Personally literate leaders share this trait of insatiable curiosity—about themselves and the world around them. What's unique is the way in which they each express it, depending on their culture.

Without curiosity, global leaders live in the past, lost in a world of limited relevance. Change occurs so rapidly that "old world" views, even those of six months ago, won't work anymore. And these leaders know it.

Personally literate leaders know where they excel, where they have shortcomings, and what their blind spots are. They question assumptions and ask for feedback from others. Theirs is an aggressive insight because it is proactive—they constantly seek opportunities to test themselves and learn from their successes and failures. Constant self-reexamination allows them to shed old baggage and reinvent themselves.

Personally literate people are psychologically astute. They understand their own emotional intelligence—what excites and inspires them and how they trip over negative emotions of anger, anxiety, and depression. They understand how negative feelings can destroy people and organizations. And they know how to counteract their impact without short-circuiting themselves.

While they appreciate the universal need for aggressive insight, personally literate leaders also understand that each person has his own approach to self-knowledge.

Why, how, and where we seek self-awareness reflect our cultural roots. North Americans, for example, seek self-knowledge primarily from external sources—hence the billions of dollars spent on personal therapy, religious affiliation, and self-help books and tapes in the United States—while Eastern leaders look inward for awareness and meaning through yoga or meditation.

Relationship style matters, too. People in individualistic societies such as Great Britain and Australia approach self-knowledge as a personal act of courage and discovery, while people in collectivist societies such as Korea and Taiwan see the development of oneself as inextricably intertwined with the community.

Confident Humility

Aad Jacobs speaks and dresses humbly. He drives an old car and spends the same amount of money he did twenty years ago, when he was a manager. He's an open, honest, unassuming man who recently retired as CEO of the ING Groep, one of the world's most powerful financial institutions with assets of more than $250 billion. He's humble enough to ride his bike to work and confident enough to march unnoticed into Barings Bank and buy it, cash on the barrel.

As Jacobs demonstrates, the second building block of personal literacy is being confident and secure, yet humble enough to listen and learn from others.

Healthy self-esteem stems from being comfortable with who you are, knowing clearly what you can and cannot do, and being at ease with your own power. Confident leaders are bold in their actions. But confidence unabated is arrogance, which personally literate leaders can't afford.

They must balance personal security and confidence with a quiet humility. By recognizing that they're only human, they accept their imperfections and learn from their mistakes. By seeing people as equal but different, they're open to learning from others and asking for advice—something only confident leaders can do.

Confident humility means having a healthy ego without feeling self-important. For many leaders who have risen to the top by being bold and outwardly confident, balancing their strong-willed behavior with a quiet confidence about who they are is a new skill.

Our capacity to express both confidence and humility in combination is culturally determined. Ambitious self-esteem and confidence look different in Asia than in the West. Our comfort with "selling" our abilities is different among people in the United States and Great Britain: Americans tend to exaggerate their accomplishments, while the British understate them.

Confident humility also poses different challenges for developed and developing worlds—and creates an opportunity for mutual learning as well. North America and western Europe stumble over humility, while nations in the developing world struggle with confidence.

Authentic Flexibility

Motorola chairman Bob Galvin stands for a strong value: uncompromising integrity. The architect of Motorola's modern success, Galvin supports that sacred principle with a constantly redefining and changing sense of personal renewal among all Motorola associates. He constantly reinforces the value of integrity and ensures that it, too, has room to grow and renew.

Like Galvin, personally literate leaders must have a teachable point of view and stand by their values and ethics. They must also develop a life purpose. All are elements of living an authentic life.

There are three key elements of authentic flexibility: a personal purpose, a set of ethics and standards, and a teachable point of view. The challenge is to be authentic in a world with confusing or conflicting values and with ethics that seem to contradict our own. And that's where flexibility comes in.

In a world of fewer black-and-white and more gray areas, leaders must embrace change, uncertainty, and contradiction while letting others know that their own personal integrity is simply nonnegotiable. By retaining our core principles and developing personal ethics, we will be able to navigate through the moral morass.

Personally literate leaders must have a point of view, a moral position, a solid platform of principles. Their followers and businesses demand it. But what's missing—and vital—is flexibility. Skyscrapers without sway can't withstand earthquakes.

Can we be flexible and also have a sense of right and wrong? The answer is that we must. It's important to have clear ground rules yet be able to adapt to changing circumstances without compromising our core principles.

Being flexible requires us to be principle-driven with integrity, enabling us to be open to conflicting ideas. We must learn to adjust our perceptions and moral lens, but not our principles. Our character interacts and evolves with changing circumstances. We understand that culture influences ethics and that there are different ways of conducting business around the world.

Our comfort with the concept of flexible values and how we exhibit authentic flexibility differs by culture. The Asians do it best: their heritage of being able to hold two opposing concepts in their minds, where it's difficult to tell where one starts and the other stops, makes them innately more comfortable with ambiguity and uncertainty. Other cultures, such as those in western Europe and North America, demand and seek distinctness, clarity, and order with clear borders and outlines. But authentic flexibility is vital because as business moves into the twenty-first century, borders and order are becoming increasingly extinct concepts.

Reflective Decisiveness

When Tenneco's Dana Mead makes decisions about quality packaging, he's less concerned with process than with results. Halfway around the world, Toyota's Hiroshi Okuda cares as deeply about results, such as the number of new car models each year, but he's also passionate about the *process* and ensuring that the result is consensus-driven.

Both Mead and Okuda know that to lead is to act and that we measure our leaders by results. But here are two leaders from opposite ends of the world who create results differently. Both value thinking and acting, but each does so in his own culturally unique way.

Reflective leaders think carefully and talk through their concerns. They thoughtfully consider all options, ask for assistance, and draw on past experiences to make decisions. They are concerned about future consequences and question how various decisions will help or hinder their desired future.

Decisive leaders are bold and forceful. They are matter-of-fact thinkers who test ideas and grasp situations quickly. They feel free to take action, are quick to form judgments, and are direct and to the point.

Together they exhibit reflective decisiveness—knowing when to think and when to act, effectively balancing thought and action. Achieving this level of personal literacy requires leaders to carve out space for reflection, seek information, and then act boldly. They must strive to understand the past while leveraging that knowledge to make decisions for the future. Then they must act with urgency; they cannot afford to be paralyzed by visions of limitless possibilities.

Personally literate leaders actively manage alternative scenarios in their head, imagining both possibilities and their consequences. They are comfortable not knowing everything and give themselves the freedom to make bold decisions.

But people differ in how they make long- and short-term decisions, partially because of their cultural marrow. Culture influences who is to make decisions and how quickly. How decisions are made—alone or in a group, quickly or slowly—and the amount of information needed before they can be made is also culturally determined.

The Japanese practice of *ringi* is a relatively slow process of consensus building that illustrates how decisions are made in that culture. Sometimes Westerners express impatience with *ringi*'s endless consultations. Meanwhile, the Japanese find fault with the swift, unilateral decisions of Western businessmen.

Decisive leaders operating in reflective cultures are often perceived and discounted as impulsive, insensitive, and superficial; alternatively, reflective leaders operating in action-oriented cultures are perceived as slow, bureaucratic, and overly process-oriented. Leaders who merge those two behaviors exponentially enlarge their leadership capacity across many more cultures.

Realistic Optimism

Rolf-Ernst Breuer, managing director of Deutsche Bank, was enough of a realist about the changing dynamics of world banking to recognize that his company needed a partner. And he was enough of an optimist to seek out Bankers Trust. Breuer is realistic about the German past and about his company's role in financing Auschwitz, the German death camp. Stepping up to the plate about the past, he's able to anticipate Deutsche Bank's future. He's realistic and optimistic simultaneously.

We're drawn to inspiring leaders who demonstrate their passion for possibility and tell us we can achieve impossible things. But we also need leaders who bridge hope and reality, who have one foot in the future and one in the present. Personally literate leaders do both.

Realistic people are direct. They talk about what's really going on in the business. Honest about business drivers, competition, and opportunity, they're also comfortable giving true, direct feedback.

Optimistic people, on the other hand, are imaginative. Always traveling into the unknown, they see possibilities that others cannot see. They have a great capacity to dream, break with tradition, envision a better tomorrow, and excite others about the future.

Because globalism both enables and threatens business, we need leaders who are simultaneously idealistic and realistic. Balanced between a desired future and current reality, they can stretch themselves and others to be better than they are, all within a framework of honesty. Leaders with realistic optimism articulate hope through their commitment to the truth. Simply put, personally literate leaders dream of what should be while telling it like it is.

Capacity for realistic optimism reflects our culture: Are we future-oriented dreamers, or are we present-focused and pragmatic? Surprisingly, the United States is one of the most skillful nations at both ends of the continuum. It is a society driven by an urgent quest for new technologies and

THE TOP FIVE PERSONAL LITERACY SKILLS

When asked to identify the two most important personal qualities for leadership, business executives said:

- Leading by example: 56%
- Facing change and uncertainty with confidence: 45%
- Being motivated by strongly held principles and beliefs: 38%
- Knowing one's own strengths and shortcomings: 31%
- Being committed to continuous learning: 30%

ideas. At the same time, U.S. business leaders are dramatically realistic: they are direct, short-term, transparent thinkers, combining the strongest venture capital system with one of the shortest-term mentalities in the world. Americans embrace the tension between realism and optimism every day. By contrast, Europeans are deeper thinkers. Intellectually driven to debate, their values emphasize history and a search for the truth.

The key to achieving personal literacy is learning from leaders themselves, in companies around the world.

In this chapter, we'll meet the Netherlands' ING Groep CEO Aad Jacobs, who teaches us humble, yet confident, honesty. In the United States, Ogilvy & Mather CEO Shelly Lazarus urges us to practice what we preach. Young Kumar Birla, CEO of India's Birla Group, models emotional maturity. Deutsche Bank CEO Rolf-Ernst Breuer shows us how to look reality straight in the eye, and the Samsung Group's chairman Lee Kun-Hee demonstrates how to make change from the inside out. Each is personally literate in his or her culturally unique way. Their stories show us how to be personally literate ourselves.

LIVE AN OPEN, HONEST LIFE
AAD Jacobs and Ing Groep N.V. *(Netherlands)*

Title: Chairman (retired)
Headquarters: Amsterdam
Business: Integrated financial services group and world's largest publicly held life and health insurer. Net profits and shareholder equity have increased by 70% since 1991, total assets by more than 30%; share price has tripled in a five-year period.
Employees: 64,162 in 59 countries

When Her Majesty Queen Beatrix named Aad Jacobs a knight in the Order of the Netherlands Lion, the chairman of the ING Groep composed a handwritten note to all ING employees: "I feel like a soccer player who scores the winning goal in the last minute and is carried on the shoulders of fellow players. That final goal was scored because the whole team—which is you—played a perfect match. The Royal Order is for the entire ING Groep, and I thank you for your contribution."

Aad Jacobs's honesty and simplicity are his foundations, not only for his life, but for his company. He believes in teamwork. A lifelong soccer player, he uses the game as a metaphor for synergy at ING. Jacobs has built an open, aggressive, and transparent company by living consistency and authenticity himself and passing those principles down through the company. Folksy and unassuming, Jacobs has transformed ING into one of the world's most powerful financial institutions. With assets of more than $250 billion, it has been called the greatest global experiment in "total finance."

Yet Aad Jacobs still rides his bike to work.

Be Authentic and Consistent

Surrounded by money and power, Aad Jacobs isn't influenced by them: He lives in a small house and considers himself "still the same guy I was when I came to this group thirty-six years ago." If he's not riding his bike, he's driving his old Toyota Camry, not the typical European executive's luxury sedan. "I'm spending the same money as when I was head of the research department, making in a year less than ten percent of the money I'm making this month." This frugal determination, born of Dutch culture, defines Jacobs as a leader. He is bold and aggressive, yet unassuming. But don't be misled—the typical Dutch CEO is more glamorous than he is, he says.

Jacobs wants people around him who are just as straightforward and honest and who will tell it as it is, rather than what they think he wants to hear. That involves a trust he cultivates by modeling authentic communication himself. "Open communication is key," he says. "I want my people to be critical, not only downwards, but also upwards." Because employees won't criticize upward when they're afraid of repercussions, Jacobs rewards honest communication. "I'm much more inclined to promote the guy who's been critical to the group, rather than one who just flatters me," he says.

Why are the Dutch so open? "Part of that is our heritage—we're very tolerant, which can also be one of our weaknesses. One of the things I regret is that I've been too tolerant of my people. I've treated them very well and probably haven't been tough enough."

Jacobs takes his responsibilities seriously: "You've got a job to do, and you have the responsibility for eighty thousand people in this world to do it as well as you can. And that's what I've done for the last six years since I've been chairman." He doesn't mention that during those six years, ING Groep has made world financial headlines by buying Barings Bank and Belgium's largest bank, BBL. Admittedly, incorporating Barings into the group hasn't been an easy transition, with losses in emerging markets and severe cost cutting and layoffs, but ING is working hard to ensure it does it well—and for the long haul.

Jacobs's lessons? That character matters, that you have to accept yourself for who you are and live the principles of trust: listening, being consistent, being predictable, and being safe enough for other people to get close to.

Know Your Strengths, Weaknesses, and Blind Spots

Jacobs retired in June 1998; true to form, he talks simply about the process of leaving ING after almost four decades there: "My only reward is that when I retired, I could say, 'I had some talents, I wasn't too stupid, I expressed myself well, I had an open character, I used all my talents, and I couldn't have done better.' "

While Jacobs knows he's done some things right, he realizes he's also made mistakes—and learned from both: "Hopefully, the balance is positive. I try to look at myself in quite a critical manner."

This self-awareness, commitment to personal learning, and willingness to compensate for personal weaknesses make Jacobs a strong believer in collective responsibility. "Nowadays, the world is so complicated that it's beyond a normal human being to know everything. I rely quite heavily on my colleagues. I'm a strong believer that the team can do much more than an individual person," he says. "I know in the United States the CEO is very close to Jesus Christ and his colleagues are not more than his assistants," he says. But that's not how Jacobs operates.

He demonstrates his reliance on colleagues by delegating wisely, something less personally literate executives do with great difficulty. After ING bought a U.S. company, Jacobs met with its chairman. He asked his American colleague about the firm's strategy moving forward. "Well, you're the boss now," came the answer. "No," Jacobs replied. "I'll look over your shoulder and give guidelines of what ING expects strategically and financially, but you're in the show and I'm not the expert you are."

Balance Confidence with Humility

If you are self-aware and committed to personal learning, you stand on solid ground. That allows you to be confident yet humble. It enables you to be honest and open about who you are, building the foundation for a direct, honest company.

ING came to reflect Jacobs's character in its transparent structure and relationships, both inside and outside the company. One of the first integrated financial services companies in the world, ING was voted the most respected European financial institution in a recent major survey of Europe's top companies published in the *Financial Times*.

In response to globalization and increased competition, Jacobs combined the disparate cultures of banking and insurance to create ING. Because he understood that both industries face extraordinary margin pressures, Jacobs knew that growing the business was critical to its success. He created a strategy of synergy and global growth. The two companies that merged to form ING were very clear about their strengths and weaknesses. By freely acknowledging the holes in their strategies, they built an aggressive, but not arrogant, company.

Like Jacobs, ING is direct about its intentions. In 1997, it announced that it had three acquisitions on its wish list: a major insurer in the United States, an American investment bank, and a bank in Europe. It bought all three. Now it has told the world it wants to expand further in Europe with the purchase of French and German financial institutions and a mutual fund. Jacobs applies an honest approach even to these global acquisitions: "It's important that all of your people, the shareholders, and the investment world know your intentions—no surprises."

ING and Jacobs demonstrate this open transparency by the way they interact in the global environment. True to Jacobs's philosophy, he learned transparency from the inside out by investing in personal learning. "I joined the company because I have more talent for figures than for languages. After two years they sent me to the U.S. I also worked in Switzerland and Japan," he says. ING demands of its managers that they understand not only their own culture, but others as well.

ING and the Dutch have a great capacity to adapt to foreign cultures and embrace cultural differences with tolerance and flexibility, which Jacobs credits to the Netherlands itself: "We have a lot of international experience. We're a small country, so we have to. We generally speak languages better than others and have a capacity to adjust ourselves to foreign cultures. We feel at home if we're in China or Peru—and we don't feel we have to change the Chinese or Peruvians. How to manage different cultures and bring cultures together in one company is a typical Dutch phenomenon."

And Aad Jacobs, with his bike, his small house, his honesty, and his large business, is a typical Dutchman. "There are," he explains, "very, very few questions I don't answer honestly."

NETHERLANDS: "Tolerant Traders"

National Snapshot

Compared to other executives, Dutch business leaders say:

- It's critical for senior executives to have multicultural experience.
- They know their strengths and shortcomings.
- They are less motivated by strongly held principles and beliefs.
- They are more likely to share knowledge and give employees decision-making authority.
- Helping people adapt to change is key to success.
- They speak the most languages.
- They give the greatest degree of autonomy to local offices.
- 89% have customers, 84% have suppliers, and 66% have employees in six or more countries.

The Dutch are traders who believe that everything can be molded by human effort and determination, whether land, society, or business. Their orderly, peaceful society has a reputation for tolerance, political stability, and an open economy.

JUST WHO, EXACTLY, did the Dutch think they were? Only a few generations after rebelling against Spanish rule, they created their own powerful empire, with a distinctive culture and commercial success admired throughout the West. They drew creativity from materialism—this imperative of being both rich and good is central to the Dutch character. Dutch Calvinist attitudes about the importance of hard work and thrift, along with a disdain for ostentation, have shaped this land of open traders.

Surrounded by very powerful neighbors—politically, militarily, intellectually, and culturally—the Netherlands has learned three basic skills: to adapt, to trade, and to respect others.

A Legacy of Entrepreneurial Traders

A tiny country bordered by Germany, Belgium, and the North Sea, the Netherlands enjoys fertile lands in five major river deltas. More than one fourth of the country is below sea level on land reclaimed from the ocean. One of the most densely populated countries in the world, the Netherlands is ranked ninth in the world in terms of the value of its imports and exports.

Although only 4 percent of its labor force is agrarian, it produces enough food to rank the Netherlands third, behind the United States and France, in the value of its agricultural exports. Its tulips are legendary and contribute to its control of 60 percent of the international flower trade.

Like other small countries with limited resources, the Netherlands had to look outside its borders to make its mark. By the 1100s, it was trading globally, by the 1600s it was one of the world's major economic and trading powers, and by the 1700s, it had lost control of the seas, watching as British power rose. The famous Dutch East India Company was one of the first global trading businesses, discovering rare commodities such as salt and pepper in Indonesia and introducing them to the rest of the world.

Rotterdam remains the world's busiest port, handling twice as much cargo as New York; Schiphol Airport ranks tenth in the world for cargo shipments; a third of European Union goods are transported in Dutch trucks; the Amsterdam stock exchange is the twelfth largest in the world; and Dutch companies are the third largest foreign investors in the United States, after Japan and the United Kingdom.

Shaped by Tolerance and Pragmatism

The Netherlands has been invaded by almost all the major European powers. In the sixteenth and seventeenth centuries, the Dutch rose up repeatedly against foreign domination to secure their republic, winning independence from the Spanish Empire and developing trading colonies in places as diverse as New York's Hudson Valley, South Africa, Sri Lanka, and the Dutch East Indies (now Indonesia).

They learned to adapt to their invaders' cultural and social norms—and refused to impose cultural rule on their own colonies. An orderly people, the Dutch hate being ordered around. Their feeling free to break the complex and impressive-looking rules they have devised isn't a recipe for anarchy because prudence prevails: the Dutch distrust extremism and prefer balance. Dissent can thrive when it doesn't interfere with business.

Their history has made them tolerant. As early as the Spanish Inquisition, the Dutch allowed Jews and others to settle in their country. Since then, countless refugees have felt welcomed in tolerant Dutch cities, especially Amsterdam.

The Netherlands may be 96 percent Dutch, but it's no cultural monolith. It has a long history of freedom of thought, in which the legacies of Dutch Humanism and Dutch Calvinism continue to interplay, creating a mixture of the Humanists' piety and knowledge, rigid Calvinism, and a more tolerant Protestantism and Roman Catholicism.

As in Belgium, politics, trade unions, education, employers' organizations, and the media divide along religious lines. Individual regions have their own distinctive subcultures. The Zeelanders of the north possess an asceticism developed through centuries of struggle against the sea—in contrast to the more easygoing life in the south.

Intuitive Globalists

A good Dutchman is described as *handig,* meaning clever and handy, able to persuade, obtain agreement, and bring people together—they're sought after to work abroad because of it. This directness and honesty make it relatively easy for them to get along with others. Their pragmatism, modesty, and comfort with compromise make them good candidates for global leadership positions. They don't expect others to know their language and culture; rather, they learn the languages and cultures of many different peoples. Most Dutch speak three or four languages in addition to their native tongue. They are among the most culturally literate peoples in the world.

And they are intermediaries to the world. The Netherlands promoted the founding of the Benelux Customs Union in 1948, which transformed into a full economic union by 1960. It was among the first signers of the 1958 Treaty of Rome, creating what has since become the European Union. The Netherlands was a strong supporter of the single-currency movement in Europe provided for by the Treaty of Maastricht, which led to the euro making its debut in 1999.

A Business Culture Emerges

The Netherlands' long history of trading has created a business culture respected globally for its productivity, international savvy, and openness, as well as a modern entrepreneurial business sector that is evident in the plethora of small companies there. More than a quarter of all Dutch workers are employed by just a handful of major global companies; the majority of the Dutch work for small companies of one to ten employees.

Productivity in the Netherlands currently exceeds that of Germany, Sweden, and Japan. Many say the reason is the egalitarianism and openness in the workplace. Organizational structures tend to be flat, with flexible boundaries. Employees can cut across reporting lines, and power is camouflaged rather than flaunted. Relationships among people are generally open and highly tolerant. Communication reflects a frank, no-nonsense informality with strictly observed etiquette.

Management styles tend toward the participative rather than authoritative; authority derives less from position than personal credibility. Lower-level managers are encouraged to make innovative decisions to get things done, creating an environment that empowers workers. With omnipresent government regulations and collective labor agreements, Dutch managers must find creative ways to reward and motivate employees. Participants in business meetings recognize a clear distinction between ideas and people:

Netherlands: ***At a Glance***
Official name: Kingdom of the Netherlands

Economy type: European Union
Trading bloc: European Union

Location: At the delta of five major rivers; between Belgium and Germany
Capital: Amsterdam **Population:** 15,731,112
Head of state: Queen Beatrix **Official language:** Dutch
Religion: Roman Catholic 34%, Protestant 25% **Literacy:** 99%

World GNP ranking: 14 **GDP (US$ bn):** $345.9
GDP per capita: $22,101 **Unemployment:** 5.6%
Inflation: 1.5% **World export market share:** 4.1%

Major industries: Metals, machinery, chemicals, oil refining, diamond cutting, microelectronics, tourism
Major crops: Grains, potatoes, sugar beets, vegetables, fruits, flowers
Minerals: Natural gas, oil
Labor force: 73% services, 23% manufacturing and construction, 4% agricultural
Computers per 1,000 people: 230.0

Assets: Well-educated, skilled workforce. Modern infrastructure. Low inflation. History of high-tech innovation. Managers with extensive international experience. Excellent marketing skills. Solid and stable financial institutions.

Liabilities: Costly welfare system; one third of the national budget is spent on social security. High labor costs. High income tax rate on individuals. High government spending.

ideas can be vigorously challenged without reflecting an attack on their originator. As with Japan, it's important in Dutch business culture to attribute blame and reward to the team—but without the extremely collaborative and conciliatory nature of the Japanese.

An aversion to the nonessential permeates all aspects of Dutch life, including business. Dutch organizations aspire to be lean and practical but not overly bureaucratic. The more bureaucracy there is, the more the Dutch are likely to feel that the rules don't apply to them. Accumulating money may be a virtue to Netherlanders, but spending it is a vice. Clothes are subdued, offices are simple, and even letterheads are basic and unadorned.

From the Dutch, we learn to be more open and tolerant. Cross-cultural by nature, they adapt easily to other cultures; their frankness and humor enable them to build bridges and be internationally savvy traders.

PRACTICE WHAT YOU PREACH
Shelly Lazarus and Ogilvy & Mather Worldwide *(U.S.A.)*

Title: CEO
Headquarters: New York, New York
Business: A subsidiary of WPP Group plc, the world's largest advertising and marketing services firm, with a network of 40 companies in 83 countries. Clients include American Express, IBM, Ford, Mattel, SmithKline Beecham, and Mattel.
Employees: 8,500 employees in 359 offices in 100 countries

Shelly Lazarus sacrifices nothing of her personal life to the fast-paced, global world of brand advertising. With confident humility, aggressive insight, and authentic flexibility, the Ogilvy & Mather CEO fosters a creative environment for people to excel while enjoying a life outside work.

Every firm has to be clear about what it does and how it does it, especially if it's in the branding business. Lazarus knows that strong principles make strong brands, and Ogilvy & Mather is brand maker for some of the most famous products in the world. It has created its own brand as a lean-forward company that stands by its principles and unleashes creativity around the world.

Lazarus exemplifies the changing role of women in America. She shows her cultural heritage in her strongly held values, direct style, and commitment to self-development and creative individualism.

What do Eastman Kodak, Kraft Foods, Jaguar, Shell Oil Company, Timex, and Unilever have in common? Ogilvy & Mather manages their global identities—and so successfully that it has created a strong brand for itself in the process.

As part of that brand, Shelly Lazarus lives the principles of personal literacy, principles supported by O&M's vision in a constant interplay of personal and business values. She uses her principles to create an atmosphere that enables an unconventional, diverse, creative workforce to feel valued and excel. It takes a mature, secure leader to lead these "creatives" around the world. She does it by standing up for her principles, putting her life into perspective, and celebrating people's diversity and creativity.

Stand Up for Your Principles

"We pursue knowledge the way a pig pursues truffles."

Leave it to one of the world's image powerhouses to talk about its operating principles in such visual and memorable terms. Founder David Ogilvy created an intensely personal document when he wrote these words, intuitively recognizing what globally literate leaders know—that personal and business principles constantly interact, each influencing and informing the other.

Just as our personal principles drive how we interact with others, our corporate principles reflect our philosophy about creating value in business. They are inseparable.

Ask David Ogilvy: "We encourage individuals, entrepreneurs, and inventive mavericks. . . . We have no time for prima donnas or politicians. . . . We value candor, curiosity, intellectual rigor, perseverance, and civility. . . . And we see no conflict between a commitment to the highest standards in our work and to human kindness in our dealings with each other."

Today these shared values glue the O&M global network together. As the chief steward, Lazarus stands up for these principles every day. And she's maniacal about three of them: commitment to brand, respect for people, and a focus on the work.

The principles must be shared by all for worldwide execution: "Today we must deliver global solutions for clients who realize they have global brands." The real challenge is to create global brands executed locally with local customs and values.

"What is universal and what is local is the whole game," notes Lazarus. "The real art is finding a central idea, giving it to a country or a region as a nugget, and giving them the freedom to execute it in a way that makes it relevant for that region."

Take creating the new IBM brand, for instance. A global brand, IBM is known for its size, scope, and image as a technology powerhouse. And while it had become a fallen giant in the United States, O&M understood that there were different emotional reactions to IBM around the world.

"It was seen as a brilliant brain without a heart and soul. We needed to warm it up," Lazarus explains. O&M's solution was IBM's "solutions for a smaller planet" campaign, which brought the world together and made it smaller and friendlier, using foreign languages. "We then delivered the concept to different countries and told them the focus was on having human impact by bringing people together through technological advances. In Japan,

Thailand, and the U.S., we saw our affiliates use this campaign very differently, depending on their local circumstances."

The "brand" of personally literate leaders is that they know themselves: "Being comfortable with yourself gives you confidence and perspective to determine what is and what is not important. You must stand up for your principles. I have to be consistent in my management style because that will allow people to know and trust me." That's why Shelly Lazarus works hard to keep her life in perspective.

Put Your Life into Perspective

Lazarus once refused to forgo a family ski trip to attend a worldwide board meeting in Paris. "People were horrified," she reported.

Like any personally literate leader, Lazarus knows what she can and cannot control. And she knows that having a personal and family life gives her a valuable perspective on life. "You must keep your perspective," she says. "It's only business.

"I'll never forget being in my boss's office one day when I first came to Ogilvy. One of our media planners was literally running around in circles because she was so distraught about an upcoming meeting. At least once a week—even now—I think about how he handled that situation. He got in front of her, stopped her from running, and said, 'What do you think they're going to do to you, take away your children?' "

Lazarus never forgot that image. When people get upset in meetings, she often asks if anybody is going to die or lose their children as a result of the decision being made. "Having a personal life reminds us about the nature of the decisions we are making. The worst they can do is fire us, and we will survive," she says. We each have three legs under life's stool: personal, work, and family. If one is loose or not there, we're vulnerable. And that doesn't make for good leadership. "People don't like people who don't have life in perspective; they don't trust them," she says.

She remembers a man from another agency who worked hard to win a contract. Celebrating with staff afterward, he stood up to thank everyone and proudly acknowledged the personal costs of the project: even though he had promised to attend his six-year-old son's birthday party, he had dropped everything and run when the client called. Though he expected applause, his remarks drew an audible gasp. "We were all thinking, 'How could you do that to your son?' "

Lazarus is a strong advocate of bringing one's full self to work. She isn't afraid to tell people what she feels and thinks, and she believes that her authenticity and transparency help people feel comfortable to be themselves. This is especially critical in a creative work environment, where people need to feel as well as think.

Celebrate People's Diversity and Creativity

Personally literate leaders know that different people need to be led differently.

Lazarus knows that. Creativity is the lifeblood of this company, which has an eccentric, diverse, unconventional, and ego-oriented workforce. "You have to really want people to be creative and not be threatened by it," she says. "Then you have to be willing to let go. We must celebrate creativity. This is a meritocracy based on contribution, not on background. It's a place full of eccentrics that do get ahead."

You have to be prepared for what people bring you. Lazarus started a creative council to stir up the pot: "They have real power; their job is to provoke us and set high standards for the company. We have to be brave enough to let the creative people pass judgment on our collective work. If you don't really want them to solve it in a way that has never been done before, don't ask for it."

To celebrate people's diversity and creativity, O&M uses a lot of global multicultural teams: "We ask who's got the best ideas regardless of country or discipline. We're known to be 'dangerously experimental' and proud of it. If you try something, you begin to know the answer."

Lazarus uses "test beds and experiments" throughout O&M: four or five offices doing things in different ways at all times, with lessons shared around the world. "The heads of our country offices get together regularly to share innovations," she says. "For example, North Americans, Asians, and Europeans are all invited to 'heads of office' meetings in Latin America. This is all about internal intellectual development."

Creativity works best in person: "It's critical for people to work face-to-face. After you've met somebody, it's much easier to call up and have discussions about creativity. The more difficult the global conversations are, the more important it is that we know each other as human beings—because it's all about creativity, negotiation, and compromise."

Lazarus thrives on the challenges that arise when working with global "creatives": "Doing things globally adds a level of complexity and fascination that I would never want to lose."

In fact, she's as happy as a pig in truffles.

MODEL EMOTIONAL MATURITY
Kumar Mangalan Birla and The Birla Group *(India)*

Title: CEO and Group Chairman
Headquarters: Mumbai (Bombay)
Business: The Birlas got their start in the opium trade in the nineteenth century, before diversifying into manufacturing. Now India's second largest industrial empire, the Birla Group is a $4.1 billion business encompassing 37 companies, with lines of business ranging from steel and cement to textiles and financial services. It is the world's largest producer of viscose staple fiber and the sixth largest carbon black producer.
Employees: 61 plants with 140,000 employees in 37 companies in 14 countries

THE IMAGE OF A RISING SUN *evokes meanings of rebirth and divine guidance in Southeast Asia, as does the very name of Aditya Vikram Birla, CEO of the Birla Group until his untimely death in 1995.* Aditya *means "rising sun" in Sanskrit.*

The elder Birla's death at fifty-two catapulted his son Kumar Mangalan Birla to the head of this vast business empire when only twenty-eight. To honor his father, the young leader designed the Birla Group's first corporate logo: a rising sun.

It's a unifying image for the rapidly growing global organization. "The sun embodies values we stand for: its journey is never-ending, and we never stop in our own search for excellence. The sun stands for progress, dynamism, and universality, just as we do," says the younger Birla.

Birla himself is a rising son, leading his company humanely into the twenty-first century.

"He must be at least twenty-five years younger than me, but he's very wise," says one of his senior managers of Birla, who has mastered personal literacy by drawing on an emotional maturity that belies his youth. Birla recognizes the power of mentoring, long practiced in his own family: his grandfather mentored Gandhi, who mentored Birla's father, who mentored him—and now Birla mentors his senior managers. He has cultivated an inquisitive mindset, serves as a trustee of the business, and models emotional maturity for others.

"I have the same hopes, aspirations, and insecurities as any other thirty-year-old," he says humbly. "The difference is that I've had the advantage of a very extraordinary orientation. But I'm just like most people in my generation—we know our own mind." He's also the richest man in India.

Cultivate an Inquisitive Mindset

Birla is clear about where he's going because he continually invests in his own personal learning, offering what he's learned as guideposts for others: "Know what you enjoy doing and go after it. Aggressively seek out learning. Have a vision for your own career. Know what you don't know, which skills you don't have, and what you need to understand better." He has embedded those values in the group's mission, which focuses on a "ceaseless quest for knowledge, perfection, and technological innovation."

Birla shook the foundation of the group by embracing Western management methods, placing young MBAs in senior positions, and abandoning his family's hiring preference for fellow members of their *marwari* business subcaste. In a culture focused on saving face, Birla has begun eliminating unprofitable businesses, balancing tough decisions with respectful benevolence. And he relies on the group's seasoned leaders, building relationships with them by showing respect for their knowledge and experience.

While the group's unwieldy mix of businesses has prompted some to call for streamlining, Birla is taking the time to get it right. His Knowledge Integration Programme (KIP) links pockets of excellence and best practices within the group: "We're focused on moving knowledge around. If one of our Thai managers has a great idea, we make sure it's shared throughout the company, around the world."

Despite India's history of bureaucracy, castes, and passivity, Birla has created a results-driven, decentralized, networked group of independent companies, a structure that demands knowledge integration. Every morning, each factory reports to the head office, giving Birla the status of each operation, on-line and in real time: "It's a very charged environment; my challenge is to quickly integrate that knowledge into the company worldwide."

The group constantly benchmarks against global standards: "If you ask the manager at Hindustan Aluminum about production figures, he can tell you exactly where he stands against the global benchmark." Because the group is so diverse that different parts of it produce exactly the same product, business units may know the external global benchmark, yet find it harder to measure internal competition. Birla is determined to change that.

"This kind of reporting keeps people involved," he says, "and we also have black phones throughout the company that people can use to make suggestions, even on the shop floor. We've received tremendously good suggestions, and we tell people why they're accepted or not." In that way, each employee becomes a trustee of the company, responsible for its growth and success.

Be a Trustee

Adherence to the concept of trusteeship forms the cornerstone of India's unique leadership style. "The most important influence on my career—and on the company—is the concept of trusteeship I learned from my father. He believed everything you do is in trust for the stakeholders. That philosophy is the bedrock of everything we do," explains Birla. "We see ourselves as trustees who do things to create value for the shareholders, employees, society at large, and our families."

With an MBA from the London School of Economics, Birla is a blend of European and Indian management philosophies. "We're trying to merge the best aspects of a multinational with those of a family business," he says. "We bring structure, consistency, institutionalization, and at the same time, we work like a family. As the younger generation, we don't hesitate to put forth our own ideas and compete, but we do so with respect for the family and for our older leaders." It's that kind of respect that moved Birla to name a group-owned hospital after a senior director who died recently with forty years' tenure in the company.

Birla combines his competitive spirit with a culture of passivism and nonviolent caring and benevolence. The teachings of Gandhi and Hindu tradition have made the enterprise more benevolent and family-oriented, yet still competitive with the outside world.

Mentor Others

At the Birla Group, mentoring is a tool to improve the business. "Before his death," Birla notes, "my father cleverly involved me with all aspects of the business. He would let me sit with him in meetings, explain why he dealt with a particular situation the way he did, and ask my opinion.

"He gave me independent responsibility early on—from running stable businesses, those in the implementation phase, some that were still on the drawing board, and some in crisis. I didn't realize it, but he was letting me see different business scenarios at a very young age—situations I would have to face in the future.

"My father believed you'll learn to swim if you're in the deep end of the pool. The independence he gave me—coupled with the training he put me through—was very good learning."

Birla's determined to pass that learning along. "Our top managers need to be what I call 'cocktail managers,' with an all-round perspective. A cocktail manager has broad-based skills. He doesn't work in isolation, isn't a groaner, and knows how to motivate people. He's a person who seeks success and is yearning to learn and improve all the time." Whether he realizes it or not, Birla is describing himself.

"From a leadership standpoint," he continues, "we're investing in a decentralized, delegated structure—having the right people in the right places and giving a lot of leeway in how they work. To succeed, they need to understand clearly what's expected of them, what the organization's philosophy is, and a clear understanding of where we're all headed."

He aims to instill a sense of direction by example. "In meetings, I try to involve people in a common understanding of the situation rather than dictating results or letting a few of the senior managers hijack the conversation," says Birla.

Despite his wealth, education, and power, Birla remains a humble man with great respect for others. He's a mature, modern, modest person with a sense of confidence and humility, a man with extraordinary aspirations and self-awareness. He believes that when employees underperform, a part of the fault lies with the boss. Birla learned a great deal from his father, who gave him room to lead his own way. "My leadership style differs from my father's," says Birla, "but if he were here today, I think he'd agree with everything I'm doing."

ACKNOWLEDGE REALITY
Rolf-Ernst Breuer and Deutsche Bank AG *(Germany)*

Title: Chairman
Headquarters: Frankfurt
Business: The world's largest bank, as a result of its recent acquisition of U.S.-based Bankers Trust, with more than 2,200 offices in over 50 countries.
Employees: 95,847

ROLF-ERNST BREUER is a proud man in a country that struggles with pride.

An optimistic realist, Breuer has a vision of where he wants to go, helping Deutsche Bank become the world's largest financial institution. Reflective about its past, he is also decisive about its future—willing to buy Bankers Trust for $10 billion, he was just as willing to scrap the deal if the return on investment wasn't just right. He's not afraid of the realities he faces: satisfying regulators in two continents, eliminating jobs, and handling revelations about the bank's support of the Nazis.

Proud of his roots, Breuer is frank about the past, present, and future. He's honest about Deutsche Bank's past mistakes in going global and its need for a new corporate culture that thrives on speed and delighting customers. He doesn't fool himself about the strengths of German quality—or the country's bureaucratic shortcomings. And he's clear about acknowledging the bank's part in the World War II Holocaust. He even commissioned historians from around the world to write The Deutsche Bank: 1870–1995, *a book documenting the bank's past.*

Says Breuer, "There is a difference between guilt and responsibility."

Though based in Germany, Deutsche Bank is "in the heart of the borderless world of finance," says Breuer. He wants to be best in class in a field already ahead of many others in its readiness—and requirement—to be global. Deutsche Bank is creating a multinational corporate culture, one deal at a time. But it's remaining German in the process, even though one third of its employees is non-German and one in three works outside Germany: "Although the world is globalizing, we are experiencing a reemphasis, a renaissance, of national values and local approaches."

To create this new DB culture—one that is German, global, and high-performing—Breuer knows that he must demonstrate personal literacy by being frank and authentic, accepting his mistakes and those of his company, and having the courage to move on.

GOOD LEADERS HELP PEOPLE ADAPT TO CHANGE

(Percentage of executives reporting that this was most important for leadership)

- Europe: 54%
- Australia/New Zealand: 49%
- North America: 44%
- Asia: 32%
- Latin America: 25%

Be Frank and Authentic

Something of a maverick, Breuer is proud in a country that is struggling with its pride as a result of its Nazi past. He's participative in a country known for command and bureaucracy. And he's a German with a global mindset.

Breuer is frank about his vision: "Think of a worldwide enterprise with a centralized manufacturing entity but a decentralized distribution network. That's the structural idea for Deutsche Bank," he explains. "We have strong roots in our home, Germany and Europe, but at the same time, we're a multinational distribution network. Being bilingual—English and German—is one of our strategic assets."

Breuer is frank about his values. Deutsche Bank adheres to global human values and upholds clear universal ethics, such as its ban on bribery—in a country where special gifts are embedded in the fabric of business practices. To institutionalize the mission statement globally, he makes sure it applies all over the world. He constantly espouses key values such as loyalty, openness, trust, and performance, cornerstones of the bank's new culture.

And Breuer is frank about Germany's strengths. Deutsche Bank reflects the German national emphasis on quality. "We're never the low-cost producer; our emphasis is on quality, not output. We pride ourselves on customized, high-value-added relationship business," he says. Its commitment to quality products is an outgrowth of its commitment to quality education.

Breuer is well aware of that European bias for educational achievement: "There's a story of a man whose dog was named Dr. Mueller. When he took the dog for a walk in Berlin and called his name, every window down the street opened in response." The DB board is full of people with Ph.D.s, a sign of the respect that Germans—and Europeans in general—have for the academic world.

This emphasis on the quality of people, products, and education are all things that Germany's young people should emulate for the future. "The new generation is European, not shackled by the past. They are of a different generation and with different attitudes and a new pride," he explains.

Accept Your Mistakes

Deutsche Bank bankrolled the Nazis and the Holocaust. It's that simple. Along with Dresdner Bank, Deutsche Bank is a defendant in an $18 billion lawsuit filed in June 1998 claiming that the banks hid assets stolen by the Nazi regime from victims in World War II concentration camps. Rather than shrinking from that awful revelation, Breuer is determined to accept the mistakes, respect the learning, and move forward. He's doing it with a personal openness and trust that models the kind of behavior he seeks from others. "Those dreadful things that happened during the Third Reich are part of the history of this bank," he says, "and we stick to our history in good and bad. We profited in our 128 years from our strengths, so at the same time we have to accept that some things happened in our past of which we cannot approve and where we have to take responsibility."

Breuer is committed to being authentic and transparent about that past, but he doesn't believe we should hold a company hostage to its past legacy—

just its future one: "It's very true that we're not guilty—I wasn't involved, nor were my colleagues or even this generation. Yes, we do feel responsible—but not guilty—for the things our predecessors committed. That's why I do everything I can to bring to light what might not have been discovered in the history of this bank. It's my duty and obligation to bring that awful, shocking past to the surface, both internally and externally. As soon as we discovered in February 1999 that we had funded the Auschwitz concentration camp, we told people."

Like most companies, Deutsche Bank has made its share of mistakes. In particular, it has had uneven success as a global player, especially in the poorly executed integration with Morgan Grenfell in 1989. "This is not the same Deutsche Bank," Breuer patiently explains. "We're now absolutely international, and it's no longer the story of German meets American, with culture clashes."

Here's where Breuer learned to be speedy: "The integration with Morgan Grenfell didn't happen immediately. And it should have, in hindsight. We didn't interfere in their management for five years, but just tried to learn from them. That's a long leash. So after five years of independence, it didn't work well when we tried to integrate."

It's a mistake the bank learned from. It now knows that time doesn't stand still. And while Breuer is committed to facing the bank's past, that doesn't slow his race into the future. He is a man comfortable with making tough decisions. "You need to know when you've listened enough and when to make a decision. Now the theme is speed, speed, speed. No endless discussions. No committees. No meetings," says Breuer, in a country known for consensus decision making. "Now it's time to make things happen."

Have the Courage to Move On

It was 1995 when Deutsche Bank made a play to become a global investment banking powerhouse. Having wanted to enter the American marketplace for some time, it first expanded internally with its investment banking arm, Deutsche Morgan Grenfell, but it couldn't move fast enough that way, so it targeted an acquisition instead.

Deutsche Bank's recent purchase of Bankers Trust is the largest takeover of a U.S. financial company by any foreign company, and has created the world's largest financial institution. Through the process, Breuer has been committed to an honest information campaign, inside and outside the company. His obligation is to communicate openly and keep everyone concerned informed. The bank's new employee newsletter, *Fast Track*, is dedicated solely to news of the pending acquisition.

Breuer is moving ahead with management changes as well, some of which are creating new business models for Europe: "People believe that Germans are too bureaucratic and not very competitive. We tend to overengineer people and products. But that doesn't mean all German companies are like that. We're trying to move from a top-down to a participative environment and bring customer focus, transparency, energy, and conflict into the DB culture. And we're making progress." The challenge for Breuer is finding the right balance among speed, consensus, and collaboration.

"As CEO, I strive for a decent majority of support for decisions, but you never get one hundred percent buy-in." In the case of the Bankers Trust deal, Breuer knew if it didn't move fast enough, he would need to pull the plug: "If there had been too many delays, the acquisition of Bankers Trust would have become economically unreasonable."

It takes personal literacy to look reality squarely in the face, take responsibility for your part, be accepting, learn, and move on. Rolf Breuer focuses on doing that every day, in a culture that has struggled with the process for more than fifty years.

GERMANY: "Quality Perfectionists"

National Snapshot

Compared to other executives, German business leaders say:

- Knowing your strengths and shortcomings is important.
- They are highly committed to continuous learning and training.
- Leadership development at all levels is very important.
- They help people adapt to continuous change.
- They focus on developing new products.
- Inspiring others to excellence is less important, and they are less competent in doing so.
- 98% are native Germans.

The Germans are quality-, task-, and process-oriented. Germany is central to the European Union, and its complex past weighs heavily on it. Rational, disciplined, and efficient, this nation is remaking its identity in the new world order.

THE REICHSTAG, built in 1894 as a symbol of Prussia's imperial grandeur, was partially destroyed during Hitler's early rise to power, and for many years the ruins stood as a memory of World War II. Rebuilt and reroofed with a glass dome, it is now a symbol of a country struggling with a complex past and trying to be transparent about its national rehabilitation. It is the nation's new capitol and one signal of Berlin's revitalization for the twenty-first century.

A nation of storybook castles and great cathedrals, many of which were damaged or destroyed during World War II, Germany is now reemerging as a modern landscape important to the European Union both physically and economically.

United Germany

Since the Neanderthals left their remains in the Neander Valley near Düsseldorf, Germany has had a long history of being united, disunited for long stretches of time, and reunited. Now a decentralized collection of states, this most populous nation in Europe, after Russia, is 91 percent German and 9 percent other, including Turkish *Gastarbeiter,* or guest workers.

Forty-five percent Protestant in the north and 37 percent Catholic in the south, Germany has been united for fewer than seventy of the past 1,100 years. United under Bismarck from 1871 until 1918, divided by the Treaty of Versailles after World War I, united again under Hitler from 1933 to 1945, and divided by the Allies at the end of World War II, Germany was finally reunited in 1989, when the Berlin Wall fell.

From that symbolic moment, real moments of pain and possibility have emerged: the pressure to meet Maastricht Treaty criteria, high unemployment, the economic burden of supporting eastern Germany, all coupled with the rebirth of German pride and the potential for greatly increasing the number of German customers. Europe's largest market, it is considered the gateway to eastern Europe, controlling the heartland of a changing continent.

Yet contemporary Germany exists in the ever-present shadow of Nazism. Devastated after World War II, Germany benefited from the Marshall Plan to rebuild. Based on that model, a staggering $390 billion in western German assistance has been given to the eastern states since 1990. Even so, experts estimate that it will take at least another fifteen years to truly reunify the country. Though the two parts are physically similar, there are unseen differences between their psychologies. The concept of a work ethic, for example, is just one such difference that is now coming to light.

Germany is not as homogeneous as many believe. Regional characteristics are a source of pride and staunchly defended. This federation of regions, each with a great deal of autonomy, is grappling with the mix of an older generation, children of Nazi Germany, and a younger generation who have grown up as proud Europeans, children of a united Germany. Its highly urbanized and educated population expects excellent living standards, abundant leisure time, and comprehensive social welfare benefits. Theirs is a rich artistic heritage, from Goethe's *Faust* to the challenging cinema of Rainer Werner Fassbinder, Werner Herzog, and beyond.

Order and Authority Rule

From precision engineering to the beer gardens of Oktoberfest, the Germans are a surprising juxtaposition of orderliness and freedom. Businessmen who toil in formal, structured work environments may end the day by sunbathing nude on the manicured lawns of Munich's Englischer Garten, one of the largest city parks in Europe.

Yet for all this surprising abandon, the overriding social norm in Germany is for order: *Alles in Ordnung*, or "all in order." This is both a commitment and a way of life. Rational and industrious, Germans strive for discipline and efficiency.

Until recently, their desire for order was personified in their support for former Chancellor Helmut Kohl, a conservative leader who came to power in 1982 on the slogan "No experiments." Even so, it was Kohl who reunited east and west and pushed for a united Europe. And when Gerhard Schröder replaced Kohl, it was with a promise of change: "Our task will be to thoroughly modernize our country and unblock the backlog of reform." Germany is ready to change but must do so in an orderly manner.

The national value of orderliness creates some of the most efficient managers in the world with high needs for social organization and respect for universal regulations. This requires conformity and consensus and leads toward risk aversion. The Germans' paradox is their high degree of hierarchy and deference to authority coupled with their highly cooperative labor-management relations, work councils, leisure clubs, and the disturbing emergence of young racist skinheads.

Germany's Nazi period temporarily destroyed this culture of order by discrediting many of the country's ruling class and destroying the property of millions of families. Modern Germany is now relatively classless, with status more closely linked to wealth than to birth.

Families and whole industries were victims of World War II, though some were reimbursed for their losses. A quarter of Germany's industrial capacity was destroyed in bombings or dismantled after the war and shipped to France and England. What emerged was a people who believed the only way Germany could redeem itself was to rebuild—and well. Hence the Germans' insistence on quality workmanship and great admiration of intellectual power.

Quality of Workmanship

Human capital is the major German strength. This nation has high skills and productivity, a superior educational system, and a commitment to training. It is a country organized to prove that learning really does matter.

Committed to rebuilding the "German way" through an immense pride of workmanship and work ethic, Germans are proud of their economic miracle. Rebuilt from ashes, the country has made the transition from a debtor nation to a world-class leader.

The country is dominated by a strong manufacturing sector. Its reliability for product quality and precision engineering are its strengths; creativity and innovation are not. Innovation in Germany takes place in an orderly, prescribed fashion. Perfection is the goal; making mistakes should be avoided. But in a chaotic global environment, the question is how Germans will deal with conditions of discontinuous change.

A nation that values science, engineering, and Ph.D.s, Germany makes a strong investment in research and development. Germans take long-term planning seriously and maintain a keen eye for detail. Task-oriented, they are frank people who get straight down to business. Time is central to German culture.

A Business Culture Emerges

The world's third largest economy, Germany has two business cultures: the west and the east. Overall, Germany has 11 percent unemployment and high taxes and labor costs, with average wages at $30 per hour. With high unemployment in the east, the costs of integration are turning out to be higher than was ever imagined, and there is resentment in the west at the strain. Manufacturing accounts for 32 percent of GDP; it is dominated by mechanical and electrical engineering, vehicle building, precision instruments, optical goods, and chemicals. Because of escalating labor costs—and their impact on the ability of German businesses to be globally competitive—the emphasis is shifting from "made in Germany" to "made to German standards."

Most German companies are exporters, primarily into Europe, and many see themselves as European companies. In fact, large corporations such as DaimlerChrysler have adopted English as their corporate language. Banks and businesses work closely in Germany, creating a governing elite that sit on each other's boards and cross-fertilize ideas and financing. Corporate leadership is largely the purview of men with engineering backgrounds who are used to traditional management hierarchies. But it is a hierarchical and formal business culture with deep threads of consensus-oriented decision making and collaboration—at least since World War II and the ensuing trepidation about any one individual being too bold as a leader. Clearly, Jürgen Schrempp of DaimlerChrysler and Rolf Breuer of Deutsche Bank are exceptions to that rule.

The Germans have a tradition of slow-moving, rigid, and bureaucratic organizations. This is changing, though, with companies such as software

Germany: ***At a Glance***
Official name: Federal Republic of Germany

Economy type: European Union
Trading bloc: European Union

Location: In the heart of western Europe
Capital: Berlin **Population:** 82,079,454
Head of state: Chancellor Gerhard Schröder
Official language: German
Religion: Protestant 38%, Roman Catholic 34% **Literacy:** 100%
World GNP ranking: 3 **GDP (US$ bn):** $2,055.8
GDP per capita: $25,049 **Unemployment:** 12.7%
Inflation: 1.8% **World export market share:** 11.8%

Major industries: Steel, ships, vehicles, machinery, electronics, coal, chemicals, iron, cement, foods, beverages
Major crops: Grains, potatoes, sugar beets
Minerals: Coal, potash, lignite, iron, uranium
Labor force: 41% industrial, 56% services, 3% agricultural
Computers per 1,000 people: 227.2

Assets: Efficient industrial sectors: strongest in the manufacturing of cars, heavy engineering, electronics, and chemicals. Highly skilled, well-educated population. Strong science and engineering sectors. Dedication to employee training.

Liabilities: High unemployment. High social security cost. Costs of rebuilding and equipping the eastern sectors have slowed economic growth. High income tax on individuals and companies.

leader SAP intent on adapting to change and exploiting the global technological revolution. It is home to some of the most environmentally conscious companies in the world because of the appeal of *die Grünen* or "the Greens," to younger, more left-leaning people.

Even with the third highest GDP in the world, Germany is twenty-fourth on the World Economic Forum's competitiveness index, largely because of the high degree of state intervention in business. The powerhouse of the German economy is the *Mittelstand*, the small to medium-sized family businesses that employ the great majority of German workers.

The trappings of the social welfare state have become elaborate and expensive. While a new generation of business leaders is demanding revolution, some are leaving Germany instead. Fortunately, years of hyperinflation led to a conservative, stable currency—the deutsche mark was one of the strongest currencies in Europe before the euro, and Germany boasts some of the soundest financial institutions in the world, including the Bundesbank, famous for protecting the mark against inflation.

The pressing question for Germany is whether she can preserve her social market economy and remain competitive while still paying her workers more than any other country in the world.

Germans may not be proud of their past, but they are proud of what they've created and how they define success today and for the future. They teach the world about the courage to remake themselves, using quality people and processes to create quality products.

CHANGE BEGINS WITH YOU
Lee Kun-Hee, and Samsung Electronics *(South Korea)*

Title: Chairman
Headquarters: Seoul
Business: Consists of 28 companies and seven not-for-profit organizations that were part of South Korea's largest, most innovative *chaebol* until the recent financial crisis in Asia. Now decentralized, major Samsung companies include electronics, machinery, chemicals, finance and insurance, automotive, and others including hotels, newspapers, and medical centers.
Employees: 267,000 worldwide in 390 offices and facilities in 63 countries

LEE KUN-HEE is reinventing Samsung for the twenty-first century. Called the "bright light in Korea," Lee feels responsible for defining a new business era in his homeland. "Change," he said, "begins with me." This kind of insight is grounded in personal literacy. The following are ten lessons of Chairman Lee that are relevant to leaders around the world.

Change begins with me: "*Each of us must initiate change, not passively wait for others to act. Mere words are not enough. And because change begins with me, actions are what I will show you.*"

Know your true self: "*Once you have made the decision to change, you are strong. Once you have recognized your limitations, you can transcend them. Once you understand what you know, and don't yet know, you begin to realize wisdom.*"

Rediscover humanity: "*We must avoid distrust, selfishness, and irrespon-*

sibility to help those in need. All the profit in the world won't make me happy if we cannot attain this goal."

Value the basic principles: "*In every sport you undertake, learn from it and apply the lessons to yourself." Golf is characterized by rules, etiquette, and self-discipline. Baseball contrasts the value of the star player with the spirit of the catcher, silently leading without demanding the spotlight. Rugby teaches decisiveness and a spirit of struggle.*

Don't fear criticism: "*If you agree with your superiors no matter how wrong they are and disagree with your subordinates no matter how right they are, you are letting the company down.*"

There is no rank in human rights: "*We need to learn what it's like to stand in others' shoes. We're not the only ones with rights. 'Chairman,' 'president,' and so on are simply positions; 'human rights' refers to our all being equal.*"

Stay on the right path: "*It would be better to close the company's doors than harm others simply to make a profit. Violating the law 'for the sake of the company' is disloyalty to the Samsung spirit.*"

Good manners are essential: "*We must adapt customs for modern times. Until now, manners in Asian society have been one way and vertical: people in higher positions receive deference while people in lower positions remain subservient. This must change.*"

Etiquette is global: "*In Western society, etiquette applies to individuals and society. In the Orient, its emphasis is on individuals within families. We must be comfortable with international business etiquette—not only around the world, but at home as more visitors do business in Korea.*"

Be honorable and socially responsible: "*We must separate private from public interests and maintain our personal honor. And we must understand the 'unseen responsibilities' of our company—to play a social role, not just make money.*"

These ten lessons are creating a new corporate culture for Samsung, one that blends the wisdom and traditions of the past with a twenty-first-century spirit of success. Yet Lee alone can't make this happen: "All Samsung employees must participate. But first they must trust my commitment. I pledge my wealth and reputation to ensure we reach our goal."

Lee puts his money where his mouth is. During the Asian financial crisis, he took a 90 percent cut in his salary to demonstrate his commitment. In a time when Korea is rebuilding from the inside out, Lee is helping Samsung do exactly the same.

He's making change happen in a country of proud pragmatists with a long, fragmented history and in a company that once personified the vast power of the *chaebol*s in Korea.

SOUTH KOREA: "Proud Pragmatists"

National Snapshot

Compared to other executives, South Korean business leaders say:

- Beating the competition is a cultural value.
- They help people adapt to continuous change.
- They encourage common goals and values.
- They are highly committed to learning.
- They develop leaders through role modeling and formal training.
- 100% are native Koreans, yet 39% of board members are non-Korean.
- 59% have customers, 50% have suppliers, and 50% have employees in ten or more countries.

A JANUARY 24, 1999, *New York Times* photo showed workers at Samsung Motors protesting the government-mandated merger of Samsung and Daewoo. But if it weren't for the caption telling you it was a protest, you might never know. Their hurt and anger are perfectly contained in geometrically precise rows. Don't let the picture fool you—they are as hungry for change and full of tension as the surging masses of humanity marking South Korean student protests in the past.

Samsung is just one of South Korea's government-supported, export-oriented, entrepreneurial business systems known as *chaebols*, a system that built the Korean economy from nothing and very nearly destroyed it in the course of forty years. *Chaebols* are huge, family-owned conglomerates—the top thirty account for two thirds of South Korea's GNP—born of close cooperation with the government and benefiting from subsidies, tax breaks, and political favors.

Economic crisis forced dramatic change, including the partial restructuring of the *chaebols* about which Samsung's workers protested: they were ordered to reduce debt levels and focus on key businesses while divesting unrelated ventures. The government's "Big Deal" imposed a radical restructuring on the top five *chaebols*, including the swapping of peripheral businesses to focus on their core competencies. South Korean workers will be the biggest losers: 170,000 will lose their jobs in addition to the 1.6 million already unemployed.

Such radical change cannot help but affect a culture dramatically. South Korean management style is traditional and authoritarian, with some individualism and team orientation. Recent changes have created more distance between business and government, decentralized and professional management, and increased participative environments in which merit and education matter, paving the way for more opportunities for women. Some fear that the Westernization of Korean business culture will mean a focus on the bottom line to the detriment of the culture's traditional emphasis on relationships.

In a country anchored by its pride and need to save face, such changes are difficult and culturally costly.

Reinvented History

This isn't the first crisis in Korean history, which dates to 2300 B.C.E. The country has had its share of setbacks, including domination by the Mongols and repeated invasions by the Japanese. Its ethnically homogeneous people lived in tribes or clans until about 76 B.C.E., interacting only in war. Ultimately, three major clans were united in the Shilla Kingdom, beginning a long dynastic rule ended only by Japanese annexation early in this century.

The Japanese suppression of Korean culture created a hierarchical society in which everyone knows his place and shows great respect for superiors. It also influenced Korea's withdrawal into isolation: it was known as the "Hermit Kingdom" until the late nineteenth century, when neighboring giants loomed.

Russia coveted Korea's warm-water ports, China wanted a special trading relationship, while Japan wanted more land and resources, which it got when it annexed Korea in 1910. Japan's harsh rule over Korea created an enduring legacy of resentment that to this day is a stimulus to surpass Japan's business success.

The end of World War II divided Korea. Just before the Japanese were defeated, Russia occupied the northern half of the peninsula and established a Communist government, while the Americans, in conjunction with the United Nations, fostered democracy in the south. The 1949 withdrawal of American troops sparked the Korean War, which in three years destroyed much of the Korean economy and infrastructure. But by 1997—less than fifty years later—South Korea was one of four "Asian Tigers," the eleventh largest economy in the world and second largest in Asia.

Pride and Saving Face

The South Koreans have insisted that all segments of the economy share the pain of this most recent crisis, a concept grounded in Korea's Confucian and Buddhist value system. Unions have allowed workers to be fired, *chaebol*s have restructured their vast holdings, and the agriculture industry has given up some of the subsidies that have protected it from foreign competition.

In South Korea, as in other Asian countries, saving face is vital. To hurt someone's *kibun*, or feelings, causes him to lose face, requiring that one constantly assess another's state of mind.

Despite the current pain and the turmoil of restructuring, the Samsung workers' respectful and orderly protest underscores the centrality of relationships and *kibun* to this Asian culture.

South Koreans remind us that the relationship between business and government makes a difference. Having created the system that led to Korea's economic crisis, business and government are now partnering in a new way to lead that nation's economic recovery.

South Korea: ***At a Glance***
Official name: Republic of Korea

Economy type: Asian Manufacturing
Trading bloc: APEC (Asia-Pacific Economic Cooperation Group)

Location: Occupies the southern half of the Korean Peninsula in Asia
Capital: Seoul **Population:** 46,416,796
Head of state: President Kim Dae Jung
Official language: Korean
Religion: Christianity 49%, Buddhism 47% **Literacy:** 97%
World GNP ranking: 13 **GDP (US$ bn):** $248.3
GDP per capita: $5,402 **Unemployment:** 2.6%
Inflation: 3.5% **World export market share:** 3.3%

Major industries: Electronics, vehicles, chemicals, ships, textiles, clothing
Major crops: Rice, barley, vegetables
Minerals: Tungsten, coal, graphite
Labor force: 27% manufacturing and mining, 21% agricultural, 52% services and other
Computers per 1,000 people: 130.5

Assets: Builds 45% of the world's ships. Highly educated, skilled workforce with a dedicated work ethic. Strong domestic savings.

Liabilities: Instability in the financial sectors. Difficult to start new businesses. Large bureaucracy. Inadequate financial regulations. Lack of managers with international experience and foreign language skills. Powerful business conglomerates called *chaebols* dominate the economy.

CHAPTER FOUR

SOCIAL LITERACY

Engaging and Challenging Others

Technology has created a world of speed and complexity. Only collaborative leaders who build productive networks will thrive. By communicating deeply, they inspire others to action and greatness.

Socially literate leaders unleash the power of collective intelligence. They assemble extraordinary people, focus them on meaningful work, connect their wisdom, and motivate them to do great things. They build strong teams (and break down and rebuild them) faster than ever.

The following behaviors of social literacy make that happen:

- Pragmatic trust
- Urgent listening
- Constructive impatience
- Connective teaching
- Collaborative individualism

In mathematics, one plus one equals two. But outside the world of integers, that equation doesn't hold. If we deconstruct cathedrals, tunnels, or bridges, we are left with simple structural parts—bricks and pipes and wiring—the "ones" in the equation. Bricks are not enough to create a cathedral unless they're combined in the proper way.

The same is true of the building blocks of social literacy. Pragmatic trust and constructive impatience are built from two simple concepts. The building blocks themselves aren't intriguing or new; rather, it's their combination that creates a new meaning, something far greater than the sum of the disparate parts.

As with personal literacy, there is a natural tension between these polar concepts. How can you be trusting while understanding others' agendas? How can you listen deeply and quickly at the same time? How can you celebrate people's individualistic efforts in a collaborative environment? To be successful, you must manage the tensions imbedded in these questions, both within yourself and for the people around you.

Pragmatic Trust

Stan Shih, CEO of the Taiwan-based Acer Group, is building independent businesses around the world with a sense of pragmatic trust. His philosophy of "fresh," his "smiling curve" business model, and his creative organizational structures are all designed to liberate employee talents and build a virtual network of entrepreneurial companies under one global brand.

To fully engage others, we have to share openly what's inside our heads—a kind of honesty that requires deep, enduring trust among the people at the table. Without it, relationships falter. With it, diverse people can work and play together. Trust creates a safe space in which people can share their best selves.

We don't simply need trust, we're drawn to it. We seek out trustworthy leaders who will tell us where we stand, good or bad. We crave realistic information about conditions, choices, and financials. We demand that leaders' words ring true with our experience of them. And with instantaneous World Wide Web access to corporate data and CNN broadcasting twenty-four hours a day, trust and credibility become even more important—and more elusive.

Trust isn't built easily or quickly but painstakingly, by consistent performance over time. Yet in our environment, time is exactly what we don't have. Instead, we're forced to trust quickly or lose opportunities to partner.

Creating informed trust—combining the believer and the pragmatist in each of us—is the answer. Socially literate leaders are skilled at doing just that. They gather data to assess the full story. Acting quickly but cautiously, they ask good questions and share their intentions. They communicate honestly about what's going on inside themselves and the business. Predictable and benevolent, they respect the confidences of others. They're able to handle both the good news and the bad.

Balancing their own self-interest for the good of the group, these leaders work hard not to abuse people's health, feelings, self-image, or values. They believe in other people and tell them so. And they seek opportunities to provide sincere rewards and penalties.

As pragmatists, socially literate leaders choose wisely what information to disclose—and to whom. Always leaning toward trust and openness, they know that people who have information can contribute more to the business.

Different cultures differ on several concepts embedded in pragmatic trust: What is a promise? Should I define self-interest as the interest of myself or my group? Should I place more value on relationships or on rules?

Pragmatic trust requires disclosure. But the way people disclose truths about themselves or their professional lives varies from culture to culture. Americans tend to provide incredibly personal details very quickly, while continental Europeans are much more guarded about their personal lives. And while Americans trust too superficially or rely too heavily on legal contracts, western Europeans tend to take longer to trust, but do so more deeply. The mark of globally literate leaders is their ability to build trust in the way different societies value it.

Urgent Listening

CEO Blair Pickerall leads Jardine Pacific as a fast-paced Hong Kong company while retaining the civility and politeness of the British people. He balances urgency with deep listening, valuing respect, relationships, and loyalty as much as speed. This helps him balance acceleration with deliberation and listen with urgency to the environment around him.

Knowledge may *be* power in the global workplace. But knowledge must be communicated to *have* power. Social literacy fosters the communication of knowledge.

Effective communication has two basic goals: first, to clarify priorities and expectations—to tell people what needs to be done—and second, to create the right tone—to help people feel good about doing it. Achieving both requires us to listen as well as talk.

While we spend more than seven hours each day at work communicating—ineffectively, for the most part—we develop bad communication habits: unproductive meetings, junk e-mail, misread intentions, and long bouts of telephone tag. We can't even process the sheer magnitude of the information bombarding us, so we often ignore it, creating chaos for everyone.

Socially literate leaders create meaning and clarity out of communication chaos. They create predictable workplaces by sharing facts and putting them into context. They work hard to listen to people's needs because they understand the dangers of uninformed, disengaged associates who are self-interested, angry, and unable to work together. To these leaders, challenging and engaging these employees requires more than outward communication: it requires listening.

Listening isn't a new skill. Urgent listening is.

It starts with self-awareness. Listening deeply to your own experiences brings a rich understanding of human behavior to others. True self-dialogue helps you communicate deeply to the words, head, heart, and gut of others. Smelling, feeling, and seeing nonverbal cues, socially literate leaders have inquisitive conversations. They listen with all their senses, never dismissing people's "voices" based on their level or appearance.

Yet socially literate leaders are also driven. They have a destination in mind and, though always willing to listen, do so without being paralyzed by the process. They make themselves accessible but feel free to say when they cannot or should not listen any more.

Socially literate leaders know they can't produce unless they learn—and they can't learn unless they listen. To really hear others, they must engage in true dialogue. Asking questions, involving others at the right time, and engaging in healthy conversation drives learning. The equation is simple: Productivity equals listening plus learning plus caring.

By helping others communicate effectively in our high-speed environment, these leaders turn a passive skill into an active asset. Their challenge is to listen deeply in a world that requires constant dialogue.

Some cultures are better than others at urgent listening. The skill implies a certain kind of intimacy that is less acceptable in some cultures than others, depending on norms of space and distance. Whether a culture is predominantly verbal or nonverbal, direct or ambiguous will also determine how urgent listening is expressed. In their high-context, nonverbal culture, the Japanese, for example, have developed a special skill for listening deeply. And while they listen for nonverbal messages, their German counterparts listen for verbal ones.

Westerners are good verbal communicators; Easterners are good at the nonverbal. The challenge is for each to learn the skill of the other.

Cultural norms often determine who enjoys access to information in organizations, whether in egalitarian cultures such as Denmark or in hierarchical ones such as Mexico. Australians, with their emphasis on individualism and nonconformity, practice urgent listening differently from Venezuelans, who are family-focused and conformist.

Constructive Impatience

Lars Ramqvist, chairman and CEO of Sweden's Ericsson, is driven by an industry of speed and information overload. He leads a company in which 900,000 e-mails are exchanged daily and in which technological innovation and changes in customer demand occur just as quickly. To keep up, Ramqvist constantly demands higher quality, faster speeds, and better service—from both himself and others.

The challenge of any leader is to inspire greatness by raising the bar for themselves and others. By asking for the slightly impossible, they create what Ramqvist calls "constructive impatience": healthy anxiety with a destination.

Inspiring greatness requires:

- Understanding what's personally meaningful to others
- Articulating a higher purpose for work
- Creating healthy organizations that are fun and focused
- Providing good benefits and a safe environment
- Respecting the diversity of all people

But great companies aren't built on safety and respect alone. Globally literate leaders must foster a hunger for getting ahead. They must be impatient enough to bring out the best in their people, setting challenging goals that tap into people's discretionary efforts. Only then can people attain performance levels above and beyond themselves, characterized by courage, creativity, and commitment. The leader's vision for other people is simply greater than people's vision for themselves.

Socially literate leaders are unwilling to settle for mediocrity. By creating bold, audacious goals and expecting a great deal, they stretch people beyond their comfort levels. Yet unchecked, their impatience can be damaging, creating an unhealthy need for instant gratification that destroys constructive work environments.

But melding the best of impatience with a constructive push for excellence creates just enough anxiety to move people forward, not paralyze them. Like a rubber band, if you pull it too hard, it breaks. If you don't pull it hard enough, you don't maximize the potential of the band. But when you optimize the stretch, amazing things happen, matching dreams with deadlines. In the United States—with its short-term horizon—constructive impatience runs in the blood. In China, a long-term time horizon makes citizens less restless about changing immediately. Changes that feel quite radical to the Chinese may seem quite slow to the rest of the world.

Most important, our ability to balance impatience with constructive patience is shaped by our culture's approach to time and relationships. For example, many Latin Americans are adept at doing several things simultaneously, have a different concept of time than others, and focus more on relationship than task; contrast that with the punctuality and sense of time as a fixed order of the Swiss, who are more focused on tasks than relationships.

Connective Teaching

Mads Øvlisen, CEO of Denmark's Novo Nordisk, leads a knowledge company in an expert culture of researchers, scientists, and engineers. Øvlisen knows that connecting all the company's intellects with shared visions and values is the only thing that will set it apart. He is dedicated to personal learning and the development of others, giving them space and opportunity to grow and learn.

Great leaders are great students *and* great teachers. This sounds obvious, but for a company to grow, it must learn every day. Companies that learn the fastest have the best chance of remaining on the cutting edge. And those that engage people in collaborative learning will win in the global marketplace.

Work must be a place of insatiable curiosity, a breeding ground for the lifelong development of all employees. Learning emerges from the creative juxtaposition of people, ideas, and technology, not from the isolated endeavors of individuals. Connective teaching makes this happen.

Socially literate leaders are imaginative and probing teachers, picturing possibilities that others don't see. They know that real change can't happen without learning and that creativity and innovation arise from people's ability to expand their perspective and skills—together.

These leaders see every interaction as a learning opportunity, teaching people about business, psychology, the marketplace, and one another. They teach by telling colorful stories about the past and painting pictures about the future. As teachers, they have an immense power to shed light or cast darkness on the learning process.

Socially literate leaders demand that people around them teach the same way. By creating webs of mutual learning in which each person learns from the ideas and talents of others in the group, they cultivate a collective intelligence that is greater than the sum of its parts. People learn collaboratively and across boundaries. Only then can companies expand their capabilities.

Connective teaching engages all the skills of personal and social literacy. Leaders are willing to ask for help from others without losing self-respect. They know that learning requires reflection, but must be achieved with a sense of urgency and decisiveness. These leaders also balance the belief in others with a realistic appreciation of people's capacity to learn. They hear deeply what people yearn to do and link their talents to the tasks at hand. By setting inspiring goals and stimulating people to think in different ways, they liberate the human spirit.

People who don't learn these literacies risk sabotaging learning around them. Their arrogance makes it difficult for them to appreciate the systemic nature of problems and solutions. And where they are blinded by their personal success, they don't embrace their teaching role.

How we learn—and how we learn with one another—is also culturally determined. In some cultures, leaders are hesitant to seek learning from their subordinates, thinking it shows weakness. The Japanese, German, French, and British tend to learn in structured environments, focusing on incremental improvement, while the Americans and Italians excel at unconventional, creative improvement that occurs in a flash of innovation.

In the United States, learning is an active, experiential activity; in the East, it's more passive—listening to the wise leader and learning. Yet both cultures are changing in the globalized world.

Collaborative Individualism

CEO Helen Alexander hires the best thinkers to write for *The Economist*. They must have strong points of view and possess the ammunition and will to argue against the best. She wants individualists with strong minds. Yet she links them into collaborative teams that cherish debate and work together to write anonymously, merging their unique individual talents with the strength of collaboration.

Alexander is living proof that something interesting is happening in the world. First, it's becoming more difficult to separate leaders from their groups. We can no longer easily differentiate the specific contribution that each person at the table makes. Today's leaders are catalysts and facilitators of collective intelligence, not lords of information. They are evolving into team coaches because they know that two minds are better than one, and many minds are best.

Second, individualistic and collective societies are moving closer, becoming more like one another. Collective societies are asserting their individualistic side; individualistic societies are becoming much more collectivist than before. Hiroshi Okuda at Toyota is extracting the best thinking of individuals in the collaborative culture of Japan, while Alexander's collaborative teams at *The Economist* thrive in the largely individualistic United Kingdom.

The combination of these two trends creates collaborative individualism, a critical skill of social literacy and the blending of individualism and collectivism.

Individualistic cultures tend to be marked by the elevation of self-interests, focused on personal agendas and skills. Australia, the United Kingdom, and the United States have been built on concepts of creative individualism and competitiveness. The individual takes precedence over the group, and original thinkers are rewarded based on merit and performance.

By contrast, collectivist societies are grounded in group interests, common rather than individual purpose, and group power and influence. Societies such as Japan and China emphasize conformity, group power and influence, harmony, and team performance.

When these two mindsets come together, a new concept emerges: collaborative individualism, the blending of self-interest and common purpose. The results are striking: coordinated teams of original thinkers that merge individual and group voices. Collaborative individualism focuses on harnessing complementary skills by engendering creative interdependence. Teams are the hallmark of this new paradigm. Shared vision coupled with individual and group accountability creates teams in which individuals all work for themselves while working together.

In this scenario, the leader serves as an orchestra conductor, hires the best "musicians," often better than herself, and combines their "voices" to create music in a performance that's bigger than any one of them. As in any symphony, each instrument enjoys moments of individual celebration, and the whole performance is made possible by mobilizing individualists in a collaborative setting.

Socially literate leaders test ideas by challenging people. They're willing to confront and resolve destructive conflict, managing their own anger. They connect their own personal interests to the shared interests of the business and demand the same of others. They openly share the tools of collaboration: information, skills, responsibility, and rewards. And they demand that people operate as mature business partners, taking initiative, providing feedback, and acting responsibly. By creating a sense of partnership among all players on the team, they reduce cautiousness and conflict. By giving everyone a voice, they model the very behavior they seek.

Egalitarian cultures such as New Zealand, Denmark, and Sweden do this best; hierarchical ones like India and Singapore have more difficulty with allowing the equality of voices that marks collaborative individualism.

Collaborative individualism balances individual and collective perspectives, as well as hierarchical and egalitarian ones. Many cultures have developed expertise at both ends of that continuum; the best leaders move toward the center by blending the best qualities of each.

The men and women whose stories follow are socially literate leaders who blend the best of all these skills: people such as Ping An Insurance CEO Peter Ma from China, who helps us craft social ground rules, U.S.-based Westin Hotels & Resorts CEO Juergen Bartels, who stretches people beyond their dreams, and Novartis CEO Daniel Vasella from Switzerland, who communicates deeply about change; Coca-Cola CEO Doug Ivester from the United States, who pays as much attention to "soft" issues as "hard" ones; Japan-based Toyota CEO Hiroshi Okuda, with his penchant for listening for the future; and Guillermo Luksic, CEO of the Luksic Group, who teaches us how to build networks for success in Chile and beyond. Each of these leaders has a story to tell and a lesson to teach.

THE TOP FIVE SOCIAL LITERACY SKILLS

When asked to identify the two most important aspects of working with and influencing others, business executives said:

- Inspiring others to action and excellence: 70%
- Listening and communicating effectively: 63%
- Encouraging others to adopt common goals and values: 29%
- Teaching and coaching others: 23%
- Transforming conflict into creative action: 16%

LISTEN DEEPLY BELOW THE SURFACE
Hiroshi Okuda and Toyota Motor Corporation *(Japan)*

Title: President
Headquarters: Tokyo
Business: Founded in 1925 by Sakichi Toyoda. In 1996, the 90 millionth Toyota automobile rolled off the assembly line. Well known for its frugality, Toyota has cut $2.5 billion in costs since 1995, and Okuda has ordered $800 million a year in extra cuts from his managers, launching the biggest expansion the auto industry has ever seen, at a cost of $13.5 billion.
Employees: 159,035

WHEN HIROSHI OKUDA isn't climbing mountains, earning a black belt in judo, or preserving primeval forests, his passion is becoming the number one car maker worldwide and regaining Toyota's 40 percent share of the Japanese market. He listens to the market as urgently as he listens to the silence on the world's mountain peaks. It's a strategy that has already paid off.

Every fall, Toyota's executives travel to the spiritual home of the Shinto sun goddess to receive blessings on new Toyota models. In 1997, instead of the customary six new models, a whole caravan pulled up to the two-thousand-year-old shrine—one of the largest new product offerings in Toyota's history. Even more recently, Toyota shocked the automobile industry by promising to fill custom orders in just five days, compared with the industry standard of thirty days. This product speedup had been achieved by aggressively listening to the market.

While the Japanese are good at both listening to their past (revering their long heritage) and listening to the present (copying what they see around them), Hiroshi Okuda is also good at listening for the future (hearing what people want and anticipating their needs in local markets around the world).

Madame Marie Curie taught us that "dysymmetry causes phenomena." She recognized that real learning—and breakthroughs—occur only when we are jarred loose from our set patterns of thinking.

Curie might as easily have been addressing Hiroshi Okuda's recent revolution at Toyota Motor Corporation. Okuda at once exemplifies and defies Japanese culture. His frank talk in a culture of obfuscation, youthful spirit in a culture grounded in reverence for seniority, and swift action in a culture of deliberate consensus making all seem to contradict Japanese cultural traditions such as *tatemae, ringi,* and *kaizen.* But the mathematician Henri Poincaré reminds us that even when there is great change in a system—in his case a mathematical system, in Okuda's a management system—"there is something that remains constant." And while Okuda is accelerating the evolution of both Toyota and traditional Japanese cultural concepts, both the man and the company remain firmly Japanese.

In an environment where speed to market is a major competitive advantage, Okuda understands the importance of listening. He combines speed with the depth of the Japanese style of listening to create a three-pronged approach to listening: listening urgently and deeply, listening to the unspoken and the spoken, and listening to global and local voices.

Listen Urgently and Deeply

When Okuda was named president in 1995, he knew Toyota had become a slumbering giant. *The Economist* reported that "For most of the 90's, Toyota has arguably been dozing." Its market share had dropped below 40 percent in Japan for the first time in fifteen years, after Toyota missed the sport utility vehicle trend, which its major domestic competitor, Honda, had caught. Okuda then began revolutionizing the way Toyota operates. He moved swiftly, creating a company "ready to unhesitatingly pounce on new ideas."

Okuda's strategy worked. "By the latter half of the decade," *The Economist* continued, "this [situation] had turned around. Toyota launched 11 models between 1996 and 1997." In other words, it woke up.

Okuda has spent his adult life working for the Toyoda family, with more than forty years of experience encompassing every phase of the Toyota operation. The first non–family member at the helm since 1967, Okuda confronted organizational inertia by developing "Toyota 2005 Vision—Harmonious Growth," his vision of an energetic, quick, and socially responsive enterprise. "I want Toyota to be a company full of youthful spirit and vitality," he notes.

First he needed to revitalize decision making, beginning with a massive overhaul of product development and corporate culture. His broader strategy is to rekindle the killer instinct at Toyota: "The faster I make decisions, the faster Toyota can move forward. I have to make quick decisions and anticipate what might happen in the future. To do that, I have to listen to people."

Okuda has institutionalized speed into the fabric of the company. He reduced the average age of the Toyota board members, flattened the hierarchical structure, replaced Toyota's seniority-based promotion system with one based on merit, and instituted casual Fridays.

"We have to operate globally, which requires new knowledge," says Okuda. "We have to nurture young human resources quickly. We have to give responsibility and authority to younger workers to capture a new cus-

IS "BEATING THE COMPETITION" A CULTURAL VALUE?

(Percentage of executives reporting this as their highest value)

- Asia: 30%
- Europe: 23%
- Australia/New Zealand: 19%
- Latin America: 19%
- North America: 14%

tomer base." Through its Toyota Young Generation Project, Okuda expects managers to "create energetic workplaces, in which younger employees feel secure to make their stand without hesitation, and to make full use of their spontaneity, intelligence, and senses."

With this new emphasis on youth comes changes in management style as well. "We're reducing the number of layers in the organizational structure," he says.

Traditional Japanese decision making is also being modernized. *Nemawashi* describes the process of bringing soil from where a tree is going to be replanted to where the tree is now so it can adjust to its new environment. This process of laying the groundwork before launching a project is followed by the process of *ringi*, "where you get the seal of approval throughout the organization before anything is official." The *ringi* system is documented by gathering signed approvals by all those affected by a decision in a bottom-up process. As a result of these "chops," Toyota—never known for its creative innovation—suffered from a slow, indecisive production development process. "We've attempted to reduce the number of chops needed from twenty to three—and the last chop will be mine," Okuda explains.

Under his leadership, designers have been given a freer hand to talk to the market. The result? Toyota has successfully reduced its new-product development time from twenty-seven months to a new industry standard of fifteen months. Okuda wants to create "high-speed, flexible carmaking with aggressive overseas expansion" that will allow Toyota to "pounce on consumer trends, drawing inspiration from human lifestyles."

Hear Both the Spoken and the Unspoken

Much of what's said in Japan isn't really said at all.

The Japanese are highly attuned to the unspoken and intuitive elements of communication. Japanese businessmen have always been good listeners because harmony and the preservation of relationships is central to Japanese business strategy.

Urgent listening is listening deeply to the head, heart, and gut of the organization: listening at all levels and to moods, verbal and nonverbal signals, body language, and tone of voice to gain a sense of how people feel.

Okuda speaks openly and directly, giving people opportunities to express real concerns. He sees himself as an "intermediary between the younger and older generation." Says Okuda, "I serve as the persuader." He might better call himself the "harmonizer."

Okuda's leadership is the foundation of a management style known as "Toyotaism," which seeks to achieve harmony among supervisors and workers and mutual trust between labor and management by institutionalizing a friendly, open attitude. Toyota is more tolerant of individualism than other Japanese companies. It balances individualism with harmony, independence with individuality, and it does this by listening to the spoken and unspoken word.

Hear Both Global and Local Voices

Toyota now has a localized strategy, in which it listens to customers around the world, tailoring cars to local markets. By aggressively listening to the changing global marketplace and customer preferences—and by listening urgently to competitors—Okuda ensures that Toyota is on target. He never loses the pulse himself, still personally reviewing every television ad before it appears and test-driving every Toyota under development.

Okuda knows that Toyota must become a master of *omoiyari*—filling anticipated needs—in a world in which anticipating needs is becoming ever more difficult. Urgent listening is Toyota's strategy for keeping up.

Toyota spends years in countries learning about culture, videotaping consumers at work and play to understand their needs. They disassemble BMWs and Mercedes-Benzes to determine how these mechanical marvels function. And they work to improve relationships with local dealers, tailoring brands such as Corolla and Lexus to local environments and tailoring advertising to local tastes. Their ad campaign featuring muscled bodies on the beaches of California spoke directly to Americans with its tag line, "We build hard body trucks." All these adaptation strategies support Toyota's twenty-first-century business plan to have plants outside Japan produce two thirds of the vehicles it sells in the global market, versus less than half in 1994.

Toyota's founding motto is "Enriching society through carmaking." It aims at nothing less than "harmonizing the global village by accepting cultural differences and improving communications as a basis for a more affluent society." And it knows that the most effective communication is listening, now a core competency for Toyota.

Its global vision is one of "harmonious growth." To Okuda, that means sharing the benefits of growth with all the people involved: shareholders, employees, and business associates, while at the same time working in tandem with people, society, the global economy, and the earth. Local managers are free to interpret the vision as they see fit.

"It might take fifty years to establish this vision," Okuda says without apology. He knows that contrary to Western perceptions, Japan is actually short-term, not long-term, focused. "We're good at work-arounds and quick fixes," he admits. "If we had been good at long-term thinking, I doubt World War II would have happened."

In a business driven by intense competition, Okuda is keenly aware of the paradox of fighting to succeed and seeking to harmonize: "I'm not trying to strike a balance between the two. Performance comes first."

And it's performance he's got: Toyota's stock price performance has been at the top of its class, increasing more than 70 percent faster than the overall Tokyo market. It's been voted the world's most respected engineering company and Asia-Pacific's most respected company. And its handling of the Asian economic crisis has been exemplary.

USE "SOFT SKILLS" TO YOUR ADVANTAGE
M. Douglas Ivester and The Coca-Cola Company *(U.S.A.)*

Title: Chairman and CEO
Headquarters: Atlanta, Georgia
Business: Global soft drink leader, with more than 80% of profits from outside the United States. Every day, consumers enjoy more than 1.1 billion servings of Coca-Cola, Sprite, Fanta, and other products of the Coca-Cola Company. In overall market value, the company ranks number 3 on the *Fortune* 500, doing business in 200 countries.
Employees: 29,500

DOUG IVESTER rose quickly through the ranks at the Coca-Cola Company—and not by accident. He was the youngest vice president in the company's history at thirty-three, CFO at thirty-seven, COO at forty-six, and chairman and CEO at forty-nine. Years earlier, he had committed to paper the dates by which he intended to attain those positions—and he wasn't far off the mark. His trademark is his focus on developing people and his penchant for walking the world's streets to see how easy it is to buy an ice-cold Coca-Cola in tiny corner markets from São Paulo to Shanghai.

On the cover of its recent annual report are forty-eight Coke bottles. One, colored red, represents Coke's share of the 48 billion beverages consumed in the world in one day. Ivester wants two red bottles there. "Every one counts," the report says. Under Ivester's leadership, you could also read it a different way: "Everyone counts."

To color that second bottle red, Ivester is narrowing the gap between vision and execution, a legacy of his American roots. By emphasizing the soft infrastructure—communication and learning—the Coca-Cola Company links business purpose with resources and results.

The Coca-Cola Company has been called "one of the most noble business systems on earth." Delighting all its stakeholders imparts a unique integrity to the business, creating a value far higher than the cans of Coke it's so well known for. Coca-Cola clearly knows that its competitive advantage rests in its people, brands, and systems—and that when you have something that creates value for everyone, you create real admiration.

Doug Ivester is the personification of Coke's emphasis on value. A strong, restless leader, Ivester is the son of factory workers from a tiny Georgia mill town. When he got an A in school, his dad would simply ask, "They give A-pluses, don't they?"

Ivester believes that leaders are "elected every morning in the elevator. People gravitate toward people from whom they're getting real leadership—it's an election that takes place by the actions of the people. They're looking for you to add value to the conversation; they're looking for trust and for consistency. And management usually lags behind that informal election."

Ivester delivers all three: value, trust, and consistency. His long-standing commitment to communication and learning has made him a leader who lives the social literacy skills of urgent listening and connective teaching every day. Both are critical to the Coke "machine" that consistently ranks number one among *Fortune*'s most admired companies.

Be Precise in All Your Communications

Doug Ivester listens and watches—a lot. Both in management meetings and out on the street, he watches people, their body language, and their conversations. He believes that soft drinks are for everybody, everywhere, everyday. Coca-Cola can't afford to be the least bit elitist: "I don't eat in fancy French restaurants anymore; I want to go where the guy is eating a piece of meat, french fries, and Coke." Leaders must be observant, live outside their own head, and learn from the uncomfortable. By employing urgent listening, Ivester does just that.

"I've always tried to listen deeply to two levels of communication—the surface level of words that people use to be nice to each other, and the unspoken level," he says. It takes real skill to hear that second level—an intuitive ability to read people at a deep level and an urge to constantly seek out the nonverbal. "In today's fast-paced world, we've reduced the margin for error. There aren't as many layers and filters; we can't afford the luxury of imprecision."

Deeply committed to interpersonal communication and building global communication systems, Ivester knows that your office relies on the brainpower you carry with you. He intends to ensure that that brainpower has the globally wired technology to support it. Creating communications toolboxes allows Coca-Cola to use a spectrum of tools to address any situation, whether voice mail, e-mail, or videoconferencing. Above all, Ivester demands communication that is simple, easy, global, technological—and human. That's why he's made a conscious decision to create a voice-mail culture in this globally wired company, rather than relying solely on e-mail.

"Voice mail allows people to detect and communicate the full human message between people," he comments. "When you use voice mail, it is instant and personal. You get tone, heart, and emotion: you can hear what's underneath the words. If I read an e-mail, I can't hear the stress or the emotion." E-mails provide the hard-fact information. "But I don't look to e-mails for insights; most of that comes out of voice mail."

And because Coca-Cola is a global company, many of those voice-mail conversations take place across cultures. To be effective, Ivester and his team debrief what is appropriate in each culture.

Ivester advocates that Coca-Cola operate in a "corridor of behavior": "A straight line is very difficult—it's easy to fall off that tight wire. So we say, 'Here's an acceptable corridor of behavior for us.' Then we look at the other company or person we're dealing with, and say, 'Their corridor is a little bit off of ours.' We have to find out what's outside their corridor of acceptable behavior and stay away from that. If we can get the corridor wide enough so both of us can fit in, then we can make progress."

Consider Ivester's recent trip to the Middle East: recognizing that his hosts wouldn't be working on Friday, he knew he'd have to contain his eagerness to get down to business when he arrived. In India, he appreciates the fact that there is little physical contact. But while traveling in Brazil, he expects big hugs from fellow executives.

Yet Ivester believes cultural barriers are going up as trade borders come down, and he knows that Coca-Cola must manage around those cultural obstacles. Ivester's job—any leader's job—is to widen his own corridor of behavior without altering the nature of the company. By listening, interacting, and communicating across cultures, companies expand their corridors of behavior. That's why Ivester's trying to build an organization centered around learning and the rapid transfer of knowledge.

Teach People How to Learn Together

When Doug Ivester doesn't know something, he finds a way to learn about it. Because he hated getting wet in the rain as a supermarket bag boy in rural Georgia, he worked for free on his days off for four months to learn how to run a cash register. An accountant by training, and an introvert by nature, thirty years later, he is still learning that way. "I try to go into any situation with a point of view that says, 'I'm going to learn something.' If I'm a little uncomfortable, I'm probably growing."

"If you hate the symphony, you should go to the symphony; if you hate country music, you should go to a country music concert," Ivester argues. This is especially true in a business that seeks to sell to all people, no matter what their background or interests.

To widen Coca-Cola's corridors of behavior, Ivester is building a learning organization. He has hired a senior executive learning officer to institutionalize the wisdom of experiences, country to country, and to turn Coca-Cola into a learning machine. Coke has developed a global toolbox to augment its communications tools, one that includes lessons in dialogue, learning coaches, management routines, a worldwide intranet, and a global learning catalogue: "I want this organization to have the very best tools available, both hardware and software, to improve the overall performance of the company—tools that help people learn how to communicate and learn how to learn."

One tool the company uses aggressively is learning coaches assigned to operating divisions to improve overall communication in business meetings. "Learning strategists at our meetings debrief us on our communication styles and help us clarify what was said and how it was received," says Ivester. "Otherwise, we'd finish the meeting and part ways without having good, crisp understanding of what was taking place. We can't afford that."

For Ivester's strategy to work, his managers must be willing to learn from those coaches. That's why they have invested a great deal in teaching managers the art of dialogue: "Either people have a passion for communication and developing people, or they have to have a wide enough corridor to give these new skills a try."

Coca-Cola's "Project Infinity" is helping develop a new information system, a global transportation system for data: "Like a trucking system that can wear out and needs to be replaced, Project Infinity is our 'new truck,' improving the overall information technology system around the world."

Another tool now in development is "Coca-Cola Management Routines." Ivester knows that effective managers have productive daily routines and ineffective managers don't. In his case that means listening to voice mail in the shower, reading five newspapers when he gets to the office, and meeting monthly without fail with his worldwide quality team and the group that manages the company's McDonald's account. "I've got a very specific routine that I go through to keep my day efficient," he says. "Mine may not be the best, but there's something valuable about routine."

The company's Management Routines program is designed to serve as best practice for managers to emulate or alter to fit their own style. Other management tools include a worldwide intranet and global learning catalogue on which management speeches are placed, allowing people to access wisdom throughout the company.

These are "soft innovations" inside a company known for its hard results. Ivester's philosophy centers on destination planning, inspired by ideals and aspirations: "We've tried to move to a destination point, defining the aspiration and goals as best we can, asking what the obstacles are, the tools and resources you need to put in place, the plan of execution, and the metrics for success—and it's a continuous loop of learning."

Ivester should know, having applied destination planning in his own life with great success. With such a thirst for learning and communication, it's a good thing he works for the world's leading thirst quencher.

CRAFT SOCIAL GROUND RULES
Peter Ma and Ping An Insurance Company *(China)*

Title: President and CEO
Headquarters: Shenzhen
Business: Founded in 1988, Ping An is one of China's three national insurance companies. Its formation was a breakthrough in the reforms of China's insurance system. Ping An maintains relationships with 160 foreign insurers, enabling them to provide services in more than 700 countries and cities.
Employees: 130,000 in 400 branches in China, Hong Kong and the United States, plus offices in London and Singapore

WALK INTO THE HEADQUARTERS of Ping An Insurance Company and look up, and you'll see a bust of Confucius—not at all surprising in this Chinese company. But look again. Facing Confucius from across the lobby is none other than Sir Isaac Newton. In fact, paintings of great Eastern and Western thinkers serve as a backdrop all the way down the entry hall to where Confucius and Newton peacefully coexist.

Ping An blends the best of Chinese and Western traditions—and not just in artwork. "Confucius says people should love each other, obey the rules, and respect each other. Yet in modern society, we must advocate change and innovation. By blending the past with the present and integrating foreign experience into the Chinese environment, we've created a highly competitive enterprise," says the company's CEO, Ma Mingzhe, or Peter Ma, as he's known outside China.

Ma has a deep understanding of the principles of human relationships and knows that a fast-changing world requires a set of guidelines to clarify commitments and responsibilities—not unlike those of Confucius himself.

Ping An Insurance Company continues to break new ground, as it has since it was founded in 1988 as China's first joint-stock, partially employee-owned company. From $30 million in assets in 1988, it has grown to a $30 billion company today, and from 10 to more than 130,000 employees. Income and profits have doubled almost every year in the past seven years.

Ping An Insurance represents a breakthrough in China's reform of the insurance business; in 1994, it became the first company to sell life insurance in China. It is considered one of China's most innovative private companies, highly aggressive and entrepreneurial, with a bright future in a huge market. Yet even with a massive domestic market, it is keen to internationalize to insulate itself from fierce domestic competition—and it plans to recruit more overseas staff to do so.

Amid these breakthroughs, Ping An remains solidly based in Chinese tradition. Its CEO blends this new, innovative, young business with its ageless past by merging Chinese and Western philosophies, by clearly defining employees' commitments and responsibilities, and by supporting people with a strong team culture.

Blend the Best of Chinese and Western Philosophies

Great leaders are great teachers, and Confucius was one of them. He had a teachable point of view and passed on his wisdom through stories. A former university professor, Peter Ma is doing much the same thing.

The secret of his company's success is its ability to keep one foot in traditional Chinese culture and one foot in the world, constantly learning and modernizing Chinese culture. Ma identifies the mission, lays out core values, fosters a strong corporate culture, and invites people to work according to those principles.

He believes that many Western cultural values are rooted in Western religions. "But Chinese culture is different," he explains. "Our values are rooted in the teachings of Confucius and in our history; we're very focused on relationships and social interactions." Confucianism is not a religion but a way of life followed by Chinese people for more than three thousand years.

It is woven into the fabric of Chinese life itself rather than simply being a creed to be accepted or rejected. Ma has woven Confucianism into Ping An's life—and he's brought it into the twenty-first century to make Confucian principles relevant to modern business realities.

Confucian tradition is based on six values: "To love each other like brothers and sisters, be responsible to society, behave cordially and courteously, be intellectual and wise, be innovative and reforming, and be trustful and trustworthy." These values are the cornerstone of Ping An's corporate philosophy.

Ironically, those values are being eroded in contemporary Chinese society, a trend Ping An is trying to reverse. "In China today," Ma laments, "traditions of Confucian thought have been lost, the cultural revolutions and wars have caused us to lose many of the country's traditional values. Our company is taking the lead in helping to reteach these values. Every year, hundreds of managers come to the home office to study and practice these principles; we teach managers how to be teachers of these principles."

To compete, Ping An's culture integrates Confucian values with Western concepts of service, planning, analysis, and investment strategy. "From the West, we've learned about professionalism, devotion to one's job and profession, and the need for people to love and respect one another," Ma says.

"China is a rapidly changing society," he acknowledges. "It's a fast-paced and dynamic marketplace." In the face of such rapid change, he still looks to traditional Chinese culture for guidance. Blending Confucian tradition with new business realities, he's turning to storytelling with *New Ideas on Ping An Spirits*, a published collection of famous Confucian and other traditional stories with modern interpretations.

Ma believes young people are best positioned to integrate Western and Eastern thought. While state-owned companies are hesitant to hire young people, Ping An welcomes them: "Young people are very smart and open to the principles of free markets, initiative taking, and adapting to change." More than 80 percent of Ping An's employees have college diplomas and higher degrees, 70 percent have insurance experience, and most are under twenty-eight years of age.

Define People's Commitments and Responsibilities

Ma understands that talking about mutual obligations inspires others to higher levels of purpose and performance. He assumes that Ping An's employees are adults who are eager to make and keep commitments to one another so they can excel intellectually *and* spiritually.

Just as Confucius outlined a clear path for living, Ping An's principles clearly define employees' responsibilities and commitments to one another—and their customers: "Commitments are a set of promises, duties, and obligations, and a pursuit that will never change. The fulfillment of these commitments is our everlasting mission."

Ping An's commitments are to their customers, to whom they pledge best services and sound protection; to their employees, to whom they pledge career progression and pursuit of happiness; to the shareholders, to whom they pledge stable returns and asset appreciation; and to society, to which they pledge to repay society and build the country.

Nurture a Team Environment

Ma has built a culture that personifies "teamness." By nurturing collaboration, he challenges people to live a life of Ping An commitments by being social stewards.

"The requirements for a Ping An manager," he says, "are to identify with the corporate culture, have good technical skills, inspire subordinates, keep a calm mind in adverse circumstances, and motivate people to work together. Since we don't have a lot of experience, we have to work hard with a clear, shrewd mind.

"My main tasks are to identify company mission, lead strategic planning, and foster a strong corporate culture." It's this culture setting that Ma focuses on and that accounts for Ping An's phenomenal success: "Our aim is to develop Ping An into a full-service, first-rate international financial services group."

To achieve those goals, Ping An has created a culture of teamwork that permeates not only day-to-day operations but all of the company's relationships, structures, and systems. Ma calls this the "Ping An Spirit." Ping An has intentionally worked to create its own corporate culture, with its own set of values, rituals, standards of behavior, and fun. Through a company song, intensive education, and a nationwide videoconferencing capability, it carefully nurtures its corporate culture. In weekly speeches to all employees throughout China, Ma urges the staff to work together. This year alone, Ping

HOW REGIONS DIFFER IN SOCIAL LITERACY

Our survey reveals these top social literacy skills for each region:

- **Asians** encourage others to adopt common goals.
- **Latin Americans** transform conflict into creative action.
- **Europeans** inspire others to excellence.
- **North Americans** listen and communicate effectively.
- **Australians/New Zealanders** teach and coach others.

An plans to train at least 70 percent of staff members at its training center or abroad.

"Our corporate culture," says Ma. "should be based on long-standing Chinese traditions. We should learn and rely on past traditions, adapt to present-day business challenges, and adapt the foreign ideas of great companies around the world to Chinese needs." Ping An is quickly becoming a global company, internationalized in management, intellectual ability, capital, and development.

As in the lobby of Ping An's corporate headquarters, Ma is as comfortable with Sir Isaac Newton as he is with Confucius.

CHINA: "Ancient Modernizers"

National Snapshot

Compared to other executives, Chinese business leaders say:

- Formal training rather than natural ability influences the development of leaders.
- They encourage others to adopt common goals and values.
- They are less likely to share knowledge throughout the organization.
- They are less likely to help people adapt to continuous change.
- Understanding one's cultural roots is very important to success.
- They recognize the need to improve senior executives' multicultural experience.

More than four thousand years of history and Confucian values have shaped the Chinese. From that rich heritage has sprung a collective yet pragmatic culture, inventive minds, and a people intent on saving face by communicating ambiguously. From this densely woven fabric, revolutions have periodically emerged onto the world stage, such as the clockworks the Chinese were the first to invent.

CHINA HAS GIVEN THE WORLD a lot more than the Great Wall. Paper, the wheelbarrow, umbrellas, matches, movable-type printing, gunpowder, rockets, the spinning wheel, watertight compartments in ships, guns, decimal fractions, the magnetic compass, and the relief map are just a few of the inventions that originated in this vast Asian nation. Imaginative and pragmatic, the Chinese were also—ironically—the first capitalists, though now their capitalism is tempered with Confucianism and communism. They were the first to use paper money—as long ago as the ninth century, though some say they had it as early as 2600 B.C.E. Europe didn't circulate paper money until the 1720s and the United States not until the American Civil War.

While Westerners may perceive China as a monolithic country, more than fifty recognized nationalities comprise its rich ethnic blend. The Han people make up 94 percent of the population and speak Mandarin Chinese, the world's most widely spoken language. More than 1 billion people—25 percent of the world's population—live on 7 percent of the earth's surface in this country where 80 percent of the land is uninhabitable.

More Than 4000 Years of Recorded History

By their own admission, the Chinese are at the middle of the world. Their "Zhong-guo," or "Middle Kingdom," was the largest in the world long before the Roman Empire. Big and centralized, it often behaved as if it needed no one from outside its borders. When Cheng Ho set sail in the sixteenth century with hundreds of ships on a trading expedition throughout Southeast Asia, he returned to China's shores never to sail again. When the king of England suggested trade with China in the late eighteenth century, the emperor responded that China was completely self-sufficient. It enjoyed a "splendid isolation" that it has entered into several times in its history.

But during the nineteenth century the Chinese began showing signs of wear as the Industrial Revolution made Europe sufficiently powerful to impose humiliating unequal treaties on them. The Japanese also invaded and devastated China. It was a period of history the Chinese have never forgiven, creating an intense national pride and xenophobic ethnocentrism that shape Chinese culture.

Modern Chinese history centers around five key periods: socialist transformation (1949–58); the Great Leap Forward (1958–62); the period of recovery from the Great Leap and preparation for the Cultural Revolution (1962–66); the Great Proletarian Cultural Revolution (1966–76); and reform and economic modernization (since 1978). The Communist Party, for all its many faults, has given the country some stability. The Chinese people are wealthier and better fed, housed, and educated than at any time in history, though their lives could hardly be described as stable during the Cultural Revolution and Great Leap Forward. Chinese per capita income doubled between 1978 and 1987, and again between 1987 and 1996.

With one economic door open to the world, China still keeps the political door shut, creating ethical and human rights dilemmas for foreign companies doing business there. In the last six months of 1998, the Chinese government carried out the most systematic crackdown on political rights since the 1989 Tiananmen Square massacre.

Though vastly different in outcome, earlier periods of Chinese history were based on Confucian principles, values that were—and continue to be—translated into modern terms by the Chinese, allowing them to hold straight the rudder of their society through calm and storm.

Imbued with Confucianism

Strong ancestor worship, a belief in demigods and goddesses, as well as belief in Confucianism and the Taoist, Buddhist, and Christian religions mark the spiritual life of China. And whereas Westerners may see conflict among these various belief systems, the Chinese see true interrelatedness and utilitarianism.

Chinese life is a largely Confucian one, characterized by its unblinking focus on the *tao*, or "Way," and on *te*, the quality by which people can tread the Way. Four basic virtues of Confucianism play out strongly in Chinese life: loyalty, respect for parents and elders, benevolence, and righteousness—any of which, taken to extremes, may be detrimental, as Chinese history has often demonstrated.

Above all, Confucianism is based on five crucial kinds of relationships, or *guanxi*, as is most of Chinese life: that of ruler to people, in which the ruler receives loyalty without question and gives wisdom in return; of husband to obedient and faithful wife; of loyal children to parents, particularly the father; of younger people's deference to their elders' wisdom; and of friend to friend, the only relationship between equals in Confucianism.

Almost everything in China revolves around relationships. The Chinese word for "self" even carries a negative connotation because the group always comes first. Chinese business letters bear a seal or red circular stamp of the company or government agency rather than one individual's signature. China's collectivism has, unwittingly perhaps, supported the revolutions that have marked its modern history. Yet there is a tension in China: this is a culture of individualistic means focused on collective ends, a paradox reflected throughout its history.

Prone to Collective Revolution

When Mao Zedong announced the birth of the People's Republic of China in 1949, he said, "The Chinese people have stood up." En masse. As a group.

Individuality is squelched in Chinese children from birth. Loyalty and unquestioning submission are of the highest value and come at great cost: China's suicide rate is three times the average of the rest of the world. Rural women in China commit suicide at a rate five times that of other countries. It is a nation where males are valued more highly than females, infanticide of girl babies is rife, and an entire generation of women are named "Zhaodi": "looking for a little brother."

The collective nature of the Chinese people engenders not only *guanxi*, the strong "bamboo network" that links them together, but also a reluctance to do anything for which there is no established, officially approved procedure. Children are trained from an early age not to do anything that might be criticized or cause embarrassment, nor anything that hasn't been approved in advance by everyone concerned.

The secret of understanding Chinese behavior is *keqi*, or "guest behavior." Being polite, considerate, and moral while downplaying your status or wealth is expected. As in many of its Asian neighbors, saving *mianzi*, or "face," is critically important—not only to one's own reputation but also to the reputations of others. Causing someone else to lose face means creating a loss of face for yourself as well.

Simply saying "No" can cause someone to lose face. As a result, conversation is an intricate dance of ambiguous terms, often leading to misunderstanding or unrealistic expectations yet allowing the participants to save face by maneuvering toward polite escape without committing them to anything directly.

But in the twenty-first-century world, China cannot isolate itself from MTV and the World Wide Web, both of which are opening new windows into this previously inaccessible society. The full impact of the resulting cultural influence—driven in large part by business itself—is yet to be seen.

A Business Culture Emerges

In China, "business has become the ultimate expression of individuality," says activist turned capitalist Li Lu in *Fast Company* magazine. "The Tiananmen generation understands that business, not politics, is the force driving social change." Bill Gates's digital manifesto, *The Road Ahead*, has sold 400,000 legal copies in China—and countless more bootleg copies. Business is the new Chinese Confucianism. This growth of business nurtures individualism in the Chinese psyche and puts pressure on the collective principles of the culture.

The explosive growth of the PRC is destined to continue for some time to come, transforming the world's largest nation into the world's second largest economy. Though China is rich in human resources and cheap labor costs, its real unemployment runs as high as 17 percent in the cities and 33 percent in the country.

China is attempting to create a new economic order called "market socialism," combining state-owned, private-owned, household-operated, and Chinese foreign-owned joint-venture enterprises, all directed by the market but under the guidance of the state. Nowhere in the world are politics and business more closely interconnected than in China, where some of the most powerful business organizations are village enterprises, giving local leaders great power. China has the world's oldest bureaucracy, including a national civil service examination dating to the sixth-century Sui Dynasty.

Powerful military enterprises, some quite entrepreneurial, help shape the complex fabric of Chinese economic life, although they are being forced to abandon their business interests. Government ministries behave like huge commercial conglomerates, yet wholly owned Chinese enterprises—small, family-owned businesses in fields such as retailing, bicycle repair, and handicrafts—are also thriving.

In 1978, state enterprises accounted for 80 percent of the gross output value of industry. This figure fell to 50 percent by 1990 and is less than 25 percent today. The Chinese government's fear is that the trend to smaller and more independent private enterprises will encourage the growth of segmented political fiefdoms of the type that led to the chaotic Cultural Revolution. Its leaders know they must nurture these small entrepreneurial enterprises, but they're unwilling to give up the political control they've learned to exert.

Fostering economic freedom without political freedom may discourage foreign investment and place onerous restrictions on companies that do enter the market. But the unprecedented task of serving so large an untapped market has proved overwhelming, and joint ventures have become increasingly important to the Chinese economy.

China is becoming intoxicated with material goods as its more liberal coastal cities such as Shanghai flourish, creating a growing middle class. A new and increasingly influential generation, born of China's "one-child" policy, is Internet-savvy. Major global corporations are seeking to tap this growing demand: Procter & Gamble, which spent only US$17 million on advertising in China in 1996, increased that figure to more than $US138 million in 1997.

The International Monetary Fund predicts that China will overtake the United States and Europe to become the world's largest economy around 2007, even though the average per capita income will remain low. Obstacles to growth do exist, including corruption, the excessive growth of credit, excess industrial capacity, and nonperforming loans. China's embrace of ancient values supports its business economies in many ways but can be dangerous when taken to extremes. Chinese frugality, for example, can produce astonishingly high savings rates but can also create excessive greed.

Government and business in China depend on each other, but have rarely gotten along. Historically, the northern, governmental region of China controlled education, which in centuries past was the main route out of poverty. Because of poverty, the southern Chinese were forced to go abroad, creating the powerful network of Overseas Chinese businessmen and the dichotomy between education and business, north and south, that exists even today. The Chinese have lived for centuries in that creative tension between living their values and modernizing their society.

The Chinese balance their respect for ancient value systems with a deep-seated desire to modernize their society. They stand true to Confucian values, but have pragmatically evolved them into the modern context, using Confucian philosophy like a palpable asset to explain and shape their future.

China: ***At a Glance***
Official name: ***People's Republic of China***

***Economy type:* Asian manufacturing**
Trading bloc:* APEC (Asia-Pacific Economic *Cooperation Group)

Location: China spans a massive area of eastern Asia and is bordered by 14 nations. Third largest country in the world. **Capital:** Beijing
Population: 1,236,914,658 **Head of state:** President Jiang Zemin
Official language: Mandarin **Religion:** Officially atheist; Buddhism, Taoism, some Muslim and Christian **Literacy:** 78%
World GNP ranking: 7 **GDP (US$ bn):** $903.0
GDP per capita: $736 **Unemployment:** 3.1%
Inflation: 17% **World export market share:** 4.4%

Major industries: Iron and steel, textiles and apparel, machine building, armaments
Major crops: Grain, rice, cotton, potatoes, tea
Minerals: Tungsten, antimony, coal, oil, mercury, iron, lead, magnesium, molybdenum, tin
Labor force: 54% agriculture and forestry, 26% industry and commerce
Computers per 1,000 people: 3.0

Assets: Huge domestic market to develop and sustain. Vast mineral reserves. Low wage costs. Low income tax on individuals. Significant domestic savings. Self-sufficient in food.

Liabilities: Challenges of overpopulation. Underemployment of many of its citizens. Poor infrastructure. Huge government bureaucracy. Not enough competitively skilled managers with international experience or foreign language skills. Banking system and support for business is not mature. Use of high technology for competitive advantage remains low. Many hidden barriers to business. Inefficient state-owned enterprises still exist.

STRETCH PEOPLE BEYOND THEIR DREAMS
Juergen Bartels and Westin Hotels & Resorts *(U.S.A.)*

Title: Chairman and CEO
Headquarters: Seattle, Washington
Business: From 74 hotels in 17 countries in 1995 to 113 hotels in 23 countries, with 49,300 guest rooms. Ranked number one upscale hotel chain by the 1997 *Frequent Flyer* Magazine/J. D. Power and Associates Guest Satisfaction Survey, and number one upscale U.S. hotel chain for an unprecedented third consecutive year, according to *Business Travel News*. Purchased in 1988 by Aoki Corporation of Japan and sold in 1995 to the partnership of Starwood Capital Group and Goldman Sachs & Company. Bartels was named CEO of Starwood Hotels in 1999.
Employees: 44,000

When Westin Hotels named Juergen Bartels CEO in May 1995, he promised to add one new hotel each month for sixty months—in a chain that had traditionally added one hotel a year. In his first eighteen months as CEO, Bartels almost doubled his original target.

An aggressive marketer and expert motivator, Bartels personifies constructive impatience. He is a driven man with an intense desire to be a world champion. He has institutionalized his growth-oriented philosophy by setting bold goals, stretching others beyond their image of themselves, and creating a culture of urgency.

Though German-born, Bartels proudly sees himself as an American leader. He's comfortable working in a U.S.-based company that's future-focused and always striving to be bigger and better. He believes that Americans are the best marketers and hoteliers in the world, and he loves the fact that his company is measured on merit and performance.

Juergen Bartels inherited a winning team that was losing the game. He brought a fresh vision, bold growth strategy, and energy to the company to enhance its quality, improve its marketing, and increase its profitability. In the process, he transformed Westin from an operations-driven company to a marketing-driven one.

Creating this culture of urgency started with Bartels himself. He set bold goals, created self-induced anxiety, and built a positive, self-fulfilling momentum around him. He was relentless, navigating around people's negativism and cynicism and demanding results. His formula for success was simple: quality plus marketing plus growth equals financial success.

Set Audacious Goals

Bartels knows that if he asks for small results, that's exactly what he will get: "Those early days were quite a ride. I had made enormous promises to the board, and I had to deliver." But he got the results he needed: "The key is to get results before the honeymoon is over. If you do, the honeymoon will go on. I got results month by month until even the doubters were saying, 'Yes, wow, hallelujah.' "

To transform Westin's culture to a more growth-oriented one, Bartels needed 100 percent buy-in: "It couldn't be implemented by people who didn't believe in it." His strategy was to communicate his plan clearly, get others to understand the numbers, and demand that people take personal responsibility for their performance. Bartels measures everything. "We must all know the numbers," he explains, "and we must not fib about them."

He sets targets for people and follows up aggressively: "I go over every single piece of our monthly report cards. Because I have a photographic memory, I can remember all the numbers, without the spreadsheet in front of me. You can't fool me on that."

Inspire and Stretch People

The hotel business is built on daily interactions—millions of them—among staff and guests. "We have an average of fourteen interactions with a customer every twenty-four-hour period," says Bartels. "We can't just win some of those interactions—we have to win all of them. I can win thirteen times, but if Mike the front desk clerk tells a guest who's questioning a phone charge on their bill, 'Sir, the computer says you made that call,' that customer thinks he's being called a liar. And an unhappy customer will tell ten others, while a happy customer only tells three. The question is, How many Mikes can we afford?"

The team Bartels inherited had been tolerating too many "Mikes." It needed someone to say, "I'm going to run the business, I'm going to take responsibility and push accountability down through the organization while I lead the charge."

That someone was Bartels. He stretched people to think positively about their future: "We have to continually navigate around the nattering nabobs of negativism and not get pulled into other people's negative conversations. I look for people who have energy and empathy and complete customer focus, because the business of hotels needs to be much less formal and more human.

"We have over forty-four thousand employees. I've given speeches to thirty-one thousand employees personally over a thirty-month period. And when I speak to our employees around the world, I tell them I bring the greetings and respect of their forty-four thousand cousins."

Finally, Westin's new "People Make the Difference" philosophy emphasizes the human element, empowering employees to reach higher standards in their guest interactions by infusing every Westin encounter with a spirit of energy and enthusiasm. It's clear to Westin employees that it's their duty to keep the customers they have—and it's Bartels's duty to bring new sets of customers to them. "So we each do our part."

Westin's $500 million renovation and aggressive training are part of its new marketing strategy. "It didn't take a genius to figure out that training is marketing," says Bartels. His greater challenge has been marketing his internal message. Through spontaneous pep rallies, he models the message as Westin's global cheerleader.

Build a Global Culture of Urgency

Westin had a stodgy, sixty-seven-year-old culture when Bartels arrived. He told people that their jobs were theirs to keep or lose. It was critical that he be a role model, holding himself personally responsible, in order to make demands on others: "In order to build a merit-based, entrepreneurial culture, I needed to work on everything simultaneously." By instilling a sense of urgency at all levels, and in all countries, he achieved a quick culture change.

Westin is a heterogeneous company with a strong global brand: "When I speak to our employees, I tell them, 'We are a global village with all languages, religions, and colors.' My challenge is to build connections around the world so people see they are working for one company. 'Did you know that when Shanghai does something good, it does so for you in Ixtalpa?' I tell them."

Westin's global village depends on local roots: "When you're invited into another country, you should respect their traditions. You can't go to Poland and disrespect the Poles. You're not going to be accepted, and it's not good business. Americans must overcome their sense of arrogance."

Sometimes you must be gracious and act out of the ordinary, as Westin did in Moscow. "There are ten million people in Moscow, and we had four thousand applications for six hundred fifty jobs. We needed to hire the right people with the right attitude who spoke English. We had to teach them about lipstick, rouge, and personal hygiene, even installing employee showers for them to use. We need employees who show a cheerful face to customers," he recounts, "and in Moscow that meant we even had to pay for dental work so they could smile with confidence.

"If you respect people," he adds, "they'll respect you."

COMMUNICATE DEEPLY ABOUT CHANGE
Daniel Vasella and Novartis AG *(Switzerland)*

Title: President and CEO
Headquarters: Basel
Business: Johann Geigy began selling spices and natural dyes in Basel in 1758. After World War I, the Swiss formed a chemical cartel of Ciba, Geigy, and Sandoz to compete with the Germans. The cartel dissolved in 1951, Ciba and Geigy merged in 1970, and in 1996, Ciba-Geigy and Sandoz reunited to create Novartis. Now the number two maker of generic drugs and pharmaceuticals, number one maker of crop protection products, and largest producer of jarred baby food (Gerber) in the United States.
Employees: 87,000 operating in 275 affiliates in 142 countries worldwide

AT THE TIME, *this was the largest merger in history, a $30 billion deal to bring together two large multinationals, Ciba-Geigy and Sandoz, to form one of the largest pharmaceutical and life sciences companies in the world. It was a "merger of equals," says Novartis CEO Daniel Vasella, a forty-five-year-old former hospital physician.*

To symbolize the company's fresh image, it began with a new name, Novartis, from the Latin term novae artes. *And while Vasella and his team didn't know the meaning until after it was chosen, it was the new start they needed: "Novartis" means "new skills."*

"As Andre Gide wrote, 'One doesn't discover new lands without consenting to lose sight of the shore,' " Vasella noted in one of his quarterly communications to all Novartis employees during the merger. "We must courageously and boldly push ahead, surpassing the standards we set for ourselves and achieving the 'slightly impossible.' " His strategy to communicate deeply throughout the organization led to a 43 percent increase in net profit the first year, and the company is moving full speed ahead.

The merger of Ciba-Geigy and Sandoz brought together two companies, each with more than a hundred years of history, know-how, and assets. "But they also had their own baggage and weight," says Vasella. "Our challenge was to know what to keep and what to get rid of. There's always some kind of discontinuity between the history of the past and the potential of the future. That's why it was essential to have clarity about where we wanted to go.

"We wanted a new name. We didn't want anchors to the past, we wanted to send a signal of looking forward. If you decide to do something new, say it to people," he adds. Vasella communicates deeply about change, expectations, and the future.

With more than 130,000 employees—now down to 82,000—Vasella knew he had a big job ahead of him. He had to navigate people through the merger, develop change leaders at all levels, and use communications as a strategic tool.

Develop Change Leaders at All Levels

There were three phases of the merger, he explains: "First was the analytical phase, in which small teams on both sides worked to determine the business strategy of the new company. Next came the design phase, with over eight hundred teams determining how we would design our business processes, reporting into an integration office, which I chaired. Finally came the 'do it' phase, where all employees were involved."

In all three phases, Vasella needed not only to navigate toward common goals but also to help people deal with the sometimes devastating impact of change: "We needed missionaries and advocates at different levels to ensure success of the merger integration. The right people in the trenches put the big picture changes into the appropriate context," he says. "We needed leaders who could have honest, deep conversations about what's happening without mistakenly believing this is a democracy."

Change leaders are messengers of the new company vision. They understand the process of change, know how to motivate in the face of uncertainty, understand the complexities of operating in a global environment, and prepare for the future. These leaders must have personal and social literacy. "They must understand the wide scope of human emotion that accompanies change and move quickly to reduce the anxiety that comes with it.

Most people react the same way to change; it generally means a loss before you gain anything," Vasella explains. "In the process, you have normal behaviors of mourning, giving up, seeing new things that are possible. As a company, you can help facilitate that process or you can make it more difficult. If you communicate change with ambivalence, it makes it very difficult for people to take the tough decisions by themselves." He opted for quick, decisive change—and consistent, honest communication about that change—to minimize people's anxiety.

"What is happening inside individuals is happening in the company as a sum of individuals," he says. "Our challenge was to synchronize our communications throughout." To do that, he needed change leaders to take the temperature of the people and communicate information honestly and consistently up and down the company.

But change leaders aren't just good at communicating shared vision and implementing shared plans. They're also natural motivators, he says: "You have to put your own enthusiasm into other people. During the first period of our merger, I was going up in the elevator with an employee, and I asked her how she was doing. 'Good,' she replied. 'How are you doing?' When I hesitated, she said, 'Oh, come on, it's great, everything's going so well.' She really motivated me. My mood was completely turned around—you have to have people who can do that."

Change leaders must also understand the complexities of operating in a globalizing world. Through retreats held around the world, individual businesses created their own common purpose under the larger Novartis framework. The key was knowing what should come from the top (mission and purpose), what should be top down and bottom up (objectives), and what should come from the bottom up (implementation and tactics). "Operating in a globalizing world is complex—languages, religions, beliefs and behaviors differ—and creating common purpose while respecting difference becomes very important," Vasella says.

Novartis leaders meet regularly to exchange experience and share expertise, work together on new concepts, formulate approaches to developing new markets, and shape a new Novartis culture. "It's very important that our top four hundred people go through the same team learning and team-building experience," Vasella says, touting a program he created with Harvard University.

Cultivate a Culture of Trust and Results

Vasella's greatest challenge was creating an environment of trust and performance, with a focus on candor, expectations, and engagement. Vasella has little tolerance for people who drag their feet after agreements are made.

Only in an environment of trust are people willing to strive for the "slightly impossible," to make bold moves, to accept the inevitable risk, he says. "Trust is essential for empowerment; it's a core value for team building, and we can't just ask for it. We must earn it with integrity, openness, fairness. And, above all, with credible, consistent, convincing behavior."

But the soft side of trust has to be combined with very clear and ambitious objectives. Trust and results are the "soft" and "hard" sides of business, and the two must be balanced. Vasella pushes people—there's no doubt about that—but he constantly assesses if he's pushing too hard: "It's important to put stretch goals out there and create enough healthy anxiety so people are leaning into the future. If you go overboard, you create paralysis, and if you go too low it's too cozy. So the question is, How far can you go?"

Stretch goals are tricky, he warns: "You know you're stretching yourself when you have an empty feeling in your stomach and don't really know if you'll be able to make it—you know it's not impossible but that you can't achieve it just sitting down. I always ask myself if I'm being unrealistic. Is the objective achievable?"

Use Communications as a Strategic Tool

Ultimately, change cannot happen, trust cannot be built, and the impossible cannot be achieved without consistent, honest communication. The socially literate leader recognizes that people are always interpreting his clarity and authenticity: "One of the big challenges is to communicate deep into the organization. Messages get diffused and distorted, so you need to repeat, be consistent, and communicate by many different means."

Especially during a merger, he says, people need to know why and how they're going to reposition, how they are going to be successful, and what will be needed to implement the merger. While the CEO is vital to the process, communication is every manager's responsibility: "Symbolic and regular communication is key—it becomes a strategic business tool."

Vasella sends quarterly letters to everyone in the company electronically, getting reactions from around the world that help him understand where the company is at any given time. "Between my ideal of where we should be and the reality of where we are, there's always tension—and I'm somewhere in between," he notes. "But I can't stay where everyone is; I have to lead. So it's a leading and a pulling process, and I need many missionaries in the organization who do the same at different levels.

"What's my real duty?" he asks. "I am a platform where people can meet from different countries to share best practice and learn from each other."

Communication provides the context, he continues: "When you don't communicate well, people don't commit, don't understand, don't say what they mean. And that undermines your success."

Vasella also knows that Novartis has to communicate deeply with its local communities. The Novartis Annual Community Day provides an opportunity for employees to volunteer in community activities around the world, respecting their local roots and meeting other people in real-life situations. "It's not *without* self-interest that I care," says Vasella, recognizing that this community activity is good publicity. "But it's not *because of* self-interest that I care." It's an important distinction.

Vasella and Novartis are products of a Swiss culture shaped by the Alps and surrounded by powerful neighbors, a nation of independent cultures that model coexistence by valuing strong localism, thrift, precision, and a tradition of working together.

SWITZERLAND: "Thrifty Precisionists"

IN SWITZERLAND, the trains all run on time. The whole country, in fact, runs like clockwork, just like the products for which it's best known. And while much of the rest of the world is preoccupied with effectively managing diversity, Switzerland handles that like clockwork as well. Its culture of precision is bound up with its smallness, its independent and locally powerful government structures, and its multilingual citizenry.

The Swiss include German-, French-, and Italian-speaking people who identify with commune or village, canton or region, and country—in that order. Switzerland has deliberately kept its three major linguistic, economic, religious, and folkloric cultures fully alive through its more than 350 years of confederation. The German Swiss can be found in banking and industrial centers such as Basel, the French Swiss in Geneva's center of world organizations such as the International Red Cross, while the Italian Swiss are concentrated in southern resort towns.

A History of Local Independence

On August 1, small villages, or "communes," throughout Switzerland light up with the dazzle of bonfires in honor of Independence Day, the day in 1291 when three cantons of the future Switzerland signed a joint defense treaty to avoid being swallowed by their more powerful neighbors. By 1848, Switzerland enjoyed stability as a federal state, following a period of national crisis and civil war.

The "new" Switzerland boasted an egalitarian democracy and a federation with twenty-six sovereign cantons, each with its own constitution, laws, and government. Patriotic societies and festivals of all kinds—songs, gymnastics, and marksmanship competitions—link these diverse cantons and nurture national unity. Even so, differences among the cantons have been maintained.

A Business Culture Emerges

Switzerland's political and economic stability make it most attractive to the business community. Its value on education directly benefits its corporations—fully 25 percent of the Swiss are in school at any given time. Its teachers enjoy high social status and salaries as much as 50 percent greater than those of its European neighbors. Yet most Swiss CEOs learned about business on the shop floor, not in school.

The Swiss see themselves as highly efficient and ethical. Yet recent rev-

Switzerland: ***At a Glance***
Official Name: Swiss Confederation

Economy type: Entrepôt
Trading bloc: EFTA (European Free Trade Association)

Location: The center of western Europe **Capital:** Bern
Population: 7,260,357 **Head of state:** President Ruth Dreifuss
Official Languages: German, French, Italian, Romansch
Religion: Roman Catholic 48%, Protestant 44% **Literacy:** 100%
World GNP ranking: 18 GDP (US$ bn): $252.8
GDP per capita: $34,918 **Unemployment:** 5.2%
Inflation: 2% **World export market share:** 1.8%

Major industries: Machinery, chemicals, precision instruments, watches, textiles, foodstuffs (cheese, chocolate), banking, tourism
Major crops: Grains, grapes
Minerals: Salt, marble, gypsum
Labor force: 67% services, 29% manufacturing
Computers per 1,000 people: 400.1

Assets: Highly skilled workforce. High level of spending on R and D. High access to foreign capital markets. Reliable provider of banking services. Low inflation rate. Low corporate tax rate. Ability to innovate to capture mass markets. Strong chemical, pharmaceutical, machine tools, and precision engineering sectors.

Liabilities: Protected cartels result in overpriced goods. No ports and rugged geography. Highly subsidized agricultural sector. High withholding tax on non-Swiss earned income, which stifles direct foreign investment in business.

elations of Swiss banks profiting from Jews who lost their lives in Nazi gas chambers have challenged the myth of Switzerland's wartime neutrality.

Given its geography and limited natural resources, Switzerland is forced to trade internationally. The Swiss export 90 percent of their goods and services, 60 percent to other European countries. Their main trading partners are European Union members. Germany is their major trading partner, accounting for more than 20 percent of exports and more than 33 percent of imports.

Recently, Swiss business management has moved from hierarchical to cooperative, nonhierarchical, and pluralistic. The Swiss have the second highest savings rate in the world, after Japan. There are no prestige executive expenditures in Swiss firms, no fancy buildings or extravagant lifestyles. The Swiss were among the first to begin the industrialization process. Their fine workmanship, for which they are known worldwide, has helped their image enormously.

> ***From the Swiss, we learn valuable lessons about being independent and connected at the same time. They've learned to embrace the creative tensions of living together among differences, in their own country, in Europe, and around the world. Precise and educated, they teach us the value of autonomous cooperation.***

BUILD SOCIALLY LITERATE RELATIONSHIPS
Guillermo Luksic and the Luksic Group *(Chile)*

Title: CEO
Headquarters: Santiago
Business: Founded by Andronico Luksic in the early 1950s with investments in the mining industry, in a country with the richest copper deposits in the world. Now a huge conglomerate with more than 60 companies and a net value of $3 billion, it has investments in industries from beverages and pasta to telecommunications, banking, hotels, and mining.
Employees: More than 26,000

As a young boy, Guillermo Luksic remembers his father gathering him and his brothers around the dinner table, telling them about his business challenges, and asking their opinions about what he should do.

As the boys grew up in this typical Chilean patrician household, their father brought them into the family business. Today, the Luksic Group is one of the most entrepreneurial groups in Chile, a country that has the fastest-growing and most competitive economy in Latin America.

Head of the Luksic Industrial Group, Luksic understands the power of social literacy and the value of family and relationships in a Latin culture focused on who you know and the relationships you build. With brothers, sisters, and cousins involved, the company has a broad diversity of holdings; each sibling oversees part of the business.

From those childhood dinner-table conversations, Luksic learned the power of engaging and challenging people. By understanding people and their emotions, he is building collaborative networks of employees, partners, and subsidiaries—first in Chile, next in Latin America, and then around the world.

Value the Human Side of Business

Luksic truly understands the principles of people management—in both himself and his company. And he sees it as a simple equation: "One side of the leadership equation is talent, creativity, experience, and expertise," he says. "But those abilities must be balanced by an equally strong understanding of people. After all, our customers are people, and so are our suppliers, coworkers, and shareholders. The human side of the equation is as important as technical abilities.

"Good leaders don't act alone," he adds. "They build teams of talented managers, each with a distinct point of view. I don't believe in the term 'personal leadership.' That's why we hire people who work well on teams, stress group participation, and know how to seek team input."

To get his own team working together, Luksic takes executives on team-building experiences in the Andes Mountains and promotes informal time together outside of work. All this requires urgent listening, connective teaching skills, and the ability to cultivate individualists in a collaborative team. This might be a surprise coming from a business leader in Chile, known for its hierarchical Latin American culture.

Build Connective Networks with Shared Information

The model for Luksic's business success is one of networks and information flows, at many different levels: "We've built a powerful network of people and companies uncovering new business opportunities and constantly learning about markets. The value of our network depends on how easily information flows."

He prefers the human touch in sharing knowledge and works to get employees and customers to meet in person. After all, the Luksic networks are made up of people. "We must communicate by being there face to face, visiting people, partners, and facilities throughout Chile and Latin America," he says. "There is no substitute for working hard and being there."

In Latin America, Chile has led the way in free-market reforms and deregulation. Luksic is leveraging this good news about Chile and working hard to expand throughout the region: "Our challenge is to build a network of relationships and information channels through subsidiaries and partnerships. Now that we are international, we must continue building and improving our network so it's equally strong throughout the region."

With one quarter of the company revenue from international sources,

Luksic is clearly focused on Chile's neighboring countries—Argentina, Peru, Bolivia, and Brazil, nations with similar languages and cultures: "Just by staying in our own backyard, we're tapping into a $1.1 trillion GDP marketplace with many underserviced markets."

The company's threefold strategy involves first exporting products, then establishing manufacturing facilities, and finally developing strategic partnerships, such as the brewery it built with Anheuser-Busch in Argentina and the jointly owned banks it owns in Peru with a Spanish company.

"Partnerships give us access to world-class brand names, capital, and know-how," says Luksic. "Our partners gain access to our market knowledge and network of companies in the Southern Cone." They also gain a foothold in one of Latin America's shining lights: Chile.

CHILE: "Relationship Capitalists"

WITH HIS LOCAL, regional, and international strategy, Luksic understands clearly how his company's being Chilean affects the business: "Many of Chile's values are ideal for business. We have a tradition of democratic, constitutional government and respect for the rule of law that dates back to the early 1880s. Though interrupted by a military government in the 1970s and 1980s, it was renewed in 1990 with a peaceful return to democracy."

It is Pinochet's military government to which Luksic refers, a coup that toppled the economically damaging rule of socialist Salvador Allende. And though Pinochet's military junta achieved its goals of stability and growth—bringing Chilean inflation down from 500 percent to 10 percent—there was a human cost. Between two thousand and six thousand opponents of Pinochet simply disappeared before he was toppled in 1990.

In many ways, Chile is unlike its Latin American neighbors. Though Chileans are largely Catholic, theirs is not the strident Catholicism of much of the region. And bribery and graft aren't prevalent here. "Corruption has never been a part of our culture," says Luksic, "so we've avoided many of the distortionary forces that hurt the economies of our neighboring countries." In the 1990s, its economy grew an unprecedented 6 to 7 percent per year, though one third of Chileans still live below the poverty line.

The Luksic Group capitalizes not only on Chile's abundant natural resources but also on its rich agriculture and Mediterranean climate. Chile's strong free-market ethic, low corporate taxes, and high business ethics create a corporate environment where reputation and relationships count.

The racial makeup of Chileans—a European-Indian mix—is the result of three hundred years of Spanish influx and the intermingling of Spanish soldiers with Indian women. It is the longest, skinniest country in the world; around one third of its Spanish-speaking population lives in and around the capital of Santiago. It is a land of long-standing conflicts between the conser-

Chile: ***At a Glance***
Official Name: Republic of Chile

> ***Economy type: Latin American***
> ***Trading bloc: MERCOSUR (Latin American Southern Zone Common Market)***

Location: Occupies most of the western coast of South America
Capital: Santiago **Population:** 14,787,781
Head of state: President Eduardo Frei Ruiz-Tagle
Official Language: Spanish **Religion:** Roman Catholic 89%, Protestant 11% **Literacy:** 94%
World GNP ranking: 44 **GDP (US$ bn):** $76.3
GDP per capita: $5,260 **Unemployment:** 6.1%
Inflation: 8.5% **World export market share:** 0.4%

Major industries: Fish processing, wood products, wine, iron, steel
Major crops: Grains, grapes, fruits, beans, potatoes, sugar beets
Minerals: World's largest producer and exporter of copper; deposits of molybdenum, nitrates, iron, and gold
Labor force: 38% services, 34% industry and commerce, 19% agriculture, forestry, and fishing
Computers per 1,000 people: 44.8

Assets: The world's largest producer of copper. Political stability and progressive free-market policies have brought foreign investments, which have propelled economic expansion since 1991. Low income taxes on individuals. Significant natural resources. Healthy percentage of citizens choosing engineering and the sciences as professions.

Liabilities: Vulnerability to shifting U.S. trade policies and to shifting value of copper on the world market. Vulnerable to inflation. Infrastructure needs improvement. Difficult geography. Lack of environmental protection and regulation.

vative oligarchy of the landowners, big business, the church, military, and right-wing politicians on the right, and the workers, intellectuals, and sometimes the middle class on the left.

Luksic benefits from a nation where the people work more hours per year than any other country, according to the International Labor Organization. A conservative, somber, and serious people, Chileans harbor some arrogance toward other Latin American countries. The Chilean culture is a male-dominated one, but even so, women in Chile are more liberated than in most other Latin American countries.

The Chileans teach the world about relationship building and integrity. Staying true to their principles, they are focused on ethics and free markets in a turbulent continent.

ARE EXECUTIVES PROMOTED FROM WITHIN?

(Percentage of executives responding positively)

- Latin America: 73%
- Asia: 61%
- Australia/New Zealand: 60%
- North America: 57%
- Europe: 56%

CHAPTER FIVE

BUSINESS LITERACY

Focusing and Mobilizing Your Organization

Relentless change forces companies to be fast and flexible as they navigate through chaos to create value for customers. By creating environments that bring out the best in people, and teaching them how the business works, business-literate leaders build cultures of learning and innovation. Liberating leaders at all levels of the business is the secret of success.

ON THE BRINK OF CIVIL WAR, U.S. President Abraham Lincoln warned, "the dogmas of the quiet past are inadequate to the stormy present." Organizations today are in a constant state of disequilibrium, blurring boundaries of time, geography, and language. We need new maps to navigate through the chaos.

To ride out the storm, our companies must be resilient and adaptable. But are our management practices ready for this brave new world?

Success isn't simply a matter of seeing clearly the chaotic environment around us; we must also act on what we see, leading our people through the chaos. To thrive, leaders must move fluidly between thought and action, able to think while acting and act while thinking; that fluency of thought in motion is at the core of business literacy. Leaders must institutionalize business literacy throughout their organizations. To succeed, business-literate leaders must embrace these key roles:

- Chaos Navigator
- Business Geographer
- Historical Futurist
- Leadership Liberator
- Economic Integrator

These abilities—riding waves of chaos, taking the lay of the land, respecting the past while meeting the future, liberating leaders at all levels, and modernizing our yardsticks for success—all help leaders ride the crest of change.

Chaos Navigator

First Pacific CEO Manuel Pangilinan sees crisis as opportunity. From his vantage point in Hong Kong, all hands were jumping ship during the recent Asian financial crisis. Not Pangilinan. He knew opportunity was there for the taking if he didn't mind the danger that accompanied it. Rather than forsake Asia, he embraced it.

Around the globe in Sweden, Electrolux CEO Michael Treschow had his own set of challenges. Since 1970, Electrolux—the world's leading producer of vacuum cleaners and Europe's number one producer of household appliances—had acquired more than three hundred companies. The company had become both big and global but was not very profitable. By involving people inside the company to help trim plants and employees, he changed that. Treschow balances optimism about the company's future with a healthy dose of realism about what needs to change. He trusts his own intuition and past experiences yet believes in his senior team and knows when to rely on their judgments. And his decisiveness is built on a foundation of reflection, as he embraces change and uncertainty with confidence.

Business literacy requires us to see and think differently, to manage complex, adaptive human systems. We must learn to suspend our beliefs about what is true because the facts of life alter daily. From simplicity to complexity, from clarity to ambiguity, from certainty to unpredictability, the chaos navigator quickly develops an entirely new mindset for change.

Business-literate leaders are comfortable with ambiguity because they understand that linear mindsets of cause and effect are inadequate in the new world. They learn to trust their intuition and seek patterns in and through experience. They also develop the capacity for systems thinking. They understand the systemic nature of economies as well as the interconnections within their businesses. They use these insights to tap the expertise of everyone in their organization.

Leaders of boundaryless organizations operating in a borderless marketplace need to have a fluid view of the world. Rejecting past concepts of stability and control, they need a mental toolbox that is full of flexibility.

But it's a structured flexibility. Leaders must stay positive and proactive while learning to thrive in a world of uncertainty. To succeed, they must learn the art of mental agility. They must be quick and nimble, and they must instill those qualities into those around them.

Business literacy entails understanding the psychology of change while managing one's own emotions during change. Able to cut through denial and resistance, business-literate leaders explore new challenges and commit to fresh opportunities. They're simultaneously excited, hopeful, scared, and confused.

Business-literate leaders must help everyone around them develop this capacity. To do that, they must know instinctively how much change people can handle. Sensitive to how people differ in reacting to change, they must tailor their style to those differences. They must provide constancy in the face of chaos.

Chaos navigators guide people through change, making sense out of confusion, clarifying what is important, and creating nimble environments where people can learn to be resilient and flexible. They deal with the unanticipated, deploy the appropriate human and financial resources, and orchestrate multiple reconfigurations. Their ability to manage the unexpected is a strategic asset to the company.

People in some cultures, especially those that are comfortable with ambiguity, contradiction, and paradox, are more natural chaos navigators than others. They think more systemically, are more individualistic, and try to control nature rather than be controlled by it.

Partial solutions to each of these literacies lie in different cultures around the world—you have to borrow the best of those cultures to become globally literate. To be a good chaos navigator, you need to combine the unconventional thinking of the Italians, the individualistic can-do spirit of Americans, the polychronic thinking of Latin Americans, and the intuitive, collective, systemic orientation of Asians; together, these cultural mindsets will allow you to master this competency.

Business Geographer

Alfred Zeien is a man in search of the perfect shave. Recently retired CEO of the Gillette Company, Zeien is globalizing a company with American roots by understanding the world outside the United States. He has created a strong culture of "interchangeable management" to navigate this unsure terrain. An intense economic competitor, Zeien is a business geographer who knows his local markets better than anyone and who demands the same kind of intelligence in others.

Business geographers such as Zeien continuously survey the countries where they buy and sell products, to understand the context of their business. In local stock markets, railroads, or child labor laws, they read national maps that they then use to chart new territories, alerting people to hazards along the way. Where the terrain is unfamiliar, they seek out experts. They are knowledgeable about the national realities of geography, politics, and history, and how management philosophy and practice emerge from them. And they are familiar with local raw materials and perceived as insiders in the local countries in which they operate.

As students of history and corporate topography, they think like explorers, always imagining something interesting just beyond the horizon and working to uncover that unknown. As explorers, they know that every country has its own banking system, telephone service, and litigation philosophy, and they create vivid legends to accompany their maps. Like a surveyor's string, business-literate leaders connect all these things.

These geographers are also business geologists, digging beneath the surface to find where there's gold. Able to decipher what's most important, business geographers map what's essential, nonessential, and irrelevant to their business. By tapping unexplored mines, they know what core capabilities distinguish them from others and which ones they still need to acquire.

Seeing the world through a geographer's eyes helps mobilize their business through the same lens. Using global criteria, business-literate leaders define and meet world standards. They benchmark the best.

Their toolbox includes a wide spectrum of world-class business practices that help them mobilize people. They connect to the world through alliances and joint ventures, and nurture those connections to develop new ideas and products.

Business geographers must operate in the past and future simultaneously, like the Taiwanese; hold several balls in the air simultaneously, like the Brazilians; and have the can-do spirit of people from Hong Kong; the holistic and circular thinking of East Asians, and the passion for change of Americans. Alone, each trait doesn't mean much; together, they create real global competence.

Historical Futurist

George Fisher inherited a culture that needed changing. He looked back to go forward: he knew that if he didn't understand Kodak's history, he would be condemned to repeat it. Respecting and honoring Kodak's 120-year tradition, he began to map its future: articulating new values, clarifying leadership competencies, and setting bold performance goals. Today, Kodak is moving from a culture of entitlement to a culture of performance.

Business-literate leaders know themselves and their companies—inside and out. They explore and celebrate the past, understand and own the present, and imagine and create the future. Each phase builds on the next. They know that people and organizations face different challenges at different stages of life, learning lessons throughout. They think in the short term, the medium term, and the long term simultaneously.

By understanding the ghosts and angels within your company, you learn how myths and stories affect its current culture. As a business historian, you need to use that rich past as the foundation on which to explore the future. Uncovering your heritage allows you to understand where you are today.

Business-literate leaders know intuitively that companies' challenges evolve and that they must craft current strategy while simultaneously planning for the future. As hockey great Wayne Gretsky says, "You must go where the puck is going to be, not where it is." So too do business leaders need to move to where great new opportunities will surface.

Historical futurists rarely see the world as completely clear or totally unpredictable. They believe that varying levels of uncertainty can be managed by identifying knowable trends, exploring alternative scenarios, and tailoring strategies to the levels of uncertainty.

Historical futurists are always asking, "What kind of company are we, and what kind do we want to be?" These leaders are "inside-outsiders," living within the company's culture while standing above to assess its strengths and shortcomings.

They also have a passion for self-assessment. By understanding deeply how the business works, how people relate, and how value is created, these leaders identify the obstacles to success.

Ultimately, historical futurists build on the core values of the business, which provide consistency through time. By ensuring that people live these values, business-literate leaders help people link yesterday's stories with tomorrow's work.

Culture influences our understanding of the past, present, and future. The business-literate leader combines the best of the European Union by living in the past, present, and future simultaneously; of Japan by balancing short- and long-term thinking; of the United Kingdom by managing change and the status quo simultaneously; and of the Netherlands, by respecting old relationships but being willing to value and reward new performers.

Leadership Liberator

Coles Myer CEO Dennis Eck knew that Australia's largest retail chain had been through a few rough years. He knew he needed to recharge his employees, upon whose collective intelligence the company's survival would depend. His job was to figure out how to tap those human assets aggressively. He helped build his employees' self-confidence and unleash their leadership abilities to put meaning back into their lives and value back into the business.

A leader's most important job is to create leaders every day at every level of the business. Executives have always provided leadership by contributing vision and influencing others. But in the twenty-first century workplace, leadership is just the beginning. Our survey shows that leaders everywhere believe that their most important job is to create other leaders. How they do so is culturally conditioned.

We need line leaders with bottom-line responsibilities who mentor, coach, and develop people. We need experts and troubleshooters who provide technical competence. We need internal networkers who plant seeds in the corporate culture. We need independent contributors who take responsibility for learning and doing. And we need helpers who follow directions and support the company's mission. All of these are the leaders of tomorrow's corporations.

Leadership liberators understand that human capital is an expandable resource and leadership can be learned. These leaders know that to have a successful company, everyone should want to contribute. The secret is learning how to make that happen.

Business-literate leaders are comfortable sharing power and control. By constantly seeking to liberate the human spirit beyond people's wildest expectations of themselves, they are a living model of how to access more ideas and more creativity. They foster a winning attitude of energy and entrepreneuralism.

Good leaders also know what doesn't work. If they're not credible, or if they are too self-interested, they undermine other people's best efforts. If they're chronically anxious or blinded by their own success, they have trouble letting other people shine. And if they are threatened by subordinates or blame others for problems, they cast darkness on those around them. The result is workers who feel indifferent, even hostile or destructive; they have no concern if a job goes unfinished, a product is shoddy, a customer walks out, or money is wasted.

Business-literate leaders encourage people to step into leadership roles by communicating confidence, clarifying expectations, and demonstrating respect. By setting bold goals, asking people to take initiative, and demanding accountability, they focus on people's strengths and manage around their weaknesses, inspiring discretionary effort.

Business-literate leaders also promote courage by altering the way people experience their own power and identity, building their self-esteem, and challenging them to do their best. Leadership liberators generate this sense of urgency by encouraging employees to take risks and creating conditions that allow them to discover leadership qualities within themselves.

These leaders let people's minds loose. By building a mature workforce committed to its own development, they become knowledge capitalists in the truest sense, shaping and expanding the company's intangible human assets.

To truly liberate leaders, we need to combine the egalitarian nature of the Dutch, the change orientation of Americans, the achievement orientation of the Overseas Chinese, and the humility of the Scandinavians. Combining these four national mindsets will help us value and unleash leaders at all levels in our organizations.

Economic Integrator

Cows, milk, and butter are nothing new in New Zealand. But New Zealand Dairy Board CEO Warren Larsen realized that this two-hundred-year-old industry wouldn't make it to its next birthday without adapting to change. So in 1997, he created a global organization for the Dairy Board, one with cross-functional teams linked virtually. He refocused the Dairy Board on a new metric of success built around value-adding relationships and results.

Like Larsen, economic integrators are obsessed with success. They focus on what excellence looks like, building a fast, flexible organization to achieve it. Instinctively, they know that successful companies are values-based, performance-driven enterprises. Their success depends on delighting all their stakeholders: shareholders, customers, employees, suppliers, and the community. By serving and balancing these needs, these leaders create companies that last.

Leaders need to create a seamless whole that is more valuable than the sum of its parts, turning aspirations into action and connecting the entire value chain, from suppliers to employees to customers. They must seek the appropriate mix of centralization, decentralization, and outsourcing to balance low costs with high service.

Creating alignment within the enterprise is their greatest challenge. Business-literate leaders must ensure that people's values and behaviors support the corporate culture goals. And the organization's structures, systems, and processes must enhance the vision, or the company will work at cross-purposes internally and undermine itself. By getting people to work in alignment and linking their actions to measures of success, leaders play a major role in gluing their companies together. Execution creates organizational consistency from top to bottom, vertically and horizontally, and across relationships and processes, jobs and teams, structures and systems.

Business-literate leaders are alliance brokers and relationship builders. They see their companies as virtual enterprises, made up of both internal and external networks. By building productive partnerships with customers, suppliers, distributors, and venture partners, they connect to the outside world of allies and competitors across divisions, companies, and countries. They create multiple centers of expertise and encourage people from diverse functions, disciplines, and organizations to work together. Their companies are connected in a boundaryless, fluid, continually changing way.

Creating a results-oriented culture is their final act of execution. Here people are focused on outcomes and results. By creating world-class standards and rewarding and penalizing people for excellence and mediocrity, they confront head-on the discrepancies between intentions and faulty execution. This requires an economically literate workforce, people who understand the business and know how to read a profit-and-loss statement. Economic integrators teach them about how the business functions and makes money.

Business literate leaders are even changing the yardsticks for success. Their companies focus less on moving materials and more on moving information: the intangible assets—human, intellectual, and learning capital—that are becoming the real value creators. By building corporate scorecards that measure success in new ways, these leaders leverage knowledge for competitive advantage.

Again, there are national traits that in combination create powerful competency: the future, active, and change-ready mindset of the United States, the integration and alignment capacity of New Zealand, the collaborative partnership-building capacity of Canada, and the caring harmony and social responsibility of Denmark—together they create the organizational capacity for economic integration.

The real lessons are in the stories themselves. From Gillette CEO Alfred Zeien, we learn to navigate the world's business geography by fostering interchangeable management. In a different part of the world—and in a whole other industry—Sir Peter Bonfield is leading British Telecommunications by creating energy through alignment. And Ted Kunkel is not only brewing beer but also leveraging knowledge everywhere as CEO of Foster's in Australia. In China, First Pacific's CEO, Manny Pangilinan, shows us how to embrace chaos and prepare people for constant change; and Nobuyuki Masuda, CEO of Mitsubishi Heavy Industries in Japan, shows how powerful a corporate creed can be in linking the past, present, and future.

THE TOP FIVE BUSINESS LITERACY SKILLS

When asked to identify the two most important ways of mobilizing people, global business executives said:

- Building a culture of learning and innovation: 65%
- Helping people adapt to continuous change: 41%
- Focusing on leadership development: 40%
- Giving all employees decision making authority: 34%
- Educating people about how the business works: 17%
- Promoting the importance of employee job security: 3%

PREPARE PEOPLE FOR CHANGE AND CHAOS
Manuel V. Pangilinan and First Pacific Company (*China*)

Title: Managing Director
Headquarters: Hong Kong
Business: One of Asia's most diversified and one of Hong Kong's largest companies, with operations in 50 countries and interests in banking, real estate, telecommunications, trading, and packaging. Controlled by the Salim Group of Indonesia, built by one of the wealthiest and most powerful overseas Chinese tycoons.
Employees: 51,300

MANUEL "MANNY" PANGILINAN'S PICTURE *was splashed all over the* South China Post *the day we interviewed him in Hong Kong. His claim to fame was the massive change First Pacific was facing as a result of the dramatic economic crisis in Asia, which had left the company more than $900 million in debt.*

Because he knows that the Chinese character for crisis, weiji, *combines the strokes for "danger" and "opportunity," he has embraced, not forsaken, Asia. His response to the crisis was a major restructuring in a chaotic market. The result? The company's share price has almost doubled since the restructuring was announced in January 1998.*

Pangilinan is a leadership liberator, pushing decisions down by developing leaders at all levels. He maintains a vision of Asia's recovery rather than focusing on its crisis; he clarifies the chaos around him for his employees; and he mirrors the Asian juxtaposition of opposites in the way he demands both entrepreneurial and *managerial excellence in his leaders, the* "yin *and* yang" *of business.*

First Pacific is an entrepreneurial company in a region where confidence was shaken and businesses were bailing out, not entering. "Business is tough these days," says Manuel Pangilinan, a Manila-born former banker who founded this Hong Kong financial and telecommunications conglomerate in 1981.

"It's a very new ball game," he continues. "This crisis isn't limited geographically; it's endemic. It's not limited to currencies, but has an impact on liquidity and profit position. This is the first time I've seen this sort of crisis." But his faith isn't shaken: "Even though we've had to redo our assumptions, we will continue to be a growth company with a bold vision."

Pangilinan knows that the Asian long-term view of history helps put this crisis into perspective. After all, First Pacific's home is in Asia, even though this region, which was First Pacific's greatest asset, has become its greatest liability. "Can you choose your parents?" he asks rhetorically. "Our parents were Asian, we're Asian, and we're in Asia. We have deep roots in the region." He knows that Asia is at a crossroads: "We either embrace globalization and surrender some sovereignty to foreign markets and investors, global competitors, and international standards, or we separate from the rest of the world—the equivalent of imposing economic sanctions on ourselves."

Pangilinan is trying to build the next phase of Asia's life—from Asian Miracle to Massacre to Momentum: "It will be marked by conservatism, reform, transparency, and moderate growth rates. Efficiency, productivity, and adherence to global standards of excellence will determine survival."

Pangilinan is globally literate. Reflective decisiveness marks his personal literacy; he relies on social literacy to build deep, strong, long-term relationships; and he cultivates cultural literacy by building diverse international business teams. But his real strength is his business literacy: he develops leaders at all levels, thinks in the past, present, and future, and manages the human side of change.

Think Strategically and Plan Proactively

Leaders must be thoughtful and strategic—and they must understand the past while planning the future. Pangilinan does that by imaging a better future, living day to day, determining what is in and outside his control, and admitting his human feelings all the way.

One of Asia's strengths is accepting the way things are and being comfortable with ambiguity. "In Asia, we generally accept nature's way of doing things," he notes. He has made peace with "not knowing": "We're comfortable with both crisis and opportunity. We understand paradox; we can hold different ideas in our heads at the same time without a problem."

In that mindset, crisis helps define prosperity: "An ancient Chinese philosopher said that you can't feel the pleasure if you don't feel the pain. There can be no up if there's no down." This heritage of the *yin* and *yang* of life helps Pangilinan understand that a new economic order will be created out of today's economic strife. "Those who adapt will do well; those who don't will fail," he predicts.

Adaptation and change inevitably involve pain of some magnitude: "If the business feels the pain, the people feel the pain. And if the people feel the pain, so do I. CEO or not, I'm a human being." By experiencing the pain himself, Pangilinan is able to help people handle their emotions with open and honest communication—something unusual in Asia, where disclosure isn't widely practiced and where a high value is placed on "saving face."

Pangilinan models open and honest dialogue: "Don't just bring me good news, bring me *all* the news," he insists. Pangilinan faced the pain of the Asian crisis head-on and insisted that First Pacific rethink its assumptions about the business. Among its first decisions: to sell its Dutch trading company, Hagemeyer, a First Pacific "crown jewel." "We're taking the money from some of our blue-chip investments in blue-chip countries and putting it to work in Asia," he explains.

He has a three-part formula for leading change: (1) accept that there is a problem—don't be in denial; (2) develop your options; and (3) just do it: "You'll never know whether your decision was right until after the fact."

Develop Leaders at All Levels

There are only 42 people working at First Pacific's headquarters, but they run a business of more than 53,000 employees worldwide. Pangilinan has cultivated a small-company culture in a large organization by decentralizing management and pushing responsibility through the ranks. "Our virtuous circle goes like this," he explains. "Produce strong results that enable you to hire good people at the local level, and then create an exciting environment that enables you to produce strong results."

He has youth on his side—new companies don't have 150-year-old rules: "We manage by flexibility, not framework. We provide the soil in which people grow their own unique way of managing. People bring their experience to the table in many different ways. The Scottish are strong in finance; Filipinos are good entertainers, for example. We complement each other."

To decentralize, Pangilinan needs people who are both entrepreneurs and managers. When he's looking for leaders, he asks himself: Does this person understand the business, the industry, the economics, and the environment? Can he tell me how he's going to grow the business?

Pangilinan himself is both entrepreneur and manager: "I pride myself on being a strategic manager, but I'm also a hands-on manager who likes to build businesses." Since he can't be everywhere at once, he knows he can build businesses globally only by constantly pushing decisions to the lowest level. To develop local CEOs, he has to give them full responsibility *and* accountability: "If my local manager just follows the dictates of somebody from head office, it doesn't work. You don't develop your managers to be future CEOs that way. If they don't take responsibility, they don't know what real bullets feel like or how to make life-and-death decisions." Instead, Pangilinan helps them think, urges them to make up their own minds, and expects them to take responsibility for their decisions.

Entrepreneurial managers tend to achieve more successes and make more mistakes, which is why they need a greater understanding of how to manage, something entrepreneurs often lack. "You've got to manage those companies once you've invested in them," Pangilinan explains. "They're like human beings that have to be fed and nurtured. They need capital and people to grow."

He examines the business through several lenses: "We first look locally and then regionally. We only look globally to see if there are trends that will affect the company locally and regionally."

After all, Pangilinan explains, battles are fought in the battlefield, not in the Pentagon.

LEVERAGE KNOWLEDGE FOR COMPETITIVE ADVANTAGE
E. T. "Ted" Kunkel and Foster's Brewing Group *(Australia)*

Title: President and CEO
Headquarters: Melbourne
Business: One of the world's ten largest brewers whose flagship brand, Foster's, is the third most widely distributed beer brand in the world. Global assets include joint ownership of Canada's largest brewer, Molson Breweries. Exports to more than 130 countries, with international growth of more than 40% since 1993.
Employees: 8,207

"CONSIDER A BEER CAN," begins Thomas Stewart's recent book on intellectual capital. It is, he says, "an artifact of a new economy, evidence of how knowledge has become the most important component of business activity."

A beer can?

The transition from heavy steel to lightweight aluminum marked the transition to the knowledge age, Stewart explains. "It still holds twelve ounces of beer, but the can contains dramatically less material and energy—and more brains." Knowledge and innovation have been substituted for raw material.

Ted Kunkel just hopes it's a Foster's inside that smart beer can. According to the company's ads, Foster's is "Australian for beer." And according to CEO Kunkel, not only Foster's beer but the company itself is "unashamedly Australian": fun, egalitarian, and optimistic, like its commercials. But don't be fooled into thinking Foster's is just a beer company. Behind that frothy, happy-

go-lucky, work-hard-and-play-hard Australian facade lies a company that has fully recognized the power of knowledge.

Ted Kunkel is as concerned with how to unleash knowledge capital as he is about the brewing process. He pushes hard to make Foster's a knowledge-based "lead enterprise," moving from market leader to best in class. Aluminum cans with that slogan sit on the desk of everyone at Foster's to remind them of that goal.

Kunkel understands business literacy—the fact that knowledge, not sheet metal for cans or hops for beer, is his business's primary asset. Untapped ideas and skills are lying dormant inside people, and his challenge is to let people's minds loose to create an enormous pool of intellectual capital within the company. "The real asset value of Foster's," says Kunkel, "is the knowledge of the people. They simply must understand the business inside and out. That's our only competitive advantage."

Unleashing the Power of Knowledge

Ask Kunkel to describe Foster's, and he talks not about beer but about brains. "We're a global brains company and investing in knowledge and development is the flame for us to create a sustainable enterprise," he says. "When you actually think of the knowledge base in an organization, it's just impossible for the top twenty people to know what's down there. You've got to believe that unleashing knowledge at all levels is crucial for the success of the business. And you need leadership skills to make that happen."

When Kunkel became CEO, Foster's was unprofitable and overdiversified. He first sold off underperforming assets and changed the company leadership, realizing that it needed a fundamental mindset shift. He also realized that he would have to explain his business goals to employees across the company.

Kunkel examined every "chain" in the company and looked for possible changes, though knowing what he wouldn't change under any circumstances: "There are only three things in the company that we won't touch: we won't compromise our brands; we won't change the product; and we won't touch training. That's our knowledge budget."

Other than those three things, Kunkel has examined every process for possible change: "We've eliminated the term 'fixed cost' in the company; everything is variable cost."

The other ingredient for making this transformation to a knowledge-creating business is information—and lots of it. "The access to knowledge here is huge," Kunkel notes. "Everything is on our computer system and people can have as much information as they want, whenever they want it.

It's a risk, and if they use the information unwisely, we have to deal with that quickly. This kind of information transparency requires not only a lot of trust but also leaders who are willing to share power. "That's difficult for people who were raised in a 'knowledge is power' environment and who were historically 'takers,' not 'traders,' of information. But if the interfaces and exchanges fail, you're dead."

The depth of information available is mirrored by the breadth of knowledge Kunkel expects of his employees: "It's not only knowledge in manufacturing, it's knowledge of your customer, marketplace, and channels in which you're operating. It's constantly asking yourself, How can I look at the enterprise differently from all angles?"

For example, when creating a new packaging line in its Sydney plant, Foster's used cross-functional teams with representatives who shared knowledge from all the stakeholder groups. "Nothing is done unless it has shareholder value," Kunkel says. "And we've made everybody in the company a shareholder by giving them a few thousand shares a year and an interest-free line of credit with which to buy discounted shares."

As shareholders, all employees are responsible for the company's results. "We put ten percent growth per year as our stake in the ground," Kunkel explains. "Ten percent of our success depends on each employee growing ten percent as a person, expanding their knowledge capacity, wisdom, and creativity. If I achieve my KPIs [key performance indicators], then my KPIs added to everyone else's will give us ten percent growth."

Let People's Minds Loose

"We let people's minds loose through this knowledge transfer," explains Kunkel. "That's our job as leaders—to help people at all levels understand the external environment, including where they fit into the value chain and the language and numbers of business." Once Foster's employees understood that, the amount of knowledge stored in the company was unbelievable, he says. "And I'd believe that's true in every company. The real value of a company is much greater than the book value of its assets—the difference is knowledge."

Foster's whole business is looked at differently now. Kunkel's challenge was getting employees to understand transformational change: "Changing a company like this requires a huge amount of talking day to day. We had to create a road show, a communications blitz, to talk about the lead enterprise concept."

The results are impressive. "Our goal is to build a sustaining enterprise," Kunkel says. "Our market share is up from forty-eight percent to fifty-six percent, our profits have doubled from 180 million to 360 million

[USD], financial results that can be linked directly to the company's success in unleashing knowledge capital inside the business. The potential of the process is limitless."

Create Knowledge Transferers and Eliminate Knowledge Blockers

Knowledge transfer is the most critical component in building a knowledge-based business. "The interfaces among people are critical," Kunkel notes. "Knowledge transfers between and among businesses, people, and countries are paramount—and require walking around with your antennae up."

"Knowledge transferers" can't be just at the top of the organization: "Personal assistants used to be gatekeepers. They'd put you in your office and decide who was worthy to come see you. But a personal assistant in our new organization is a knowledge transferer. It's their job to make sure everyone who's associated with a particular issue has the knowledge they need to do their job."

Kunkel created knowledge transferers and "frontiersmen" throughout Foster's, people who, like the PA, ensure that all employees have the knowledge they need to do their jobs: "We're giving people enough knowledge to help them exert an influence on their job—and those issues will change every day." Part of the knowledge transferer's role is walking around like a big sponge picking up information, he says.

Yet he knows that in any culture change, there are blockers you must deal with, people who sabotage and undermine your vision and strategy. Foster's has sustained more than 30 percent growth for nine quarters. To make that happen, it changed the performance management and reward system, emphasizing individual and team KPIs and eliminating knowledge blockers. Foster's employees are now rewarded for three things: increasing their knowledge and skills; increasing the productivity of the enterprise as a whole; and increasing the share price.

Kunkel knows that book learning isn't all his employees need to be globally literate: "You never start off being good at all the literacies, and you don't learn them at Stanford and Harvard. You acquire those by falling into and climbing out of dry gullies."

And Ted Kunkel will have a nice cold Foster's in a smart beer can waiting for you when you climb out.

Australians are gregarious and individualistic, with a desire for equality and sport. Their ancestors were pioneers, and their large land of wide-open spaces has created a culture of openness and informality that permeates life and work.

AUSTRALIA: "Rugged Individualists"

National Snapshot

Compared to other executives, Australian business leaders say:

- They are strong at communicating global vision.
- They know their strengths and shortcomings.
- They help people adapt to change.
- They understand and respect their own cultural roots more than they respect the traditions of others.
- They are less likely to value multicultural business teams.
- Recruiting efforts are critical.
- 50% of CEOs and 31% of board members are non-Australians.

IF YOU FLY INTO ANY AUSTRALIAN CITY, the phrase you're bound to hear most frequently in the first few hours is "No worries." A word of caution to the business traveler: It's contagious, both linguistically and psychologically. After a week in Australia, you'll be saying it too—and meaning it. Work—and taking yourself too seriously—comes into clearer focus on this massive island continent.

Molded by Hardy Stock

Heavily British in culture and history, Australia was founded in 1788, largely by some people who rejected—or were rejected by—the Old World of Europe and others who were drawn by the promise of fast fortunes and wide-open spaces. With its convict heritage and proud Aborigines, it was—and is—a land with a pioneer spirit and a healthy defiance of authority. Proud but isolated, these hardy people created a friendly, accepting culture where people could live life as they wished, as long as they were careful to maintain the environmental beauty they found there, without the social strictures they had left behind. Australia's extreme, beautiful geography has continued to draw visitors since its founding; tourism is one of its biggest industries, though it has recently been hurt by the Asian economic crisis.

Yet despite its rough-and-tumble reputation and its reliance on such employments as farming, ranching, and mining, Australia is a cosmopolitan, industrialized society that ranks third in the world for the number of computers per 1,000 inhabitants and twelfth in the world for competitiveness. An early adopter of ATMs and mobile phones, Australians have embraced high technology with open arms, making Sydney a "call center" capital of the world. They enjoy a high standard of living and temperate climate that facilitates their love of both the outdoors and sports, Australia's "national religion," according to some.

It's a nation of literate, cultured people with a keen sense of humor, and it ranks second only to the United States in its citizens' individualistic nature. They are modest and self-made, with a disdain for pomposity and a preference for the "school of hard knocks" over formal education. Australians like to appear equal with their peers and will even hide their expertise for fear of appearing boastful. And although Australian culture is an individualistic one, Australians consider it sport to cut down "tall poppies," people who stand out from the crowd and are pompous about their accomplishments. This sometimes translates into a relative lack of positive feedback in business settings; Australians simply expect you'll do a good job and usually don't offer that kind of encouragement.

Straddling the Commonwealth and Asia

Australia is the world's sixth largest country and one of its most urban—only 15 percent of its population live in rural areas. Geographically and psychologically, Australia straddles the British Commonwealth and Asia. And while Australians consider themselves Europeans, not Asians, they've begun to develop closer ties with their Asian neighbors; 60 percent of their exports are to their local region.

But the historical separation of Australia from Asia is a feeling shared by Asians themselves. In fact, until very recently, the only regional neighbor that has been ready to accept increasingly closer ties with Australia has been New Zealand.

One reason for this regional isolation is that one of Australia's earliest pieces of legislation clearly snubbed the Asians. Its ban on Asian immigration and its "whites only" policy barred nonwhite brainpower from entering for almost a century, not to mention the antagonism they caused among its Asian neighbors. Small wonder that Asia ignored Australia and left it out of the Asian economic miracle.

While more than 90 percent of its population remains Caucasian, more than 4 million new immigrants have settled in Australia since 1945, creating new diversity challenges. Even so, there remains a strong minority opinion that the days of economic, racial, and social isolationism were best for Australia that is akin to the conservative backlash against immigration and diversity in the United States.

From Isolation to World-Class Business

By the 1970s, Australia's history of protectionist policy had severely isolated it. Its economy slid from being one of the world's most prosperous to one

Australia: ***At a Glance***
Official name: Commonwealth of Australia

> ***Economy type: Anglo-Saxon***
> ***Trading bloc: APEC (Asian-Pacific Economic Cooperation Group)***

Location: Island continent in the Pacific Ocean, southeast of Asia
Capital: Canberra **Population:** 18,613,087
Head of state: Queen Elizabeth II, represented by Governor-General Sir William Patrick Deane **Official Language:** English
Religion: Anglican 26%, Roman Catholic 26%, other Christian 24%
Literacy: 100%
World GNP ranking: 15 GDP (US$ bn): $343.5
GDP per capita: $21,158 **Unemployment:** 9.7%
Inflation: 1.9% **World export market share:** 1.5%

Major industries: Mining, steel, industrial and electrical equipment, chemicals, autos, aircraft, ships, machinery
Major crops: Wheat, cotton, fruit, sugar
Minerals: Bauxite, copper, coal, iron, lead, tin, uranium, zinc
Labor force: 36% trade, manufacturing, and industry, 34% finance and services, 6% agricultural
Computers per 1,000 people: 309.1

Assets: Strong agricultural and mining sectors. Significant mineral deposits. Highly developed tourist industry. Solid and experienced financial sector. Good infrastructure. Effective police force.

Liabilities: Unemployment remains high. Continued susceptibility to market damage caused by unstable and volatile Asian economies. Competing with Asian nations with low wages and poorer working conditions is a difficult endeavor. Tax rate for businesses and individuals is high. Low gross national savings. Difficult geography and location. Lack of managers with international experience and foreign language skills.

struggling to maintain a slowly deteriorating base. And though its citizens currently enjoy one of the highest standards of living in the developed world, it's widely acknowledged that its economic performance has lagged behind many of its neighbors'.

By the 1980s, productivity levels in Australia were woefully behind those of its international competitors and Australian companies were characterized by many business leaders as being strangled by inertia and fear of change. Declining world market share, lower productivity gains and economic growth rates, and rising unemployment were among the symptoms. Sweeping government reforms, begun in the 1980s, focused on making the country more open to international markets and operating methods.

Visitors might be surprised by the open, informal nature of Australian business. Influenced by strong labor unions, Australian business culture is now focused on international success, looking to the world for models, and engaging business and government in a unique, powerful partnership in the process.

Australia's "Best Practice Programme" (BPP) is creating a climate for change, with up to 70 percent improvement in productivity in some participating businesses. The Australian government has fostered an innovative model linking industrial policy, leadership, and benchmarking to effect change. As with any transition in an economy, leaders must change, too. By the beginning of the 1990s, Australia showed the world a new class of business leaders who demonstrate the best of Australian culture and infuse it with a broad knowledge of international best practices.

From Australians, we learn to take life, but not ourselves, seriously. Individualistic in outlook, these proud, informal people teach us to have a pioneering spirit in the context of strong relationships.

FOSTER INTERCHANGEABLE MANAGEMENT
Alfred M. Zeien, and the Gillette Company *(U.S.A.)*

Title: Retired Chairman and CEO
Headquarters: Boston, Massachusetts
Business: World leader in grooming products, including blades, razors, and shaving preparations. World's top seller of writing instruments, toothbrushes, oral care appliances, and alkaline batteries. With 64 facilities in 26 countries, Gillette sells in 200 countries. Seventy percent of its sales are international, and 1.7 billion people use Gillette products every day. The company spends 2.2% of annual sales on research and development, two times the consumer products average. As a result, 50% of sales are from products introduced in the last five years.
Employees: 44,000

IF YOU VISIT THE GILLETTE COMPANY, be prepared to enter what it humbly calls "World Shaving Headquarters." At this Pentagon for the war against whiskers, hundreds of unshaven employees arrive every day, saving their morning ritual for computer-equipped cubbyholes stocked with shaving cream and Sensor ra-

zors, stacked one on top of the other like "Hollywood Squares." Here, researchers poke and prod, even filming the process with a "whisker-cam," a razor with a tiny video camera attached—all in search of the perfect shave.

Gillette's retired CEO, Alfred Zeien, is a man who gets excited about the perfect shave. To ensure they keep the innovations flowing, Zeien moves employees around the business so that all can bring fresh perspectives to their new assignments. Zeien has created a strong culture of "interchangeable management with different management styles," a marriage of product and process technologies in a hotbed of innovation.

In the process, he's globalizing a company with American roots. And he's capitalizing on the uniquely American approach to work as a place to celebrate your own ambition and self-interest. By creating an environment where champions flourish, he's combining the best of American initiative with the wisdom of the world.

In a 1977 interview, Fidel Castro confessed that the only reason he had grown his famous beard in the first place had been a disruption in his supply of Gillette razor blades. Talk about influencing the course of history—or at least the "look" of history.

Gillette is one of America's truly international companies, and it's a place where world leadership is critical. Only 15 percent of Gillette's operations people are from the United States, and only eight of those in the eighteen top operating jobs have U.S. passports. "I've got a special drive going on to keep the Americans from being depleted," Zeien insists.

Seeking to be a "one-world business" of world-class brands, products, and people, Gillette is committed only to businesses that are "globalizable." International even before World War I, it wants to "Gilletify" the world by gaining technological supremacy and charging a premium for innovative products.

Zeien's greatest challenge is to develop management talent around the world. He does that by systematically assessing what skills are needed, conducting regular career reviews, and offering diagonal promotions across geography, functions, and product lines.

Determine What Skills You Need

Zeien doesn't worry about solving problems; he's got a whole staff of good people to do that. Rather, his job is to be an opportunity seeker. One of his toughest challenges is matching opportunities with the management needed to lead them. Building a global management culture at Gillette—finding, utilizing, developing, and retaining good talent—is really what keeps him awake at night, not developing a better toothbrush or closer shave.

From Oral B toothbrushes to Duracell batteries and Gillette shavers,

Gillette is in six businesses, including Paper Mate and Parker pens and Liquid Paper. It sells six blades outside the United States for every blade sold in the United States, and it's in businesses only where it can be a leader. "We shouldn't be in any core business unless we are the worldwide leader or have a plan in place to be number one," Zeien explains.

In the early 1990s, Zeien inherited a company with a strong foundation of trust from his predecessor and then globalized it. In the process, he built a matrix organization in which the skills needed to excel were different. Today he needs interactive skills, the ability to delegate effectively, personal awareness, and reciprocal trust.

"Our problems are not cash flow, product development, or basic geography," he says. "Our problems are management talent. How can we throw the right talent at these opportunities? You know for sure you can't do it from Boston, you have to do it on site, wherever that happens to be.

"Our managers must grow twenty percent for the businesses to grow twenty percent. That's why we put so much emphasis on internal management development. Recruiting is a challenge because some people can't handle this environment. The organization regurgitates them because of the complexities of coming to work inside a matrix organization in which everyone has responsibility for far more than they have direct authority over."

Gillette is basically a simple business, Zeien says. He can tell you about every product it makes, how and where it makes them, and how it makes money from them. At least part of his day is spent monitoring the comfort level inside that simple business, seeking to create a balance between the business risks his people face and the learning opportunities he's creating for them. He speeds up that process by aggressively moving people around the company.

Offer Diagonal Promotions Around the Company

At Gillette, it's simply not true that the shortest distance between two points is a straight line. Here, a zigzag will get you to the top more quickly than a vertical line.

Each year, Zeien and senior management review the top eight hundred people inside Gillette, looking at their careers and making recommendations for diagonal promotions across product lines, geography, or functions. In 1995, the company made it a rule that no more than 10 percent of promotions in Gillette would be vertical.

These diagonal promotions induce cross-functional sharing of skills and introduce a lot of change and innovation into the system. Because employees must be recognized by a large number of people as high potentials in order to move up, they focus less on just satisfying the boss and more on developing other employees and serving customers in changing markets. That encourages greater collaboration and leads them to help others achieve their goals.

By contrast, vertical promotions induce little change inside a company, as bosses often promote replicas of themselves. "If you want change," Zeien says, "disrupt the vertical promotion." He's intent on breaking the cycle of bosses who hire only people who do things their way.

Diagonal promotions also foster international careers. One half of Gillette's expatriate employees are in their fourth country. "If you asked anybody who joined this company in the last five years how to get ahead," notes Zeien, "they'd say you probably won't get ahead unless you're willing to move."

Interchangeable management is Gillette's central internal business strategy: "We won't be in any business where we can't move people from one business to the other. And since we've run the world on the same palette concept, selling the same products in relatively the same way no matter where we are in the world, we can move people geographically from one country to another as well."

By fostering diagonal moves in the business every three years, Zeien creates constant change, giving a fresh look to the business and creating an environment in which creativity and innovation flourish. From batteries to toothbrushes, from marketing to operations, from Singapore to Chile, people bring their unique experience to reinventing their new job.

This model of interchangeable management also encourages creative approaches to the way the company markets and sells its products: "We tend to look at the world as having five hundred states, each with their own markets. We recognize that Oregon is different from Louisiana and that Argentina is different from Bangladesh, but we tend to market and sell the same products to them. Our goal is to create 'captive customers' who enter Gillette as a buyer at the bottom of a product line ladder. Then we walk them up the rungs of the ladder."

Gillette makes creative use of its product and process innovations. That's why it has created an atmosphere of champions, consciously fostering an environment where it's essential to be creative and take risks.

Create an Atmosphere of Champions

In 1952, the United States had 52 percent of the world's GDP: half of everything produced and marketed was from the United States. That number is down to 21 percent today because the rest of the world has been growing at a faster rate. "There's hardly an American company that doesn't accept the fact that somebody's coming in here to hurt my business here at home," says Zeien. Building a culture of innovation is a key defense against that possibility.

This fact makes Gillette take innovation very seriously. As the pharmaceutical industry does, Gillette designs and builds its own equipment. It's taking this process even further by developing its own machinery-building business. "We try to identify new technologies that will have a major impact on our business in an ever-evolving marketplace," comments Zeien. "We ask, 'How do they apply, how do we master them, and how can they be a resource to our seventy-five profit centers?' "

Interchangeable management works only if people are able to go into their new jobs and be wildly creative: "U.S. companies are attuned to letting people be champions. They're collaborative, allowing people to wrestle with 'What do I stand for, what can I accomplish?' " But not all people are like Americans. The world outside the United States has a different attitude about the work relationship, Zeien acknowledges. "In western Europe and the Middle East, the job relationship is viewed as a contract; in Asia, it is viewed as a duty, and employment is service. In America, the job is a place to do your own thing," and the job of the leader is to unleash all these self-interests of ambition, money, and career.

To create a culture of champions, Gillette gives people lots of opportunity to stretch. And it tries not to shoot the messenger if things go wrong: "We don't do postmortems at Gillette. Sure, we lose something by not doing them—experience, analysis, and lessons—but we avoid witch-hunts and protect our champions. We start with the attitude that if there's an employee problem, we did something wrong. We didn't prepare them adequately, or perhaps we mismatched skills and circumstance."

Gillette's culture of champions creates a real, tangible result: product innovations. These innovations often result in new product lines for Gillette, such as the Mach 3 Razor or the new toothbrush line launched at Christmas of 1998. There's nothing new about toothbrushes; they were invented by the Egyptians in 1550 B.C.E. But 3,500 years later, Gillette has fundamentally changed the way one is made. To figure out how, it built a mouth bigger than a table, using robots to examine how the mouth and toothbrush work. By developing new materials for the toothbrush and changing the design of how the bristles work on the teeth, they created a new technology for an old application. "Without being arrogant, you have to have confidence in your own wisdom about where the business is going versus being so dependent on market research," Zeien says.

Because the company has developed managers in many different jobs over their lifetime and allowed each business to benefit from their fresh perspective, the world has opened up to Gillette. The international markets for new and improved Gillette products are growing, and Zeien wants to keep up with the demand. Russia's previously $10 million market is now a $200 million market, growing at 40 percent a year. In the same time, India has gone from a $25 million to a $150 million market, he says. That's a lot of razors.

THE MITSUBISHI CREED: LINKING PAST, PRESENT, AND FUTURE

Nobuyuki Masuda and Mitsubishi Heavy Industries *(Japan)*

Title: CEO
Headquarters: Tokyo
Business: Founded in 1870, Mitsubishi means "three diamonds," from the fact that it is a trinity of companies: Mitsubishi Heavy Industries, Mitsubishi Corporation, and Mitsubishi Bank.
Employees: 39,980

COMPANIES DON'T CELEBRATE *113-year anniversaries without a clear understanding of how their past, present, and future are linked. For Japan's largest heavy machinery maker, Mitsubishi Heavy Industries, the common thread is its corporate creed and its CEO, Nobuyuki Masuda.*

Masuda is a historical futurist who understands why telling stories creates constancy from one generation to the next. The Mitsubishi Creed is one such living story—it is a creed for all times, all places, and all people.

For all times: *Like many things Japanese, the Creed is designed to hold a lot of meaning in a small space, with only three points: customers come first, the company must grow and be innovative, and the company must make a societal contribution.*

In Japanese fashion, the Creed is deliberately ambiguous, with goals that set into motion a process of exploring meaning, stimulating communication, and creating an atmosphere where people work incredibly hard to fulfill its general intent.

For all places: *"We have a saying in Japanese," says Masuda, "that if you go to a different village, you follow the rules of that place. Our Creed doesn't do battle with the philosophies of other countries—it's universal and can be applied anyplace."*

After all, the gap between cultures isn't as large as we think. "In America," Masuda notes, "being honest means being aggressive, while in Japan it means respecting the harmony of relationships and seeking group understanding—different definitions of the same concept." Even the enigmatic public "face" the Japanese show the world—their tatemae*—isn't that different from how people operate around the world. "Every country has its own form of* tatemae*—the face we show others and the real feelings we keep inside."*

For all people: *Creeds are one thing, daily behavior is another altogether. Masuda makes sure there's no gap between the two by aggressively communicating three aspects of the Creed—the company's historical traditions, his principles for the year, and specific managers' philosophies—thus bringing it to the operational level for employees.*

INTEGRATE AND ALIGN YOUR COMPANY
Sir Peter Bonfield and British Telecommunications *(U.K.)*

Title: CEO
Headquarters: London
Business: A $23 billion telecommunications giant. Its Concert Communications Services is the world's leading provider of seamless global communication services for multinationals, with more than 3,700 customers in 50 countries, including 40% of the *Fortune* Global 500. BT recently formed an alliance with AT&T; together they bought a 30% stake in Japan Telecom.
Employees: 129,000, down from 245,700 in 1990

"THE DATA WAVE IS BREAKING *higher every day. Monopoly, bureaucracy, and stagnation are out; competition, choice, and innovation are in."*

Sir Peter Bonfield knows what he's talking about, having led British Telecommunications' dramatic transformation from monopoly to global competitor with the administrative ability that has marked British history. The company's transition from regulated to unregulated, from public to private, from national to global, and from voice to data has been dramatic—and fast.

BT has emerged as a fast, market-driven business riding the crest of that data wave. To make it work, Bonfield had to create a business-literate workforce: employees know where they're going and how to weather adversity, develop aspirational goals, and measure success. It's the complete alignment of vision, values, strategies, goals, and success indicators that has made this company world-class.

In 1998, British Telecommunications had revenues of $26 billion, but it had traveled a rocky road to get there: it had laid off over 100,000 people and stopped short of a major deal with MCI after years of work. But rather than lose course, Sir Peter Bonfield applied his business literacy—the clarity with which he mobilized his company toward a common goal—to provide the elasticity and cohesion BT needed to succeed. He's making profits today because for the past five years he has hammered BT's strategic plan into place with a constant focus on organization-wide alignment and consistency.

Bonfield has shaken up this telecom giant with straight talk and by paying attention to his home market, where BT earned most of its estimated $5 billion in pretax profits in 1997. But its international deals are what really grab investors' imaginations, according to *Business Week*: "As deregulation takes hold around the world," it reports, "BT seems poised to become the first truly international phone company."

As Britain's biggest TV advertiser and Europe's fastest-growing Internet provider, BT is at the very beginning of a convergence among telecommunications, information technology, and broadcasting, a fusion that will give rise to a new generation of opportunities. No other company has joint ventures, partners, and operations in every single major liberalizing market in Europe. "We're seizing opportunities for growth and making things happen," says Bonfield. BT is doing it by aligning its corporate values, strategies, and core priorities with its leadership team and success metrics—measures of the company's future, not its past.

Link Vision, Values, Strategies, and Goals

As a leader navigating through chaos, Bonfield knows he has to thoroughly understand the psychology of change and provide constancy in the face of it. He creates meaning for people, realizing that he's the focal point for everyone in the organization. And he knows that the data waves BT is riding require a change mindset at all levels of the organization. As a business geographer, he has to understand business drivers, local markets, and the history of BT itself and let those drive the change it undertakes but not limit it.

To set direction in this swelling sea, every company needs to have a stretch vision that is just about impossible, values to help guide it there, and a leader who can navigate toward that horizon through chaos. For Bonfield, that means having an aspirational vision that all employees can really sink their teeth into.

In BT's case, the vision is unequivocal: to be the most successful worldwide telecommunications group. Bonfield has set a high bar and has simultaneously broken the company into smaller units so people can get their arms around the business and move quickly. "We're trying to get people to believe the vision is achievable, not just pie in the sky," he says. "We want them to say, 'Yes, that looks tough, but I can see a way of achieving it.' " That's how Bonfield gets his people to make bold moves.

BT's vision and values have to be its rudder no matter what. When BT stepped back from its impending deal to buy MCI and lost out to WorldCom, its very public loss could have easily damaged its corporate vision. People could have lost their way, but they didn't. They knew that the vision of BT was still intact, and they knew the values that would help get them there: professionalism, respect, a unified team, and continuous improvement.

BT employees know that living those corporate values is a good career move. "We promote people who have the corporate values, not just people who are good at running the P and L," says Bonfield. "As long as we do that consistently, people will believe our management team."

Success is a moving target, and business geographers have to continually scan the environment for ways to get there. Global telecommunications revenues are expected to increase from around $650 billion in 1996 to about $1.2 trillion in 2002. And liberalization means that the size of the market that is open to free competition will grow fivefold in the next five years. To capitalize on those opportunities, BT's priorities are to grow its core operations, stake out a major claim in the U.S. market, achieve rapid growth in Europe, and seek out joint ventures in Europe, Latin America, and the Far East.

The advocate for leading change has to be the leader at the top. "Change must start with me and my management team," says Bonfield. To be credible and have impact, change programs have to be driven by Bonfield and his team, not by the quality team or human resources department. People will decide how serious leaders are about change based on how much time they spend communicating and how much time they invest in it personally. In other words, leaders have to be free to lead change.

Liberate Leaders to Lead

Bonfield knows that symbols help develop people, and he opts for positive ones, not hatchet jobs: "I want to concentrate on people doing the right thing; I want to break the mold and surprise people with my promotions." He's constantly looking for ways to identify, train, and reward international mindsets and leadership at all levels of the organization. The top two hundred to three hundred executives receive continuous 360-degree feedback in five areas to assess their leadership skill: leadership of change, direction setting, getting results, personal style, and managing relationships.

With twenty-five joint ventures worldwide and more in the works, BT is looking for internationally minded risk takers. Bonfield knows that growing a global business requires a new cadre of people who know how to operate across Europe and beyond, are multilingual, can work in partnership with other shareholders and boards, and are professional and can listen. "In the end," he explains, "you've got to understand that all these places are different, and you've got to do a lot more listening than you normally do."

Bonfield also knows that the personal transformation of company leaders is key: "You've got to lead from the front and do what you want other people to do. Great leaders have always been very consistent in all their relationships: up, down, sideways, no matter the difference, you treat all the same, with the respect they deserve, and you never deviate from that no matter what circumstances you find yourself in."

Bonfield seeks out and rewards that kind of consistency. And he knows that this kind of personal transformation doesn't happen overnight—it requires a major investment in learning: "I told my folks to put fifty percent on top of their training budget and then double it. You must go overboard with money and resources, and then people will know you're serious about it. You can't make the progress you need without putting money into training."

But that's not all that's required. Bonfield is pushing BT to hire more graduates from international universities; encouraging more people to be multilingual; and moving employees around internationally. He's creating a global-centric company by promoting an international language of global metrics for success.

Create Corporate Scorecards to Measure Success

Ultimately, people want to be measured. But knowing what success looks like, learning from failure, and balancing the needs of all your stakeholders requires that you modernize your yardstick: "If you just do revenue and profit measures in the short run, you'll be dominated by the past. To have a successful future, it's more important to get customer and people scorecards right. Future measures assess how well you're cultivating your value in the long term."

And it's long-term value that BT is after. It has combined its aspirational visions with the metrics of success to create corporate scorecards that reward leading indicators, not static ones. Bonfield helps people understand what "best in class" means by breaking it down into several different scorecards: Who's the best with people, customers, and shareholders? Who has the best financials, processes, and organizational learning?

It takes years to create an alignment between vision and success measures. To do so, you must have a vision of your company that is consistent with how people are rewarded; and the measures of success must be fair, clear, and applied to everyone. "If customers, employees, and your stakeholders think you're wonderful and you have aspirational targets and metrics of success, then you're moving in the right direction," Bonfield says. "These are leading indicators of the business."

Two of BT's indicators are quality and people. It measures quality using a scorecard based on the European Quality Foundation and people through its "Investors in People" program, a BT-developed leadership model. Less than two years after privatization, BT began its quality program. Ten years later, it won the European Quality Award, on the first try.

The company's investment paid off when it decided not to spend $20 billion to buy the remaining 80 percent of MCI—after years of working to do just that. It would have been the biggest takeover in British corporate history, but it failed—and very publicly. Because the British are known for keeping their word, "not completing the MCI deal was the most difficult decision I've made in my career," Bonfield says. "We had to convince our people that the wheels hadn't completely fallen off."

How was BT able to weather that deal? Because it had good alignment and internal cohesion. When the deal went wrong, the employees trusted Bonfield. Together, they managed the psychological process of losing the deal. While the failed MCI deal was a disappointment, it wasn't a killer blow. "Amazingly, employee surveys after the MCI situation were significantly better than they were two years earlier," Bonfield says.

Maybe that's not so amazing after all. "We were brutally frank, as a matter of fact," he recalls. BT had worked hard with MCI for years. But with its strategies in clear alignment, its employees were confident they'd get to their goals—with or without MCI.

The British have always been considered highly cultivated and well educated, with an emphasis on individualism and tradition in a heritage culture. Some say they are cool and detached. What's clear is that they're grappling with change and emotion on a national scale.

UNITED KINGDOM: "Modernizing Traditionalists"

National Snapshot

Compared to other executives, British business leaders say:

- They value executive multicultural experiences and cross-cultural teams.
- They lead by example.
- Beating the competition is a cultural value.
- They are less likely to focus on leadership development.
- Listening and communicating is the best way to influence others.
- 68% have customers, 52% have suppliers, and 43% have employees in ten or more countries.

Beefeaters, Big Ben, Buckingham Palace, and red double-decker buses are all symbols of Britain. But as powerful and recognizable as they are, they have more to do with this country's heritage than with its future.

The arrival of a new government might have sparked it, or perhaps it was caused by a new millennium or their losses in global competitiveness—whatever the reason, people are trying to reposition this country, which was once synonymous with trade and enterprise. Labour Party leader (now Prime Minister) Tony Blair first hinted at his desire to "rebrand" Britain in a speech to the Labour Party Conference in October 1995: "I want us to be a young country again." Blair wants to promote what some call "Cool Britannia."

The United Kingdom is being pressured to change by the growth of global markets, the influx of immigrants from Third World countries, competition from other EU countries, and women entering the workforce, among other forces. Traditions and symbols once held sacred are being challenged, reformed, or even abolished, including that of Britain's once powerful empire.

Britain is a country shaped by an island mentality and emerging from the legacy of a powerful empire, moving from being a cultural exporter to a cultural importer.

Shaped by an Island Mentality

Britain's island geography has both saved and isolated it.

The English Channel certainly helped save Britain from being invaded by both Napoleon and Hitler; unlike many of its European neighbors, Britain hasn't been invaded since the Normans came calling in 1066. Island nations tend toward strong naval forces, and Britain's is the model for a navy that not only defended its own shores but literally ruled the waves for more than a hundred years. Its insularity has also kept its citizens from feeling truly European and has created a healthy dose of xenophobia toward foreigners.

Britain tried to stay out of the European Economic Community (EEC) when it began in 1958, but by 1975 the economic pull of the EC was so great that it had no choice but to join—and now it has resisted joining the European Monetary Union, which came into existence on January 1, 1999, but has reserved the right to join at some later date. Britons' fear of losing sovereignty and national identity is keeping them out now, but economic pressures will likely make it impossible for them to stay out indefinitely.

Whatever xenophobia still exists in the United Kingdom is concentrated mainly in the lower socioeconomic classes and in small towns and rural England—and certainly isn't found in the world-class businesses that are shaping Britain's future.

Emerging from an Empire Legacy

In the last half of the eighteenth and all the nineteenth century, when Britain was most powerful, it was true that "the sun never sets on the British Empire." The ruler of one of the largest empires the world had known, controlling a fifth of the earth's surface and a quarter of its population, Britain had a profound impact on the cultures of countries worldwide. It started the use of English as the de facto international language, and as of 1999 more than half the countries formerly part of the empire still use English as one of their national languages, or even as their only one, even if there are dozens of other languages indigenous to the country.

The British didn't create and maintain this large, diverse empire by accident; they invented a worldwide administrative system that was able to run and perpetuate the enterprise, shored up by social and military domination. Their administrative mindset allowed them to institute a system that decentralized power to the areas they governed, while maintaining control from London. They recognized that various locations had to be ruled differently, a forerunner of global/local strategies in modern business. The British East India Company was itself a forerunner of modern multinational corporations.

Some of Britain's holdings were "Crown colonies," run by governors taking orders from London and with direct responsibility for building infrastructure: roads, harbors, hospitals, and schools. Other areas were ruled indirectly by Britain, through local traditional rulers. And still others weren't officially ruled by the British, but representatives of the Crown were sent to ensure that foreign policy and trade were conducted to the benefit of Britain.

World War I weakened Britain, and World War II showed that it no longer had the power to rule an empire. Once the economically most powerful country in the world, it is now sixth in terms of GDP, behind the United States, Japan, Germany, France, and Italy—a fact that particularly galls Britons.

The "post-British" era began when that great symbol of Britain, Winston Churchill, was defeated by a socialist government after World War II. Whole industries were nationalized, from the Bank of England to steel mills and even the British health care system. Growth in the United Kingdom slowed enormously, and British industry fell behind other countries. Many parts of the system just didn't work.

Until Margaret Thatcher. For eighteen years, beginning in 1979, the Thatcherite Conservatives ruled with a probusiness mindset, privatizing more than two thirds of the industries that the Labour Party had nationalized. Suddenly, Britain was a place for foreign investment again, with Japan leading the way. As the longest-serving prime minister of this century, Thatcher used her stability in office to enable business to plan, invest, and make profits in a way the country had seldom witnessed. The Conservative governments, led by Thatcher and her protégé John Major, were founded on a philosophy of free enterprise, competition, and less state intervention.

The Labour Party also needed a makeover, which it got from Tony Blair, who became prime minister in 1997. Young and dynamic, Blair began changing the party's image in 1994, abandoning its socialist policies, distancing it from the labor unions, and embracing the European Union. The Labour Party, no longer perceived as a party that fights only for working people's rights, moved to represent the middle class itself.

Repositioning Its Heritage Culture

It isn't just British business and politics that have changed, but British culture itself. In 1990, the ad agency DDB Needham asked foreigners which adjectives best described "Britishness." Proud, civilized, cultured, arrogant, and cold, it was told. The British have always taken a particular pride in these descriptions and their ancient institutions, such as Parliament and the monarchy. There's a Britishness about their products, though, that sometimes works against businesses and the country as a whole—identifiably British products were found to have a staid image among foreign consumers, a problem that has led some large multinational firms such as BT and British Airways to play down their Britishness. But the tide of communal emotion and outrage at the monarchy that surged through Britain after the death of Princess Diana didn't compute with these stereotypes of British behavior. Today, the British are finding that in a nation where their second largest city—Birmingham—will soon be a majority minority city, the old rules simply don't apply.

As a nation, the British are now embracing a new national pride that's the patriotism not merely of the monarchy, warm beer, or village greens, but of a profoundly urban and contemporary sort. This modern Britishness is inclusive rather than exclusive, based in the present rather than in the past, urban rather than rural, and genuinely multicultural—and much creative energy is growing out of this juxtaposition of the past, present, and future.

The results of a recent inquiry into national identity suggested that Britain's new brand be based on key features of modern Britain: as a "global hub" where goods, messages, and ideas are exchanged; as a "creative island" with an outstanding record of originality, from scientific discovery to pop music; as a "hybrid nation" whose ethnic and cultural diversity is a source of strength; and as a "silent revolutionary," leading the world in managing nonviolent change, from privatization and deindustrialization to constitutional reform. They called Britain a "nation of buccaneering entrepreneurs" and the "nation of fair play."

A Business Culture Emerges

The tools that helped Britain build its powerful empire are being used today by British businesses to succeed in the global marketplace. Britons' history of administrative excellence has nurtured a mindset that easily crafts policies and procedures, creating alignment between mission, goals, and priorities—just as they did in building their empire.

Much of British business culture today is a carryover from the time when it was the economic superpower of the world. During that period of more than a century and a half, many of the currencies of the world were pegged either to the British pound sterling or to gold. And while that glory has faded, the United Kingdom is still one of the world's great trading and financial centers. Its economy is still the fourth largest in Europe and sixth in the world. It remains a world leader in financial services, pharmaceuticals, precision engineering, and high technology, including telecommunications. And it has the largest energy resources of any EU state.

British industry is labor-intensive, with manual workers making up 45 percent of the workforce. In Europe, the United Kingdom is comparable with Spain and Portugal as a cheap labor market and is the least restricted by labor legislation; companies have greater freedom to hire and fire workers than in any other EU country. The British business community is dominated by banks, insurance companies, and other financial institutions collectively known as "the City." The London stock market is the largest and most active in Europe and the principal source of capital for companies.

The British are individualists and risk takers. Short-term thinkers, they seek quick returns on their investments, with great pressure to make the bottom line look good now, not later. That kind of short-term perspective can mean cuts in R and D, employee training, and, in some cases, product quality—which might bode poorly for British firms in the future.

While many older British executives fit the stereotype of the upper crust Englishman who studied classics and is "well bred," managers are increasingly coming from more diverse, less upper-class families and from less prestigious schools than Oxford or Cambridge. There are now more women and more northern English, Scots, and Welsh, who place more stress on straightforward, uncomplicated relationships and are much less class-conscious themselves. That's not to underestimate the power of the class system in Britain: it may be changing, but it's still very tight, with disdain on each side for the other. The "right" schools and family still increase the likelihood of rising to the top of the British business establishment.

British businesses tend to be hierarchical in terms of structured decision making but are increasingly willing to decentralize and give division heads great latitude in carrying out corporate policy. Younger British execu-

United Kingdom: ***At a Glance***
Official name: United Kingdom of Great Britain and Northern Ireland

Economy type: European Union
Trading bloc: European Union

Located: Island nation in northwestern Europe **Capital:** London
Population: 58,970,119 **Head of state:** Queen Elizabeth II
Official languages: English, Welsh, Scottish, Gaelic
Religion: Anglican, Roman Catholic, other Christian, Muslim
Literacy: 99%
World GNP Ranking: 6 **GDP (US$ bn):** $1,300.7
GDP per capita: 22,584 **Unemployment:** 5.6%
Inflation: 3.6% **World export market share:** 6.8%

Major industries: Steel, metals, vehicles, shipbuilding, banking, textiles, chemicals, electronics, aircraft, machinery, distilling
Major crops: Grains, sugar beets, potatoes, vegetables
Minerals: Coal, tin, oil, gas, limestone, iron, salt, clay
Labor force: 63% services, 25% manufacturing, 9% government
Computers per 1,000 people: 191.1

Strengths: A global leader in banking services, pharmaceuticals, and defense industries. Efficient aerospace, precision engineering, telecommunications industries. Progressive working practices and lower wages than in continental Europe. Excellent supply of venture capital. Significant investment in R and D. Strong global brand names.

Liabilities: Outmoded industrial machinery. High consumer and governmental debt. Lack of engineers. Tendency to high inflation. Lack of managers with international experience and foreign language skills.

tives recognize the importance of incorporating lower-level managers into decision making and encouraging bottom-up feedback. As a result, there's sometimes a split personality among managers that mirrors the split personality of the country itself: they attempt to respect traditional cultural guidelines yet utilize managerial reforms that may run counter to tradition.

Though often called a nation of shopkeepers, the English as a whole actually display mixed emotions about business. Even their educational system stresses the arts and classics over engineering, technological, and professional business training. In a recent survey asking about the most important factors in getting ahead, the British ranked hard work, education, ambition, ability, and knowing the right people, in that order.

Having done business in virtually every culture of the world for more than a century should have taught the British a great deal about how to use culture to their advantage. And while many did learn those lessons and are among the world's great global businessmen, many took their own culture with them wherever they went and expected the "natives" to adjust: to having tea, speaking English, and so forth. Like their American counterparts, a surprising percentage of British business executives lack the sensitivity to leverage cultural differences to their advantage.

Resting on a solid foundation of administrative savvy and buoyed by their pragmatic commitment to fairness and integrity, the British teach us how to be historical futurists. They embrace change by keeping one foot firmly in the past to honor their strong heritage and one foot firmly in the future to create new business empires.

CHAPTER SIX

CULTURAL LITERACY

Valuing and Leveraging Cultural Differences

All business is global, yet all markets are local. This globalized, multicultural world needs leaders with a keen understanding of national cultures. By learning from other countries, these leaders develop the best thinking and best practices from around the world, enabling them to leverage culture as a tool for competitive advantage.

Corporate survival and prosperity increasingly depend on our ability to interact with and manage people of different cultures—locally, regionally, nationally, and globally. Increased multicultural connections, driven by technological revolutions, have created new tensions and opportunities among groups. New cultural identities and mixtures are emerging as boundaries between cultures blur and become permeable. We are confronted with greater complexity than we can handle: uncertainty, contradictions, ambiguities, and contrasting interests abound, as do boundless opportunities.

For years, megacorporations cornered the market on crossing cultural borders. By sending expatriates abroad to search for international customers and suppliers, they experienced the benefits and pitfalls of the multicultural world. Local companies stayed home, and through their diverse workforces got a taste of internationalism and the challenges of managing across cultures.

But today everyone is part of the global marketplace, even though many companies don't yet realize that fact. Service firms, law offices, even taxi services are global companies. Small bookstores in South Africa, independent wine merchants in New Zealand, even co-op galleries in Finland—all buy from and sell to the world. The Internet is the great equalizer.

To thrive, all companies must adopt a global-centric approach to business. They must develop a multicultural perspective, an international knowledge base, and a global imagination—in other words, cultural literacy.

In this globalized world, culture is no longer a soft concept but an asset to be leveraged. Cultural literacy allows us to understand our own culture and the culture of others deeply, enabling us to mobilize diverse people, serve diverse customers, and operate across cultures around the world.

To be culturally literate, we must take on new roles:

- Proud Ancestor
- Inquisitive Internationalist
- Respectful Modernizer
- Culture Bridger
- Global Capitalist

To succeed in these roles, we must value our own culture, be literate about others', and use this knowledge to strengthen our own culture, create connections, and leverage culture for our advantage.

Proud Ancestor

Zhu Youlan reveres the stories that are an integral part of her Chinese culture. As CEO of Hong Kong–based China Resources, she adds to that heritage every day, using images of boats and shirt collars to describe her leadership philosophy. Zhu knows that learning how to exchange business cards is superficial; what really counts is a much deeper understanding of her culture. She's proud of the fact that the Chinese do things differently.

Zhu Youlan is a strong leader with a proud legacy, intent on learning from her ancestors. She understands what it truly means to be a progenitor, to accept the responsibility of "going before," passing on the culture from one generation to the next. Zhu understands her cultural roots and how they affect her style of thinking and behaving.

Proud ancestors understand the psychology of cultural self-awareness. With a healthy knowledge of their country's history, strengths, and shortcomings, they come to the table willing to share their past. They understand the cultures in which they live and recognize that each of us is the product of more than one culture—we can be German, Bavarian, female, and an accountant simultaneously, each identity providing cultural tendencies and data that inform how we live our lives.

Culturally literate leaders also have an honest sense of themselves in the world. By exercising cultural self-esteem, they value their roots and build confidence in themselves, enabling them to come to the international table as a mature adult.

Proud ancestors also know that feelings of cultural inferiority create resentment and diffidence. Worse yet, feelings of cultural superiority create arrogance and antagonism. When we believe our values are better than others, we are unable to listen cross-culturally. People who try to impose values on others expect others to fall into line with their view of the world.

DOES MULTICULTURAL EXPERIENCE MATTER?

(Percentage of global executives responding as a priority)

- New Zealand: 52%
- United Kingdom: 47%
- Singapore: 45%
- Philippines: 44%
- Netherlands: 44%
- France: 44%
- Brazil: 41%
- Hong Kong: 40%
- Sweden: 40%
- China: 40%
- Germany: 39%
- Mexico: 36%
- South Korea: 33%
- United States: 28%
- Canada: 26%
- Australia: 25%

Inquisitive Internationalist

Istanbul sits squarely at the meeting place of Europe and Asia, with a bridge literally spanning the distance between these two continents and mindsets. Sakip Sabanci, chairman of Turkey's leading global conglomerate, Sabanci Holdings, clearly mirrors that span in his business leadership. He is a proud Turk, balancing his nationalist passion with his keen desire to learn from others. At Sabanci Holdings, he travels abroad incessantly, enters into international joint ventures, and incorporates outside business practices—such as Japan's *kaizen*—into his management toolbox.

Like Sabanci, inquisitive internationalists know they must be literate about other cultures. Insatiably curious and sensitive about people and places, they analyze their own cultural biases and act like polite guests when traveling abroad, always respecting local customs.

Culturally literate leaders look beyond their own culture for business solutions. By seeking markets, competencies, and resources in the farthest corners of the globe, they enlarge their ideas and expertise. Like bees with pollen, they are incessant cross-fertilizers who take the best from one place to another, understanding the need to synthesize multiple perspectives.

Inquisitive internationalists don't shy away from diversity and debate—instead, they're drawn to it, unafraid of differences. They prefer to talk about, question, and celebrate these differences rather than be paralyzed by them. Because they know that one-size-fits-all leadership doesn't work, they cherish the fact that people differ in ability, background, and personality.

All of these qualities enable Sakip Sabanci and others like him to meet cultures as equals in the global marketplace.

Respectful Modernizer

Keshub Mahindra manufactures vehicles in Mumbai. As CEO of India's Mahindra & Mahindra, the world's largest manufacturer of tractors, he sees himself as much more than a carmaker. He is a trustee of his company and his country. As such, he has a dual responsibility: to both respect India's past and modernize its future. Keeping one foot in his own culture and one foot on the world stage, Mahindra is a respectful modernizer.

Becoming culturally literate requires an honest sense of your own culture, creating a national pride tempered with an awareness of national flaws. You must be aware of your personal biases and prejudices and cultural strengths and shortcomings and careful not to let these blinders obstruct your vision. You must be confident and clear about who you are and express the best of your country.

Understanding and valuing others is the natural next step. By developing the capacity to see the world from another perspective, you open yourself to learning what each country has to offer. By looking globally for new ideas and business practices, you expand your worldview and open up the possibility of bringing something of value back into your own country.

The final step is to modernize your own country with the new ideas you learn abroad. By integrating others' worlds into your own, you enlarge and enrich your perspective and become enlightened and elevated in the process. Inevitably, you become a broader person and modernize your country. But you must be open to change.

Culture Bridger

Leo van Wijk, CEO of KLM Royal Dutch Airlines, literally bridges cultures every day, flying 13 million people a year from one place to another. "We are culture bridgers, listening and sharing what we learn from around the world," says van Wijk. A culturally literate leader, he is able to bridge other cultures to form alliances and connections, such as KLM's extensive partnership with Northwest Airlines.

Building connections with other cultures doesn't happen just with airplane flights. The opportunities exist for everyone every day in the global environment. Being successful requires a special mindset and a commitment to collaborating cross-culturally.

Culture bridgers are true integrators. They get excited by seeing similarities and differences among people. Accepting that others may have different

CULTURAL DATA BANK

- If the world were a village of 100 people, there would be 56 Asians, 21 Europeans, 9 Africans, 8 South Americans, and 6 North Americans. There would be 30 Christians, 18 Moslems, 13 Hindus, 6 Buddhists, 5 animists, and 21 without any religion. Of these 100 people, 6 would control half the total income, 50 would be hungry, 60 would live in shantytowns, and 70 would be illiterate.
- *Fortune* magazine reports that cross-border mergers and acquisitions now account for more than half of all new foreign direct investments worldwide.
- The top 100 multinationals own nearly $2 trillion of assets outside their home countries, a quarter of the world's stock of all foreign direct investment.
- Most of the estimated 45,000 U.S. firms that operate internationally employ fewer than 250 people.
- In 1998, the total revenues of Mitsubishi Corporation were $128 billion. That same year, the gross domestic product of South Africa was $129 billion.
- The combined wealth of the world's 225 richest people is $1 trillion. The combined annual income of the world's 2.5 billion poorest people is $1 trillion.

values than their own, they look for ways to discover those differences, destroy the walls between them, and celebrate their commonalities. They connect on some things and extract lessons from what's different, always using the differences to build sturdier bridges.

Like civil engineers, culturally literate leaders know that building bridges depends on a strong, solid foundation. You must first like yourself and your national culture. Then you must survey the distant shore to know where you're going. Taking the time to understand another culture is critical to building a permanent bridge. Bridge builders also value balance and rely on the creative tension that holds the arch of the bridge together. By combining the solidity of knowing yourself with the flexibility of being open to others, you too can manage the creative tension.

Bridges are also built brick by brick, just as relationships are built one person at a time. It's inevitable that conflicts and miscommunications will arise, but culture bridgers know how to resolve them with grace. When bridges rust or have a loose foundation, they require upkeep and attention. Cultural relationships require the same.

Global Capitalist

Jean-Louis Beffa is French, European, and global. As CEO of Saint-Gobain, one of France's largest industrial conglomerates, which created the windows of Versailles, Beffa embodies the concept of a global/local mindset. With a French appreciation for history and strategic planning, a European love of truth and debate, and a global appreciation of diversity and world markets, Beffa is a true global capitalist.

Like Beffa, global capitalists develop a global/local mindset, use the diversity of their employees to respond to the diversity of markets, and broaden the definition of business success by focusing on their corporate social responsibility. They understand the global marketplace, see regional opportu-

CULTURAL ILLITERACIES

- McDonald's took thirteen months to realize that Hindus in India don't eat beef. When it started making hamburgers out of lamb, sales flourished. Today it serves beer in Germany, wine in France, and kosher beef just outside Jerusalem.
- In Africa, companies show pictures of what's inside bottles so illiterate customers know what they're getting. When a baby food company showed a picture of a child on its label, little wonder the product didn't sell very well.
- An American television ad for deodorant depicted an octopus putting antiperspirant under each arm. When the ad flopped in Japan, the producers realized that octopuses don't have arms there, they have legs.
- An American firm sent an elaborate business proposal to Saudi Arabia bound in pigskin to dramatize the presentation. Since pigs are considered unclean by Muslims, the proposal was never opened.
- The names of European products don't always translate well in the United States. Some examples: an English candy called "Zit," a French soft drink called "Sic," and a Finnish product that unfreezes car locks called "Super Piss."
- Conversely, Kentucky Fried Chicken's "finger lickin' good" became "eat your fingers off" in Chinese; General Motors' Nova sounds like "no go" in Spanish; Ford's Pinto means "small male appendage" in Portuguese slang; and "Fresca" means "lesbian" in Mexican slang.
- A Swiss restaurant sign boasted, "Our wines leave you nothing to hope for"; a bathroom sign in Finland read, "To stop the drip, turn cock to right"; and a Swedish vacuum cleaner producer was proud to claim, "Electrolux sucks."

nities, and are sensitive to local markets—and they recognize, hire, develop, and nurture local managers with global literacy skills.

Culturally literate leaders understand the interconnectedness of the global economy, always looking globally for customers, capital, suppliers, and talent. In so doing, they bring global power to local problems and local solutions to global opportunities. They tap into the world's resources, utilizing them to create new products around the globe. They know how to access new talent, information, and experience from around the world.

Global capitalists leverage a diverse workforce to serve diverse customers. They know that different people bring their own experiences and habits to work and that all these differences are vital for creativity and innovation. By learning multiple languages, building an international board of directors, and creating multicultural teams, these leaders create a sense of wholeness, incorporating all that diversity.

And these leaders truly understand their corporate social responsibilities. By broadening the definition of success to incorporate a triple bottom line of financial, social, and environmental measures, they enhance the role of businesses as global citizens and environmental stewards.

These leaders understand deeply their role in building a healthier, sustainable planet for all our citizens. They use their cultural wisdom to manage the public-private interface between consumers, environmentalists, investors, human rights activists, governments, and societies.

No matter how global they become, they try hard to protect their local communities. With their enlightened self-interest, they know only too well that nothing is worse than alienating a local community of customers.

MAKE "INTERNATIONAL" A PART OF YOUR BLOODSTREAM

Helen Alexander and The Economist Group *(U.K.)*

Title: Managing Director
Headquarters: London
Business: Flagship publication is *The Economist.* It conducts top-level business seminars and conferences and offers worldwide analytical expertise to continuously monitor and forecast trends in 195 countries. Since 1928, half the shares of *The Economist* have been owned by the *Financial Times,* a subsidiary of Pearson, the other half by a group of independent shareholders, including many members of the staff.
Employees: More than 1,500 editors and analysts

It may look like a magazine, but Helen Alexander insists that it's a newspaper. Whatever you call it, The Economist *is one of the most highly respected publications on earth. It goes to press every Thursday like clockwork, to be printed simultaneously in six countries.*

"A newspaper like The Economist *is classified with frozen peas when it goes through customs because it's no good tomorrow," says Alexander, chief executive of the Economist Group, owner of* The Economist *and other intelligence-gathering publications, products, and services. Every week, business and world leaders—more than 650,000 readers per issue—depend on* The Economist *to analyze world events with insight, integrity, and intellect.*

Its leader is culturally literate, talking urgently about the world around her, debating issues, and exploring what it means to be a global leader, sometimes irreverently but always globally. "The international nature of our business is deep in our bloodstream," explains Alexander.

One of its own editors penned the best description of *The Economist:* "It is a Friday 'viewspaper,' where the readers, with higher than average incomes, better than average minds but with less than average time, can test their opinions against ours. We try to tell the world about the world, to persuade the expert and reach the amateur, with an injection of opinion and argument."

"We're supplying perspective, analyses, viewpoints," agrees Alexander. "To do that, we need people with an international mindset who know how to cultivate diversity and debate across cultures; linking people and knowledge around the world." The Economist Group needs urbane, articulate, and opinionated employees who serve sophisticated global customers.

Develop an International Mindset

Admirers of *The Economist* have included no less than Queen Victoria, Benito Mussolini, Helmut Schmidt, and John F. Kennedy. For years there's been speculation about who receives the solitary copy allowed into Cuba.

With an audience like that, the company has had to be international to its bones, serving a global audience by trading in intellect, from the pages of *The Economist* to its powerful Economist Intelligence Unit, new Web-based tools and databases, and high-level conferences. It thinks, prints, and delivers across borders, using local successes such as *CFO* and *Roll Call* magazines in the United States to start new publications in Europe such as *CFO Europe* and *European Commission* magazine.

Its business is nothing less than enhancing the executive intelligence quotient around the world—constantly and urgently. "We supply analysis to the thinking executive who sits above their business, their country, the marketplace, the world," says Alexander. "We communicate the context of things; we teach people the international perspective." It's a British company, dating back to 1843, with British shareholders, headquarters, and traditions, but it has mastered the international mindset so well that Europeans think it's U.S.-based and Americans think it's European-based, Alexander says with a smile.

She thinks the Economist Group is in the right place, because in the vortex of this technological world of information, debate, and global implication, the British continue to make contributions as world traders and proud administrators. "The British are individualistic, honest and fair, and we're good at being slightly dispassionate about a lot of things, so we're the observer—not the conscience, exactly, but a combination of balancer and observer," she notes. Her description of the British is also an apt description of *The Economist.*

"We're good at getting things across borders, both physically and mentally," says Alexander. To excel at that, they need people with the right international mindset, but Alexander doesn't put too much faith in "how-to" books about international work: "I don't think books that teach you how to say 'Hello' in Japanese and what not to do when a Japanese person takes you out to dinner are particularly relevant—that's superficial sensitivity."

Instead, being international is more deeply embedded in the fabric of the Economist Group: "We look for highly educated and flexible, open-minded people who can work across borders, who can be international and local at the same time, and who are naturally culturally sensitive; we want people who can think beyond superficial cultural differences."

That kind of international mindset isn't a technique; it's a way of thinking and acting in the world. Alexander is looking for people who are culturally literate inside their own heads and in relationships with others. And while a deep international perspective is vital to the Economist Group, its people must also know how the world works—how government and business influence each other—yet still respect their local roots. In Alexander's book, nationalism and national self-esteem still count: "You can't be on an airplane all the time, because in the end you have to come down to earth. You have to operate from somewhere, and you have to know where you come from."

Cultivate Diversity and Debate Across Cultures

The Economist Group is well respected because it has a point of view. It pushes forward argument, and it provokes and debates. And it isn't fearful of saying what it thinks. Take the no-nonsense cover headline after the Clinton sex scandal broke: "Just go." There's no ambiguity about its perspective: "It is religious about free trade and stands for clear thinking, quickly trampling anything that is muddled or fake," says Alexander. "In some instances, it even stands for free speech in nations where there is little."

How does it continually succeed in being clear, insightful, and shining a bright light on the workings of the world? To bring the kind of clarity it does to the analysis of fast-changing, complex world events, the Economist Group has built an environment that cultivates diversity of opinion and debate across cultures, with an underpinning of Quakerly politeness in the strong British tradition. The environment is informal, open, and fair. "All the debate that goes on here is nevertheless really quite polite," says Alexander. "People who are plain rude don't work here. Even when we're quite foul on paper, it's all done in a polite way. Social etiquette matters at the Economist Group" as does a keen sense of humor.

Debate is woven into the process. "It's a highly educated team who will debate anything from 'Is your coffee cup half empty?' to 'What's the future of the world?' " admits Alexander. "If you work here, you have to be able to make up your mind, because the team sniffs out anything that's less than complete. We thrive on real openness to information, cultures, diversity, and debate. It's a tough culture and highly unforgiving; it demands a clarity of thought and personality and a certain robustness."

It also requires strong, proud, opinionated people who believe that what they're doing makes a difference. Remarkably, these bright, outspoken, sure thinkers don't sign their work; look closely at a copy of *The Economist,* and you'll find it difficult to locate a single byline, even though its contributors have ranged from Soviet spies to prime ministers and presidents.

Many hands write the paper, but it speaks with a collective voice—its correspondents and editors are strictly anonymous to preclude the information hogging and byline grabbing that often mark journalism. It's a practice that has given *The Economist* a personality far stronger than that of any one mind. "Self-promoters self-select out of our culture; collaborative leaders with strong points of view are our role models," Alexander says.

This is a culture of collaborative individualists, a unique cooperative experience that has an edge to it—and is underscored by strong leadership. "From the newest young recruit to the oldest established venerable journalist, everybody has their say, but then someone decides. At that moment it's no longer a democracy at all," explains Alexander.

The Economist Group blends the individualistic West and the communitarian East, celebrating individual initiative with a higher purpose and harnessing talented individuals to strive toward a common goal. Its group profit-sharing plan for every staff member helps support this community of common purpose. It's a performance-focused and sometimes individualistic community of thinkers, but with a quieting of the individual personality for the good of the higher purpose. "This is a collection of feisty, smart individuals who say 'I work for *The Economist*' with pride and pleasure," says Alexander. "Somebody has an idea, somebody else develops it, and somebody else runs with it. That's a very common theme through the organization."

Link People and Knowledge Around the World

In today's world, people, information, and technology are interdependent and interconnected. "We need leaders," says Alexander, "who can think across borders, sectors, and institutions to see connections among them."

The Economist Group is a changer of and reactor to global business: "The media force companies to have no secrets, to have complete exposure in a world where there's no time delay. In some ways, it plays the role of conscience for global business; it's tougher for business to hide, and your customers are exposed very quickly to whatever it is you're doing."

When more than 80 percent of your product sales are foreign and your product itself is international news and analysis, your whole mission is to link people with information globally. *The Economist*'s worldwide circulation has grown by 37 percent since 1990, reaching more than 180 countries. To serve its customers, the Economist Group depends on access to the best information—and it knows it can't access that without technology: "With the advent of technology, it's like a couple of layers of skin have been peeled off so we have much more interface with customers. We don't have agents and newsstands and telephone customer centers." Its revenues from electronic delivery methods are growing by 37 percent annually, making the digital future important to the Economist Group.

The group knows that its customers are technologically savvy and international, so at an absolute minimum it has to build its own internal infrastructure to keep up with the best: "We're determined to benefit from the opportunities that arise from the convergence of computing, telecommunications, and media. By managing the businesses as a coherent group while retaining the flexibility and entrepreneurial nature of our business units, we can create competitive advantage."

The experience of Alexander, a leader in the unique position of teaching the world's business leaders about the world, provides lessons for all companies: build an environment that nurtures collaborative individualists with

DO YOU VALUE MULTICULTURAL EXPERIENCE?

(Percentage of executives responding positively)

- Europe: 44%
- Latin America: 41%
- Asia: 39%
- Australia/New Zealand: 33%
- North America: 28%

an international mindset, and institutionalize a global perspective that is comfortable with diversity and debate across cultures.

BE A MIRROR AND A MODERNIZER OF YOUR CULTURE

Keshub Mahindra and Mahindra & Mahindra, Ltd. *(India)*

Title: Chairman
Headquarters: Mumbai
Business: Tenth largest private sector business in India. World's largest manufacturer of tractors and India's biggest manufacturer of utility vehicles.
Employees: 17,000

KESHUB MAHINDRA is both a mirror and a modernizer of his rich Indian culture. He understands how his view of the world is influenced by the rich mix of cultures, languages, and religions that is his homeland.

Mahindra accepts that others have different values; he remains constantly curious about other people, places, and cultures. Because he sees opportunity outside India, he looks globally for new customers, capital, suppliers, and talent—but he doesn't stop there. Instead, he brings the best of the world back to India to modernize this country for a new era.

Value Your Own Roots

Keshub Mahindra's work and life reflect the values that permeate culture in India: a deep respect for family and relationships, a basic concern for people, and a sense of benevolence and service: "I learned from Gandhi my sense of being a trustee to the company and the country. If you're going to act as a trustee, you have to create confidence—and you can only do that if people have faith in you. Faith and confidence come not only from the dividends you pay but from how you run your business and your life. You can't speak one language in business and lead your life another way."

Mahindra's program to educate employees' children is one tangible expression of that stewardship—and of his belief that education is the answer to India's social ills. He knows that with only a 50 percent literacy rate, India has failed to educate its people. The program allows employees' children to receive educational subsidies not provided by the Indian government.

M&M is based on this strong values orientation; it builds faith among its stakeholders through these types of social programs. And Mahindra's understanding of himself and his culture influences how he runs his company—by knowing and valuing his cultural roots, he's able to reach out, identify, and link with business partners in different cultures around the world.

Link Your Culture to the World

"As Buddha says, 'You can't clap with one hand.' " says Mahindra. "If you can't build an honest relationship with your partner, you can't succeed. 'People rapport,' finding the basic, common values and ethics we share, is extremely important to our success." He links his company—and India—to the world by meeting with business partners one-on-one to learn about their values.

Partnerships must be reciprocal. Mismatched, by all external measures—size, financial clout, and global branding—with its partner Ford Motor Company, the American giant, M&M has formed a mutually beneficial relationship in which M&M learns business practices from Ford while Ford learns how to manage effectively in an Indian environment. "We don't agree on everything," Mahindra says, "but when we disagree, we do it in a manner of understanding and of reaching out that is rooted in Hindu culture."

He's also pragmatic about the relationship: "You've got to deal with local conditions, yet meet global competition at the same time. We'd be foolish to try to compete with Ford, but we can learn a lot from partnering with them."

Mahindra & Mahindra's mission is to be "The Moving Force." Mahindra himself focuses on being a "driver with a destination," appropriate for a company founded on its automotive division. But what drives Mahindra? He is "driven by India, by the market, by goodwill, by technology, and by people," according to the company's corporate brochure. He's also driven to change India by knowing its strengths and shoring up its weaknesses.

Modernize Your Country and Retain the Best of Your Culture

Mahindra, an engineer trained in the United States, knows he needs to understand the strengths and weaknesses not only of his company but also of his country. His corporate brochure says it most clearly: "A truck moving uphill hardly does so on its own. It demands a firm foot on the accelerator, a firm hand on the wheel. It needs a driver with a destination. The force that moves the truck is the force of a person who needs to attain a goal. Where lies the force that moves a nation?"

Mahindra is determined to be that force. He knows what resources India lacks—and he builds relationships to bring in technology, ideas, and financial capital. Because his company has grown up with India, he feels a paternalistic responsibility to help India reinvent itself, a role many large businesses play in Indian society.

Because the government controlled India's business environment until liberalization, some of India's workers lack discipline and a work ethic, according to Mahindra. He wants to change that. He knows well the challenges of the Indian business environment—increased competition, the end of the "license raj" that thwarted competition for so long, the draconian laws that destroyed initiative and entrepreneurship, and the recent liberalization of the economy—yet he's very bullish about the future. "When you're insulated like India was until 1991, your parameters get distorted," he says. "You have protected markets, no global competition, and no access to the latest technology or marketing techniques. Indian business is in a massive learning curve."

Access to global markets and partners is critical to India's—and M&M's—success. "We have to expose our leaders to world-class thinkers and new technologies. They need to travel like hell and see what's happening in the world."

Mahindra is a great mediator of many cultures: his own, his company's, India's, and those of the countries in which he does business. And he sees culture as a resource, not an obstacle. He's a catalyst for change, yet, as he says knowingly, "I provide a link to the past, too."

INDIA: "Serving Merchants"

India's chaotic surface and underlying calm and its rapidly growing culture of entrepreneurs embracing ancient ritual are all reflections of this richly diverse, enigmatic culture. This melting pot of castes, languages, regions, and faiths is full to the brim and has created a culture of modest self-reliance and trusteeship.

YOU'RE TAKING YOUR LIFE in your own hands if you try to drive in Mumbai, formerly known as Bombay. Nothing can prepare you for the seeming chaos on the roads and highways of India. You'll find yourself in a national game of "chicken" where cars barrel toward one another at high speeds, disregarding any semblance of order, traffic regulations, or lanes, leaving thousands dead each year in road carnage alone.

When your car finally does stop, hoards of impoverished children swarm toward it as if in a reflex action, hands outstretched, begging for money or a stick of gum. Behind them, billboards of some of the world's largest multinational corporations announce the new India, a modern land linked to the world through high technology and global business.

The magic of this largely Hindu land is that what lies beneath this chaotic surface is a clear, true sense that none of this highway chaos really matters, that you will get to where you were meant to go. As *The New York Times* recently reported, "Although a great many Indians are instinctively entrepreneurial, Hindu beliefs have engendered an abiding respect for those holy men who abjure the material world." There is a sense in India that beneath the chaos lies a deep calm that has no use for the things of this world.

Weaving a Rich Tapestry of Culture

India is a grand tapestry of castes, languages, regions, and faiths, all coexisting—sometimes peacefully, as Gandhi hoped, and sometimes not so peacefully—in more than 650,000 villages across this vast land. What divides Indians? What class they belong to, what caste they're from, what education they've received, whether they're urban or rural, and what language they speak.

It's a land with a 3,500-year-old history, lush and rich with natural resources; more than 56 percent of India is arable land, compared to 12 percent in the United States and a mere 8 percent in China. And it's an old land of young people: 35 percent of Indians are fourteen years of age or younger, compared to 14 percent in the United States and 15 percent in China, which means that India's population will continue to grow rapidly for at least the next two generations. Dense with people already, the country will see its population surpass China's by the year 2025.

India is a nation of fourteen official languages; its people also speak hundreds of unofficial languages, all with different dialects, using English as the unifying force and sometimes as the only way to understanding in this modern-day Babel. English is the language of business, government, and urban areas, home to one quarter of the 970 million people living in India.

A mix of religions adds to the stew that bakes under a hot Indian sun: Hindu, Muslim, Christian, Sikh, Buddhist, Jain, and Parsi. Eighty percent of India's people are Hindu, which is a religion, a way of life, a philosophy, and a social system unto itself.

Blending the Past and the Future

"India can only be compared with India," argues Yogendra Singh, a professor at Jawaharlal Nehru University in New Delhi. He's right: How else can we reconcile the juxtaposition of the new India of high technology and software with the old India of bullock carts and Hindu chants?

Economic reforms have empowered a thriving class of entrepreneurs, creating a culture both focused on participating in ancient ritual and embracing the Internet, on maintaining peaceful coexistence and constructing nuclear weapons, on revering sacred texts and launching communications satellites. It is a place where opposites meet, small wonder in a nation that invented the concept of zero, so important and yet so empty, a cornerstone of the binary language of computers, now one of India's greatest strengths.

India is at once home to the world's largest middle class and to the largest concentration of people living below the poverty line. It is a leader in software development, yet one half of the population—and two thirds of women—over the age of fifteen are illiterate.

A four-layer caste system still exists, though untouchables are now called the *dalit.* The castes, or *varna*s (meaning "colors"), include the *brahmans* (priests), *kshatriyas* (warriors), *vaisyas* (traders), and *sudras* (serfs and workers). The 15 percent of the population who belong to the *dalit* are outside these four layers. The caste system is essentially a hierarchical social system that proclaims the fundamental inequality of humans. This concept of hierarchy carries over into work, as well.

Shaped by Religion and Colonization

Hinduism—the religion of 80 percent of its population—shapes India. Even the tension between Hindus and Muslims literally shaped this country's borders when Pakistan was formed. Hindus are formed by the passivity, benevolence, and service orientation that the religion engenders. Its central theme, concern with issues of the "self," centers around the quest for enlightenment and the perfection of the human person, both the material and the "inner," or spiritual, self.

Hinduism legitimizes three secular goals of life: experiencing desire or pleasure; achieving wealth and possessions by honest means; and living one's life according to the sacred or moral law, the quest for Dharma.

For many years, India was a Hindu nation with a British lord. As early as the end of the fifteenth century, its lush riches were known to the rest of the world. Attracted by the spices of Malabar, Portuguese explorer Vasco da Gama landed in Calicut in 1498. Less than five hundred years later, the British grew so enamored of India that they annexed the country into their own empire, establishing one of the finest civil services in the world there, as well as a functioning infrastructure, legal system, and a concept of Westminster democracy that flourishes to this day.

The popular political awakening in India that has been evident since the late 1960s has made India a more genuine democracy and in some ways a more difficult country to govern. Indians are particularly proud of the persistence of their democracy and contrast their country to Pakistan, the nation carved out of British India when Muslim leaders demanded a separate state. Since independence, Pakistan has had a series of military governments that have come to power through coups, while India has had uninterrupted democracy. Despite the massive illiteracy in India, the voter turnout there is consistently higher than that in the United States.

The Serving Merchants

Given this long, rich history of colonization, this tapestry of diverse cultures, ethnicities, and languages, and the burgeoning competitive environment, what are the Indian culture and character that have emerged?

Out of this diverse culture has emerged a business environment that is primarily family-owned, patriarchal, hierarchical, and with a rigidly class-based structure. No matter how Western the professional, international businessmen from India may appear on the outside, the Indian ethos infuses their deepest beliefs. Reincarnation, predetermination, and karma are internalized values that affect the behavior of even the least "religious" of Indian business leaders. They accept logical reasoning but believe that other kinds of thinking, such as intuition, insight, and mysticism, are also valid ways of seeing the world. And they may use all four methods of thinking simultaneously to make their decisions, baffling some Western businessmen in the process. Indians are among the least time-conscious people in the world; they believe that things will happen when they are meant to.

Economic reforms are beginning to show results in India with far-reaching changes to India's creaky, largely state-controlled economy. Before they were instituted, India was a market where almost everything was controlled, including prices, quantities of products produced, wages, labor force size, and investment. This controlled environment actually led businesses such as Birla and Mahindra to look outside India and start down the path to globalization before they would have otherwise.

Liberalization has happened slowly—and differently in India from any other place on Earth—and has made foreign investment possible in key infrastructural sectors such as road building, telecommunications, port facilities, and electricity generation. As a result of this forced competition, India's companies are becoming world class; they're slimming down and benchmarking themselves against their global competitors. The government has also done away with the restrictive "capacity-licensing" regime, the "license raj" that stifled domestic businesses for so long by limiting the amount of goods that companies could make. Some companies feel threatened by this new competition, suspicious that they'll be taken over by the large multinational corporations that are salivating over the potential of the market in India, which has a middle class the size of the entire U.S. population.

The new division in India is between north and south. The south, with

India: ***At a Glance***
Official name: Republic of India

> ***Economy type: Emerging***
> ***Trading bloc: SAARC (South Asian Association for Regional Cooperation)***

Location: Occupies most of the Indian subcontinent in South Asia
Capital: New Delhi **Population:** 984,003,683
Head of state: President Kocheril Raman Narayanan
Official languages: Hindi, English
Religion: 80% Hindu, 14% Muslim, 2% Christian **Literacy:** 52%
World GNP ranking: 16 **GDP (US$bn):** $342
GDP per capita: $354 **Unemployment:** N/A
Inflation: 9.1% **World export market share:** 0.8%

Major industries: Textiles, steel, processed foods, cement, machinery, chemicals, mining, autos
Major crops: Rice, grains, sugar, spices, teas, cashews, cotton, potatoes, jute, linseed
Minerals: Coal, iron, manganese, mica, bauxite, titanium, chromite, diamonds, gas, oil
Labor force: 65% agricultural
Computers per 1,000 people: 1.5

Assets: Produces exceptional engineers and scientists. Huge source of inexpensive labor. Massive home market of 980 million. Highly efficient textile and garment manufacturing sectors. Low income tax rate for individuals.

Liabilities: Poor roads, ports, and telecommunications. Mass unemployment and underemployment. Mass poverty. Politically fractured. Ethnic and religious tensions.

24 percent of India's people, has 35 percent of its knowledge-based workers. Its literacy rate is markedly higher than India's as a whole, its infrastructure more developed, and its divisions over caste and religion less troublesome than in the north.

A new breed of Indian businessmen is eager for change—and quickly.

India's potential weaknesses? 350 million people in India live below the poverty line; 100 million city dwellers live in slums known as *jhuggis* where homes are mostly structures of metal and timber scrap; 70 percent of Indians have no access to toilets; 30 percent have no access to a safe water supply;

and millions live on the streets with no shelter whatsoever. All this leads to a culture of violence that is India's worst failure, many say. The big gap between the haves and the have-nots continues to widen, and India's abysmal infrastructure is a major constraint to growth.

> ***From Indians, we learn how important it is to combine modesty, benevolence, and a desire to serve with a keen ability to trade with others. From this combination emerges a capacity to be world-class merchants.***

BE A CULTURE BRIDGER
Leo van Wijk and KLM Royal Dutch Airlines *(Netherlands)*

Title: President and CEO
Headquarters: Amsterdam
Business: Established 1919, KLM is the world's oldest and fourth largest international airline with interests in catering, computer reservation systems, and regional air service businesses. Its partnership with Northwest Airlines was formalized in 1997, creating the first global airline alliance. The Dutch government owns 25% of KLM, down from 38% in 1996.
Employees: 26,811 (excluding subsidiaries), with 350 offices in 94 countries

Imagine flying from Amsterdam to London in an open two-seater plane in freezing weather. Welcome to KLM Royal Dutch Airlines in the spring of 1920. In preparation for the four-hour flight, KLM provided flying essentials: a leather coat, helmet, goggles, gloves, scarf, parachute, and—of course—a hot-water bottle.

The in-flight amenities, flying times, and choices of destinations have changed, but KLM'S CEO, Leo van Wijk, still sees what the airline offers in essential terms. "We're focused on the quality of our connections," he says. It's a role that comes naturally, created by the history of the Netherlands as a land of explorers and traders.

Van Wijk's essentials? You must know yourself; accept that there are differences between cultures; tell people what you believe in and listen to their perspective; and be flexible, tolerant, and balanced.

And you can't let a little cold weather stand in your way.

Understand and Value Your Cultural Roots

Geography and history matter. Because of their proximity to the sea, small size, and lack of natural resources, the Dutch were and still are a nation of explorers and traders. "The Dutch have been sailing the seas and trading around the world for many years," says van Wijk. "Holland started commercial trading early on, with the Dutch East India Company operating in Indonesia and Japan. We'll celebrate four hundred years of trading with Japan in the year 2000."

This long heritage of trading overseas drove KLM founder Albert Plesman to position the airline as a global carrier from the beginning. He was, says van Wijk, "an adventurous man who took the airline to all parts of the world, exploring new routes."

Van Wijk is a modern-day Plesman in many ways—minus the hot-water bottle, perhaps. He understands his cultural roots and leverages them in international business. His deep understanding of his own culture makes it possible for him to bridge to other cultures to form alliances, such as the extensive partnership KLM forged with Northwest Airlines. He says their cultural grooming, history of trading, tolerance, and flexibility all make the Dutch good culture bridgers.

But there's a streak of independence in there, too—a perfect balance of stubbornness and pragmatic tolerance. "The Dutch are not followers," says van Wijk. "we are independent and have our opinions, yet we're also extremely tolerant. We balance being stubborn with listening to others."

He knows firsthand the balancing act that mediating between strong cultural norms and independent opinions can entail: "People who go abroad for the first time have to realize that having strong opinions isn't respected everywhere around the globe. This perspective of having and sharing opinions is embedded in Dutch culture, but sometimes we must keep our mouths shut when other cultures simply don't understand."

It's this tolerance and acceptance, underscored by their pride, that distinguishes the Dutch and their ability to bridge cultures. Personal literacy—understanding and valuing yourself—is the grounding for cultural literacy—knowing and leveraging cultural differences.

Accept That Others Have Different Attitudes and Values

The Dutch have also finely honed the skill of cultural adaptation. "We're a relatively small country that has been invaded—occupied, really—by the Spanish, the French, and the Germans," says van Wijk. "We're not a big power that can dictate the ways things have to be, and in order to trade you have to make the best of it and adapt." When the Netherlands itself became a colonial power, it didn't interfere very much with running other countries, in contrast to other colonial powers. "Instead," says van Wijk, "we adapted to local circumstances."

This art of cultural adaptation has served van Wijk and KLM well in establishing flying partners in Europe, North America, and Asia while respecting the local cultures of their partners and employees overseas. Van Wijk knows that cultural literacy begins with basic human respect and accepting that others have different attitudes and values. "Cultural awareness starts not just in bridging culture," he says, "but in all human relationships. And it starts by respecting the other person's opinion, by being open to others' ideas and trying to see how they blend with your own beliefs."

What's fundamental in this process of bridging cultures is your own personal literacy. "It's imperative," he says, "that you start with your own beliefs and build them. If you don't have beliefs, how do you judge whether you like an idea or not?" And if leaders don't clearly communicate their core values and beliefs, how can others judge them? "You can only communicate and be a leader if you tell what your beliefs, values, and ideas are," he says.

You must know and like yourself before you're able to embrace others. One of your core values must be respect for other people, van Wijk maintains, "whether black or white or from country X, Y, or Z, male or female, sane or insane, healthy or unhealthy. They all have their own particular situation, opinions, and habits, some of which you may like and others you may not like."

Van Wijk's commitment to personal learning is a natural outgrowth of the Dutch norm of exploration. Rather than dismissing others' cultural norms, he urges learning from them: "Start by assuming you can learn something from others' values. If you decide they don't fit into your value scheme, then you can decide not to adopt them. I tell you what my beliefs are, but I don't expect you to take them on and endorse them. If you have different beliefs, then fine, as long as we can live in peace."

His process of culture bridging is a little like using spices in cooking: "We are continuously listening, putting in elements that are not necessarily Dutch, things we picked up in different parts of the world, mingling them in, and then bringing it all together in a melting pot."

It's this comfort with adaptation, flexibility, self-knowledge, and cultural respect that makes van Wijk and KLM so globally powerful. He's put both personal and cultural literacy into action to create a truly global airline.

Understand the Interconnectedness of the Global Economy

For evidence of the Dutch culture-bridging capacity, look no further than the global joint venture agreement forged between KLM and Northwest Airlines in September 1997, creating a deeply integrated, worldwide airline network. It's the first truly global airline alliance, with synchronized schedules covering more than four hundred cities in more than eighty countries on six continents. That's a lot of culture bridges.

The first bridge to be built was with KLM's American partners at Northwest Airlines. The common value on direct communication between the two helped. "We get along with Americans because our cultures are both very direct; we basically have the same values and open, direct communications styles. And being direct minimizes the chances for misinterpretation," van Wijk says, having learned from firsthand experience. "The first time I was in Indonesia, I asked a direct question of the president of Garuda Airlines. They didn't tell me that they had prepared a list of questions to ensure he wasn't exposed to questions for which he didn't have an answer. If he didn't have an answer, he lost face, which is terrible. I only made that mistake once."

Van Wijk learned to adapt to the Indonesian style, but he still prefers direct, open, honest communication. In the Netherlands, he says, there are fewer yes-men than you might find in corporations elsewhere, including the United States: "Here it's very natural that people tell me, 'Well, that's nice, but we think it's bullshit.' And I always benefit from the dialogue."

But he knows that bridging cultures depends first on clarity of understanding: you have to be clear about whether you are providing information, giving an order, asking a question, or engaging in dialogue in which you'll be open to feedback: "You have to be very explicit in your leadership, letting people know when you're really open for discussion and when you're not."

The history of KLM's strategic alliance with Northwest Airlines is a good example of the need to be clear and directive: "In the early days, everyone wasn't necessarily in agreement. We didn't have a formal position but were exploring our options, saying, 'Let's see whether this will work.' Yet at a certain point, there had to be a management decision about moving forward or not—we had to say, 'Let's stop the debate about whether this is the way to go, we're going to go this route now, and it can't be discussed anymore.' "

The alliance is built more on common respect than on legal documents: "They had a need, and we had a vision. Both sides didn't necessarily know how to do it; we just started with the dynamic of a relatively small number of people unhindered by legal constraints and top management rulings. We still have a relatively marginal legal document, which is uncommon for such a large alliance of a few billion dollars." Over time, KLM and Northwest have expanded the scope of their alliance to information systems, cargo, sales and marketing, and operations; their CEOs sit on each other's boards.

When there was conflict in the early stages of their global alliance, it was helpful that there was a kinship between the two companies: "The small

COUNTRIES WITH THE MOST INTERNATIONAL CUSTOMERS

(Percentage of companies with customers in ten or more countries)

- Netherlands: 86%
- France: 84%
- Australia: 73%
- Sweden: 70%
- New Zealand: 70%
- United Kingdom: 70%
- Germany: 63%
- Singapore: 63%
- South Korea: 60%
- Brazil: 56%
- Japan: 47%
- United States: 47%
- Canada: 45%
- Philippines: 39%
- Mexico: 36%
- Hong Kong: 33%

cultural difference between Scandinavian Americans and northwestern European Dutchmen certainly helped. It definitely would have been more difficult with Texans, who are as culturally close to Minnesotans as Dutchmen are to Italians."

Cultural bridge building with Americans, he says, is both helped and hindered by the fact that both sides speak English—there's still room for misunderstanding even though the words seem the same: "We tend to think the values being created on the other side are exactly the same because we speak the same language, but that's not the case. It takes a long time to understand the mental and cultural setting of a statement, even if the words are the same."

To cope with all this cultural complexity, KLM needs people—from pilots to baggage handlers—who are able to deal with ambiguity, are focused on quality and reliability, and are hardworking and compromising. In other words, they're looking for people who have a Dutch blend of order and flexibility but who retain their own culture and local identity: "We leave a lot of freedom for local people to keep their own cultural elements intact as much as possible. We understand they do things differently other places; as long as it doesn't interfere with our overall objectives and image to the customer, that's fine with us."

There's that Dutch adaptiveness again.

CULTIVATE A GLOBAL/LOCAL MINDSET
Jean-Louis Beffa and Saint-Gobain *(France)*

Title: President and Director-General
Headquarters: Paris
Business: Founded in 1665 by order of the Sun King, Louis XIV. With 580 companies in 42 countries, it has many international markets and product lines, including glass, ceramics, plastic, and iron businesses. In 1986, after a change in France's political climate, it became the first company to be reprivatized.
Employees: 108,000

WHEN JEAN-LOUIS BEFFA VISITS *the Palace of Versailles, he can't help but notice the windows. His pride in the craftsmanship is well founded: those windows were created by the company he now leads, Saint-Gobain.*

The market for palace windows has dwindled in the ensuing 330 years of Saint-Gobain's corporate history, and Beffa has focused on balancing products, sectors, and geographies to allocate opportunities and risks worldwide. "By being in different businesses around the world, we buffer the cyclical nature of the business," he says. "It's not good to be dependent on any one business; we overcome that by becoming more global."

A diversified group with decentralized organization, Beffa sees his role as CEO to be one of spreading limited resources around: "My job is to get senior executives to share risks and money. There is ongoing pressure for each business to provide cash to the holding company, and we allocate net cash flow back to the businesses."

By developing a global/local identity, strategy, and leaders, Beffa has created a flexible consumer-oriented strategy with emphasis on local execution. With the company achieving its highest net income in history in 1997, his strategy must be working.

When you read about the long history of Saint-Gobain, the one word that keeps coming to mind is "balance."

CEO Jean-Louis Beffa's leadership strategy is focused on balance in many areas: finance, human resources, product development, leadership, and global risk, among others: "If you want to have a good price for shareholders, it's better to have the same numbers, but not all from the same place."

Going international is its answer, with mass customization of its wide diversity of products: "I don't like anything that's too standardized, and I don't like winning by cost. I like to win by being customized and listening to the consumer. That's why we finely tailor the product to the local needs."

To do that, the company's structure, strategy, and leaders must be flexible and culturally literate, understanding and appreciating different cultures and developing a truly global/local mindset in all it does.

Craft a Global/Local Identity

Imagine three concentric circles, and you've created a mental image of how Beffa sees Saint-Gobain: the internal circle is French, the next is European, and the outer circle is global: "French is at the center because the essential nationality of a company is that of its shareholders."

Beffa's tripartite strategy has heavily depended on them being global *and* local at the same time. "We are more a 'Euroland' company than a French company," he says, "and we're surely global." Saint-Gobain was in Germany by 1914, Latin America by 1937, and the United States by 1968, among other countries. Much of its recent history has been characterized by aggressive internationalization.

Beffa expects leaders to operate effectively in all three circles. And he recognizes that while the company's operations are global, it's still more French and European than American. Everyone must have French headquarters experience at some point in their career and must understand the value of each of the circles.

From the French, Saint-Gobain derives its appreciation of history, its capacity for good planning and strategic thinking, and its love of truth and debate: "Frenchmen have a sense of appreciation for history. We wouldn't go into Russia without learning Russian history and without understanding that country's past. We love cool, dispassionate pursuit of the truth and like to be convinced by an argument, not a fight." But as a culturally literate leader, Beffa knows that there's a balance of good and bad qualities in each culture: "We're good strategic thinkers, but perhaps less good at the practical, and certainly less innovative than U.S. managers."

From its place in Europe, Saint-Gobain has learned to appreciate diversity and operate cross-culturally: "European companies have an advantage in managing culturally; they know there's not one best way because they're in such a diverse market. By contrast, because of the size of their market, the U.S. thinks they have the best way."

And finally, its global approach helps Saint-Gobain see world markets, world-class practices, and worldwide opportunities. As a European company, Beffa thinks, it's particularly well suited for global success: "European multinationals are more likely to understand cultural differences and give autonomy to local businesses. We historically balance country and division management; we align branch and country systems." And Saint-Gobain mixes its people around in its global operations: "In our Flaglass operations, for example, there is a German marketing manager and a Spanish financial director; all our executive teams are deliberately international."

Yet he knows that for all the good news about being a European company in a global world, there are competencies the company lacks: "What Europeans need to do more of is create socially responsible leaders who mix economic efficiency with social creativeness."

This identity as a French, European, and global company helps facilitate cross-fertilization of ideas and cooperation. "We don't want anything that is run as a country or division idea," Beffa says. Saint-Gobain's multilayered identity breaks down those kinds of silos; job flexibility and rotation keep change alive: "We must totally adapt to the modern world, but we must also keep our culture, our people, our reputation, and the way we do business."

And while Beffa clearly respects his French history, he wants to ensure that Saint-Gobain moves forward seamlessly: "French society tends to move only in crisis—the French Revolution is a good example. We're unable to make reforms smoothly." While respecting the French past and culture, he wants to change that mindset.

Develop a Global/Local Strategy

To be a global, regional, and local leader, Saint-Gobain also needed to develop a global/local strategy across the whole business. To be a "diversified group with decentralized organization," it needed to centralize its vision, values and strategies and decentralize its tactics, executives, and customer service.

It has done so by organizing around businesses and countries and by balancing risks and product lines across regions. Masters at mass customization, it tailors its business strategy to different businesses in different regions.

When the company was privatized in 1986, its global/local strategy jelled. To increase competitiveness and change the business portfolio, it sold one half of the company and acquired the other half: "We looked for businesses with different ideas. We were buying leaders, specialized companies, noncyclical businesses, and higher growth potential." And it's always still on the lookout for new acquisitions. Having been named chairman at a very young age has allowed Beffa to invest in this long-term strategy. "We didn't have to rush with the execution," he explains. Today Saint-Gobain's management shares the responsibility for implementing the company's strategy by focusing on local management, divisional planning, national coordination, and general oversight by corporate headquarters.

The CEO's job, as Beffa sees it, is to steward this global enterprise and play a multitude of roles, including adviser, decision maker, and balancer of risks and resources. "It's not too difficult to be accepted as a decision maker," he says, "but it's more important to be accepted as the adviser." But he knows he can't fill those roles alone, and he works hard to create culturally literate leaders at all levels; there, too, his strategy is one of balance, creating leaders across product lines, businesses, and geography.

Cultivate Global/Local Leaders

There's no ambiguity about what Beffa is looking for in leaders; he wants people with energy and a driving force for entrepreneurship: "They must have common sense, hate to lose money, and be innovative."

They must also be willing to move in a company with three-year job rotations. And they must be culturally literate: "Leaders who can accommodate different countries along the way naturally rise to the top." But Beffa doesn't just wait for the cream to rise to the top; he and his team constantly search for talent around the globe: "We have ongoing conversations all the time about what talent exists and who's available for moving around. There is a person whose sole job is to facilitate the movement of executive talent around the company."

To counter French parochialism and level the playing field for non-French executives, Beffa concentrates on value and potential. "We are a global company based in France that promotes on talent, not on nationality," he explains.

Saint-Gobain cultivates the global, regional, and local perspective so central to its corporate strategy by expecting executives—the top two hundred of whom get stock options—to gain a lot of international experience and work on one of the many multicultural teams Gobain runs across businesses, regions, and disciplines. Leaders must appreciate and understand different cultures in order to customize their products and delivery, and operating managers must have wide experience. At a minimum, they must work in two divisions and two countries, and they must understand the world.

Saint-Gobain employees rotate jobs across businesses and regions, gaining cross-cultural experience on the job. And everyone is obligated to share talent, which spreads risks and resources around the company. Beffa doesn't tolerate any unwillingness to share that talent: "If you're not prepared to give somebody up, it means you're not organized enough. That's your problem, and your performance rating will suffer." Each country branch runs its own talent pool for the rest of the company.

The aggressive global/local identity, strategy, and leadership that Beffa engenders at Saint-Gobain is working: since 1986, Saint-Gobain's value as a company has grown from 13 billion francs to more than 100 billion francs today.

USE YOUR NATIONAL NATURE TO ADVANTAGE

Guglielmo Moscato and ENI S.P.A. *(Italy)*

Title: Chairman
Headquarters: Rome
Business: Italy's third largest company and the world's number 5 oil company, ENI operates in three industries: oil and natural gas, petrochemicals, and oil field contracting and engineering. Wholly owned by the state until 1995, ENI is now 51% owned by the Italian government after three stock offerings. Recent development deals outside its traditional bases of Africa and Italy include China, Croatia, Kazakhstan, the North Sea, and the Gulf of Mexico. The company is number 58 on the *Fortune* Global 500.
Employees: 80,000 in 77 countries

FROM STATE-OWNED TO WORLD CLASS, *Italian energy company ENI once served as a virtual slush fund for Italy's political parties. But with Italy's massive anti-corruption campaign came housecleaning and deregulation at ENI, ending with arrests and the suicide of a former chairman in prison. "Over the last three years," writes an analyst at J. P. Morgan, "ENI's management has successfully reinvented the company." Since 1995, ENI has shed two hundred noncore operations, such as flower growing and publishing, halved its debt, cut its workforce by 42,000, and accelerated its global presence among top competitors such as Exxon, Mobil, and Royal Dutch/Shell.*

Guglielmo Moscato's secret of success as ENI's chairman is using his Italian nature to build relationships around the world. Friendly and flexible, he leverages those national tendencies to create synergy and innovation worldwide.

ENI is known as the engine of Italian development. Called "a people's privatization" because so many people were involved—including the 70 percent of ENI's staff who became investors—it has spearheaded the public acquisition of wealth in Italy. ENI is the fifty-eighth largest global company, producing more than 1 million barrels of oil a day.

Realizing that "bureaucracy destroys business," ENI has slashed its time to market and today acts much more like an integrated business. In contrast to many hierarchical, macho Italian firms, ENI focused on decentralization and participation, changing from a vertical organization to a horizontal one. By installing radically new business systems, ENI became a high-performance enterprise responsive to global markets and shareholder demands.

Moscato, along with ENI's well-respected CEO, Franco Bernabè, led the change by instilling values of friendliness and flexibility abroad, linking to others with international alliances, and being a socially responsible global capitalist.

Be Friendly and Flexible Abroad

Moscato sees this Italian company from a global perspective, having spent much of his career in Africa and the Middle East: "I spent almost twenty years abroad, beginning in Nigeria, when they were coming out of the civil war. I lived with local people in a very temperamental situation. We learned a lot from working in a situation where the possibility of intervention from our headquarters in Milano was technically impossible—we had no communications link. It was a big responsibility to have such independence, and we tripled production in four years."

One of the reasons Moscato and his fellow Italians are so successful in international situations is that they have an unconventional, friendly, engaging nature. Being comfortable with chaos and ambiguity enables them to be free and flexible in their dealings with others. "I was crowned chief of a village in Nigeria of over ten thousand people—and I still visit them," Moscato says, providing one striking example of his good harmony with people abroad. "Our flexibility comes from our Mediterranean culture and our history of invasion by the Arabs, the Spanish, the French, and the Germans. We had to please other people, or we wouldn't have survived."

But it wasn't just survival skills the Italians learned from their history of invasion; they also developed the capacity to learn from other cultures. Out of that legacy has come a nation of unconventional innovation. "We are creative in how we enter new markets, build important business bases around the world, invent new instruments for future growth, and forge creative alliances. Italians are more comfortable jumping into the chaos and craziness," Moscato says.

Not all people thrive in this chaotic global environment: "To live abroad, you need the capacity to fully enter another culture. When I was in the Sinai, we didn't have newspapers or barbershops. After two months, one of our people came to me and said, 'I'm used to waking up in the morning, drinking my espresso, reading the newspaper, and getting my hair cut once a week.' What he didn't realize is that he had to invest in learning that new culture and be flexible enough to live their way."

Build International Alliances and Partnerships

Because of its small internal market and limited natural resources, Italy has always looked outside its own borders for growth. Founded as a small local firm after World War I, ENI needed to tap energy-rich foreign markets to survive. Because more powerful oil companies had already entered the most lucrative markets, ENI was forced to enter regions such as Iran, Egypt, Libya, and Nigeria. As a young, maverick company, it had to build creative partnerships with these countries, tapping promising but challenging markets.

"The real driver for growth," says Moscato, "was beyond our national borders. We had to strengthen our skills by embracing a partnership approach that didn't limit us to certain projects. Through that strategy, ENI became the first Western oil company to develop relations with Soviet Russia and among the first in Central Asia and China.

"The strategy of alliances and partnerships was one of the key elements driving our growth. Companies that think they can make it on their own will lose out. There needs to be a pooling of resources to allow continuous, mutually enriching exchanges of skills and expertise."

ENI thinks unconventionally about opportunities. "One factor that makes ENI unique," emphasizes Moscato, "is the leadership philosophy the company adopted to pursue its geographic growth. We took risks, breaking up the status quo dictated by the powerful players. With time, these elements became an integral part of the corporate culture of the company."

To succeed, ENI had to invest in leadership education: "Key to a successful people strategy is fostering a learning environment at all levels of the organization. Italy, unlike other countries such as the U.S. or France, does not have universities that provide training in petroleum engineering and petrochemicals. So we created our own groupwide training institution; in Italy alone, ENI collaborates with over twenty-five universities, providing over a million hours of training to 115,000 employees in 1997." Part of that training is how to be a culturally literate and socially responsible corporate citizen.

Be a Socially Responsible Capitalist

Italy is the world's fifth largest economic power, with strong national industries, few multinational corporations, and a revitalizing national economy. Its economy is fueled by tourism and supported by extended families in small to medium-size companies.

In that environment, Moscato focuses the energies of ENI on moral leadership both at home and abroad, making investments in the social and physical infrastructure of developing countries such as the Congo, Kenya, and Nigeria. And while many companies get involved in philanthropy after a crisis inside a foreign country, ENI does not wait for a business conflict. Instead, it acts proactively. "We created a campaign to vaccinate forty thousand children in the Congo, built hospitals in Kenya, and gave tools and training to local people to teach them how to cultivate their land," Moscato says. "We are extracting natural resources from these countries and want to give something back."

Governing all these good works is a code of conduct created at ENI after the bribery scandals of 1993. Created by benchmarking against other countries, it ensures that workers adhere to the new code by using a general audit system inside the company. "ENI," says Moscato, "considers the company's reputation a primary value which results from the responsible, honest behavior of all its managers, and from their respect for the law, in all businesses and countries where ENI operates."

The frontier spirit of ENI comes from being open to the world. Says Moscato, "By cooperating with diverse cultures and respecting the communities in which they operate, ENI manages the social, economic, and cultural diversity in a spirit of friendship and cooperation."

ENI's first public offering in 1995 sold 1.2 million shares and netted US$5.2 billion, the largest secondary cash offering in the world and the largest public offering in Italy. The advantage of ENI, now a world-class public company, comes from retaining its Italian roots.

ITALY: "Resourceful Innovators"

The Italians are creative, flexible, and comfortable with ambiguity and chaos. Understanding the depth of human relationships, they have a limitless exuberance about life and business. They seek the best things in life and make enjoyment a national pastime.

IT WAS AN ITALIAN PAINTER—Masaccio—who first presented objects in perspective on canvas. Now taken for granted, Masaccio's invention of perspective was revolutionary in fourteenth-century Europe and is felt even today. In fact, the Italians have nurtured a different perspective on how to live in the world ever since the Roman Empire.

This is the country of Dante, the cradle of humanism, and the birthplace of the Renaissance, Leonardo da Vinci, Michelangelo, and Machiavelli, not to mention Galileo. From Neoclassicism to the Futurismo movement of Italo Calvino and Umberto Eco, Italy has been one of the leading cultural centers for fields from science and art to fashion and design—for so long that the name of the country is synonymous with cultural advancement.

The Two Italys

In reality, there are two Italys, north and south. Northern Italy, the industrial capital of private enterprise, includes Milan. Southern Italy, a largely agrarian culture, with government subsidized businesses, includes Naples and Rome. A nation that is 98 percent Roman Catholic and a major exporter of Catholicism to the rest of the world, modern Italy is the inheritor of Roman history. Italians honor the Roman Empire as one of the greatest in recorded history. The impact of Latin, central to much of the world's linguistic legacy, is still felt.

For centuries, the history of Italy was largely the history of Rome. From the ninth century, the Holy Roman emperors, Roman Catholic popes, Normans, and Saracens all vied for control over segments of the Italian peninsula. Large city-states, such as Venice and Genoa, whose rivalries were intense, and many smaller principalities, flourished in the late Middle Ages. Although Italy remained politically fragmented for centuries, it became the cultural center of the Western world from the thirteenth to sixteenth centuries.

In 1861, these disparate city-states became the United Kingdom of Italy. The annexation of Venetia in 1866 and most of Rome in 1870 marked the complete unification of peninsular Italy into one nation under a constitutional monarchy. Yet even today there is much regional identification and pride in Italy.

A land of beautiful scenery, Mediterranean weather, and no significant natural resources, Italy is revered for its food, wines, and olive oil. Primarily agrarian after World War II, by 1987 Italy had become the fifth largest economic power in the world.

A Political Society

Italy is a "chaotic" country that has always balanced chaos and order in a highly politicized environment. It is a country with a reputation for government corruption, yet it is a leading democracy of the world, one of its many paradoxes.

Modern Italian history starts with Benito Mussolini, a former socialist, who in 1919 organized discontented Italians into the Fascist Party to "rescue Italy from Bolshevism," becoming premier in 1922. Transforming Italy into a dictatorship, he embarked on an expansionist foreign policy by invading and annexing Ethiopia in 1935 and allying himself with Hitler in 1939.

When the Allies invaded Italy in 1943, Mussolini's dictatorship collapsed and he was executed shortly afterward. Following armistice with the Allies in 1943, Italy joined the war against Germany. In 1946, monarchy was rejected and a republic was proclaimed. Italy became an integral member of NATO and the European Economic Community as it successfully rebuilt its postwar economy. But even as it grew, volatility remained a constant. A prolonged outbreak of terrorist activities by the left-wing Red Brigades threatened domestic stability in the 1970s, but by the early 1980s the terrorist groups had been suppressed.

Scandal brought the long reign of the Christian Democrats to an end when Italy's fortieth premier since World War II, Arnaldo Forlani, was forced to resign in the wake of disclosure that many high-ranking Christian Democrats and civil servants belonged to a secret Masonic lodge known as "P-2." By 1994, more than 4,500 people had been arrested, including leading businessmen, former ministers, and even former prime ministers. In 1996, Italians elected a government dominated by a center-left coalition for the first time since the proclamation of the Italian Republic.

This history has created a highly politicized nation where socioeconomic status, family lineage, and rank matter. Italy appears to have one of the most unstable governments in Europe; yet even with fifty-five governments since World War II, this may be a function more of its multiparty system than of instability—and could also be a reflection of Italians' comfort with change. Italy's history of national, bureaucratic government undermines business through state ownership and protectionist policies, fomenting a large black market, an underground economy, and the infamous Italian Mafia. Its high levels of organized labor and bureaucracy—and the resulting labor inflexibility and poor financial infrastructure—are mirrored by a high degree of political intervention in large companies.

But that's changing. Recognizing that membership in the European Monetary Union is vital, Italy has responded aggressively to the requirements for affiliation, including cleaning up government, privatizing state-run businesses, and expanding its global activities.

Creative and Communicative

The Italians have great pragmatic skills—adaptability, flexibility, and improvisation—that enable them to manage through adversity. They are individualistic people with a strong commitment to family, which serves as their safety net.

Passionate people, Italians are affable and socially engaging, enabling them to build strong, respectful relationships with others. Like the perspective painters of their early history, they see the depth of life and people around them. Comfortable with uncertainty, they are able to work in complex, confusing situations and see the connections between different planes of experience. Some people say they live in a world between chaos and creativity that gives them their flair for design and visual appeal. Others say it's simply unstructured and disconnected thinking and action that is at the heart of the Italian experience.

Whatever your interpretation, their out-of-the-box thinking enables them to create fresh solutions to social, business, and even design problems. Resourceful people who are always changing the rules, Italians are risk takers. They are the creatives of the world, entrepreneurs who are excellent communicators. Gregarious and flexible, they have a modesty that helps them accept both praise and criticism well.

A Business Culture Emerges

For all their creativity and ebullience, they are businessmen at heart. It was the Italians, after all, who in the fourteenth century invented the promissory note, so essential to banking, as well as double-entry bookkeeping and insurance. These advances led to early specialization in business and the formation of the early city-states.

Italian businesses are traditionally male-dominated, with commanding, paternalistic leaders who seek input from subordinates. Fluid, unstructured enterprises, they are now witnessing a new generation of young Italian businesspeople, the *giovani imprenditori*.

Four giant firms account for 30 percent of Italian sales. These large, state-run enterprises traditionally have been inefficient, and Italian industry on the whole has been hampered by poor infrastructure, difficult labor-management relations, political expediency, and government bureaucracy. It's not surprising that Italian business leaders have developed their pragmatic skills as a way of overcoming these challenges. Today, these large firms are increasingly being privatized.

Each region of Italy has its specialty and its own concentration of similar industries. For example, two small regions account for half of the world's jewelry exports, with "constellations of collaborating companies" nearby. Italy is known for small, flexible, creative enterprises, many of them among the 500,000 entrepreneurial family firms that account for 70 percent of Italy's exports in textiles, apparel, footwear, and housewares. These firms produce quality artisanry, depend on skilled labor, and are very customer-savvy. The world's second largest exporter after Japan, Italy is known for its finished products, creative design, and flexible specialization.

CEO Francesco Trapani leads one of the shining constellations of Italian family firms: Bulgari, a brand that has a tremendous cachet. The world's number three jewelry company, behind Cartier and Tiffany, Bulgari's 114-year-old history is one of refining precious metals and creating jewel-encrusted baubles. Today, Trapani is leading this global brand into new, upscale markets by making watches, leather goods, fragrance and skin care products, and eyewear. By personifying and protecting the cachet and prestige of the global brand, Trapani is using his national nature to advantage.

Italy: *At a Glance*
Official name: Italian Republic

> ***Economy type: European Union***
> ***Trading bloc: European Union***

Location: Southern Europe's peninsula into the Mediterranean
Capital: Rome **Population:** 56,782,748
Head of state: President Carlo Azeglio Ciampi
Official language: Italian **Religion:** Roman Catholic 98%
Literacy: 97%
World GNP ranking: 5 **GDP (US$ bn)** $1,098.9
GDP per capita: $19,337 **Unemployment:** 12%
Inflation: 5.7% **World export market share:** 4.8%

Major industries: Tourism, steel, machinery, autos, textiles, shoes, wine, clothing, chemicals
Major crops: Grapes, olives, fruits, vegetables, grains
Minerals: Mercury, potash, marble, sulfur
Labor force: 61% services, 32% industrial, 7% agricultural
Computers per 1,000 people: 92.1

Assets: Competitive and innovative small to medium-sized businesses. Strong tourism industry. Efficient agricultural sector. A world-class leader in innovative product design.

Liabilities: High unemployment. Large public debt. Inefficient public sector. Frequent strikes decrease productivity. Uneven distribution of wealth. Influence of organized crime has diminished but remains detrimental to achieving Italy's full potential.

"The success of Italian designers is one incredible example of creativity and flexibility," Trapani says. "We're good at creating entrepreneurs, people who are not fully happy with what they have today and want to do more. We develop products in Rome, produce them in Switzerland, and sell them in Japan." For those networks to work, Trapani creates cross-cultural teams that create global brands tailored to local markets around the world. For Bulgari, cultural literacy works. In 1998, sales were up by 28 percent and operating profits were up by 39 percent, providing healthy dividends for shareholders.

The Italians teach us how to spark creativity in business and how to learn from complex, ambiguous situations. They show the world the power of deep relationships and an irrepressible love of life and beauty.

DEVELOPING CULTURAL LITERACY FROM THE INSIDE OUT

Sakip Sabanci and Sabanci Holdings *(Turkey)*

Title: Chairman
Headquarters: Ankara
Business: The leading private-sector industrial and financial conglomerate in Turkey, with more than $10 billion in revenues. Its 50-50 global joint ventures with fifteen multinational companies include Toyota, Bridgestone, IBM, du Pont, Philip Morris, Danone, Hilton International, Dresdner Bank, and Hoechst.
Employees: More than 30,000

DARTING FLAMES OF REAL GOLD highlight the vast collection of Islamic art that Sakip Sabanci has amassed over the years. On display at New York's Metropolitan Museum of Art, this exquisite collection of Ottoman calligraphy and Koranic verses clearly illustrates Sabanci's love and reverence for his cultural heritage. At once a businessman, philanthropist, and cultural ambassador, Sabanci and his company exude the qualities of cultural literacy.

Proud ancestor: Proud of his cultural roots and the rich, seven-hundred-year history of his country, Sabanci demands equal partnership in joint ventures with powerful multinational companies. Because Turkey is a young democracy, Sabanci knows, companies aren't always willing to come in, so he takes them by the hand and helps them enter.

A producer of high-quality, inexpensive goods—like the tires it sells to the United Kingdom and the synthetic yarn it sells to Italy—Turkey is a country that knows what it can offer the world. And Sabanci clearly knows about Turkey, too, both its beauty marks and its warts.

A secular Islamic state with a strong national identity rooted in shared language and religion, Turkey dates back to Ephesus and Troy and the antiquities of the Ottoman and Byzantine Empires. An insulated, state-directed economy prior to the 1980s, it then began an economic turnaround based on market forces, export-led development, and integration into the world economy. Tensions exist between the secular state and Islamic fundamentalism. Racially diverse, Turkey has a bumpy human rights record and a class of wealthy entrepreneurs.

Inquisitive internationalist: A tenacious businessman, Sabanci learns from the world while sharing Turkish culture and business globally. He's not only proud but also inquisitive, bringing back ideas, businesses, know-how, and other companies into Turkey. He wants to develop Turkish businesspeople, so he sent some Turkish engineers to the United States as part of Sabanci's joint venture with Philip Morris and others to Tokyo to learn from Toyota. "There is no limit to my learning," he says. "I will learn until my death." To make sure others do the same, he and his family have endowed Sabanci University, which he chairs.

Rapid growth has gained Turkey a GDP that has outpaced all of western Europe's, except Ireland's. The gateway to East Asian markets, Turkey also wants to become a member of the European Union; Germany is its largest trading partner. With chronic high inflation, cheap labor, and a population of 67 million, many of them young, Turkey, with its male-dominated society, has a strong, reputable military, a high growth rate, and a large informal economy.

To play his part in that transition, Sabanci has brought in outside management techniques and foreign-trained managers. In a country where there is chronic underinvestment in most firms, Sabanci companies invest for growth, winning the European Total Quality Leadership awards for the past two years.

Culture bridger: By loaning his Turkish art collection to the museums of the world, Sabanci wants to change attitudes about Turkish history and culture and enhance the world's understanding of Islam: "To help build good relations between Turkey and the U.S. was good for all Muslim countries. Economic bridges aren't enough; culture bridges are important."

As Sabanci Holdings moves onto the world stage, Sabanci understands the cultural implications of globalization: "A country culture is important. But to enter the global market, an international culture is needed. We have partners from Japan, America, Egypt, Israel, Belgium, and France. We cannot have a different culture for each of them. But this doesn't mean that national culture is forgotten."

His goal is nothing less than to help Turkey become globally competitive and savvy in all those cultures. And he's determined to introduce competition into Turkey so that international businesses will go there. Sending a piece of his nation's culture around the world on a traveling PR campaign is just one tool he uses to do that.

Respectful modernizer: At once an industrialist and benefactor, Sabanci embodies a spirit of philanthropy stemming from his Muslim desire to give something back to society. Active in Turkish business organizations, he has a passion for modernizing the society around him—such as changing the role of women in a country that is 80 percent Sunni Muslim: "Twenty years ago, women were not working—it was not on our agenda or in the Muslim mentality. Come into our company today, and you'll find that one third of the employees are women."

He wants the company's success to drive success in the country itself: "Turkey started from nothing, establishing industry with scant resources and little knowledge. As a country, we passed rapidly from a planned to a free market economy, from import substitutions to exports, entering foreign markets, forming joint ventures, and succeeding in growing and remaining strong even in a twenty-two-year inflationary crisis environment."

Yet unsteady politics, chronic inflation, and the Kurdish insurgency continue to hamper Turkey's global business success. During the last three years, Ankara has seen more than five coalition governments come and go. Still, the United States has declared Turkey to be one of its ten big emerging markets. Sabanci himself can take some of the credit for that. For instance, initially Dupont was unwilling to create a 50-50 joint venture with Sabanci because of its experience in Iran with the Shah. But with Sabanci's Turkish tenacity and proud persistence, together they created DuSa, a joint venture that funnels foundation monies back into Turkey. To attract Daimler-Benz

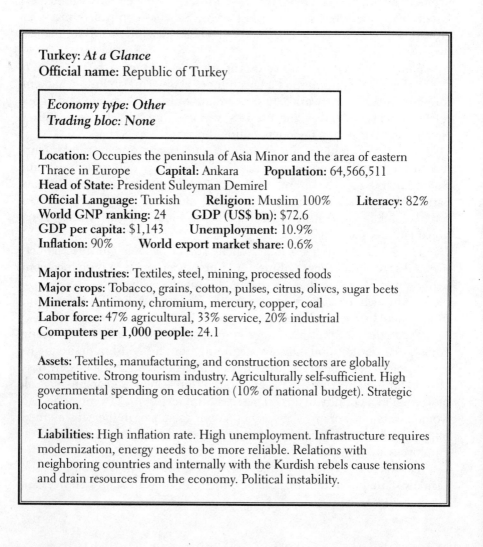

Turkey: ***At a Glance***
Official name: Republic of Turkey

Economy type: Other
Trading bloc: None

Location: Occupies the peninsula of Asia Minor and the area of eastern Thrace in Europe **Capital:** Ankara **Population:** 64,566,511
Head of State: President Suleyman Demirel
Official Language: Turkish **Religion:** Muslim 100% **Literacy:** 82%
World GNP ranking: 24 **GDP (US$ bn):** $72.6
GDP per capita: $1,143 **Unemployment:** 10.9%
Inflation: 90% **World export market share:** 0.6%

Major industries: Textiles, steel, mining, processed foods
Major crops: Tobacco, grains, cotton, pulses, citrus, olives, sugar beets
Minerals: Antimony, chromium, mercury, copper, coal
Labor force: 47% agricultural, 33% service, 20% industrial
Computers per 1,000 people: 24.1

Assets: Textiles, manufacturing, and construction sectors are globally competitive. Strong tourism industry. Agriculturally self-sufficient. High governmental spending on education (10% of national budget). Strategic location.

Liabilities: High inflation rate. High unemployment. Infrastructure requires modernization, energy needs to be more reliable. Relations with neighboring countries and internally with the Kurdish rebels cause tensions and drain resources from the economy. Political instability.

to invest more technology in and bring new models into Turkey, Sabanci first formed a joint venture with Mitsubishi to make Daimler anxious to be there as well. "They had the same models in Turkey for years, until they saw us doing business with Mitsubishi," he recalls.

Global capitalist: Sabanci's father, a cotton worker, started a small family business that his son has turned into a true global conglomerate. By moving from exporting goods to developing joint ventures and now to foreign investment in Europe, Brazil, and Egypt, Sabanci has learned to survive the high Turkish inflation, which has averaged 70 percent a year in the last twenty-two years.

Sabanci Holdings is involved in all aspects of the Turkish economy, including agriculture, banking, insurance, tires, automobiles, plastic, paper, energy, food, and tobacco. With this diversified portfolio, it's doing business in fifty countries, with a clear focus on "investing in tomorrow with strategic investments today." Sabanci knows how important it is to give back to his country and has created the largest social and cultural foundation in Turkey to do just that.

PART THREE

THE GLOBAL LITERACIES AT WORK

Solving the Five Universal Business Questions

ACCORDING TO GEORGE FISHER, recently retired CEO of Kodak, theory is great, but what he needs are results. There's no time for slow, slumbering companies; instead, knowledge must be shared around the world, everyone must be linked by technology, and we must all make and own our decisions. It's the fast, flexible, focused company of the twenty-first century.

In this section, you'll learn to leverage your leadership philosophies into business results. You'll learn to hard-wire your company with the beliefs and behaviors necessary in the global economy. And you'll learn to leverage your global assets and build a globally literate workforce for the twenty-first century.

In this chapter, we'll show how the global literacies help answer the five universal business questions: Where are we going? How do we get there? How do we work together? What resources do we need? and How do we measure success?

As leaders answer these questions, they build shared visions and values, create new structures and systems, strengthen their networks and relationships, introduce the appropriate processes and tools, and measure the right results.

And while business leaders have been asking these questions since trading began, in the twenty-first-century workplace the four world drivers—knowledge, technology, change, and globalization—are forcing us to ask these universal questions in fundamentally different ways.

More People at More Levels Must Ask Questions

Capable people all around the world are asking, "What's in it for me?" In the war on talent, leaders must show that there's a connection between what people want from work and what a company offers. Sooner or later, people will demand to know what's going on inside the business. By having more people at more levels ask these questions, companies create common understanding, shared ownership, and mutual responsibilities. And while we used to ask these questions at the end of the year, in tomorrow's workplace people will be asking them all the time.

There Must Be More Agreement About the Questions and Answers

In the twenty-first-century organization it's critical to have understanding and alignment about how these questions are answered. The goal is to create a globally literate workforce—people at all levels who know where they are going and how to create success. Without this clarity and consistency, there's serious danger of moving in conflicting directions, which undoubtedly will sabotage the company's success.

Culture Influences Both the Questions and the Answers

Our cultural mindset influences the fundamentals of a business (see Figure 3). Culture influences purpose: what principles are important and how strategy is made. It shapes our plans: what structures are created and which are employed. And it influences our networks: the kinds of people we value, the relationships we build, and our management style. Culture also influences our tools: the skills we develop and the processes we provide. It also shapes our results: the stakeholders we serve and our philosophies about social responsibility.

For instance, there's a real difference between how the linear, logical British and the intuitive, circular Chinese develop vision and values. The structured, grand French and the less structured, friendly Filipinos approach the creation of plans differently. Networks are created differently by the affable, authoritative Italians and the cooperative, egalitarian Swedes. The tools employed by the direct, verbal Americans and the nonverbal, indirect Japanese are different. And the results we aim for are expressed differently by the socially responsible Danes and the performance-minded Taiwanese.

While not every cultural tendency applies to *every* company, every tendency applies to *some* companies. For globally literate leaders, it's vitally important to understand how culture influences the basics of business.

This section is organized around the five universal business questions. Along the way, we will introduce you to leaders and their companies who are

Figure 3. How Culture Influences Business

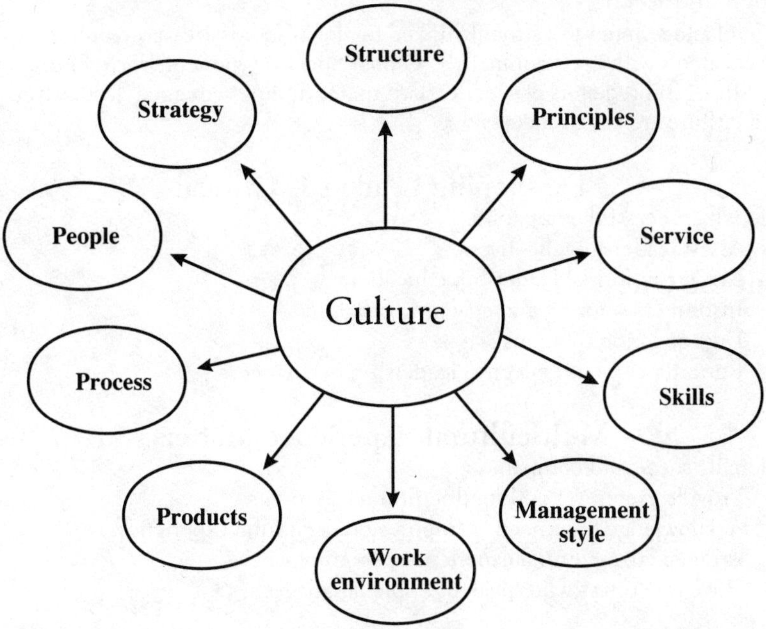

© *Robert H. Rosen 1998*

putting these global literacies to work around the world. That is their strategy for success.

THE ELEMENTS OF GLOBAL SUCCESS

What factors were most strongly linked to global success? By correlating the survey items with each company's "Global Success Quotient," we identified the strongest predictors of success. Two major findings emerged: leadership and culture are key to success.

Developing Leaders Is Critical

Globally successful companies:

- Assess leadership effectiveness
- Engage in formal leadership education
- Institute mentoring and coaching programs
- Engage in job rotations
- Reward people for effective leadership behavior

Multicultural Experience Matters

Globally successful companies:

- Provide executives with multicultural experiences
- Acknowledge their need to improve cross-cultural experiences
- Arrange cross-cultural experiences for employees
- Have executives who speak multiple languages

The Bottom Line?

Developing leaders and multicultural experiences predict global success throughout the world. Globally successful companies are more likely to assess, develop, coach, educate and rotate their leaders. And they are more likely to invest in cross-cultural awareness, experiences, and practices. In our opinion, the study confirms that an investment in leadership and culture helps to give companies a competitive edge in the global marketplace.

CHAPTER SEVEN

PURPOSE

Where Are We Going?

EVERYBODY WANTS TO BELIEVE in something that matters.

A leader's first job is to create a North Star, a purpose to believe in, something that inspires and stretches people. As pathfinders, leaders articulate a compelling vision. They must then cultivate a leadership philosophy, craft global values, and shape a competitive agenda for the future. Ultimately, the purpose must be our foundation for effective strategy.

To embed this purpose deep into people's hearts and minds, globally literate leaders communicate it aggressively. Only by articulating shared values and laying out corporate goals and priorities can we cultivate a common mindset of pride, shared identity, and ideological cohesion. Leaders must create a common set of attitudes and values that transcend the company's nationality or country of operation; they must also develop cross-cultural strategies to disseminate the value throughout the organization.

But the process cannot be just top down. There must be room for people to participate, evolve, and own the company's purpose. The core purpose must be preserved while stimulating progress, experimentation, entrepreneurship, and change. Our own personal purpose must be linked to that of the company. Local businesses must tailor the vision and values to their particular circumstances. And local feedback systems must be created to revise the vision as the world changes.

In this chapter, we will meet seven leaders who are answering the question of purpose in similar and different ways around the world: people such as Canon honorary chairman Ryuzaburo Kaku in Japan, who talks about appealing to people's higher purpose; Novo Nordisk CEO Mads Øvlisen in Denmark, who focuses on building shared visions and values; Discovery Communications CEO John Hendricks and Mary Kay Haben of Kraft Foods in the United States, who want to create reality out of dreams; Ultrapar Participações CEO Paulo Cunha from Brazil, who breaks his vision into bite-size pieces, and recently retired Eastman Kodak CEO George Fisher, who creates a road map for the future.

THE NEW RULES OF BUSINESS

- **Global reach:** Companies will need global reach to serve global customers. If they lack the capacity, they must build partnerships around the world.
- **Local markets:** All markets are local markets. Quality, pricing, and service must be globally competitive and domestically appropriate.
- **Foreign competitors:** No longer will geography bind a company's aspirations. Thousands of companies will lose their local monopolies to new foreign competitors.
- **Speed to market:** Speed and urgency will be the norm as companies change strategy and direction continuously. Flexibility and innovation will be their secrets to success.
- **Electronic commerce:** Electronic commerce will fundamentally change customers' expectations about convenience, speed, and price, giving consumers more choices.
- **Real-time delivery:** Real-time pressures for product design and development will enable customers to influence how products are made and delivered.
- **Local distribution:** Local distribution will require a much deeper understanding of local business needs and prevailing national cultures.
- **Outsourcing:** Outsourcing noncore services forces companies to rethink their basic competencies and develop relationships with suppliers to provide the others.

APPEAL TO PEOPLE'S HIGHER PURPOSE
Ryuzaburo Kaku and Canon *(Japan)*

Title: Honorary Chairman of the Board
Headquarters: Tokyo
Business: In Japanese "Canon" is the Buddhist goddess of mercy. In the last two decades, the company has seen a worldwide expansion, opening 18 factories outside Japan. With more than 80 million cameras sold, Canon is also the world's largest producer of photocopiers and the second largest maker of printers. Its laser printers claim 70% of the world market, and its sales of Bubble-Jet printers have topped 10 million.
Employees: 78,767

In a culture shaped by ambiguity, Ryuzaburo Kaku has no ambiguity whatsoever about his vision of the future: "Living and working for the common good." The Japanese concept of kyosei *literally means "symbiosis": "all people, regardless of race, religion, or culture, harmoniously living and working together for many years to come."*

Though the Japanese language doesn't have a word for "ethics," Kaku believes that kyosei *should occupy a central position in the personal ethics of each individual, act as a creed for corporations and nations, and serve as nothing less than the guiding principle of a new world order. In Canon's case,* kyosei *is a universal principle, central business strategy, and higher purpose for a company whose two main goals are wealth creation and distribution.*

At heart, the Japanese are farmers, not hunters or colonizers. Kaku's ancestors didn't conquer their neighbor's land but harvested rice while living and working together. That same spirit drives kyosei. *And in today's world,* kyosei *can teach us how to live and work together for the common good.*

As a young shipyard worker who had studied atomic physics, nineteen-year-old Ryuzaburo Kaku immediately knew what happened on August 8, 1945, when the atomic bomb fell on Nagasaki. He saved his colleagues' lives by urging them to disobey orders and stay underground for three days to avoid the fallout. This traumatic experience gave Kaku a passionate concern for ecological issues, which are today incorporated into the business philosophy of Canon.

His insight around the concept of *kyosei* emerged from this personal history. Having spent most of his childhood in China, he returned to Japan at seventeen. Considered an outsider by his classmates, he spent time with other children from nontraditional backgrounds, learning that "outsiders" were no different from everyone else—a lesson that still drives his passion for valuing diversity. Starting at Canon in the cost-accounting division, Kaku made a name for himself by writing letters to Canon's leadership team about changes he thought needed to be made.

Even then, he was driven to seek the good that corporations could accomplish while making money. "It is in the interests of the world's most powerful corporations to work for the advancement of global peace and prosperity," he says. But the question remained: How could Canon promote peace and prosperity while remaining true to its obligation to make a profit?

The answer? *Kyosei:* harmonious relations with owners, customers, suppliers, competitors, governments, and the natural environment. When practiced by a group of corporations, *kyosei* becomes a powerful force for social, political, and economic transformation.

Make *Kyosei* Your Unifying Purpose

The word may be new to others, but the concept is rooted deep in Japan's history and reflects a natural tendency of its people's cultural mindset. In the sixteenth century, a set of principles was developed to minimize conflict among traders from different nations. It mandated that trade must be carried out not just for one's own benefit but also for the benefit of others, and that despite differences in skin color and culture, trading partners should be considered equals—perhaps one of the earliest national diversity statements. It was from this historical precedent that Kaku began to develop *kyosei.*

Canon's entry into the global marketplace was one driver for *kyosei.* When it went global—building plants, hiring workers, and managing its finances in foreign countries—it encountered a new set of business challenges. Three global imbalances surfaced: the imbalance between importers and exporters, that between rich and poor nations, and that between generations, the current one of which is consuming the earth's resources so fast that little will be left for the next. In Kaku's mind, *kyosei* is the path to finding solutions to these three major global problems. But it has to be more than a philosophy or ideal; it must be operationalized.

Put *Kyosei* into Corporate Action

By adopting the practice of *kyosei,* companies will find new ways of doing business and move to the cutting edge of business strategy, organizational design, and management practice. But, as the saying goes, the proof is in the pudding. Canon shows us how it's putting *kyosei* to work in five distinct stages:

Stage 1: Commit yourself to economic survival. A company's first commitment is to economic survival. Purely capitalistic in this stage, the company focuses on making money, often with conflicts between labor and management. In stage one, Canon established a healthy business foundation. But profit making was only the beginning of its obligations.

Stage 2: Create partnerships with people. A company must share its prosperous future with its workers and each employee must make *kyosei* a part of his or her own personal code of ethics. Canon fulfills this stage by having every employee make a commitment to live and work in harmony with others. It cares for its employees, eliminating boundaries between salaried and hourly workers, for example. Canon was the first large company in Japan to adopt a five-day workweek, and it has never in its history fired a domestic employee. Nor has it ever asked any employee to take early retirement. The result? It has never had a strike.

Stage 3: Create partnerships with outside stakeholders. A solely internal focus on workers isn't enough; companies must assume local social responsibilities to reap real rewards. Customers who are treated respectfully give back loyalty, suppliers provided with support deliver high-quality materials on time, competitors invited into partnership agreements and joint ventures bring higher profits for both partners, realizing that a rising tide lifts all ships.

Canon donates technical know-how to its local communities, not just money to local charities. It distributes two U.S. products for the blind and the sight-impaired in Japan on a break-even basis, as well as a Canon-developed product for the speech-impaired. The strategy must work, because Canon has continued to grow over the last ten years in the midst of the Japanese recession, its vision and values protecting it against the national problems. Canon also works with its major competitors as part of its commitment to *kyosei.* Partnership agreements with Hewlett-Packard, Eastman Kodak, and Texas Instruments demonstrate a unique cooperation among competitors.

Stage 4: Assume global social responsibility. When corporations assume global social responsibilities, they take responsibility for cooperating with foreign companies, build production facilities where they have a trade surplus, set up R&D facilities in foreign countries, and train local scientists and workers. Canon's environmental assessment program employs three hundred people who seek ways to minimize damage to the ecosystem, from manufacturing to disposal. Its largest American plant, at Newport News, Virginia, recycles more than 90 percent of its solid waste and reprocesses photocopiers for resale; it has won several environmental awards. In Dalian, China, Canon employs more than two thousand people, who to date have recycled 9 million used laser copier and printer cartridges from around the world.

Stage 5: Be active globally. Canon aspires to this stage, in which government becomes a *kyosei* partner and works with corporations to rectify global imbalances, by doing such things as passing legislation to reduce pollution. Kaku is clear about Japan's need for economic reform, having warned ten years ago that it was courting national crisis if it continued to do nothing about its trade surplus. He sees *kyosei* as the vehicle for moving Japan into this new phase.

By succeeding in all five stages, Canon is using *kyosei* to solve the three global imbalances. It helps rectify the trade imbalance by situating factories in the countries with which Japan has the largest trade surpluses and by procuring parts from local suppliers overseas. And it helps overcome income imbalances by building plants in developing countries, creating employment, increasing the tax base, contributing to export growth, and facilitating technology transfer. Obviously the win-win for Canon is cheap labor.

And it helps rectify environmental imbalances by working in harmony with the natural world, protecting wilderness areas, cutting back on energy consumption, and recycling photocopiers as well as cartridges.

Because Kaku is convinced that *kyosei* is vital not just to Canon's success but to the future of our world, he constantly shares the philosophy with everyone, including his (the company's) archrivals.

Share *Kyosei* with the World

Kaku is now in his eighties. His goal is simple but profound: he wants to share *kyosei* with the world. "Because multibillion-dollar corporations control vast resources around the globe, employ millions of people, and create and own incredible wealth, they hold the future of the planet in their hands. Although governments and individuals need to do their part, they do not possess the same degree of wealth and power," he says. "If corporations run their businesses with the sole aim of earning more profits, they may lead the world into economic, environmental, and social ruin. But if they work together in a spirit of *kyosei*, they can bring food to the poor, peace to war-torn areas, and renewal to the natural world. It is our obligation as business leaders to join together and build a foundation for world peace and prosperity."

Kaku recognizes that each region of the world sees *kyosei* differently: leaders, companies, and countries have specific strengths, shortcomings, and obstacles to overcome. For example, the concept of human rights is interpreted differently around the world: "In the U.S., they castigate the Chinese for their human rights violations: suppressing free speech and so forth. But the Chinese look at the U.S. and see homeless people, guns, and drug addiction, while China is providing shelter, clothing and food to 1.2 billion people. So there are vast differences in interpretation in this one seemingly common concept of human rights."

Kaku clearly places his hopes on the promise of the future—the young people of the world. His legacy is ensuring that those of the next generation will understand what *kyosei* is and how to apply it as they shape the business world of the future.

ARE YOU MOTIVATED BY STRONG PRINCIPLES?

(Percentage of executives reporting that this was most important to personal leadership)

- Asia: 46%
- North America: 45%
- Latin America: 33%
- Australia/New Zealand: 30%
- Europe: 24%

JAPAN: "Contextual Harmonizers"

National Snapshot

Compared to other executives, Japanese business leaders say:

- Having strong principles and beliefs is important, but they don't do it well.
- Facing change with confidence is their most important leadership trait.
- They strongly encourage common goals and values.
- They are less likely to help people adapt to change.
- They are committed to building a culture of learning.
- Personal leadership comes from both positive and negative role models.
- Beating the competition is a strong cultural value.
- 68% were promoted from within.
- They are 100% Japanese.

The Japanese live in a land of paradox and contradiction. Their national isolation coexists with a finely honed ability to adapt and adopt foreign artefacts and innovations. Theirs is a nation in which context drives behavior, harmony is vital, saving face is crucial, and the group takes precedence over the individual—until now.

HIROSHI OKUDA AND BANANA YOSHIMOTO, born of different generations, have something in common—and both represent the new, emerging Japan. Okuda, the first nonfamily CEO of the Toyoda family's empire—Toyota—and Yoshimoto, the hip young best-selling Generation X author, both stick out from the crowd, a most un-Japanese trait. Okuda, at more than six feet tall, literally stands above the crowd and distances himself from traditional Japanese salarymen by his willingness to rethink the ways his company solves problems, makes decisions, and promotes young people.

Yoshimoto, as her self-chosen first name implies, isn't afraid to shine as an individual. Her first novel, *Kitchen*, which sold more than 2 million copies, is full of foreign influences. It is considered un-Japanese by some but is a perfect reflection of the new Japan, in which Italian restaurants are trendy and Mariah Carey advertises for English language schools. In a land of limited ethnic diversity in which more than 99.4 percent of the people are Japanese, Yoshimoto personifies the seemingly contradictory urge to embrace the foreign while maintaining the country's ethnic purity.

Japan itself is an enigma. An archipelago of four main islands and numerous smaller ones, of which only 20 percent is hospitable land, it is a densely populated nation of more than 130 million people. A modern society rooted in a feudal past, it is a secular society many of whose values stem from five great religious traditions, four of which originated in foreign cultures: the indigenous religion of Shinto, Confucianism, Buddhism, Taoism, and Western scientific materialism.

Together, they form Japan's value system. The Shinto belief that the spirit world, mankind, and nature are bound together and should exist in complete peace and harmony is alive in the Japanese business environment and society at large, where the highest premium is placed on maintaining harmony at all costs. Confucianism's basic tenets of obedience to superiors and the paternalistic treatment of subordinates form the core of strictly hierarchical working environments in which workers are dedicated and industrious and in which women play an inferior role. Zen Buddhism—the combination of Buddhism and Taoism practiced by the ancient warriors of Japan to make themselves better fighters—is one source of the intense way some Japanese businessmen operate as modern-day samurai.

And in keeping with its "early adopter" approach, Japan was the first Asian country to adopt the Western concepts of cause-and-effect relationships at the core of scientific materialism. Its businessmen used this knowledge to industrialize and develop a strong manufacturing base beginning in the late 1800s—and in the process created the foundation of the quality and continuous improvement mindset for which they're famous.

Depending on the situation, the Japanese use these five belief systems interchangeably and without any feelings of inauthenticity as they move from one to the next. While they emphasize cultural homogeneity, they welcome foreign innovations. This is a collective society founded on harmony, submerged in a high context culture, and creator of a great industrial machine known as Japan, Inc.

A Collective Society Founded on Harmony

According to interculturalist and Japan expert John Condon, "If Descartes had been Japanese, he would have said, 'We think, therefore we are.' "

That group mentality started very early in Japan—and to this day, there isn't a Japanese word for "privacy." In a land of few natural resources, the basis of this collective mindset is agricultural. Around 1000 B.C.E., rice farming was introduced into Japan from China. The very nature of the enterprise meant that a spirit of group cooperation and harmony was vital and has survived through the centuries as a fundamental characteristic of Japanese culture. As ruthless and aggressive as the Japanese were in their conquests of countries such as Manchuria and China, their first constitution in the seventh century B.C.E. stressed harmony as its central theme.

With this as their heritage, Japanese children are raised in a world in which even before kindergarten they are socialized to operate in groups, expected to consult one another before beginning projects, and encouraged to wait for everyone else to finish before handing in their work. This groupthink continues into the workplace, creating generations of traditional Japanese salarymen who wear company uniforms, live in dorm rooms, and work at long rows of identical desks.

This post–World War II value system of diligence and cooperation is changing with the advent of a "me generation" that rejects traditional values in a country in which the workforce is aging and shrinking fast. Three major changes have emerged: a greater tendency toward individuality; a need for instant gratification; and less desire for the status quo. Japan's youths want greater corporate transparency, political accountability, and immediate enjoyment of material things.

Fundamentally, the Japanese are less concerned with the rights of individuals than they are with harmonious reciprocal relationships involving social obligations. For many Japanese, this dependence—or *ahmae*—on family, friends, and company is more significant than even their relationship to a higher being.

But often the group-oriented, cooperative nature of the Japanese masks an underlying mistrust among individuals and institutions, their need for social controls, and their desire to reduce conflict. Paradoxically, their cooperative mindset often exists to curb competition.

Submerged in a High-Context Culture

Western cultures are typically organized around core values and moral guideposts such as justice, freedom, and democracy. But Japanese culture doesn't have cornerstones that govern conduct—it doesn't have a word for "sin" or "ethics" either. This doesn't mean that the Japanese are less moral than Westerners; on the contrary, acting correctly is of supreme importance in Japan. The difference is that correct action depends on the situation, not the principle.

Japanese thinking styles, communication, and behavior are usually situational rather than absolute. Correctness in all three areas is vital but is also a moving target. Nowhere in the world is it truer that actions speak louder than words. Japanese culture emphasizes the power of the nonverbal world, carefully monitoring dynamics of superiority and inferiority by mandating where people sit in meetings and how low they bow upon greeting.

And while the Japanese appear egalitarian with their quality circles and *ringi*, their consensus-focused decision-making process, there are few more rigidly structured hierarchies than Japanese companies. In fact, the Japanese rank everything: companies, universities, government, baseball teams. In every setting, it's critical to know your own rank—and that of others—since hierarchy regulates the interactions among group members. This unique combination of hierarchy and equality, clarity and ambiguity suits the Japanese perfectly.

In Japanese culture, trust and relationships are themselves situational. In this culture of clear insiders and outsiders, your position depends on your rank or situation. Insiders gain allies, information, and status; they also share responsibility and embarrassment. Foreigners, or *gaijin*, are almost always outsiders—and treating outsiders differently is accepted in Japan.

Watching how others behave drives Japanese behavior. The Japanese do all they can not to feel embarrassed; in contrast, Americans do all they can to stand up and be recognized. And while the Americans strive for innovation, the Japanese strive for perfection, a mindset that is socially appropriate when focused on quality and continuous improvement but may be taken to the extreme—and sometimes with disastrous consequences, such as the prevalence of *karoshi*, or death from overwork.

The suicides of three bankrupt businessmen in adjoining rooms of a cheap hotel in suburban Tokyo are a striking reminder of the primacy of saving face in Japan. According to what doctors call conservative estimates, at least 50,000 Japanese were hospitalized in 1998 after trying to kill themselves—a 35 percent surge over 1997.

The Japanese learn well the rules of social behavior: fitting into a group, self-sacrifice, and following superiors' commands. *Tatemae*, the art of wearing a socially acceptable mask to cover how you really feel, is raised to the level of an art form and confuses *gaijin* trying to determine the reactions of their Japanese counterparts.

The societal demand for perfection, the ambiguity of context, and the motivating force of avoiding embarrassment are magnified when fueled by the demands of economic growth and prosperity in business.

Japan, Inc.

The Japanese workplace is a controlled and controlling place with three forms of social control: group pressure to achieve the desired outcome; winning the cooperation of others by working through the system; and fierce power struggles beneath the harmonious surface. Like all business cultures, these too have societal and historical roots.

From the twelfth to the nineteenth centuries, the real power in Japan rested with the shoguns and other clan lords, creating a feudal system that prevailed until the 1868 Meiji Restoration, when authority was focused on the warlords that surrounded the emperor, marking the beginning of Japan's modern period.

Japan threw itself into the modern world by benchmarking before it was in vogue, sending envoys to gather the best of the world and bring it back to Japan. It focused on colonial expansionism, taking Taiwan in 1895, defeating

Russia in 1905, annexing Korea in 1910, taking Manchuria in 1931, and launching a full-scale war on China in 1937, taking what it wanted. But in 1945, it was defeated and occupied by the Americans, who brought with them the atomic bomb, democracy, a new constitution, and demilitarization. With independence in 1952, Japan began a period of sustained economic growth unmatched by any other modern developed nation. It was an economic transformation driven by an obsession to get ahead and remake its society—further fueling the concept of continuous improvement as a national ideal.

Japan: ***At a Glance***
Official name: Japan

Economy type: Asian manufacturing
Trading bloc: APEC (Asian-Pacific Economic Cooperation)

Location: A nation of islands off the east coast of Asia in the Pacific Ocean
Capital: Tokyo **Population:** 125,931,533
Head of state: Emperor Akihito **Official language:** Japanese
Religion: Buddhism and Shintoism 84% **Literacy:** 99%
World GNP ranking: 2 **GDP (US$ bn):** $3,972.6
GDP per capita: $31,607 **Unemployment:** 3.4%
Inflation: 1.9% **World export market share:** 10.1%

Major industries: Electrical and electronic equipment, vehicles, machinery, metallurgy, chemicals, fishing
Major crops: Rice, potatoes, sugar beets, vegetables, fruits
Minerals: Few commercially exploitable resources
Labor force: 50% services and trade, 33% manufacturing, mining, and construction, 7% agricultural and fishing
Computers per 1,000 people: 128.1

Assets: A global presence of brand names associated with quality and dependability. Global network of factories and research and production facilities enable companies to respond to local conditions. Efficient infrastructure. Productive, efficient workers. Highly educated workforce. Strong in engineering and the sciences. Efficient use of high technology to enrich global competitiveness.

Liabilities: Dependent on foreign oil and resources to maintain its success. Continual trade surplus is a source of international tension with its trading partners. Restrictions to entry into its domestic markets are an additional source of tension. Years of risky business loans have burdened the financial institutions with significant bad debt.

Retooling Japan rested on the shoulders of the Liberal Democratic Party, which ruled for more than forty years. Through a period of great postwar cooperation among government bureaucrats, businessmen, and politicians, the powerful Ministry of International Trade and Industry (MITI) protected Japan by coordinating the entire Japanese industrial complex so it could compete internationally. Known as "Japan, Inc.," the country was so successful that by the 1980s it was the second economic power in the world and the engine fueling the Asian economy. It was poised to overtake the United States in the early twenty-first century.

Then, in 1990, the economy stalled.

It turned out that Japan's banking and financial institutions were using accounting methods that masked their actual debt, bringing Japan into a recession that fueled a depression in much of East and Southeast Asia. The chink in the armor of the Japanese economic machine was clear: though they were masters of continuous improvement, they were having trouble with discontinuous change.

When the bottom fell out of their economy in the 1990s, the Japanese had to fundamentally rethink the economic model of the *keiretsu* to compete in the world economy. The *keiretsu*—large industrial powerhouses such as Mitsui and Mitsubishi, clustered around megabanks bound together by stock holdings, loans, and interdependent business and political relationships—had fueled Japan's growth, but now the country needed to create new business structures. However, in a nation in which noble failure is better than success, the traditions of saving face and avoiding confrontation made it difficult to face these problems directly.

Japan's emphasis on continuous growth, the importance of relationships, the Japanese people's resistance to reversing commitments, and lifetime employment all create the impression that the Japanese have a long-term business perspective. Their focus on long-term goals often deflects their embarrassment at short-term losses; in reality, they employ a shorter time horizon than outsiders often realize.

The strength of the Japanese is their great capacity for "synthetic creativity": combining existing technologies into new hybrids. Their collective mindset enables them to conduct national rollouts of new initiatives effectively, as they did with the quality movement. They are masters of refinement, modification, process variation, and product evolution.

But there's a downside to this: because the Japanese tend to avoid risk, their decision-making style encourages conservatism. As innovation is inherently risky, the Japanese excel at product improvement but are less skilled at creating ideas. This is clearly not true for all Japanese companies. To witness innovation at its best, one need only look to Sony and Canon or to the growing number of entrepreneurial companies in Japan.

Japan is rising to the occasion of the recent economic collapse. In 1997, knowing that the current socioeconomic system had reached its limits and constrained future development, the Keidanren—a powerful federation of economic organizations—created a new charter for good corporate behavior. As the world becomes increasingly borderless, Japanese businesses are reassessing their behavior and re-creating themselves as viable economic machines for the future.

> ***From the Japanese, we learn to listen urgently. In a society in which silence speaks loudly and context determines meaning, deep awareness of situations is vital. The keen ability of the Japanese to listen to customers and their openness to continuous innovation from outside sources will serve them well in a world of new amalgams of competition and cooperation.***

BUILD AN EXPERT CULTURE OF SHARED VALUES
Mads Øvlisen and Novo Nordisk A/S *(Denmark)*

Title: President and CEO
Headquarters: Bagsværd
Business: Novo Nordisk is a world leader in insulin and diabetes care and the world's largest producer of industrial enzymes. More than one fifth of its employees are engaged in research and development. Formed by the 1989 merger of Danish insulin producers Nordisk Gentofte A/S and Novo Industri A/S, two companies that had existed since the 1920s.
Employees: 14,175 people in 61 countries

If you have an appointment to meet the CEO of Novo Nordisk, be prepared to see him the moment you arrive. It's not an assistant who comes down three flights of stairs to greet you, it's Mads Øvlisen himself.

Once you've met him, you realize this gesture is genuinely reflective of Øvlisen's egalitarian way and his belief that leaders have to stand behind their people—not in front of them. The job of a leader, Øvlisen says, is to release personal energy by developing a collaborative culture of common values and visions. "Values," says Øvlisen, "are our fundamentals. Shared visions and values allow us to learn faster and be more competitive." In a way, they also facilitate the absorption of intellectual energy, much like the insulin and other pharmaceuticals that Novo Nordisk produces.

The Danes' values run deep. Their passion for equality stems from a her-

itage of Viking traders drinking from a common bowl, sharing to ensure that there was enough to go around.

It's not surprising that in a land such as Denmark, which has limited natural resources, people's minds become a kind of gold. Education and knowledge become investments; brainpower is its major export.

"We're living in a world where all the things that used to give business a competitive advantage—financial capital, technology, natural resources—are disappearing," says Mads Øvlisen. "The only thing left is our people. Our work on shared visions, values, and fundamentals is aimed at unlocking that potential." Øvlisen knows that he's leading a knowledge company in an expert culture of researchers, scientists, and engineers and that to excel he needs to mobilize those intellects and energize them. He does it not through elaborate reward systems but by focusing sharply, consistently, and globally on values.

"The only thing that sets us apart—perhaps the only sustainable advantage we have as a company—is the ability of our people to learn and act faster than the competition," he says. "In Denmark, it's said that we 'think with our hearts and love with our minds.' We develop and sell our know-how—that's our business."

Mads Øvlisen is culturally literate; he reflects the Danish mindset by being team-oriented, egalitarian, and values-focused: "It's more important who you are as a person than your last name or title." He is personally literate: he has thought a lot about his personal values and is dedicated to personal learning and the development of others. He is socially literate: he reveals himself to others so they can clearly see what he stands for and he challenges and nurtures clear, strong values in others. He believes people need room to achieve their fullest potential—and he gives them that space and opportunity to grow and learn. When he unleashes the potential of his worldwide organization by instilling core values, creating opportunities for global conversations about visions and values, and using those conversations to drive learning across cultures and business units, he is demonstrating his business literacy.

Create Shared Visions and Values to Drive the Company

"Values," says Øvlisen, "are not a system or program but a management style. Vision 21 [Novo Nordisk's blueprint for the future] tells us where we're going, our values tell us how we're going to get there, and Novo Nordisk's Fundamentals outline our tactics and individual responsibilities."

Øvlisen's goals are to build a world-class business and create a great place to work. Universal values—such as responsibility, trust, innovation, wisdom, and sincerity—are pillars of that strategy and drive Novo Nordisk. "Our way," he explains, "is to be accountable, ambitious, open and honest, close to our customers, ready for change, and a responsible neighbor. Building a global, values-driven culture is a fantastic experiment in changing management style around the world.

"We also recognize that universal values may have local interpretations. In Japan, for instance, there isn't even a Japanese character for the word 'openness,' which is one of our core values. We had to look outside the language to find a word and a character that would get across our meaning." This linguistic dilemma underscores the importance of local interpretation of universal values—and illustrates just how complicated these issues can be.

"There are major cultural differences that influence values, but the basic things that turn people on and make them want to run to work in the morning—those are universal. We try to not just accommodate or tolerate those local nuances but to actively learn from them," Øvlisen notes.

The Novo Nordisk worldwide intranet makes sure that employee "better practices" in India or China or Switzerland are shared with counterparts in Belgium, the United States, and Chile—in the hope that they might be beneficial there too. "For instance, our small Indian team developed cost-effective ways of reaching important doctors in their large market. Our Russian team—a very different market—invited a group of colleagues from India to set up a similar structure in Russia."

"Each unit must share and use better practices," according to the Novo Nordisk Fundamentals, a manifesto created with employee input from around the world. It's not just a list of aspirations; these are real goals against which performance is measured: individual managers, for example, are required to "buy" and "sell" three "better practices" each year through the global data system. It is these unique worldwide "conversations" that set Novo Nordisk apart and that help engrain its values in each of the sixty-one countries in which it operates.

Facilitate Worldwide Conversations

To nurture the company's shared values, a team of fourteen global culture "coaches" travels the globe, holding retreats for Novo Nordisk business units to help personalize, interpret, integrate, and operationalize these values. "They're not policemen or spies from headquarters," says Øvlisen, "they're facilitators of shared values, global messengers of the culture." The coaches work in pairs of two—one must know the business, both must be culturally sensitive, and all are highly respected professionals who meet quarterly to share their learning.

This learning comes from the top. "There is no more personal an act than that of being a CEO," says Øvlisen. "If you're not willing to share your dreams and anxieties with people, you're not doing your job. Basically, it means standing up onstage, taking your clothes off, and saying, 'This is it.' "

Denmark: ***At a Glance***
Official name: Kingdom of Denmark

Economy type: European Union
Trading bloc: European Union

Location: The most southerly country in Scandinavia
Capital: Copenhagen **Population:** 5,333,617
Head of State: Queen Margrethe II **Official Language:** Danish
Religion: Evangelical Lutheranism 91% **Literacy:** 97%
World GNP ranking: 25 **GDP (US$ bn):** $164.3
GDP per capita: $30,979 **Unemployment:** 7.9%
Inflation: 1.7% **World export market share:** 0.9%

Major industries: Food processing, machinery, textiles, furniture, electronics
Major crops: Grains, potatoes, sugar beets
Minerals: Oil, gas, salt
Labor force: 70% services and government, 19% manufacturing and mining, 6% construction
Computers per 1,000 people: 303.7

Assets: Successful high-tech manufacturing sector. Low inflation. Good overall infrastructure. Highly educated workforce. High worker productivity and good labor-management relations. Large oil and gas reserves. Creative product design and innovation. Managers with good international experience and foreign language skills.

Liabilities: High government spending. High taxation on individuals. Unemployment remains high.

Use Values to Accelerate Learning

"In 1994, we realized we needed to focus a laser beam on our competitive edge—our 'know how,' " Øvlisen remembers. "The worst thing we could do is get in the way of people's abilities. Our biggest risk is that people will only perform up to our expectations, and not to their fullest potential. To safeguard against this, we have to release their personal energy."

"We asked ourselves," he continues, "what it would take to compete as a medium-sized pharmaceutical company in a world dominated by giants. And we decided to sharpen our business focus, performance, and business culture in order to survive.

"I had to realize how important it is to keep score, even when you're talking about values. That's why we've gone beyond values statements to real, measurable, definable behaviors that we expect from our company—those are our Novo Nordisk Fundamentals. When we reorganized, some of our senior managers actually willingly worked themselves out of a job because they realized we didn't need their function anymore. That's how focused we were on our goals and our values."

The result of focusing on values-based goals? The company's sales grew 148 percent in three years.

CREATE A ROAD MAP FOR THE FUTURE George M. C. Fisher, and the Eastman Kodak Company *(U.S.A.)*

Title: Chairman and CEO (retired)
Headquarters: Rochester, New York
Business: Operating divisions include consumer, professional, digital, entertainment, health, and business and office imaging. Founded in 1881 by George Eastman. The first Kodak camera was produced in 1888 with the slogan "You push the button, we do the rest." By 1900, distribution outlets had been established throughout Europe. Today, the company is the world's largest seller of digital photographic products, with more than $1 billion in sales of digital products alone in more than 150 countries.
Employees: 95,000

"People care about their pictures, not the technology that underlies them, whether it's Spielberg making a movie, a radiologist's X rays, or you the consumer." That's how George Fisher understands Kodak.

When he became CEO, Fisher found a company confused by its vision. He sold off businesses unrelated to photography, repaid debt, and separated digital imaging from the photographic division, all in an effort to change the direction of this 120-year-old company.

With a Ph.D. in applied mathematics, Fisher combines cognitive and emotional intelligence to put all four global literacies to work. His mindset is thoughtful and decisive, his vision simultaneously realistic and optimistic. He continually raises the bar, challenging people to change. With unusual cultural literacy as an American, he uses the best of U.S. diversity to win market share from people around the world.

Kodak is undergoing nothing less than a major corporate transformation. In 1993, it was playing catch-up to Japan's Fuji Photo Film Company, losing

$1.5 billion that year on sales of $16 billion. It had lost 30 percent of its monopoly in film sales, spent $10 billion to diversify, and pushed debt up to 69 percent of total capital. Worst of all, it wasn't investing in the core business.

The first outsider to run Kodak, Fisher has a background at Bell Labs and Motorola that made him feel right at home in this technological business. He refocused the company, set strict goals for quality, and drove the company for growth through product innovation and emerging markets. His mantra was simple: "Take pictures. Further."

To change Kodak's corporate culture, Fisher had to develop a personal leadership philosophy, outline a corporate road map, and tailor that map to local traditions. When he retires in January 2000, this map will be his living legacy. The power of his vision will live on.

Develop a Personal Leadership Philosophy

To understand Kodak these days, you must understand Fisher's psychology. He knows that cognitive and emotional intelligence are essential to leadership and that leadership is essential to world-class performance: "To me, leadership is taking an organization in a value-adding way to a place it would not have otherwise gone, and doing it in a way that gives people optimism and confidence about the future."

Fisher's five leadership Es outlined his role at Kodak: to envision, energize, enable, execute, and create environments. He used these to transform Kodak's change-resistant, benevolent, paternalistic culture into a change-ready, high-performance global company.

Out of this mental philosophy he created a road map for becoming a values-based, performance-driven company: "A totally qualitative view of the world is nice but won't get you from here to there. People want to know how they're doing. The mix of quantitative and qualitative measures is essential—you can't have one without the other."

Fisher practices what he preaches. By creating a strategic business framework that starts with Kodak's values and leads to performance metrics, Fisher has fundamentally changed Kodak's culture: "Culture change is so fundamental, it becomes part of the fabric of the company, the operational principles, values, and performance-based culture we're trying to drive."

Like most companies undergoing massive culture change, the main obstacle Kodak faced was the old relationships: "We needed to define a new relationship with our employees. It was critical that people knew what was expected of them. We defined what they could and could not count on from the company. There would be no lifetime employment, but there would be lots of opportunities for continuous improvement. Then we had to live it." To do that, he needed leaders.

Fisher and his senior team had to learn to lead *and* to follow: "From time to time, I have to fall in line, become a follower, and champion their leadership. When a person with the power acts this way, you're sending a message that we're looking for good ideas." Fisher had to create an environment receptive to people's ideas and needed to develop and reward this new leadership.

It was Fisher's responsibility to plot Kodak's direction, a path into the future that is tough yet credible. His road map is just that. And it's accessible to all: posters outlining the map and its roadblocks and landmarks are made available to every Kodak employee.

Outline the Road Map for Other People

The map is a global trajectory of where Fisher wants Kodak to go in the future. Laid out in a special issue of *Kodakery*, a newsletter sent to 100,000 employees, "The New Kodak: A Road Map for Corporate Renewal" was designed to help achieve customer, employee, and shareholder satisfaction.

Fisher first worked hard to resurface Kodak's core values, starting with those put in place by founder George Eastman more than a hundred years earlier. The five corporate values that surfaced have become their North Star: respect for the dignity of the individual, integrity, trust, credibility, and continuous improvement and personal renewal. "If I were at a different company," Fisher says, "I might articulate a different set of values, depending on where they were in their life course."

These values drive long-term global performance. By building and managing a diverse corporation, investing in employee development, revitalizing the Kodak brand, developing people leadership, and striving for environmental responsibility, Fisher got everyone moving in the same direction.

Their new performance-based culture kept the momentum going. Fisher built a workforce of well-trained people who were able to deliver world-class products and services. By mapping values, principles, performance, and expectations, he created a new social compact for Kodak, one in which people have a clear understanding of goals and responsibilities. Simply put, Fisher engaged the whole company in a conversation about what it means to be a performance-based culture.

Their success metrics ensure that Kodak practices what it preaches. For starters, a 360-degree Touchstone assessment measures how well managers live the Kodak values. "The behaviors you encourage become part of your culture," says Fisher, "and culture is nothing more than the result of consistent practice of principles and values over time." A Management Performance Commitment Plan links values and performance. A worldwide communications alignment tool, this plan influences annual bonuses, encouraging the new Kodak behaviors. Twenty-five percent of the bonus is given for employees' performance, 25 percent for how well employees serve their customers, and 50 percent for the financials and shareholder returns.

To make all this work, Kodak invests in leadership, identifying high-potential employees, creating development plans for senior and junior officers, and identifying who is teachable and in what ways. Today, Fisher estimates that 85 percent of their employees around the world have a development plan in place under this new system.

Tailor the Map to Local Traditions

George Fisher's definition of globalization is simple: "What any business has to do is serve its customers better than its competitors in every country of the world. If you do that, you're global."

The challenge is that the road map must be able to be read around the world: "You have to worry about how abstract concepts translate in different cultures. We allow a certain amount of freedom by culture without losing the fundamental intent. Our values translate fairly well, yet we don't force fit something into a different culture if it doesn't have meaning there. For instance, respect for individuals plays out with interesting twists in different countries.

"Quality and cycle time play out very well globally—if anything, the rest of the world takes them more seriously than people in the U.S. Our people in Asia take them very seriously: if you write it down, you must mean it, so it gets done. In Asia, people respond to the letter of the rule—they're used to an authoritarian culture—but you haven't necessarily captured their hearts. In the U.S. and the more questioning Western world, you have to work on capturing the heart and mind, and you can't rely on authority as your only vehicle.

"Whatever your location or interpretation, you have to make people understand unequivocally that you're serious about the corporate values and they are a condition of employment."

To ensure that happens, Kodak's values and principles are aligned with its global information, finance, and human resources systems around the world. Yet the responsibility for execution lies across the four regions: "You can have a lot of local flexibility, but you've got to have a glue that holds the whole thing together. Otherwise, you're a bunch of itinerant tribes running around without coherent objectives." Fisher knows well that there are large variations in people leadership styles around the world: "The biggest difference is on the scale between authoritative and participative leadership, between Asia and western Europe and the U.S., with Latin America somewhere in between."

To be a truly global company, it's critical that your senior leadership team understands these differences: "It will be impossible to maintain large market shares in all the world's markets unless you have that understanding. If measured by market share, Kodak is one of the most global companies in the world, but in terms of management diversity, we have a long way to go."

By creating a compelling and legible road map, Fisher has created an environment for change. "You don't have anything in the end," he emphasizes, "unless you have people who believe in the future. It's as simple as that."

BREAK YOUR VISION INTO BITE-SIZED PIECES
Paulo Cunha and Ultrapar Participações, SA *(Brazil)*

Title: Chairman and CEO
Headquarters: São Paulo
Business: A diversified company with three lines of business—gas (Ultralgaz), petrochemicals (Oxiteno), and the storage and transportation of both (Ultracargo).
Employees: 5,200

PEOPLE USED TO LAUGH AT THE IDEA of flying to the moon. They stopped laughing in 1969, when a man walked on the Sea of Tranquillity. "We broke the challenge into its different parts: What kind of rocket will we need? How will we live in space? And who needs to be involved?" remembers Paulo Cunha. "Suddenly, it was doable."

That kind of destination planning and incremental execution enable Cunha to achieve his own vision as chairman of Brazil's Ultrapar Participações and CEO of Grupo Ultra. Fiercely patriotic, he knows that Brazil can no longer operate detached from the rest of the world.

Until recently, most industry in Brazil was regulated. "We just played follow the leader—whatever the government said, that's what companies did." Now state monopolies have opened up quickly, bringing competition, turmoil, and huge problems of stabilization, deregulation, and financial instability: "We've not built a decent capital market or financial structure to develop our production capacity. Our political institutions are fragmented and dysfunctional for today's capitalism."

In other words, the Brazilian infrastructure doesn't support globalization. But Cunha's determined to meet the challenge. In leading Grupo Ultra, a diversified company with three business lines—gas, petrochemicals, and the storage and transportation of both—Cunha has developed his own way of getting to the moon: he thinks big, acts small, and tells stories to engage people one-on-one.

Think Big, Act Small

Cunha's goals for Grupo Ultra involve the future of the country itself: "Our company's challenge is to help Brazil be the standard for global competitors."

That's a big vision. And Cunha knows it. "This is a huge challenge," he admits. "That's why people reacted with a lot of skepticism at first. But now excitement is picking up and the parts are falling together, like an orchestral piece. When you play music, you start by having rehearsals and making noise. But gradually, the musicians develop the skill to really play the tune."

Break Your Vision into Bite-size Pieces

First, you have to overcome the enormity of the task: "Our company's vision seems difficult, but decompose it into pieces, explain them, and evaluate what action is needed, and suddenly it looks more doable."

Get People Involved One Person at a Time

Cunha can't accomplish his vision alone: "You have to work personally with key people and get them aligned. You keep doing that in successive circles until you get the whole organization moving." It takes a lot of storytelling. Every manager has to tell stories about the future of the business and engage people's hearts and minds at every level. This is a strategy that is especially effective in a country so people- and relationship-focused.

Be an Effective Storyteller

Breaking the grand vision into more manageable parts doesn't mean you can lose sight of the big picture.

"Keep your eye on the fish and cat at the same time," says Cunha. "When Alexander the Great set out to conquer the world, he was lonely at first. But as the bits and pieces fell into place, people rallied around him. Like Alexander, most visionary leaders not only see the high-level goals but keep their eye on incremental actions at the same time."

Involve Others in Your Story

In his office, Cunha keeps a brick from the demolished mansion of a Brazilian businessman whose company collapsed when he died: "He didn't share his vision effectively and didn't have enough capable people to carry the torch after he left. This brick reminds me to share my vision to maintain the momentum over the long haul."

Timing Is Everything

The thing that keeps Cunha awake at night is timing, an important facet of the polychronic, Latin world in which he operates.

"And what keeps me awake during the day," he says, "is doing my homework, developing alternative strategies and evaluations. Timing is crucial with these kinds of large initiatives. But in Brazil, timing isn't linear. And the rest of the world doesn't stand still waiting for us to get our act together."

Share Your Dreams and Nightmares

Cunha has learned to communicate aggressively and get people sensitized to the challenges they're facing, both good and bad: "During downsizing, it was hard to get people committed. If I knew then what I know today, I would have communicated more and shared not only my dreams but also my nightmares and worries."

Cunha's strategies work: he has doubled the net present value of Grupo Ultra in four years and is well on the way to doubling it again. "My time frame," he says, "is the next three to five years. We have a window of opportunity, and either we do it or don't. I'm convinced we can." Success depends on a clear picture of the country in which it's operating: Brazil.

BRAZIL: "Affable Humanists"

National Snapshot

Compared to other executives, Brazilian business leaders say:

- Natural ability is most important to personal leadership.
- They face change with confidence.
- They inspire others to excellence more than listening and communicating.
- They are good at transforming conflict into creative action.
- They are less likely to lead by example.
- Brazil sees itself as an exporter nation.
- 26% of companies are domestic.

THE LUSH NATURE OF CUNHA'S HOMELAND doesn't stop with its Amazon rain forest. A Catholic country of immense beauty, it's also a land of deep feeling and rich personal relationships. Its heritage of mixed peoples, oligarchy, and economic tumult is being transformed into a future of diversity, national stability, and global competitiveness.

A Mixture of Peoples

Discovered by a Portuguese navigator in 1500, Brazil was colonized thirty-three years later. When Napoleon conquered Portugal in 1808, the entire royal court of 15,000 people fled to this new land. Less than fifteen years later, Brazil declared independence from Portugal, remaining a monarchy until 1889, when the emperor was deposed and a republic declared.

The ethnic and cultural mixture of peoples in Brazil further diversified with the infusion of more than 3.5 million immigrants from Italy, Portugal, Spain, Germany, and Japan at the cusp of the twentieth century, creating five regions with distinct personalities and cultures, yet each exhibiting the easygoing nature that characterizes Brazil. Though the people are diverse, theirs is a strong Brazilian nationalism, seen nowhere more clearly than in the fervor they feel for their national soccer team.

But this diversity has brought difficulties. Though denied by most Brazilians, racial exclusivity is widespread. Top management in all parts of Brazilian society is mostly white male—and while 45 percent of the population is black or mixed, the student population of the University of São Paulo, for example, is 99% white.

The Power of Oligarchy

The fifth largest nation in the world, Brazil's plantation economy and aristocratic ruling class employed some 4 million slaves from Africa. Its practice of slavery was wider spread and lasted longer than in any other country in the Western Hemisphere. Abolished in 1888, it was replaced by an unofficial but highly rigid class system of haves and have-nots that persists to this day. According to the United Nations, Brazil has the greatest income disparity of any South American country, a gap that continues to widen.

When the emperor was deposed by a coalition of wealthy landowners and military elite in 1889, a long history of military involvement in government began. While it was not as brutal as the Chilean and Argentinean military dictatorships of the same period, more than twenty thousand Brazilians were imprisoned or tortured or simply "disappeared." Thousands more fled, including current president Fernando Henrique Cardoso. This military power base lasted until 1985.

Business depends on stable governments, and the Brazilian military provided them. Between 1968 and 1973 an "economic miracle" occurred in Brazil, with growth rates of more than 7.5 percent per year. By the time the military handed power back to the civilians in 1985, Brazil had become the world's tenth largest economy. Its Amazon is the largest rain forest in the world, containing vast stores of wealth, whether trees, minerals, or land. Brazil is considered the world's most ecologically important nation; it is this wealth that pits businessmen against environmentalists, the first seeking development, the second preservation.

A History of Economic Tumult

Government took the lead in modernizing Brazil, creating many state-owned companies from oil and steel to communications and railroads. Now privatizing again, Brazil is finding it difficult to implement change. Its economic tumult between 1986 and 1994 saw six currencies, seven stabilization plans, and eight foreign ministers come and go.

By early 1994, the rate of inflation in Brazil had reached an astounding 7000 percent. It was then–Finance Minister Fernando Henrique Cardoso who ended its hyperinflation. Elected president by a landslide that same year, Cardoso deregulated and privatized business, reducing Brazil's huge foreign debt, creating a new Brazilian currency, the real, and encouraging foreign investment.

Even so, Brazil is forty-sixth of fifty-three countries on the World Economic Forum's competitiveness ranking. In 1998, a US$42 billion IMF rescue package helped prevent the Brazilian economy from collapsing. Because of its huge budget deficit and cash-strapped government, Brazil was even more vulnerable to external shocks during the global financial turmoil of 1998–99 and was the nation most affected in Latin America by the financial crisis in Asia half a world away.

A Business Culture Emerges

There are five major economic regions in Brazil, including the Southeast, which boasts São Paulo and Rio de Janeiro. With less than 10 percent of the population, São Paulo produces more than one third of its GDP. With 17 million people, this crowded city is called "the locomotive that drives Brazil." Other regions include the South, with a large German population; the Center-West, including Brasilia and its large farms and ranches; the Northeast, including Bahia—called the "heart and soul" of Brazil and one of the country's poorest regions; and the North, which includes the Amazon region.

Aware of the need to create trading blocs to compete, in 1995 Brazil, Argentina, Paraguay, and Uruguay signed the trade agreement Mercosur; Chile and Bolivia signed the next year. With reform under way, many for-

Brazil: ***At a Glance***
Official name: Federal Republic of Brazil

> ***Economy type: Latin American***
> ***Trading bloc: Mercosur (Latin American Southern Zone Common Market)***

Location: The largest nation in South America
Capital: Brasilia **Population:** 169,806,557
Head of state: President Fernando Henrique Cardoso
Official language: Portuguese **Religion:** Roman Catholic 90%
Literacy: 89%
World GNP ranking: 9 GDP (US$ bn) $800.5
GDP per capita: $4,775 **Unemployment:** 5.7%
Inflation: 33.4% **World export market share:** 1.3%

Major industries: Steel, autos, textiles, shoes, chemicals, machinery
Major crops: Coffee (largest provider), sugarcane, soybeans, cocoa, rice, corn, citrus
Minerals: Iron (largest provider), manganese, phosphates, uranium, gold, nickel, tin, bauxite, oil
Labor force: 56% services, 25% agricultural, 19% industry
Computers per 1,000 people: 17.6

Assets: Large natural resource deposits. Significant deposits of gold, silver, and iron. In the top five of the world's leading steel producers. Well-developed local industries. Low corporate tax rate.

Liabilities: Poor infrastructure: roads, railways, ports, telephones, power supply. Poor use of technology for increased global competitiveness. Confusing tax system and high evasion rate. Unstable financial institutions. High inflation. Weak political institutions.

eign corporations are now being attracted to Brazil, but heavy tariffs and barriers still stifle foreign trade.

Brazil is considered to be one of the more corrupt countries in the world, according to a recent poll of international executives; its volatile economy and enormous government bureaucracies and monopolies are in large part to blame. Brazilians have had to become adept at *jeitinho*—getting around obstacles. The rapidly changing political and economic conditions over the last thirty years have developed a flexible mindset in a world of ambiguity, as well as creating a deep distrust of people in power. Yet, as in many countries, the "old boy" network is still very strong and personal relationships are all-important. Business is often facilitated by a *despachante*, a private middleman between government and business who expedites matters to get things done.

Four types of companies exist: large and small family businesses, foreign multinationals, and state-owned companies, which are being phased out. Common to all is a first-rate managerial pool, which is this nation's best hope for the future.

> ***From the Brazilians, we gain a feel for the human side of life. The Brazilians understand deeply the human psyche and the value of people in their lives. With their appreciation of the "whole person," they have developed a deep capacity to build relationships—a quality critical to conducting business in tomorrow's world.***

CREATE REALITY FROM DREAMS
John Hendricks and Discovery Communications, Inc. *(U.S.A.)*
Mary Kay Haben and Kraft Foods International *(U.S.A.)*

Discovery Communications

Title: CEO
Headquarters: Bethesda, Maryland
Business: A top U.S. cable and communications company, Discovery reaches more than 250 million people in 145 countries, with television channels, retail stores, multimedia products, and international networks. Its award-winning programs make it the largest originator of documentary programming in the world, focused on nature, science, history, culture, travel, and health.
Employees: More than 3,000

Kraft Foods International

Title: Executive Vice President
Headquarters: Northfield, Illinois
Business: A subsidiary of Philip Morris Companies, Kraft Foods is the largest food company in the United States, formed by the merger of Kraft and General Foods. Brands include: Kool-Aid, Maxwell House, Taco Bell, and Oscar Mayer, with 50 manufacturing facilities and 260 distribution centers in the United States, along with another 90 facilities in 35 other countries.
Employees: 37,500

JOHN HENDRICKS GREW UP in Huntsville, Alabama, home of the Saturn rocket. "As a child, I was always dreaming about space," he says. Today, as CEO of Discovery Communications, Hendricks's dreams may have changed, but his passion for discovery remains. Now he dreams about being global, the power of the Internet, and offering real-time TV.

When Mary Kay Haben was a child in Chicago, her policeman father worked two jobs to make sure his family had what they needed. Now executive vice president of Kraft Foods and president of Kraft Cheese, Haben still lives the American dream: "In America, we're taught you can be anything you set your mind to."

Some leaders are dreamers, some are doers, and a select few are both. In a nation of dreamers, it's the "doing" that sets Hendricks and Haben apart—they create reality out of dreams every day by creating places and times for dreaming.

Build a Culture of Discovery

Creating reality out of dreams comes naturally for Hendricks and Discovery Communications. Insatiable curiosity and exploration are the company's mission and Hendricks's own life philosophy: "Explore your world, satisfy your curiosity."

Leaders must create environments conducive to dreaming. "By nurturing creativity, you allow people to dream independently of you," says Hendricks. "By overriding people, you're saying you're smarter than they are—and that's demoralizing."

Surrounded by creative individualists creating content, Hendricks creates an intoxicating culture to "stimulate the passion for discovery inside each person's head." By creating a place where creativity is respected, people are valued, and work is flexible, Discovery has become a "content company helping people explore their world."

For Haben, the challenge is to make time for people to dream. "You have to push people to dream big," she says. "In my life I've been more a taskmaster, but over time I've been encouraged to dream and think big." She, too, creates environments where others can dream: "I create spaces where people can think in terms of possibilities."

Haben's big dream was to take the Kraft pizza business from a $200 million to a $1 billion business by helping people understand their role—from route drivers to crust makers. "We gave them a point of common understanding. Being an old cheerleader didn't hurt," she says with a laugh, "because passion is an important piece of leadership."

Play Your Part in the Dream

To dream, you must imagine your place in history and create your own script for the future. "A leader must enroll people in a history lesson, helping them understand market trends and driving forces," says Hendricks, who does that by reminding people of the television revolution in the mid-1970s, when HBO, ESPN, and Discovery were new cable companies: "The U.S. networks at the time—ABC, CBS, and NBC—couldn't see how anyone would want to just watch movies or sports or history. So they missed the opportunity to create cable TV. Today we're facing similar decisions with our global and Internet strategies. Old paradigms don't go away, they just have their market share eroded." A leader's job is to change course and capitalize on the opportunities.

For Haben, achieving dreams is like taking a trip: "Like any journey, you have to take the first step. And that's easier to do if you know where you're going." Those steps are also easier if you're not afraid of failing: "You can't worry about whether you're going to get squashed or if what you're doing is the wrong thing."

Localize Your Dreams Around the World

Hendricks has global dreams: "We hire indigenous people in local cultures who know instinctively what is acceptable and not. We have to ask the right questions: Is this product uniquely for the U.S., or can it travel abroad? Are there cultural differences that require us to adapt it?" For Hendricks, one lesson was having one of Discovery's cooking shows in a Muslim country feature a pork dish.

Discovery realized the potential of its global reach in early 1999 with "Cleopatra's Palace," a television event broadcast simultaneously to millions of people around the world. One evening in March, the world watched as Discovery led an exploration in Alexandria, Egypt, leading to Cleopatra's ancient palace.

Successful dreaming is contagious. "If you dream about success and achieve it, that motivates you enormously to keep dreaming and creating. It's intoxicating," Hendricks says. "The goal of the leader is to get everyone else involved in these dreams; to give people confidence that we're on the right course."

Achieving dreams provides an extra benefit for the leaders themselves. "If you're doing something you really love, you'll never have to work a day in your life," he adds.

CHAPTER EIGHT

PLAN

How Do We Get There?

PEOPLE MUST KNOW NOT ONLY where they're going but how to get there. A globally literate leader provides the plan so people can execute the company's purpose. While many people can—and should—be involved in creating that road map, at some point the company must create a strategy for success.

To build a twenty-first-century organization and develop a mindset for growth, leaders must navigate through change. They do that by creating people-centered environments where the global literacies are embedded into the structures and systems of the business.

What they leave behind are old hierarchical structures, bureaucracy, and controlling systems. In their place, leaders must rely on common purpose, shared principles, empowering processes, and responsible people to do the work. They must create new, flexible business structures that anticipate and respond quickly to change. The result is leaner, looser enterprises in which traditional boundaries become irrelevant. Based on horizontal processes and boundaryless networks, these new organizations support, not sabotage, people. They are flatter and more prepared for uncertainty, able to withstand stress, and pliable enough to expand or contract as activity accelerates or slows.

In these new organizations, transparency and trust substitute for hierarchy and control, and the work is executed at the local level with maximum competence and autonomy. The great challenge is to create world-class organizations where the strategies, structures, systems, and processes fully serve the business's goals.

In a global marketplace, companies must balance global drivers and local realities—developing global vision coordinated with local practices, promoting global values yet respecting local traditions, crafting global strategies while relying on local relationships, building a global workforce yet managing local people, and creating a global corporate culture with local customs.

In this chapter, you'll meet leaders who are answering these challenges around the world: Cheong Choong Kong, CEO of Singapore Airlines, teaches us about building a high-tech, "high-touch" culture; Stan Shih, CEO of Acer in Taiwan, designs fresh organizational forms that serve people; John McFarlane, CEO of the Australia and New Zealand Banking Group, puts the right people into the right jobs. In South Africa, Warren Clewlow, CEO of Barlow, shows us how he works to integrate his global company; John Donaldson, CEO of Thomas Cook in the United Kingdom, has created a global footprint for the company; Jean-Marie Messier, CEO of France's Vivendi, is building a fast, flexible organization; and Lars Ramqvist, CEO of Ericsson, globalizes standards and localizes competence.

BUILD "HIGH-TOUCH" SERVICE AND A HIGH-TECH CULTURE

Cheong Choong Kong and Singapore Airlines *(Singapore)*

Title: Deputy Chairman and CEO
Headquarters: Singapore
Business: Singapore Airlines is the world's best airline, according to a recent poll of Condé Nast readers. With revenues in 1997 at nearly US$5 billion and contracts to purchase US$12 billion worth of new aircraft, Singapore Airlines serves 80 cities in 41 countries.
Employees: 27,516

THE CEO OF THE "WORLD'S MOST ADMIRED AIRLINE" is a mathematician by training and a pragmatist at all costs. But he also harbors a passion for drama and a secret desire to star in a local comedy.

This merging of passion and practicality is a mirror as much of the man as of the company he leads. "I don't place too much emphasis on ideologies and ideals and theoretical models," he says. Just as there is a division in mathematics between the theoretical and the applied, Cheong Choong Kong may not have his leadership philosophy written down anywhere, but it's clear from the strong culture of his company that he has mastered its application.

His company's passion is excellence in customer service; its practicality is its high-tech culture supporting this "high-touch" service.

A small city-state, Singapore has a multicultural environment and a relative lack of natural resources that focus attention on its people, an amalgam of Overseas Chinese, Malays, Indians, Pakistanis, Eurasians, and Europeans. Founded to promote commerce, its mission hasn't wavered since. A blend of Chinese and British cultural values and entrepreneurial spirit shored up by a national emphasis on education and savings makes this an ideal workforce, one that has made Singapore Airlines (SIA) one of the best airlines in the world, year after year.

SIA consistently ranks at the top of the "world's best companies" lists. It has gotten there by doing three things well: choosing the right people with the right spirit, building a multicultural community with a common purpose, and getting the fundamentals right.

Choose the Right People with the Right Spirit

"From early in life, Singapore teaches the 'three Ss': skills, social attitude, and social responsibility," says Cheong. Add "service," and you've described the cultures of both the country and the airline.

"We continue to rely on those three Ss as much as we can," he adds, "but you can't say 'I want all these Oriental strengths' and 'I want to be a global player immersed in global technology' at the same time. One would dilute the other; it's hard to have the best of both worlds."

Finding the right people with the right skills—and the right spirit—is critical. "Singapore is a wonderful starting point because we have such a strong, trained workforce," says Cheong. "But we fly all over the world—and we need to treat the whole world as our source of talent."

Social attitude is key. "We look for people with a multicultural outlook, intelligence, the right temperament, a desire to serve, and—most importantly—a sense of loyalty for the company," he notes.

"Training is also critical. We used to teach rules of etiquette, but while that made our crews efficient, it also made them something like human robots. Now we focus less on rules and more on the spirit of interacting with customers, which is harder. You should feel what a passenger needs and put yourself in his or her place. We teach this spirit through our culture and through partnering new SIA employees with cabin crews with more experience.

"Our real competitive edge is our ability to work internationally and get the best out of all the cultures in our company." By building multicultural communities with a common goal, Cheong succeeds in doing just that.

Build a Multicultural Community with a Common Purpose

Relationships are crucial in Singapore's diverse culture, as is the pressure to individualize service while adhering to a common culture. Cheong replicates both in SIA's corporate culture.

"It's harder today to preserve Eastern collective values because we do business in a worldwide community and because young people have different values now," Cheong notes. "Because they're watching *Beverly Hills 90210* on TV every night, it's risky to build plans around traditional Asian cultural norms of loyalty and pride for family, country, and community. We have to blend the ability to move fast and to preserve the past. We keep one foot in Eastern and one foot in Western values, constantly defining our culture for the future."

It's this comfort with the fluidity and interface between cultures that distinguishes SIA. "We don't have as much difficulty as some other Asian countries plugging ourselves into the global grid because we're used to working in a multicultural environment," Cheong explains. "Many of us were educated overseas—in England, Australia, and the U.S.—so we've learned what other people are like. We're not apprehensive about Westerners, and we don't have any illusions about their superiority over us nor of our superiority over them." Working together, whether on a global scale or on the scale of a cabin crew, is one way SIA breeds success.

Cheong operates somewhat counter to traditional Chinese authoritarianism in which *taipans*, or "supreme leaders," rule. He knows that an amalgam of individualism and collectivism is emerging in Asia, engendering creative tension for businesses. "We want to cultivate team spirit on every level, including the cabin crews. But in our old rostering system, every day you might be flying with different people. We now create teams that fly together for at least a year," he says. "So they know each other, help each other, and reinforce each other's values. If somebody gets out of line, peer pressure brings him back." This combination of peer pressure and a family feeling underscores SIA's success. It is grounded firmly in Asian concepts of saving face and of harmony.

"Our culture is pervasive," says Cheong, "and has acquired a momentum of its own. Take our concept of a caring cabin crew, for example. We have very detailed manuals about what our crew should do; each bit of a task is analyzed, and they're told how to do it. But even if we sent the manual to another airline, their cabin service wouldn't be the same because culture isn't so easily duplicated."

There are advantages and disadvantages to building such a strong culture: "Because of our culture, we speak a common language, and move very fast. But it may also make us blind to certain possibilities. There's a danger of mass speak or groupthink in such a strong culture."

SIA's finely honed, impeccable "high-touch" service creates the foundation that makes its high-tech experimentation possible.

Get the Fundamentals Right

"Execution matters," says Cheong. "We get the fundamentals right; we religiously live our values and stress the importance of the customer. And we're proud that most of the service innovations in the airline business were invented by SIA. We make sure our people know about the awards we win for service because corporate self-esteem helps build our strong culture."

So does succeeding against the big guys: "Since our beginnings, we've had to compete against huge odds to survive. We've pitched ourselves against the best all over the world. Because our people grew up in that kind of climate, competition is nothing new to them. They're not easily daunted by any obstacle or challenge." Cheong has made sure that in addition to "high-touch" service, SIA has technology on its side as it competes. Both are fundamentals.

SIA's high-tech environment is one of the best in the world. "Technol-

PUTTING THE LITERACIES TO WORK

Personal Literacy: How Does Cheong Think?

He is a no-nonsense pragmatist with a clear mind, an even clearer agenda, and a strong sense of ethics. He is rooted in the East with a foot in the West, merging Confucian values with a commitment to commerce.

Social Literacy: How Does Cheong Engage Others?

Cheong believes in the fundamental rights of others and seeks common languages to bind people together. Relying on interpersonal pressure to achieve results and reinforce corporate culture, he focuses on team spirit as the glue for his company.

Business Literacy: How Does Cheong Mobilize His Organization?

He infuses SIA worldwide with the strong spirit on which the company is built. He focuses on "high-touch" service within a high-tech environment, demanding excellence in execution.

Cultural Literacy: How Does Cheong Reflect His Heritage?

Though rooted in the East, Cheong understands the need for balance between Eastern and Western thinking and uses that cultural awareness as a business leverage, exploiting the best of both worlds to create success.

ogy," says Cheong, "is one of our strategic assets. Being first with new technology—like the interactive personal entertainment system—sometimes can cause problems. But if the benefits are significant, we're willing to take the risks.

"We've got the most technology of all the major international airlines, and we have the most beautiful balance sheet. It gives us the opportunity to take risks, invest quickly, and make decisions on expensive technology that can offer us a quantum leap over the rest."

Even with such a strongly embedded culture, Singapore Airlines still remains open to change. "Things change all the time," says Cheong, "and you cannot afford to take inflexible positions. In the last few years, we've slaughtered a few sacred cows. We've always said we should stick to our knitting, but now if we see a good opportunity, we explore it."

SINGAPORE: "Commercial Catalysts"

National Snapshot

Compared to other executives, Singaporean business leaders say:

- It is very important to understand your own cultural roots.
- Their organizations engage in many kinds of leadership practices (e.g., assessment, training, rotation, cross-cultural experiences).
- Compared to other Asian leaders, they are less likely to encourage others to adopt common goals.
- Only 58% are Singaporean natives.
- 79% have customers, 87% have suppliers, and 66% have employees in six or more countries.

TAKE A COUNTRY EXPELLED from Malaysia in 1965, dependent on its neighbors for raw materials and drinking water and with an economy like a rickety sampan. Add tight government regulation, loose trade relations, financial stability, and the entrepreneurialism of the Overseas Chinese network. Let forty years pass, and you've got modern-day Singapore with a per capita income greater than Great Britain's and the world's largest container port.

A Heritage of Commerce

One of the world's fastest-growing economies and ranked number one in the world for its openness to foreign trade, Singapore was founded in 1819 by Sir Thomas Stamford Raffles for the East India Company precisely to promote commerce. It is populated primarily by southern Chinese with strong Confucian and Buddhist values, many of whom came as indentured servants to work in the tin mines and at the docks.

All city with no countryside to speak of, Singapore is free-market-driven, having remade itself since World War II from a minor trading center into a booming capitalist entrepôt state. When Japan defeated the colonial powers of the British, French, Dutch, and Americans during the early days of World War II, the world saw the defeat of whites by Asians, which had a tremendous impact on the Asian psyche. If the West could be defeated in war, Asians reasoned, it could also be defeated in business.

With an active financial center, freedom from corruption, and regional headquarters for multinational companies, Singapore proved that that reasoning was solid. To become the world-leading "intelligent island," Singapore has committed to early completion of fiber-optic broadband communications networks.

This high-performance knowledge economy will require increasingly delicate decisions about how much free flow of information to allow in a nation that has been accused of censoring the Internet, barring satellite television, and controlling local media. It is open to financial investment and relatively closed to cultural imports. And it's unlikely that Singapore will give up its culture of control so easily. Even its recent decision to permit street actors and musicians in restricted areas was a difficult one. Striking a balance between the demand for individual rights and the needs of the community may become the most difficult challenge of all. And while tight government regulation has created this Asian wonder, a lighter regulatory touch may be necessary for it to move forward and innovate.

Because Singapore is an entrepôt state, it has enormous experience in dealing with foreign companies and has developed great skill in intercultural communication and modern management techniques. Large foreign holding companies dominate the modern sector of the economy, while smaller entrepreneurial businesses are run by Chinese families, part of the immense Overseas Chinese network, whose economy, if it were accounted for as a sin-

COUNTRIES WITH THE MOST INTERNATIONAL SUPPLIERS

(Percentage of companies with suppliers in ten or more countries)

- Singapore: 81%
- France: 79%
- Netherlands: 65%
- New Zealand: 65%
- Germany: 63%
- Sweden: 60%
- Australia: 60%
- Hong Kong: 54%
- United Kingdom: 51%
- South Korea: 50%
- Japan: 37%
- United States: 34%
- Brazil: 33%
- Mexico: 32%
- Philippines: 29%
- Canada: 28%

gle unit, would rank third in the world, just behind those of the United States and Japan.

Building Overseas Chinese Networks

Though created by the British, Singapore is largely populated by Overseas Chinese. Waves of immigrants have filled this 238-square-mile island nation, many emigrating from China to better their economic position, bringing with them values of entrepreneurialism, good education, and a drive for getting ahead. Willing to face incredible hardship and uncertainty, the Overseas Chinese in Singapore and elsewhere in Asia are achievement- and risk-oriented; they are focused on making money to achieve status. Few people in the world are harder working.

The largest cross-border investors in much of Southeast Asia, the Overseas Chinese hold more than 80 percent of all foreign investments in mainland China. With economic power totally out of proportion to their numbers, the Overseas Chinese network works on a small scale with a relatively simple organizational structure. They are typically focused on one product or market, with centralized decision making and a close overlap of ownership, control, and family. As they grow, their businesses are generally cautious about outside management. With their paternalistic organizational culture, the Overseas Chinese are known for their accumulation of wealth and deferred gratification, which results in very high savings rates.

In these networks, "saving face" is extremely important. Even among the *taipans*, leaders in government and big business, there are tightly networked communities in which relationships with people matter. Reciprocity is key, and losing face would make it unlikely that other Chinese businessmen would do business with the offender. In Singapore, more emphasis is on relationships with people than on products or timetables, shoring up the image of the Overseas Chinese network as a "network of networks."

Ideal People and Infrastructure

Traveling to Singapore is like finding a miniature Shangri-La. In this small, self-contained country, government controls abound to create an ideal environment. Fines for car ownership ensure use of mass transit and a lack of traffic jams. Nine of ten Singaporeans own their own homes or apartments, the world's highest home ownership rate; 80 percent of the housing is government-subsidized. There are constant celebrations of cultural diversity, acknowledging Singapore's mix of 77 percent ethnic Chinese, 14 percent Malays, and 7 percent Indian. While there are four official languages—

Singapore: ***At a Glance***
Official name: Republic of Singapore

> ***Economy type: Entrepôt***
> ***Trading bloc: ASEAN (Association of Southeast Asian Nations)***

Location: Small island city nation at the southernmost tip of the Malay Peninsula **Capital:** Singapore City **Population:** 3,490,356
Head of state: President Ong Teng Cheong
Official languages: Chinese, Malay, Tamil, English
Religion: Buddhist 32%, Taoist 22%, Muslim 15%, Christian 13%, Hindu 3% **Literacy:** 91%
World GNP ranking: 39 **GDP (US$ bn):** $86.2
GDP per capita: $25,059 **Unemployment:** 1.7%
Inflation: 1.3% **World export market share:** 3.0%

Major industries: Oil refining, electronics, banking, food and rubber processing, biotechnology
Major crops: Copra, fruits, vegetables
Minerals: Granite
Labor force: 34% finance, business, and other services, 26% manufacturing, 23% commerce
Computers per 1,000 people: 190.7

Assets: A world leader in biotechnologies. Highly skilled, well-educated workforce. Huge accumulated wealth reserves of more than US$60 billion. High institutional stability. Exceptional country credit rating. Excellent infrastructure and ports. Excellent location. High R-and-D spending. Effective police force. Little to no corruption. Easy to start new businesses. Wise use of high technology to maximize its global competitiveness. Sound government support of business.

Liabilities: Totally dependent on neighboring Malaysia for its drinking water. Nearly all food, natural resources, and energy must be imported. Limited land stifles continued development. Shortage of some key professional skills, especially engineering.

Mandarin Chinese, Malay, Tamil, and English—for political reasons only Malay is considered the "national" language, despite the fact that only a fraction of the population speaks it.

Their British colonial and Chinese cultures create companies that combine the paternalism of the Confucian tradition with Western management systems. Even the government—the "guided democracy" practiced in Singapore since independence—is a mix of traditional Chinese authoritarianism and modern Westminster democracy.

Social engineering by the government ranges from banning chewing gum to acting as a dating service. The government is focused on establishing a sense of nationhood among these diverse ethnic groups, engaging an active public relations function—some call it a propaganda machine—to establish a national ethic of patriotism, hard work, thrift, and obedience to the law.

One of the best-developed industrial, financial, and consumer economies in the world, Singapore is considered very safe and somewhat antiseptic. There is simply no tolerance for littering, illegal drugs, pornographic materials, jaywalking, weapons, spitting, smoking in most public places, or failing to flush a public toilet.

With its great harbors and ideal workforce, Singapore has built a strong infrastructure of political stability, technology, education, health care, and crime prevention. Its national strategy is to make itself, a country in a Third World region, into a First World base with standards of administration, health, security, and communications to rival those of Europe, the United States, and Japan. Its twenty-first-century challenge will be sustaining those systems in a world that requires more flexibility, less control, and more innovation.

Singaporeans teach us through their Overseas Chinese networks and effective central planning. These strong bonds of mutual trust and mutual benefit are key in the interdependent and complex environment of global business.

PLAN FOR THE FUTURE: Go Global

Three leaders on three continents have responded to the four universal business drivers by going global—in different ways. In Australia, John McFarlane matches the right people with global jobs; in the United Kingdom, John Donaldson has developed a global presence for his company; and in South Africa, Warren Clewlow has created a global management matrix.

Put the Right People in the Right Jobs

John McFarlane, CEO, Australia and New Zealand Banking Group (Australia)

John McFarlane's message is simple: "Two billion by 2000."

"To double earnings by the year 2000," he says, "things have to change materially. We have to put the right people in the right jobs with the right teams and the right businesses doing the right things to get the right results."

McFarlane puts the right people into place, gains their commitment, gives them the right tools, and asks for their performance. Matching people to jobs is the real magic—and with more than 30,000 employees, it's a challenge: "I look for people who have the three Cs: capability, commitment, contribution. Does the person have the capability to do the job? Do they have the desire to contribute? Do they deliver the desired results?"

Matching people to the right teams is also essential. "When I came here, I went into a meeting with eighty top managers of the business. There wasn't a woman in the room. When I went to senior management meetings, there was no reflection that we do business in forty-three countries. We're miles away from being a true multicultural organization, and we're going to accelerate that by running global businesses."

Commitment is key: "There comes a point where you're either committed or you're not. So even if you're capable and talented, if I can't get you committed to our vision, you have to be sacrificed."

McFarlane stretches those "right people" for results but knows he must balance demand with benevolence and care: "People have to walk out of my office better than they came in. I want people to be straightforward about mistakes so I can talk them through it. That way, we can have a real discussion and they can leave with a plan to make it better.

"Sometimes I have to back off and allow their leadership to come through. I used to run a training program and thought I'd performed well when I put on a great show. Then I realized I had it all wrong—I was showing the grasp I had of the situation, not bringing them out. Education is about bringing out, not putting in."

Create a Global Footprint

John Donaldson, Managing Director, the Thomas Cook Group (U.K.)

There's nothing subtle about the challenges facing the Thomas Cook Group. With the launch of the euro, the need for foreign exchange and traveler's checks in Europe will disappear, eroding a mainstay of the company's business.

With call centers on three continents offering service in more than forty languages, Thomas Cook provides emergency, travel, financial, and special services at three thousand locations in more than a hundred countries, with 14,000 staff serving 20 million customers each year.

Managing Director John Donaldson knows the company has to evolve to keep up. And while they've banked on their strong brand name for over 150 years, sometimes old and secure means safe and stodgy. Instead, they must be fast, innovative, and flexible.

"All businesses have threats, but few can say they're going to lose a big part of their revenues in one weekend," Donaldson explains, referring to the changeover to the euro.

Moving from a status-conscious, hierarchical civil service owned by the British government to a company that values innovation and change hasn't been without pain. For years, success meant being operationally excellent, delivering short-term financial performance and measuring shareholder value in this year's or this month's payout. But now business needed to be built to meet the future needs of customers.

Donaldson uses psychologists to evaluate the strengths and weaknesses of his top team, brings in debate coaches to teach them to deal with conflict, and challenges the team to think like the CEO. His strategy is to reinvent the leaders to step into the Thomas Cook "global footprint." And reinventing the business didn't stop with the top team. Donaldson transferred those lessons to all the global teams inside the company, giving them the tools for thinking about the business.

Together, these teams and Donaldson's top leadership are creating this global footprint for the Thomas Cook Group: no matter where you are in the world, if you're in distress they can help—whatever it takes to make things right.

Grow with a Global Plan

Warren Clewlow, Managing Director, Barlow Rand Ltd. (South Africa)

How do you manage a sophisticated business in an unsophisticated economy?

It's a question that Warren Clewlow, CEO of South Africa–based Barlow Rand Limited, has spent a lot of time pondering. The short answer? You build a strategy for global growth.

Barlow is an industrial holding company for a group of manufacturing businesses focused on infrastructure development. Of its 27,804 employees—down from 238,000 in 1989—nearly a third are now based outside South Africa.

The end of apartheid signaled the beginning of a new Barlow, sparking the transition from a highly unintegrated group of businesses—with products as diverse as steel, paint, and vacuum bags—to a business of clarity, cohesion, and coordination.

"Today, forty percent of our business is outside of South Africa. We're an international company with headquarters here." But building a successful business based in multiple countries is totally different from exporting from a single company. Clewlow has managed these global challenges by creating a new global structure, building local relationships, and using common sense.

Control centrally; use collective systems; give local autonomy. This three-tier approach starts with strong central control over areas such as finance, strategy, and acquisitions. Business challenges common to the whole company, such as logistics, technology, and industrial relations, are handled with companywide systems, leveraging best practices and drawing on collective skills. Day-to-day management is left to local managers. Their eight operating divisions are each led by an executive director who participates in the overall corporate strategy.

Going global means cultural adaptation: "When you move out of South Africa, you've got to adapt yourself to new conditions. Our challenge was to get in step with local management and to tune into another culture and management style."

Australia was the company's learning laboratory: "We had to get on the same wavelength with Australian executives. We asked a lot of questions about their country's style, products, advertising, and working there. We had to respect their culture rather than be arrogant, and build on their good points rather than focus on their weak ones." Today, Barlow's has a 25 percent share of Australia's decorative market.

SOUTH AFRICA: "Apartheid Survivors"

> ***South Africans are living proof that history matters. To understand the South Africa of today, it's critical to understand its past and appreciate its historical roots, yet not be held hostage by them. The history of this complex land is inextricably woven into the tapestry of its contemporary society.***

Cape Town is one of the most beautiful cities on earth—a jewel at the very tip of this lush, green, mineral-rich country. Yet little more than a mile separates its fashionable Victoria and Albert Hotel from the cardboard-and-tin houses in the townships outside the city. And while waiters offer cool drinks in the hotel lobby, rivers of human waste swim with animal bones and fruit rinds when it rains in the townships.

This is a nation with a long history of haves and have-nots, brutalized by injustice and early in its transition to true democracy and equality. Born and raised on conflict and oppression, rich with natural resources, and heavy with the legacy of apartheid and racial discrimination, South Africa is struggling to balance the developed and developing world within its borders.

Born of Conflict and Oppression

In 1498, Portuguese sailor Vasco da Gama was the first European to sail around the Cape of Good Hope to India; by the 1660s, the Dutch had established a fort at the cape to service the boats and sailors of their Dutch East India Company. Bringing in slaves as their labor needs grew, they otherwise built lives separate from—and in conflict with—the indigenous tribes they found there. From that time until 1994, South Africa would remain a nation of conflict and oppression among a myriad of peoples: the Dutch; the British, who took control of the cape in 1796; and the various South African native tribes, including the Xhosas, Zulus, and others.

As the Dutch farmers, or Boers, moved inward, they increasingly came into conflict with the black cattlemen in Africa's interior—primarily over land. The urban-dwelling English and the farming Boers were in conflict almost from the beginning, and in 1833, when slavery was abolished by the British Empire, the situation was only exacerbated—the Boers felt they weren't adequately compensated for the slaves they were forced to free.

To liberate themselves from what they perceived as the yoke of the British, the Boers migrated north en masse to look for farmland in the mid–nineteenth century, a "Great Trek" that moved them into direct conflict with the Xhosa and Zulu nations, which were migrating south in search of grazing land for their cattle.

The Trekboers, the British, and the indigenous African tribes—who themselves were fighting intertribal battles—were long involved in wars of tripartite hatred and greed. The second Boer War, at the cusp of the twentieth century, decided who would control South Africa's vast mineral wealth; the British won, gaining control not only of the gold and diamond mines discovered on the land of Afrikaner brothers Johannes and Diedrich de Beer but of the rest of the country as well.

Finally, in 1910, all the colonies at the tip of Africa were united and became a British dominion, the Union of South Africa. The impact of this legacy of conflict and the scars of oppression lay the foundation for the deep cracks of anger, resentment, and conflict that still exist in South African society today.

Isolated by Racism

Nothing in South Africa remains untouched by the oppression and racial separation that stemmed from these historical roots. Even among white South Africans, the separation between the British and the Dutch played out for decades in the way they sought power: the Brits in the business world, the Dutch in government.

The separation of the blacks from their own land was as insidious and devastating as the separation of the races from each other. In the 1880s, as land became more valuable with the discovery of vast deposits of gold and diamonds, the Europeans enacted a Land Act that made it illegal for Africans to purchase or lease land anywhere in South Africa except in designated preserves, later known as "homelands." By 1914, the whites controlled ninety percent of the land, forcing blacks to take low-paying, unskilled jobs in the mines and ensuring that the whites would control the economy and government of South Africa.

In all-white elections, the 1948 victory of the mostly Afrikaner National Party ushered in the consolidation of apartheid and almost forty years of unbroken Nationalist rule. As the condition of blacks worsened, the government increasingly used force to gain compliance with apartheid laws, including a massacre of blacks by security forces in Sharpeville in 1960 and of youthful demonstrators in Soweto in 1976, bringing widespread international condemnation.

New foreign investment almost ceased, and existing international businesses were pressured to divest their holdings in South Africa. Yet these economic boycotts were limited in their success because some countries and corporations were still willing to trade with the South Africans, including Taiwan, Israel, Iran, and Iraq.

By the end of the 1980s, even the Afrikaners recognized that apartheid was doomed and that South Africa couldn't continue to be isolated from the rest of the world; they opened the country to the first all-race elections in 1994.

Today, the workplace is increasingly the meeting place for these historical forces—a social laboratory and a catalyst for social change in South Africa.

Blending the Developed and Developing World

South Africa has the strongest, most sophisticated free-market economy in Africa, yet its modern financial, commercial, and industrial sector operates alongside a large Third World subsistence economy and an informal sector of numerous microbusinesses and informal retailers.

It is a diverse society that represents the great hope of the continent. While South Africa represents only 4 percent of the continent's surface and 6 percent of its population, it accounts for 18 percent of Africa's GDP, 46 percent of its generated electricity, and 45 percent of its mineral production. Its diversity may emerge as one of its greatest strengths—almost 75 percent of South Africa's population is black, representing nine major language and ethnic groups with Zulu as the largest. The minority population is 13 percent white (Afrikaner or British), 8 percent of mixed race, or "colored," and 2 percent Indian, speaking one or more of English, Afrikaans, Zulu, and eight other tribal languages that are all official languages.

Great social progress has occurred, but economic apartheid remains. The white seventh of the population have the same standard of living, health, and education that their cousins in Europe and the United States enjoy, with income on a par with that of Californians. But most of the black population is among the poorest in the world, crime is rampant, schools are crowded, and 50 percent of the adult black population is unemployed. Past political policies have created the most inequitable economic society in the world, according to the World Bank. Realistically, the African National Congress (ANC) government doesn't have the capital or skilled manpower to change that by itself—it is looking to business for expertise as well.

When elected in 1994, the new ANC government, led by Nelson Mandela, had a clear majority in Parliament and a clear mandate to act. It moved to correct the injustices of more than forty years of neglect by bringing the black, colored, and Indian populations up, not by bringing the whites down. In fact, political stability emerged surprisingly quickly; the revolutionary ideas of the ANC and the apartheid ideology of the Nationalist Party were

South Africa: ***At a Glance***
Official name: Republic of South Africa

Economy type: Other
Trading bloc: SADC (Southern African Development Community)

Location: Southernmost nation on the African continent
Capitals: Pretoria, Cape Town, and Bloemfontein
Population: 42,834,520 **Head of State:** President Thabo Mbeki
Official Languages: Nine African languages, English, Afrikaans
Religion: Christian 68%, traditional animistic 29% **Literacy:** 82%
World GNP ranking: 29 **GDP (US$ bn):** $122.2
GDP per capita: $2,895.6 **Unemployment:** 29.3%
Inflation: 7.3% **World export market share:** 0.7%

Major industries: Mining, steel, chemicals, vehicles, machinery, textiles
Major crops: Corn, wheat, vegetables, sugar, fruit
Minerals: Platinum, chromium, antimony, coal, iron, manganese, nickel, phosphates, tin, uranium, gem diamonds, copper, vanadium, oil, world's largest producer of gold (30% of world total)
Labor force: 35% services, 30% agricultural, 20% industrial
Computers per 1,000 people: 37.8

Assets: Africa's most developed economy; diversified and possessing a modern infrastructure. Strong financial sector. Abundant natural resources, especially rare and precious metals and gems. Growing tourism industry. Manufacturing sector is continuing to grow and develop with global aspirations.

Liabilities: High unemployment. High inflation. High population growth. Vast income disparity between educated professionals and uneducated minorities. Lack of skilled engineers and scientists. Lack of managers with international experience and foreign language skills.

swept away as they moved toward unification. With a remarkable sensitivity to minority fears, Mandela's main theme has been to unify the country, using a consensus building approach to policy formulation.

A Business Culture Emerges

There is still much unresolved anger and pain on both sides. And in a land of contrasts and inequities, the workplace brings all the history and conflict together. Admittedly, some companies do a better job than others in mediating the painful conversations taking place nationally.

Business did suffer to some degree during the international boycotts. Isolated from the real world of international competition, many businesses had to be government-supported and are just now learning to be globally competitive. But there were some benefits as well: the boycotts provided an incentive to develop the manufacturing sector of the economy.

Economic recovery began in 1993 and has expanded with the privatization of several large state-controlled corporations. Their biggest challenges are the lack of skilled labor and capital. They are working to mediate between Western, individualistic, hierarchical management styles and the traditional and highly collectivist African style of *ubuntu*, in which all are part of the decision-making process.

The enormous capacity of the people of South Africa is illustrated by the process of their national Truth and Reconciliation Commission, which is piecing together a patchwork quilt of personal stories and testimony to shed light on the governance systems that made apartheid possible in the first place.

South Africans teach the world to have open, honest, national conversations about painful issues. From them, we can learn how to distill lessons from adversity and mistakes in order to heal in the future.

DESIGN FRESH FORMS THAT SERVE PEOPLE
Stan Shih and the Acer Group *(Taiwan)*

Title: CEO
Headquarters: Taipei
Business: One of the world's top PC manufacturers, Acer sells products under its own name and manufactures products for companies like IBM and Compaq. They operate 17 manufacturing plants and 30 assembly plants around the globe.
Employees: 4,401

"FRESH IDEAS ARE POWERFUL because they have the broadest application and are easiest to implement on a global scale," says Stan Shih, one of Taiwan's leading entrepreneurs.

His philosophy of "fresh" shows itself in the colorful forms of Acer computers, in his "smiling curve" business model, and in his creative organizational structures—all designed to liberate people and help them move quickly around the world.

Shih looks to the fast-food industry for insight into business structure and product delivery. He looks inside his own industry to explore how its metaphors provide models for the structure of the company itself. And he looks around the world for new customers and new ventures.

He knows that leaders must facilitate innovative thinking and that organizational structures must serve the creative needs of the people and the business itself.

Language matters.

Take the word "fresh," for example. Stan Shih is probably the only CEO in the world who centers his business strategy on that concept. Called the "Bill Gates of Taiwan," Shih is a man in relentless pursuit of "fresh." When you talk with him, "fresh" is everywhere.

Shih's fresh vision centers on creating new forms for his product, his employees, his business, even his culture. Acer's vision of "fresh" translates into innovative organizational forms designed to optimize quality in a globally effective and locally responsive way—and it's in those structures that we begin to understand Shih's passion.

Design a Fresh Organizational Form

"I spend a lot of my time talking about our corporate culture and about our core value of 'fresh.' As CEO, I'm the chief spokesperson for Acer, the glue of our value system. I constantly seek consensus around vision and goals. That takes time and a kind of openness that isn't as customary in Chinese society as it is in the West."

Acer's a player in the Chinese world and beyond, a global giant in small Taiwan: long diplomatically isolated, Chinese by nature, Eastern by faith, and vulnerable to invasion. And Shih isn't just breaking new cultural ground. His computers are breaking new ground, too: Acer is known for its unique, curvy, colorful personal computers.

"Creativity is a central theme of Acer's philosophy and strategic direction," Shih says. Designer of Taiwan's first desktop calculator and the world's first pen watch, Shih personifies the entrepreneurial and creative spirit he builds into his corporate structure. He creates images—such as his "smiling curve"—to convey his vision to employees worldwide at a glance. If you understand his "smiling curve," Shih says, you'll end up smiling in the future.

Shih knows that at each end of the "smiling curve," Acer can find added value: through component design and production, on the one hand, and through marketing, distribution, and localized assembly, on the other. Where Shih doesn't find added value for Acer is at the curve's middle, the simple assembly of PC systems. His goal, then, is to optimize the value at each end of the curve; and to do that, he knew he would need to "institutionalize" the lessons from his smiling curve.

In 1994, he created three strategic initiatives to build an architecture for Acer that will keep its bottom line smiling: a "global brand, local touch" strategy, a "client-server" organizational structure, and a "fast-food" business model—"just three examples of the fresh ideas that have helped build Acer into the internationally successful operation we are today," says Shih.

Develop a "Global Brand, Local Touch" Organization

The next time you're in an international airport, take a closer look at your luggage cart. Chances are that you'll see Acer's logo on the cart, no matter where you are in the world.

That global branding is how Shih keeps Acer glued together as one enterprise. "In our 'global brand, local touch' strategy, independent business units around the world cooperate to provide PCs and peripherals to locally owned and operated assembly sites worldwide," Shih explains.

Acer is unique in its willingness to give up control of its local operations. It's clear that Shih trusts his employees and provides them maximum flexibility to do their jobs well, no matter where they are. His remarkable level of trust explains one of four core Acer values: "Human nature is basically good."

Trust translates not only into greater independent decision making but into lower-cost manufacturing, as well as innovative logistics and assembly strategies. Shih's local managers know they can make their own decisions, assemble their own product, and own their own business unit in a way almost unheard of in traditional Chinese companies.

"In Chinese culture," says Shih, "the tradition is to transfer wisdom from one successor to the next. But that won't help Acer achieve our 'global brand, local touch' strategy; we have to transfer our wisdom down to *all* our colleagues. All our managers must have one foot in Acer culture and one foot in the local environments where they are doing business."

That delicate dance succeeds only when the Acer culture is accessible, visible, and passed down to all Acer managers. Shih makes sure that happens by training Acer managers and by constantly reinforcing that learning. The company's "Sea Dragon Program" trains hundreds of managers a year. The newness of the Acer approach is that the faculty aren't just OD specialists or corporate trainers: Acer managers learn from senior executives—including Shih—who deliver their management philosophy and share their management experience with all the trainees. They share the vision of the company and explain the structures that embody that vision, such as the Acer client-server organizational structure.

Develop a Client-Server Organizational Structure

Your desktop PC is probably linked to an organizationwide server so you can share software, databases, and communication programs. These types of client-server networks have replaced the large, unwieldy mainframes of the past, offering better performance and value, plus exceptional flexibility, because they can easily be modified to meet users' changing needs.

In 1994, Shih took a fresh look at Acer's structure. He looked to his own industry for ideas, recognizing that this new computer architecture could provide a model for how he runs the business. The result was Acer's new client-server organizational model, with one significant change: in Shih's model, the clients can also act as servers and the servers can also act as clients, depending on the need and situation.

Acer's eighty-person headquarters provides legal and accounting services to the network of companies that make up the group—and depends on the dividends from those companies for its revenue. Shih has put strategy and control where they are most effective, not where they are most expected. In effect, he has adopted and upgraded the client-server model of the computer industry. His fresh approach to structure carries over into his fresh approach to delivery. PC networks provided one inspiration; hamburgers provide the next.

Learn from the Fast-Food Business Model

Most of us have eaten at McDonald's or Burger King. But most of us don't see corporate inspiration in Happy Meals. Stan Shih sees inspiration everywhere.

Based on the strategy used by global restaurant chains, Acer's fast-food business model distributes assembly operations to sites around the world. Components are defined as perishable or nonperishable. Perishable motherboards, memory, hard disk drives, and related components are sent via air transport to ensure fast delivery. Nonperishable PC housings and floppy disk drives are shipped via slower sea transport. In McDonald's language, hamburger meat is perishable and napkins are not, so their delivery systems are vastly different. Perishable components may also be bought locally, from approved vendors, to expedite the process even further. Adapting the business model of the fast-food industry allows Acer to be faster, more flexible, and more adaptive.

Stan Shih is personally literate. Believing human nature is basically good, he uses that belief as one of the grounding principles of Acer. His social literacy shows in his understanding that leaders need to touch people with his vision. By recognizing that he must create organizational structures that liberate people, he demonstrates his business literacy. And with his clear sense of Chinese roots and openness to learning from other countries, he shows how culturally literate he is.

"Out with the bland, in with the bold," reported *Newsweek* magazine when Acer launched its Aspire line of multimedia home PCs in 1995. Form and function coalesced in a product with an innovative look, a design that promoted easy access for users, fast and low-cost production, and a virtual explosion of global brand awareness overnight. It was a visual representation of the "fresh" to which Stan Shih aspires. To continue this legacy, in August 1999, Acer announced a strategic alliance with Cisco Systems, the aim of which is to take advantage of the explosive development of the Internet.

The Chinese word for "insightful and elegant knowledge," is a concept Shih literally embodies. That word is *shih.* And what about the company he leads? *Acer* is Latin for "active, sharp, clever, and incisive."

Language does matter. And so does place. To fully understand Shih, we must understand his homeland.

TAIWAN: "Efficient Manufacturers"

THE DIFFICULTY IN TALKING ABOUT TAIWAN is exemplified in the *CIA World Fact Book.* In the alphabetical index, there's no entry for "Taiwan." At the end of the index, however, there's a separate box about this island nation. This separateness speaks volumes on Taiwan's presence in the world. Economically and strategically, it's one of the Asian Tigers; politically and diplomatically, it's a night-blooming tiger lily, a nation the world deals with in the shadows.

An immigrant and exile community, mountainous, semitropical Taiwan is just 115 miles off China's southern coast. Its people are almost entirely of Chinese origin and speak various Chinese dialects. Before World War II, save for a small number of aborigines, the population consisted of the descendants of Chinese emigrants from the mainland who had arrived on the island starting in the sixteenth century.

After losing its influence in Korea in 1894, China was forced to cede Taiwan to Japan in 1910, an occupation that caused Taiwan's history and that of China to diverge. For fifty years, Japanese authorities supplanted Chinese culture and language with that of Japan. But the only remnants of their occupation include a respect for Japanese orderliness, the architecture of Taipei, Western science and technology, and a desire to expand Taiwan's economic base.

Since 1949, the island has been the seat of the Republic of China, once headed by Chiang Kai-shek. In that year, the population was augmented by 2 million Chinese fleeing the mainland, a group that included high-ranking government officials, intellectuals, and a military force of more than 600,000 men.

Taiwan was exiled in 1971 from the United Nations; by 1979 the United States and other nations had switched their diplomatic recognition to Beijing, leaving Taiwan in no-man's land. An isolated country in a world of giants, Taiwan quickly learned modesty, pragmatism, and a compromising spirit. To maintain its legitimacy with and economic importance to Western governments, it adopted a strategy of increasing its export trade with the world. Today, almost every Western government maintains a trade mission in Taiwan that serves as an unofficial embassy.

A Country of Manufacturers

Taiwan is a series of fifteen islands, the total area of which is no larger than one tenth that of Japan. With a population of 21 million and an unemployment rate of less than 3 percent, Taiwan has made the transition from a poor, preindustrial debtor nation to a modern export economy. Typically, Taiwanese businessmen are practical, simple, and compromising. Taiwan's wealth is hardly a decade old, leaving a legacy of caution about money and uncertainty about the future.

Yet in 1997, Taiwan's GDP grew by nearly 7 percent, foreign investment climbed by 14 percent, and the country's per capita income was equal to those of Spain and New Zealand. As Taiwan has grown richer, its authoritarian government has grown less so, achieving fully democratic elections in 1996. It is a spending economy, with a lot of disposable family income, new shopping malls, and credit cards.

Taiwan weathered the Asian economic crisis of 1997–98 by being a nation that makes things for the world. Constructing monitors, mice, and motherboards for the computer industry, the Taiwanese have capitalized on their industrious manufacturing mindset to achieve economic gain.

There is a saying in Taiwan that it is better to be the head of a chicken than the tail of an ox—that is, it's better to work for one's own gain than for a large corporation. Small-scale capitalism and complex distribution networks are the norm in Taiwan.

The mentality of family entrepreneurship is shaped largely by the teachings of Confucius. Obedience and respect for superiors and parents, duty to family, loyalty to friends, and courtesy are hallmarks of Taiwanese society. Work is one of the highest virtues—and businesses are built on the model of a traditional Confucian family, organized hierarchically and with clear orders of seniority and status.

> ***The Taiwanese teach us how to use external adversity to build internal competence and economic advantage. By focusing on their pragmatism, they have built up their cultural self-esteem, taking their manufacturing mindset to a new level of entrepreneurialism and competitiveness.***

Taiwan: ***At a Glance***
Official name: Republic of China (Taiwan)

Economy type: Asian manufacturing
Trading bloc: APEC (Asia-Pacific Economic Cooperation)

Location: Island nation forty miles off the coast of Mainland China
Capital: Taipei **Population:** 21,908,135
Official language: Mandarin Chinese **Religion:** Buddhist, Taoist, and Confucian 93%, Christian 5% **Literacy:** 94%
World GNP ranking: 20 **GDP (US$ bn):** $248.4
GDP per capita: $11,444 **Unemployment:** 2.7%
Inflation: 4% **World export market share:** 2.9%

Major industries: Textiles, clothing, electronics, processed foods, chemicals
Major crops: Vegetables, rice, fruits, tea
Minerals: Coal, limestone, marble
Labor force: 52% services, 38% industry and commerce, 10% agricultural
Computers per 1,000 people: 87.7

Assets: Well-educated, productive workforce. Keen work ethic. Many business leaders have been U.S.-trained and have inside understanding of the U.S. market and U.S. business leaders. Many small to medium-sized firms that are able to adapt swiftly to changes in the market. Good location. Low unemployment and inflation. Good supply of scientists and engineers. Good utilization of technology to increase global competitiveness.

Liabilities: Uncertainty of mainland China's long-term intentions for this island nation. Low level of spending on R and D. Lacks innovation and original invention. Legalized corruption remains. Standing in the international community of nations is controversial. Little protection of intellectual property rights.

GLOBALIZE STANDARDS AND LOCALIZE COMPETENCE

Lars Ramqvist and LM Ericsson *(Sweden)*

Title: Chairman and CEO
Headquarters: Stockholm
Business: World's leading supplier of telecommunications equipment. In 130 countries, with 96% of revenues outside Sweden. Lars Magnus Ericsson opened a telegraph repair shop in 1876; by 1892 he marketed his first international product. With an R&D budget exceeding 20% of sales, the company has 40% of the world market for cellular telephone systems.
Employees: 100,774

LARS RAMQVIST'S SPECIAL INSIGHT *into running one of the world's fifty largest companies started as small as you can get—at the atomic level.*

When he got his Ph.D. in solid-state physics and chemistry, Ramqvist was studying the world of crystals—the building blocks of the physical world—and the ways those minute structures react to the outside world. As Ericsson's CEO, he remembered those lessons well. He created a vast collection of local networks—the building blocks of his company—and the overarching structure and global standards that would help the company react to outside forces.

"Fully develop the concept of 'small in large,'" reads Ericsson's "Vision 2005," its blueprint for the future. This interplay of large and small, of global and local—all intricately networked together—is what distinguishes Ramqvist's global plan.

Widely regarded as the leader in wireless systems, Ericsson must catch up in the Internet field, and quickly. Through aggressive cost cutting, acquisitions, new-product development, and a keen focus on wireless Internet services, the company is working to do just that.

Imagine exchanging more than 900,000 e-mails every single day. With more than 75,000 linked terminals, Sweden-based telecommunications giant Ericsson has created one of the world's largest private information networks and the largest worldwide customer base for telephone communications—all in the fastest-developing industrial sector in the world.

This rapid-fire information and technology is held together by three global values: respect, professionalism, and perseverance. "Respect is about relationships, professionalism is about technical excellence, and perseverance is about results," says Ramqvist. These values are at the heart of his strategy: be boundaryless, globalize standards and values, and localize competence.

Lars Ramqvist is a personally literate man. He's willing to do what it takes to get the job done, but not at the expense of the organization or the people around him. The value he places on perseverance and constructive impatience fits perfectly with an industry that requires such high speed. Ramqvist is always raising the bar and challenging the organization and himself.

Ramqvist is very tough in terms of setting rules, but also realizes that leaders have to be open and generous, a juxtaposition that defines his social literacy. His business literacy shows in the world class execution of Ericsson's open systems architectures and in his insistence on their three key values. He is also culturally literate, reflective of his Swedish roots: Ericsson is a neutral, humble company, with a keen sense of being a guest in a foreign land. Like his home country, Ramqvist is oriented toward innovation and cooperation yet grounded in a solid pragmatism that demands results.

Build a Boundaryless Enterprise

Add to those 900,000 daily e-mails the 60,000 people trained yearly at Ericsson. They're encouraged to live in any of the 130 countries where the company operates, work in the technology areas they choose, and learn the "Ericsson way" through courses conducted all over the world. This access to know-how and global transfer of knowledge is an Ericsson trademark.

"We move executives globally to learn, using job rotations and cross-cultural training to eliminate any boundary thinking," says Ramqvist. "Ericsson isn't a one-country company. We're everywhere, and we must accept and embrace every culture. Our values cut across cultures and help make us boundaryless."

Ericsson's Vision 2005 was the result of intensive scenario planning by five hundred top managers worldwide. It outlines "new ways of working," all designed to facilitate this "borderless organizational concept" and create a culture for speed and flexibility. One part of that strategy is its "open systems architectures," designed to link with other companies, research parks, and universities to maximize creativity and minimize the cost of innovation. "That way, we broaden our base without paying for everything ourselves," says Ramqvist. This collaborative mindset marks Swedish culture—not surprising in a nation whose history was marked by the teamwork of Vikings aboard ships bound for the New World.

A key reason Ericsson has focused on being boundaryless is nothing more than geographic: Sweden is a tiny market and had to become export-driven early in the process. Telecommunications, by definition, is a boundaryless industry, but even so, Ericsson is uniquely connected by its communications technologies. "We train and recruit local people, but the common factors are our standardized products, systems, technologies, and values." These standards help create consistency and predictability in a complex world.

Globalize Your Standards

Sweden's small size might get lost in a "boundaryless" mentality, but not Ericsson, which created global standards to glue its boundaryless organization together.

Ericsson has literally defined GSM (Global System for Mobile Communications) telecommunications standards in 130 countries—by boldly investing in R&D. Ramqvist created the rules and standards to help guide this R&D culture: "If you need speed and a sense of urgency, you must be extremely careful in developing technical and interpersonal standards." That's even more important in the digital age, when standards are changing rapidly. Today, while Ericsson has a formidable presence in wireless and fixed-line networks, it is behind and working to catch up in the industry's hottest areas: mobile-handset and Internet telephony.

"In 1991," says Ramqvist, "we got an order to develop the first digital system for a mobile telephone system. Working from scratch, we delivered in less than two years. To do that, we had three thousand engineers in twenty-five global centers of excellence all working on the project at the same time—in real time—using our global standards as a framework.

"That same year, I met with the Japanese minister of communications to discuss development of their telecommunications standard. Our board agreed we had no choice but to spend the 500 million dollars it would cost to assist them—and we became Japan's market leader as a result.

"I remember flying to Wall Street in late 1991 to tell investors we were doubling our R&D expenditures at a time of flat profits and recession. I made a personal commitment to repay our R&D quickly. Our culture of speed and flexibility ensured we would make that happen. If you stand still only one quarter, you're a dead duck in this business."

Ramqvist is always asking for higher quality, faster speeds, better products, and better service—from both himself and others. "Our value on perseverance means that we never give up. We go through concrete walls if necessary," he says.

But Ramqvist knows that speed alone can't build a culture of excellence: "To deliver quality products in the speediest ways known to mankind, you must be extremely generous in your leadership approach. This would never work if I were an officer on a galley ship just whipping the slaves, saying that they'll get double rations of beer when they finish.

"We must balance the push for speed with the 'soft stuff,' " he adds. "We've developed external standards for products in the marketplace and internal standards for working conditions." This focus on nurturing, inclusiveness, and consensus building is a strong facet of Swedish culture and balances Ericsson's push for strong business results.

Localize Your Competence

Competence must be created when and where it counts: close to the customer. That's Ericsson's people strategy. "We're a customer-focused, networked organization that places a lot of emphasis on internal joint ventures and informal networks to get the job done," explains Ramqvist.

"Our Centers of Excellence each have their own expertise and are linked globally. For example, call centering is an Australian strength. And they export that expertise to all other Ericsson companies, which makes the Australians extremely proud and makes them more willing to collaborate.

"If there is a competence in Ericsson," he says, "there should be only one center of that competence. So our 100,000 employees work together because they know the other 99,999 will turn to the expert to buy his or her expertise."

The local experts must be empowered to do their jobs: "The first thing I did as CEO was introduce a matrix organization giving our local sales companies greater influence because they're in closest contact with our customers, and customers are the ultimate control factor."

Ericsson people are truly world-class innovators. "In 1997," says Ramqvist, "we applied for twelve hundred new patents. We issue several

COUNTRIES WITH THE MOST INTERNATIONAL REVENUES

(Percentage of revenues from sales outside the home country)

- Sweden: 75%
- France: 56%
- Netherlands: 48%
- Canada: 47%
- Singapore: 42%
- Germany: 42%
- New Zealand: 35%
- Mexico: 35%
- Philippines: 34%
- Hong Kong: 33%
- United Kingdom: 33%
- South Korea: 31%
- Australia: 25%
- Brazil: 21%
- United States: 21%
- Japan: 15%

patents every day—that's a lot of creative activity." But that's not all Ericsson delivers; Ramqvist has produced earnings growth of more than 30 percent annually while CEO.

SWEDEN: "Practical Cooperatives"

National Snapshot

Compared to other executives, Swedish business leaders say:

- Natural ability drives personal leadership more than experience.
- Educating people how the business works is very important.
- They are highly committed to continuous learning.
- They give employees decision-making authority.
- Building multicultural teams is their highest priority.
- They emphasize cross-cultural experiences and job rotations.
- They speak 3.4 languages, second only to the Netherlands.
- 75% of revenues are derived from outside Sweden and 32% of boards are non-Swedish.

Swedes are marked by reserve, collaboration, innovation, and consensus building. Centuries of struggle in a harsh environment with uncertain soils helped create their practical approach to life—and to business.

SWEDEN'S FURNITURE, some say, is a perfect reflection of the Swedish mindset: functional, simple, understated, adaptable, and above all practical. The Swedes have a word, *lagom*, that means "just right." *Lagom*, say the Swedes, is best. It shows in their chairs, and in their businesses.

The Swedes' practical inclination is seen in their social welfare systems, in their functionalist design movement of the early twentieth century, and in their census—one of the oldest such accounting systems—dating back to 1749. Their practicality grew out of needing to make good use of scarce resources in an agrarian society—lessons that serve them well when applied to industry and invention.

Shaped by Viking Traders and Uncertain Soils

Sweden is a very old country. Organized in the tenth century, it was shaped by Viking aggression and warfare as well as the growth of its Russian neighbor under Peter the Great, causing Sweden to make the transition from conquering queen of the Baltic to neutralist trading nation.

The legacy of Viking traders lives on in Sweden. Driven by its small size and relative lack of a home market, Sweden has long exported its manufactured goods in search of profits. As of 1990, 80 percent of production for the twenty largest Swedish companies was sold abroad, and more than 50 percent of those companies' employees worked outside their home country.

For the Swedes, mastering their own land was good business training. Historically, Sweden's northern location meant battling natural forces such as the short three-month growing season, during which people had to gather and hoard enough food to survive the rest of the year. Life was dominated by work; relationships were created more by actions than by words. Swedes' lives were—and still are—focused on getting things done and working together.

Seasons without sun and too much rain created harsh conditions that caused the Swedes to stress the practical. They learned to engineer practical solutions and develop technical gifts. These conditions shaped their factualness, emphasis on the concrete, and need for order, planning, and pragmatism.

Proud of Their Neutrality

Susan Sontag wrote in *Letters from Sweden* that "Swedish avoidance of conflict is little short of pathological." But what Sontag saw as absurd reasonableness and passivity, Swedes consider politeness and conciliation, notes Ake Daun in *Swedish Mentality*.

Proud of their Viking heritage, Swedes are equally proud of their twentieth-century history of being peacemakers. Sweden has balanced its history of aggression with a long period of neutrality. It was, after all, the home of the originator of the Nobel Peace Prize.

Sweden remained neutral during both world wars. Its neutrality provided another bonus for Swedish businesses—there was great demand for the steel and finished industrial goods that Sweden produced during the war, and unlike other Scandinavian countries, its factories and infrastructure weren't destroyed by bombing.

More than 90 percent of Swedes are Evangelical Lutheran, and while most are secular believers, their thinking and management style is still affected by religious beliefs of submission to authority, diligence, and being reserved and quiet with an emphasis on fairness and honesty.

Officially a monarchy, Sweden—like Denmark and Norway—is among the most democratic, egalitarian countries in the world; since the 1930s it has been ruled almost exclusively by the Social Democratic Party. Characterized by ethnic homogeneity with one commonly shared language, religion, and history, Swedes are literate: they have a high rate of library borrowership, a nearly completely literate (99-plus percent) population, and a high per capita book-publishing rate. More than 27 percent of all Swedish radio broadcasts are devoted to classical music. The Swedes are also culturally literate, the result of their ability to work in collaboration, coupled with their multilingualism. But their homogeneity is changing, with an influx of refugees that has raised the non-Swedish population to around 10 percent.

Pragmatic and Compromising

Swedish culture values innovative organization, disciplined work, and high ethical standards. Swedes are analytical and reserved, and can seem somewhat unemotional.

They have a special word for cautiousness or safety—*trygghet*—and it's embedded in their national character. The strong safety record of Volvo, stringent factory safety regulations, and their plethora of smoke alarms attest to this love of safety. Yet they tend to take risks and are bold in building international businesses. Their business environments are more feminine than masculine, with a high degree of nurturing and consensus building. They value not aggression but collaboration.

"Fairness, justice, equity" are the cornerstones of a culture in which people who can afford it are willing to pay among the highest taxes in the world to take care of those less fortunate. Scandinavian countries are among the very few who give almost 1 percent of their GDP to aid needy countries, as the United Nations has asked all countries to do. Swedes have a strong sense of civic duty: in the last national election, voter turnout was 87 percent.

What has enabled the Swedes to make the most of their resources has been their pragmatic leaders, who have learned to resolve conflict between the classes creatively and to develop the vision of fair and just societies in which everyone participates and gets *lagom.*

A Business Culture Emerges

The Swedish business world is a harmonious one in which workers are paid very well and are among the world's most productive.

Sweden's labor unions—representing more than 85 percent of Swedish workers—are influential in almost all important decision making by major corporations; by law, unions must have two members on the boards of all major corporations. Their influence is balanced by strong employer organizations.

Nordic management style is characterized by planning and order, delegation of responsibility, egalitarianism, and friendship with subordinates. Like the Japanese, Swedes spend time discussing things, but when they are finished conferring, they implement their decisions quickly.

Sweden has fallen from fifth to eighteenth place in the ranking of per capita purchasing power over the past twenty years, overtaken by such countries as Ireland and Italy. Its 1998 elections highlighted a stark choice: either it would have to hit the fast-forward button—embracing radical reform in social welfare, employment rules, and foreign and security policy—or it would have to rewind, seeking to re-create the 1950s era of jobs for all and unrivaled state care. Or seek a middle ground, where the government could "look after Sweden," while reassuring big companies that it's a good place to do business.

Companies such as Ericsson—which is threatening to relocate its headquarters to London if the tax burden in Sweden isn't reduced—are watching closely.

Sweden: ***At a Glance***
Official name: Kingdom of Sweden

Economy type: European Union
Trading bloc: European Union

Location: Scandinavian peninsula of Europe; sandwiched between Norway and Finland **Capital:** Stockholm **Population:** 8,860,738
Head of state: King Carl Gustaf XVI **Official Language:** Swedish
Religion: Evangelical Lutheranism 94% **Literacy:** 99%
World GNP ranking: 23 **GDP (US$bn):** $218.7
GNP per capita: $24,674 **Unemployment:** 8.0%
Inflation: 2.2% **World export market share:** 1.6%

Major industries: Steel, machinery, precision instruments, vehicles, processed foods, shipbuilding, paper
Major crops: Grains, potatoes, sugar beets
Minerals: Zinc, iron, lead, copper, silver
Labor force: 38% social and personal services, 21% manufacturing and mining
Computers per 1,000 inhabitants: 219.4

Assets: Highly skilled labor force virtually bilingual in English. Sophisticated technology and well-developed infrastructure. Significant annual investment in R and D with high number of patents granted. Low tariffs and quotas. Managers have significant international experience. High quality of management. High product reliability. Low inflation. Low tariffs and quotas. Very effective corporate boards.

Liabilities: Uncompetitive labor costs. High taxation. Peripheral location raises costs for producers and exporters. High government spending.

As the world becomes more complex, the Swedes teach us about simplicity, practicality, and functionality. From their disciplined minds, we learn to value and measure intellectual capital in the context of collaboration and inclusiveness.

CREATE A FAST, FLEXIBLE, FOCUSED ORGANIZATION

Jean-Marie Messier and Vivendi *(France)*

Title: Chairman and CEO
Headquarters: Paris
Business: Established in 1853 by French imperial decree, it is now the world's leading distributor of water, serving 73 million people. Ranked first in Europe in waste management, Vivendi is active in three business sectors: utilities, construction and property, and communications (telecommunications, publishing, and multimedia). Vivendi's Cegetel is France's number one private telecommunications operator; Havas is France's leading publisher of books and business information. The company operates in 90 countries and has net sales of $35 billion.
Employees: 220,000

JEAN-MARIE MESSIER IS FAST. In 1996, he became CEO of Vivendi and unveiled its new name, headquarters, and business portfolio. He swept away objections of minority shareholders, put his team in place, and took over a major communications firm.

Messier is flexible. A new kind of leader, he balances authoritative and participative styles—and French and not-so-French qualities—to achieve four goals: audacity, interactivity, ethics, and social commitment.

And he is focused. He arrives early and returns to the office late, after attending the opera. He overlooks no detail in his desire to make both money and a difference.

Messier inherited a $624 million annual loss and a $9.6 billion debt. He disposed of $5.3 billion of nonessential assets, trimmed the company's workforce by 10 percent, and sealed alliances with many non-French companies. Today, Vivendi generates more than half of its net sales in international markets.

Jean-Marie Messier's vision was bold: to transform this stodgy French bureaucracy. His plan was simple: to be fast, flexible, and focused in doing it. His style was global-centric: to weave a particular pattern of French and non-French qualities into the company.

Under his leadership, the company changed its name from Compagnie Générale des Eaux to Vivendi. Easy to pronounce and remember in all languages, the name is one under which the international company can now unite.

To reform strongly and abruptly, Messier borrowed the brasher business practices of the United States. A financial wizard from his days at investment house Lazard Frères, he focused on shareholder value and acquired America's U.S. Filter to become the world's leading water supplier.

Like many French executives, Messier is highly educated and cultured. Using his French ability to manage political, economic, and personal interests, he has navigated through the murky waters of change. His transformation of Vivendi has prompted similar changes throughout France, illustrated by the many mergers and alliances occurring these days.

Today, Vivendi and Messier have become French household names, reinforced when "J2M," as he is called by collaborators, became France's Man of the Year in 1997.

Be Decisive and Participative

The French vacillate between their love of powerful leaders and authority and their passion for democracy and the power of the people. Messier personifies both. He is a bold, decisive leader—a master of constructive impatience. Truly comfortable with his power, he's known to consult, listen, and then attack. Yet as a leadership liberator, he is equally committed to the principles of participation: building teams, creating networks, and unleashing the power of young people.

Messier is simultaneously authoritative and empowering. "Monsieur Plus," as he is called by his troops, is methodical and determined. He is always on the go, an accessible, face-to-face president who protects his private life but speaks often of his five children.

Messier embodies the French love of debate. Yet his passion for change underscores his deep commitment to resolving conflicts with creative action and desired outcomes. Leaders, he feels, must not be afraid of conflict. They must confront problems head-on and navigate through interpersonal conflicts and consequences. For example, Messier deals with unions by always telling them where he is going: "I have to deal with them directly in socially innovative ways."

Organize in a Decentralized Way

Vivendi is changing quickly from an unfocused, bureaucratic conglomerate with eighty-two lines of business to a high-performance company with just three lines: utilities and construction, telecommunications, and publishing and multimedia.

"We sold assets, reshuffled groups of businesses and people, and are now a group of services, not an industrial group," says Messier. "As quickly as possible, we want to be the global company for utilities and a European company in communications. To achieve these goals, we must find new ways to organize and new ways to network people and skills." With his bold, brash strategy, Messier emphasizes the social management of restructuring: internal job transfers, flexible work hours, early retirement, and increased job mobility among companies, business sectors, and countries.

He wants to be flexible enough to take advantage of new ideas in different parts of the group. "Our Internet, telecommunications, and TV teams work together because it's important for us to use these media as interchangeable distribution channels." This group has had double-digit growth every year as a result.

"By playing businesses off one another, we gain a competitive advantage," he explains. "We can't achieve that through a classical, hierarchical organization. It takes a ground-level network of talent and people close to the final customer. In the service arena, the most efficient companies will be ones able to create new services and businesses at the frontiers, the borderlines of their existing businesses."

To ensure this flexibility, people need to know the rules inside the company. "To be flexible today, you have to organize in a very decentralized way," says Messier. "But decentralized doesn't mean independence—it means autonomy. Independence means pursuing your own targets, while autonomy means that you're in charge of your own business but are judged by the same criteria as others. And if people don't follow the rules, there must be consequences."

To be fast, Vivendi needed to shed some national baggage: "We were too French in our way of doing things. We have taken steps to internationalize the management of the company." In the last two years, its foreign investors have grown from 30 percent to over 45 percent. "Those investors understand and respect our strategy as a global, and not just a French, company. But being global doesn't mean you don't have roots. We're quite proud of our European roots."

Invest in Young People

Messier is a big fan of young people. In his mid-forties, a youthful adult by French standards, he shows it through his commitment to hiring young people as an investment in Vivendi's future. Recently he met with five thousand newly hired young people to personally reinforce the company's welcome and answer any questions about the business. "Our future depends on these globally focused young people. Young French managers are much more international than the previous generation," he explains. "Fifteen years ago, we had to speak French at our management meetings—that's not the case anymore."

He clearly walks the talk. By signing a Global Social Reintegration Agreement with the French government, Messier committed to recruiting 7,300 young people under thirty years of age over a two-year period, the equivalent of ten young people a day every day of those twenty-four months. For all the massive change, "our commitment to hire young people is the best investment I've made since I've been here," Messier acknowledges. He also knows that hiring them isn't enough—he has to create a modern corporate culture in which young people want to work.

As a service business, Messier believes, Vivendi needs to help create "social coherence." "Priority should be given to the betterment of the quality of life in society and inside the business," he explains. In the case of Vivendi, this means supporting the thirty-five-hour workweek, hiring youths, and helping outcasts.

"People are becoming more and more strangers to their companies, with less personal commitment. Leaders need to spend more time helping people understand where the company is going, so they know the company cares what they think and feel." He works hard to achieve that right balance.

Messier knows that the proof is in the pudding: "The right strategy is not when you're expressing it. It's several years after . . . it's the last thing, the results."

COUNTRIES WITH THE MOST INTERNATIONAL EMPLOYEES

(Percentage of companies with employees in ten or more countries)

- France: 72%
- Germany: 59%
- Australia: 58%
- Netherlands: 54%
- Sweden: 50%
- New Zealand: 50%
- South Korea: 48%
- United Kingdom: 45%
- Singapore: 44%
- United States: 34%
- Mexico: 31%
- Brazil: 28%
- Philippines: 27%

CHAPTER NINE

NETWORKS

How Do We Work Together?

ORGANIZATIONS ARE LESS BRICK AND MORTAR and more communities of networks these days. Our companies are on-line now, from employee communications and customer sales to inventory management and supplier purchasing. This networked world is by definition an open, transparent world.

Leaders must be community builders. By creating a climate of trust and teamwork, they focus on three key strategies: managing knowledge, developing networks, and building alliances.

- *Managing knowledge.* Globally literate leaders know that knowledge is a strategic asset and source of competitive advantage. They must collect, assimilate, disseminate, and utilize knowledge, not accumulate information. By mining databases, distributing information rapidly, and developing intranet technology, they actively manage knowledge and build knowledge networks.
- *Developing networks.* Leaders must develop a networking capability across the entire company, creating webs of interaction that link people, information, and technology. This requires great skill in communications, relationship building, conflict management, and team learning. Globally literate managers know how to develop these networks and relationships.
- *Building alliances.* Globally literate leaders know how to link their businesses with the outside world of experts and resources. They leverage key external relationships through alliances, joint ventures, and partnerships with competitors, product developers, distributors, and marketers—all to foster collaborative research, marketing agreements, and joint ventures. These leaders use outsourcing to improve flexibility and create new ideas, and are obsessed with getting suppliers, customers, and employees to work together.

The ultimate challenge for globally literate leaders is to build multicultural, cross-functional teams across organizational boundaries. To do that, they need people who use all of the four literacies at all times.

In this chapter, we will meet leaders who are grappling with the question of how we work together: Coles Myer CEO Dennis Eck in Australia teaches us to engage people's hearts and minds; Tractebel CEO Philippe Bodson in Belgium shows us how to forge strong management teams; Jardine Pacific CEO Blair Pickerall in China urges us to be civil in high speed environments; San Miguel CEO Andres Soriano in the Philippines describes how to form global alliances; and New Zealand Dairy Board CEO Warren Larsen shows us a blueprint for building global business teams. We'll hear from China Resources CEO Madame Zhu Youlan, who tells us about the mind of a Chinese leader. Half a world away, in Venezuela, we'll meet Cisneros Group CEO Gustavo Cisneros, a master of partnering.

ENGAGE PEOPLE'S HEARTS AND MINDS
Dennis Eck and Coles Myer Ltd. *(Australia)*

Title: Managing Director and CEO
Headquarters: Melbourne
Business: Largest Australian retailer with annual sales of over $19 billion. Operates over 1,900 retail, discount, and specialty stores, including Coles and Bi-Lo supermarkets, Myer Grace Bros. Department stores, Kmart and Target discount stores, and is moving into Internet-based shopping. Is the country's largest nongovernment employer and one of the country's largest corporate philanthropists.
Employees: 148,346 employees in Australia and New Zealand

"I CAME HERE WITH NO SCAR TISSUE—I didn't know the company and had never been to Australia—so I was completely objective. What I found was the 'calcification of success,' where you no longer question decisions because they were once successful."

"Here" is Coles Myer, Australia's largest employer. The "I" is Dennis Eck, an American who became CEO of an almost one-hundred-year-old company rocked by scandal and record low employee morale. His story is important to leaders rescuing troubled divisions and businesses.

Eck knew that, given the company's bumpy past, he needed to rebuild trust and optimism, overcome the victim mentality, reengage employees in the present, and mobilize them toward a better future. He knew he had to develop a contract with employees for mutual benefit, rebuild the tarnished relationship between employees and company, and combine authoritative and empowering leadership skills to move forward.

He began to painstakingly knit back together the self-esteem of the company to achieve its goal of being "the best retailer in every market."

Build Self-Esteem Through Trust

Faced with high turnover at every level, Eck had to put meaning and "livelihood" back into the business. He wanted to give aisles in the supermarkets back to people so they could feel a sense of accomplishment.

He didn't come in with a new management team: "The talent we needed was already there. There was so much untapped potential in the business that almost any agenda for improvement would lead to early success. Any leader who thinks he can rebuild confidence with a speech is fooling himself. We had a hundred years of strong brands and quality people; I knew the problem wasn't with our people but with what the people were being asked to do." His trust was infectious.

Eck described his desired outcomes and mutual expectations. "We had to overcome the victim mentality and get people to rely on themselves to find the problems and create the solutions," he says.

There's a saying in Australia that the tall poppy gets cut down. Eck doesn't adhere to that philosophy of modesty; he thinks people should take credit for good work. "They need to shine and own the problems in order to own the solutions," he says.

In 1997 he urged a managing director to hold a staff meeting and ask his people, "When's the last time you felt good about coming to work?" "Just stand there and wait as long as it takes for people to come up with answers," he told the manager. "It might seem like a lifetime, but someone will answer." And answer they did. After much prolonged silence, a voice answered quietly from the back of the hall. "Nineteen seventy-eight," it said.

The transition began at that point. Trust was being rebuilt.

Develop a Contract for Mutual Benefit

Eck needed to create a contract with employees for mutual benefit. His Scandinavian ancestry may account for part of his collaborative nature—and his knowledge that collaboration builds commitment. He started by telling employees that the company was broken—and that he needed their help to fix it.

He designed a process for change that engaged the employees of Coles Myer and showed his belief in them. "We're dying to be fixed," he told them, "and you have my commitment that whatever you decide to do, I'll support it. It just has to be consensual, and it has to address a consumer, employee, or supplier need."

Australia, Eck realized, is a land of rugged individualists where people speak their minds and pride themselves on defying authority. "I went to the people and said, 'Look, I'm going to promise each of you one thing: we're going to bet on each other, that we're smart and talented enough to make this work."

Decisions had to be based on a mutual understanding of the business. "Reengineering has actually destroyed loyalty and emotional involvement," says Eck. "Self-esteem is a big piece of the contract between employer and employee. And the trust and respect I offer people must be balanced by our mutual commitment to performance, our clear delineation of desired outcomes and expectations." He reminds us that a mutual contract depends, in large part, on reciprocity, on "making promises and keeping them."

To engender a true reciprocity between business and employee, Eck gives people true responsibility and accountability—and he stays firmly in charge.

Set Boundaries and Stay in Charge

Leadership, Eck feels, must be authoritative and empowering at the same time: "First, when you're defining a problem, you have to create an open and democratic process. To solve it, you must create an authoritative process that defines for people what they have to do." He knows that people want independence—and they also want to depend on a power bigger than themselves.

"I initially traveled around with our top four supermarket executives to show them, not tell them, what I was thinking. I realized it wasn't what I wanted to do that was important—it was what they wanted to do. The only thing I asked during the trip was that they take notes without making judgments.

"When we got back, I put them in a conference room and said I didn't care how long it took—a week or six months, it didn't matter—but I wanted them to stay in that room until they could agree on recommendations they would make to me."

Four weeks later, they came back to Eck. "Before we start," he said to them, "let me ask you three questions: Has everyone had a chance to fully express their point of view? Is your decision unanimous? And if you go back on what you're about to tell me, will you agree that you've not just let yourself down, you've let your colleagues down, too?" By giving them free rein while clearly outlining his expectations, Eck developed a unique contract among the team.

When Coles Myer set out to launch its flagship sporting goods store in Melbourne, he continued that strategy by involving people in developing the vision. But he insisted they become business-literate: "Well-run businesses are complete thoughts, and managers must think in those terms.

"For example, in our Melbourne store, we focused on complete thoughts. I told them I wanted them to create the best sporting goods store. Then I let them know that it had to be finished in just fourteen weeks for the Christmas season. They beat that deadline by a day." Once the standard is set through empowerment, Eck says, democracy must become autocracy: "You let them decide what you're willing to let them decide."

Eck's philosophy balances empowerment with authority: "The safest structure is totally authoritative because as long as you don't get outside any of the boundaries, you can't be touched. The least safe is when people can't deal with coming to work because they don't know the boundaries. You have to find a balance between the two scenarios."

Eck is quick to give the credit to employees. "Leadership," he says, "is always defined by the followers."

FORGE STRONG MANAGEMENT TEAMS THAT THRIVE ON HONEST DIALOGUE

Baron Philippe Bodson and Tractebel *(Belgium)*

Title: CEO
Headquarters: Brussels
Business: Tractebel was founded to build streetcar lines all over the world, hence its name: "Tracte" from traction, "bel" from Belgium. An international utility and industrial services group with operations in distributing electricity and gas, waste management, technical installations, engineering, communications, and real estate, Tractebel operates in more than 100 countries worldwide.
Employees: 60,000

SCIENCE PROVIDES THE METAPHORS *for how Philippe Bodson wants Tractebel to operate: "When I was studying to be an engineer, we learned the theory of ideal gases. The image of millions of gas particles hitting against one another has stuck with me all these years; what impressed me was that the particles move at random, actually making the behavior of the whole gas very predictable. That's exactly what I want. I want everything to move, and I know if we are numerous enough and are confronting our ideas, we'll go in the direction I want."*

It's no accident that we derive the word "gas" from the ancient Latin word chaos. *It's this comfort with chaos and ambiguity—and this urge toward action—that characterizes Bodson. The molecules, in Bodson's case, are his strong management team. He knows that its members must be open, diverse, direct, honest, and constantly moving to survive in these chaotic times.*

Baron Philippe Bodson is a hard-charging, and pragmatic man. He's survival-oriented, multilingual, and a global businessman in one of the most international cities in the world. He's also well rested.

"If you don't believe in what you're doing, you're dead. For me, the major quality of a leader is to be able to sleep at night whatever happens. I never lose sleep. Even if the problems are terrible, I go home, go to bed, and fall asleep."

It's a restfulness that comes with honesty and straight talk.

Belgium is a flat border country long subject to invasion and one struggling with tensions among three subcultures: the Dutch-influenced family businesses of the Flemings, the French-influenced managerial firms of the Walloons, and the English-influenced multinationals of Brussels.

In this highly commercial environment, Bodson steps outside that dynamic of subcultures to create a company without borders. "The secret to my success is in creating a strong, global management team and building the capacity of that team to argue, create conflict, and build consensus. Our goal is simple: 'Tractebel, know-how without frontiers.' "

He achieves the vision by building a culture where it's okay to say "I don't know" and in which he and his team are as comfortable in the chaos of the moving particles—such as entering a new international market—as they are in the pattern of the final product.

Find Patterns in Chaos

In the new, somewhat chaotic environment of deregulation, Bodson is seeking to find pattern in chaos by developing four strategies: cost control, improved customer service, extended partnerships with municipalities, and a new company structure where each operation has real freedom to make its own decisions. He knows it's his strong management team that makes all four strategies possible.

Bodson constantly seeks clarity and patterns. So does his home country, which might account for Belgium's extensive highway network, so well lit that it's the second most distinctive man-made sight from outer space, after the Great Wall of China. To his training in the precise art of the engineer, Bodson added the art of forging metals, building new, stronger composites through synthesis.

"My degree in engineering and metallurgy really shaped my mind," he says. "It gave me the tools to be analytical, but also to synthesize large bits of information, one of the most difficult skills to learn. Most people are either analysts or synthesizers, one or the other, but not both." Like a metallurgist, Bodson can boldly dissect and analyze problems and put the pieces together differently to create a new amalgam: "My skill is listening to the reasoning of others, and splitting their logic into very small pieces. When I've heard everyone, I put those things back together, differently, for a new solution.

"I'm comfortable changing my mind in front of others. I think that shows humility, not weakness. I make strong, bold decisions, but I can also stand up and say I was wrong or that I don't know something. It's a form of commitment to the whole company. That's a valuable lesson for others to see, too. Seeing me stand up and admit mistakes makes it easier for them to do the same."

This high tolerance for risk is a key value for Bodson. "We just want to make sure that risk isn't fatal," says Bodson, remembering one of his executives who killed himself when called back from an international assignment because he wasn't making the necessary cultural adjustments. "I have to make sure that in pushing people, I don't give them the feeling that if they miss or if they fail, they're dead." As a result, he constantly balances his aggressiveness with benevolence.

Create Conflict to Find the Truth

"My greatest talent is my capacity to argue in a way that creates consensus. I hate one-on-one meetings, but I love meetings with ten to fifteen people where everyone talks and we put things on the board. If debate doesn't take place, then I make it happen. I push until they react. I want people to speak their mind. That's why I create conflict in meetings. My job is to unveil truth around the table."

Bodson's frankness and direct communication style set the example for a strong management team that is honest and has the capacity to learn in real time around the table, something that's not always comfortable. "I'll argue like hell to defend my point of view—and they know it. Even if I don't have a point of view on a particular subject, I'll play the Devil's advocate. If you're good enough, you're going to go against me. And that's not aggressive; it's just part of the game.

"It's illusionary to think you have no conflicts. What's more, when my people try to push an idea forward and I push back, they're really testing me. They want me to challenge them, even if they don't realize it. If I don't, they'll lose confidence in me." Bodson pushes, but he tempers that bluntness with a fairness, a caring, and an honesty that build the trust necessary for his team to operate so candidly.

By being frank and straightforward—and thoroughly Belgian in doing so—Bodson brings people together around common visions and provides the catalyst for honest conversations. Over the years, he's developed a process for unveiling truth around the table, one that starts with confrontation—confrontation with limits, that is. "I have to know," he says, "when my role is to move the conflict forward and how to manage my own anxiety." He's truer to his university upbringing than even he realizes: like metal and ideal gases, Bodson's team is made stronger by being forged in heat—in this case, the heat of confrontation.

Forge the Right Team

"Leadership is like a soup," Bodson says. "It must be a good mixture of different qualities. I like to surround myself with leaders, people who think differently than me and who will fight back. Finding the right people to run our business is one of our greatest challenges. I would expand faster overseas if I could find the right people to run the projects.

"As a team, we're constantly asking ourselves if we're making the right decision," Bodson says. "That means that we're agile, always moving back and forth from strategy to operation and rethinking our strategy even while we're working it. If there's an opportunity we think is good, bang, we go, even if it's outside our strategy. Our operation in Quebec is one example. We didn't plan to be there, but we have an advantage because we speak French, and we said to ourselves 'Why not?' and we went.

"To be agile like that, we have to be able to talk plainly and openly about the strategy. We have to be competent. We have to be committed to the vision of the company, confident in our decisions, and consistent. When the decision is made, no matter what side we're on, we have to walk out that door and support the decision—until experience tells us we need to rethink our strategy."

Those four Cs—competence, commitment, confidence, and consistency—are the basis of Bodson's leadership strategy. To those, add creativity, chaos, confrontation, and clarity.

Bodson shows his personal literacy in the way he constantly seeks honesty from himself and is comfortable with his own uncertainties. He enjoys the messiness of people and organizations, thriving on the energies and anxieties of teamwork to express his social literacy. He mobilizes Tractebel with a business literacy that demands honest dialogue at the table, and his cultural literacy shines through the clear reflection of his multilingual, frank, and pragmatic Belgian roots.

There is order in chaos; the random actions of gas particles are one example of that, as are the heated discussions around the Tractebel conference tables. Those head-to-head meetings allow a powerful management team to bump up against one another's ideas and—much like refining a metal such as stainless steel—make the company stronger through its forging procedure.

Consistent with Belgium's history of invasions, French firm Suez Lyonnaise des Eaux swept in and bought the 49.7 percent of Tractebel shares it did not already own. In the process, Baron Philippe Bodson was ousted by Suez. Yet in the typical spirit of finding order in chaos, Bodson went on to take advantage of this situation and was elected Senator in Belgium in 1999.

BELGIUM: "Pragmatic Survivors"

Belgians are masters of pragmatism, comfortable with uncertainty, and able to find creative solutions for almost any problem—skills they've developed to survive three thousand years of invasion and foreign occupation.

A WALK THROUGH BRUSSELS might prove more bewildering than you think—if you don't read Flemish, French, or both. A festoon of multilingual signs, each receiving equal space, colors the streets of this international city, reflecting the multilingual, multiethnic, multicultural world of Belgium.

Belgian culture is focused on commerce, shaped by foreign invasions, and divided by internal cultural distinctions—seen not only in the traffic signs but at almost every turn, including newspapers, churches, and businesses.

Shaped by Invasions

Belgium has been described as an accident of history, made up of the left-over Catholic pieces of Western Europe. Conquered by Julius Caesar in 57 B.C.E., the Belgians have been invaded ever since, making them critical of any form of authority and laws.

It was Belgium's flatness, rivers, and ease of access that invited the Spanish, Austrians, French, and Dutch to invade it; it is this same geography that connects Belgium to the heart of Europe, making it a choice location for foreign multinationals.

Divided by Language and Culture

Though united in its opposition to outside invasion, Belgium is internally divided into three distinct areas, cultures, and languages. Flanders, in the north, is home to the Flemings, the 55 percent of the population who speak Flemish, called "Dutch with an accent" by some. The Walloons in the south make up 35 percent of the population and speak French.

The remaining 10 percent live in the bilingual city of Brussels. Though the city is situated in Flanders, more than 65 percent of its population is actually French-speaking, an island of French in a sea of Flemish, in a country where most Walloons cannot speak Flemish and most Flemings refuse to speak French. Add to the linguistic noise a small border strip of people who speak German, making that one of Belgium's official languages even though the German speakers make up less than 1 percent of the population.

Wallonia was historically considered the wealthy manufacturing center of Belgium, in a world where language determined class distinctions: Flemish was considered the language of servants, French the language of the middle class. But when the country's mining, steel, and textiles industries collapsed in the 1970s, the tables turned, causing even more divisiveness by upsetting a long history of Walloon superiority and Flemish resentment. Flanders took the lead and began to dominate the economic life of Belgium, a transition coloring every aspect of Belgian life, including business.

The "three pillars" of Belgian society—Catholic, socialist, and liberal—are themselves split into Flemish and Walloon factions. Each language group has a political party, labor movement, unions, newspapers, and so forth. Not even the names of companies are immune. If a company is Flemish, the initials after its name are either NV, for a public company, or BVBA, if private. Walloons designate their companies either SA or SPRL.

And it's not just history, economics, and language but also culture that separates Flemings and Walloons. The Walloons are culturally like the French, whose language they share. Hierarchical in business, they are formal and comfortable with directive leadership, rules, and rank. The Flemings are like their Dutch cousins: practical and hardworking, they prefer flatter organizations with less emphasis on titles; they value participative leadership and an individualistic approach.

Versed in Compromise

It is said that Belgians define themselves as Flemish or Walloon first, European second, and Belgian third, yet there are typically Belgian traits that spring from this divided culture, such as a pragmatism in which solutions are based on compromise. A special phrase was coined for this approach: "a Belgian compromise" is the typical way in which solutions are reached—by conceding something to every party concerned.

Take abortion, for example. Normally, all laws accepted by the Belgian Parliament must be signed by the king before they can be applied. In the case of the law legalizing abortion, former King Baudouin couldn't approve it on religious grounds. To solve his dilemma, he simply declared himself incapable to rule for just one day, long enough to pass the law without his signature—a pragmatic solution to even the most sensitive of issues.

Belgium: ***At a Glance***
Official name: Kingdom of Belgium

Economy type: European Union
Trading bloc: European Union

Location: Between Germany, France, and the Netherlands
Capital: Brussels **Population:** 10,174,922
Head of state: King Albert II **Official languages:** Flemish (Dutch), French, German **Religion:** Roman Catholic 75%, Protestant and other 25% **Literacy:** 99%
World GNP ranking: 20 **GDP (US$ bn):** $234.7
GDP per capita: $23,090 **Unemployment:** 13.6%
Inflation: 1.3% **World export market share:** 2.9%

Major industries: Metal products, glassware, autos, textiles, chemicals
Major crops: Wheat, fruits, sugar beets, potatoes
Minerals: Coal, gas
Labor force: 70% services, 27% industry, 3% agriculture
Computers per 1,000 inhabitants: 166.6

Assets: Skilled, productive workforce. High trade volume as percentage of GDP. Many patents granted. Good worker education in basic science. Good foreign language skills. Excellent harbors and inland waterways. Attractive interest rates. Managers have solid international experience and foreign language skills.

Liabilities: Unemployment rate remains high. Europe's largest public debt. Huge governmental bureaucracy. Tax evasion remains high. Income tax rate on individuals is high. Political polarization between Flemings and Walloons.

Adaptability, flexibility, intellectual humility, a talent for improvisation, and an avoidance of dogmatism set Belgians apart from their immediate neighbors and are traits that surface again and again in their home and business lives. Belgians traditionally have been more concerned with finding a solution than winning an argument, but this is changing as their internal language and cultural conflicts alter their style of solving problems.

Experience gained in tiptoeing around their intricate multiparty, multilingual, and multicultural problems has led to an unlikely new export product: Belgian political expertise. It has also led to Belgium's central role in the European Union.

A Business Culture Emerges

Brussels personifies Belgium's national drive for commerce. While invasions made one use of Belgian geography, this passion for business has made more profitable use of those same rivers and flatlands, spawning three types of companies in the process: the familial enterprise (Flanders), the managerial enterprise (Walloon), and the multinational enterprise (Brussels).

Leon Trotsky once described what he called "Belgianization—the abandonment of national responsibility in favor of total commercial values." Combine Trotsky's Belgianization with an urge toward democracy, and you have created a business environment shaped by a "democratic" attitude. Unlike most industrialized nations, Belgium has experienced an enormous growth of union membership since World War II, up from 30 percent in 1945 to 70 percent in the 1990s. This urge toward democracy also leads Belgians to make little distinction between classes or social strata, an egalitarian philosophy that results in the lowest percentage of poor people in the world and the world's most productive workers because of extended automatization, highly skilled labor, shift work that minimizes idle time, and low absenteeism.

Belgium's potential weaknesses? In a country whose industry is dominated by engineers, people may spend too little time thinking about what they make and too much on how it is made. The many foreign rules, skepticism towards authority, and internal linguistic split have led to a relative lack of national pride and self-confidence. Belgium may well be one of the least nationalistic countries in the world, which means that those of us outside may lack a clear image of the country.

In a world where cultures and economies are bumping against one another, the Belgians teach us to be adaptive and flexible. Their improvising mindset and creative problem solving show us how to navigate through the inevitable conflicts of commercialism, though admittedly, their current ethnic and linguistic conflicts are testing this skill.

PURSUE THE POWER OF PARTNERING
Gustavo A. Cisneros and the Cisneros Group of Companies *(Venezuela)*

Title: Chairman and CEO
Headquarters: Caracas
Business: Begun in the 1930s when the family patriarch, Diego Cisneros, operated passenger buses in Caracas before entering the soft drink business. Now one of Latin America's largest conglomerates, with annual revenues of more than $3.2 billion. Companies include TV and radio networks, telecommunications operations, production companies, supermarket chains, beverages, fast foods, and video franchises, with a total of 70 companies in 39 countries in Latin America, the Caribbean, Europe, and North America.
Employees: More than 35,000

GUSTAVO CISNEROS IS CONNECTED, *both literally and figuratively.*

One of only seven people from Latin America on Vanity Fair *magazine's recent list of the sixty-five most influential people in the world, Cisneros was in the company of five country presidents.*

As CEO of Latin America's media powerhouse, the Cisneros Group of Companies (CGC), he's often called the Rupert Murdoch of the Spanish-speaking Western Hemisphere. His Univision is already the largest Spanish-speaking television network in the United States. With Hughes Electronics, CGC is a partner in Galaxy Latin America, leading providers of direct-to-home satellite service to Latin America. And he recently brought AOL to his region, unleashing the power of the Internet on this irresistible market—from Mexico through Argentina and Chile there are 452 million people, with a growing middle class.

Cisneros has a strong, unifying vision to guide the organization: to become one of the most dynamic, forward-looking broadcast, media, and entertainment conglomerates in the world. It's a vision that must connect people inside and outside the company and can be made possible only through building partnerships with others, like AOL.

"Our alliance with America Online was designed to bring the world's largest Internet service to Latin America. We're leveraging our experience in this market with AOL's unparalleled expertise in top-notch Internet services." Other corporate partners include Disney, Motorola, Hearst Corporation, Blockbuster, Virgin Records, Spalding, and even Playboy. Sometimes these partnerships mean that players find themselves cooperating in one venture and competing in another—such as CGC's Pizza Hut franchise in Venezuela, owned by Pepsi-Cola, a competitor of its Coca-Cola operations there.

Some CGC partnerships show Cisneros's deep sense of social responsibility. In conjunction with partners including Microsoft Corporation, the Cisneros Group is developing a satellite-based teacher-training program to enhance the skills of more than 1,800 primary school teachers in 115 schools in Latin America. Cisneros is clearly committed to learning. A major collector and benefactor, he's also committed to art and culture.

And he forms partnerships not just on a personal and corporate level but also on a national scale, having received Spain's Order of Isabel La Católica, conferred by His Majesty King Juan Carlos I, for strengthening international ties between Venezuela and Spain.

Create Partnerships in a Multicultural World

To lead in this networked world, Cisneros needs people with new competencies, able to keep abreast of new markets, move swiftly to capitalize on promising opportunities, explore synergies with strategic partners, and create environments for loyal, creative employees. Chief among them are partnering skills.

"Partnering," he emphasizes, "is key to our successful international expansion. It means being business-savvy and pragmatic to identify those times when it makes most sense to work with a business partner whose strength, insight, and experience can complement our credentials. Our challenge is to integrate the cultural differences of our expansive network of business partners."

The Cisneros Group's expertise is in the Ibero-American market, comprising Spanish- and Portuguese-speaking populations in the Americas and the Iberian Peninsula. "It's a market with a common language and culture," Cisneros says. "Relatively young and one of the most populated regions in the world, it has almost half a billion people and an improving economic

DO YOUR CULTURAL ROOTS INFLUENCE YOUR THINKING?

(Percentage of executives responding positively)

- Latin America: 75%
- Europe: 67%
- Asia: 62%
- Australia/New Zealand: 54%
- North America: 51%

Venezuela: ***At a Glance***
Official name: Republic of Venezuela

Economy type: Latin American
Trading bloc: Andean Group

Location: Located on the northern coast of South America
Capital: Caracas **Population:** 22,803,409
Head of state: President Hugo Chávez **Official language:** Spanish
Religion: Roman Catholic 96% **Literacy:** 91%
World GNP ranking: 41 **GDP (US$ bn):** $81.2
GDP per capita: $3,625. **Unemployment:** 6.6%
Inflation: 52.7% **World export market share:** 0.6%

Major industries: Iron mining, steel, oil products, textiles
Major crops: Rice, corn, sorghum, bananas, sugar
Minerals: Oil, gas, aluminum, iron, gold
Labor force: 64% services, 23% industrial, 13% agricultural
Computers per 1,000 people: 21.4

Assets: High government savings rate. Low income tax rate for individuals. General government surplus. Good location. Possesses the largest oil reserves outside the Middle East and Commonwealth of Independent States. Significant reserves of natural resources. The world's most efficient and productive producer of aluminum. Enjoys considerable foreign investment, particularly from the United States and Japan.

Liabilities: High inflation and unemployment. Infrastructure requires modernization. Lack of environmental regulations. Corruption is being tackled but remains a problem. High tax evasion rate. Difficult bureaucracy. State-run industries are overmanned and inefficient. Stability of governmental and financial sectors is questionable. Little governmental commitment to R&D spending. Ineffective use of high technology to increase global competitiveness.

and political landscape. I view Ibero-America as one market, comparable to the European Union but bound more closely by language and culture."

The company's experiences in Latin America offer lessons for the rest of the world: "Throughout history, Latin American countries have faced considerable adversity, from bouts of economic depression to the remnants of colonialism, a history that has provided us with a great impetus to overcome adversity. We've applied this historical lesson to the global marketplace, learning to compete on a par with more established, better-equipped international players. This dedication to excel, despite these shortcomings, is one of the dominant traits of Latin American multinational enterprises."

Cisneros is fully aware of Venezuela's strengths and shortcomings. It is a highly class- and status-conscious country with authoritarian leadership styles and stability provided by the Roman Catholic Church. Family is the country's most important institution; extended families are the norm, and the best interests of the family take first priority in this largely male-dominated and relationship-driven society. Though rich in natural resources and with relatively cheap skilled labor, Venezuela suffers from high inflation, unemployment, corruption, bureaucracy, and inefficient state-run companies. Yet it grows leaders like Cisneros who both mirror and modernize their national roots.

"We have a determination to put Latin America on the map," he says. "We're fully committed to bringing the best the world has to offer to Ibero-America and the best of Ibero-America to the world."

BE CIVIL IN A HIGH-SPEED ENVIRONMENT
Blair Pickerall and Jardine Pacific *(China)*

Title: President
Headquarters: Hong Kong
Business: Founded in Canton, China, in 1832, it was dubbed "The Noble House" by novelist James Clavell, amassing riches in the early years by feeding the Chinese appetite for opium. It gave up narcotics long ago but continues to amass fortunes. The largest private-sector employer in Asia, bringing brand names such as Ikea, Pizza Hut, and Caterpillar into the region. The wholly owned trading and services arm of Jardine Matheson Group has interests in five industries: marketing and distribution, engineering and construction, aviation and shipping services, property services, and financial services. Operates in partnership with companies such as British Airways, Canon, Bacardi-Martini, and Trane. Has operations in more than 20 countries.
Employees: Jardine Pacific has more than 70,000 employees; the parent company, Jardine Matheson, has more than 200,000 employees

In 1820, two Scottish merchants met in Bombay; twelve years later, they traveled to China to start Jardine, Matheson & Company in Canton. One of them—James Matheson—played a major role in founding Hong Kong just four years later. The company moved there in the 1840s and "grew up" with Hong Kong.

The Asian "arm" of Jardine Matheson, Jardine Pacific is really the "cul-

tural home" of the larger company, says CEO Blair Pickerall, and it provides the most profits for the company as a whole. It is a proud, trustworthy, and traditional company with generations of long-tenured employees and a glamorous name in the Asian region. It means a lot to work for Jardine, says Pickerall.

"We are called," he says, "either the most Western Asian company or the most Asian Western company."

Blair Pickerall uses social and cultural literacy to operate in Asia. He is an American who combines the company's British and Scottish heritage with Chinese philosophy to build networks both inside and outside the company. Married to a Chinese woman, he is a permanent resident of Hong Kong, where his children were born. He is an intense, fast-moving forty-two-year-old who personifies speed and civility. His uniqueness—and that of Jardine Pacific—is the ability to operate as a traditional Hong Kong company with speed and urgency while retaining the integrity, civility, and politeness of the British.

Respect, relationships, and loyalty matter in this company. "Putting the Jardine label on your calling card matters both in personal pride and customer value," Pickerall explains. "We're in fast food, guarding, cleaning, and building management. If you work for the world's biggest cleaning company, it doesn't go down real well when you go to the dinner party at the neighbors'. But 'I work for Jardine's' is powerful."

To capitalize on this reputation, Pickerall knows that Jardine Pacific must stay fast and flexible, walk before it runs, and be polite no matter what.

Stay Fast and Flexible

The company experienced a drastic downturn in 1997 because of the Asian economic crisis. But what has fueled Asia's growth in recent years—an industrious workforce, an entrepreneurial drive, high levels of personal savings, and a commitment to education—remains intact, and Jardine Pacific has confidence in the long-term prosperity of the region.

It has learned to adapt to changing regional conditions. By being flexible, it has been able to change its strategy from producing products to providing services, recognize that expertise matters more than geography, and apply its long-standing expertise in China to today's markets.

Pickerall knows that speed is critical and can be either a weapon or a risk in this highly deregulated region. Companies must use speed to differentiate themselves, hire good people quickly, and respond to new competition, he says. The environment demands it. "We've gone from one telephone company a few years ago to four land-based telephone companies and roughly ten to twelve mobile ones, all for one city and all in the last five years. If you're building your network and client base, you can't sit around and take your time."

But Pickerall isn't seduced by speed for speed's sake.

Walk Before You Run

Running a business is always a balancing act. Pickerall has to balance speed with deliberation to achieve the right acceleration for the company. It has to walk before it can run; he matches opposite skills to ensure that happens.

Finding the right pace is a great challenge. "I spend half of my time getting some people to go faster and the other half of my time getting others to slow down. Hong Kong draws people who are fast and focused," he notes. "Some need a kick, and others need to be bridled."

Pickerall's recent words of advice to an employee outline the company's philosophy: "I want you to run as fast as you can. Money isn't a problem; we've got all the financing you need to grow the business, but don't do eight new ventures at once. Do two. And when you've got any one of them up and running smoothly for six months, by all means do the next one.

"Where do we stumble?" he asks. "Usually by being too entrepreneurial. You can't quite keep all the balls in the air."

Pickerall tailors the right speed to the right situation, and he matches opposite skills to ensure that people slow one another down long enough to make more balanced decisions and prevent stupid mistakes. "In Asia, it's hard to find well-rounded general managers who are great at everything. We often match a Westerner with an Asian to get skills, strengths, and weaknesses that dovetail perfectly. Or we'll match finance and marketing guys—the salesmen move quickly, and the finance guys put on the brakes."

In some ways, the company itself is a match of opposite skills: "This is the merger of the good administrative skills, the carefulness, and the internal audit mindset of the good Scottish accountant combined with a get-up-and-go Chinese businessman."

To be successful, the company must be expert not only in the industry but in the country as well. Jardine Pacific excels at translating cultures, even down to the items on the menus of its restaurants: "We've switched from being the classic product trader to being a service trader. In the old days, we might be the agent for a brand of beer; now we're creating our own Pizza Hut menus for these markets. You don't have soups on Pizza Hut menus in the States; we have soups. We have something called Spaghetti Americana that looks like a can of peas and carrots dumped into spaghetti and mixed up—we sold three thousand miles of it last year. Half of the pizzas have Thousand Island dressing on them. We sell a lot of eel pizza. We told Pizza Hut, 'Don't object when we start serving chicken feet on the menu.' "

Sometimes Jardine Pacific has to fight to get these kinds of local accommodations; even though it knows the local market best, it has to educate their partners. "We had a long running battle with IKEA, the Swedish furniture company. They had this ingrained idea that you have to build a big box in the potato fields, with a thousand parking spaces around it. And we put our small IKEA smack in the middle of Causeway Bay with no parking spaces. 'This isn't IKEA, you've violated the concept,' they said. And that store is second in the world for sales per square foot." He smiles.

The company uses that formula of knowing the local market to run its business in thirty cities in mainland China with seventy joint ventures and 15,000 employees. It's extremely knowledgeable about Chinese culture and people, but it still finds it hard to "get past the mayor." "China's a tough place to do business and a hard place to make money," Pickerall explains, "partially because of entry barriers and partially because of partnership issues. Westerners are seduced by the 'Chinese dream syndrome,' thinking that they can sell a shirt to everybody in China."

Be Polite

Everybody loves action and results. But what are the consequences of so much speed? In Hong Kong, speed must be balanced with a focus on people. Hong Kong "has no natural resources, is basically populated with refugees, and is as capitalist as they come. Hong Kong is all about people," Pickerall says. Jardine Pacific mirrors that focus by investing in relationships and looking after its staff.

The first competency Jardine Pacific looks for is nothing less than politeness: "Human skills, politeness, a reasonable level of English. Not much

COUNTRIES WITH THE MOST INTERNATIONAL BOARDS

(Percentage of board members who are not citizens of company's home country)

- Hong Kong: 44%
- South Korea: 39%
- Sweden: 32%
- New Zealand: 31%
- South Korea: 31%
- New Zealand: 31%
- Australia: 31%
- France: 26%
- Brazil: 25%
- Singapore: 24%
- Philippines: 24%
- Germany: 17%
- Mexico: 16%
- United Kingdom: 15%
- Canada: 15%
- Netherlands: 14%
- United States: 14%
- Japan: 8%

more than that. We're constantly asking, 'Are they our kind of people? Are they friendly and cooperative? Are they polite and flexible? Are they willing to invest in the long term, discuss problems when they arise, and be flexible, not dogmatic?' "

"You can be here a long time," he notes, remembering that the company has employees with as many as sixty years of service, "and we want to be around nice people."

Leaders at Jardine Pacific must be human and accessible—they must touch people on a regular basis. That's one way they balance speed with civility: "We spend a lot of time informally touching base, taking the time for face-to-face meetings even when there is such a premium on speed. People want to be noticed." That's why Jardine Pacific has institutionalized a "round of visits," with executives taking time during business trips to make the rounds and visit the troops.

He experienced this Jardine "personal touch" firsthand early in his career: "I used to be amazed when I'd go to London and the chairman would call to ask me to tea. We'd spend thirty minutes being polite, with him asking how my wife liked Taiwan and how things were going. You'll never even see the chairman of many large companies, but you'll see us when you interview, when you join Jardine, and a few times a year when we visit each other."

BUILD GLOBAL BUSINESS TEAMS
Warren Larsen and the New Zealand Dairy Board *(New Zealand)*

Title: Chief Executive
Headquarters: Wellington
Business: New Zealand's largest multinational food marketing organization, with a 26% share of the global dairy market. Ranked number 1 in Top 200 New Zealand Company index with $6.1 billion annual turnover. Exports dairy products to 115 countries, with more than 80 subsidiary companies worldwide. Its Anchor brand is the world's largest butter brand.
Employees: 9,200

WHEN REVEREND SAMUEL MARSDEN arrived in the Bay of Islands with two heifers and a bull in 1814, he had no idea he was starting a national dairy industry. Almost two hundred years later, cows are still key players in New Zealand's economy, accounting for 23 percent of the nation's GDP.

According to the New Zealand Dairy Board, there are nearly 3 million dairy cows—one for almost every person—and 14,500 dairy farmers in this small island nation. There's no place for all that milk to go but out—more than 95 percent of it is sold overseas with the help of the Dairy Board, a co-op of farmers with a shared vision. "New Zealanders have been traders from way back," says CEO Warren Larsen. "And farmers have had to understand the very ethos of cooperation to survive."

The Dairy Board has its own recipe for survival: "If we're smart and form strong teams and cultural relationships—and really work at it—then performance goes up."

Milk spoils. Quickly. "In this business, degradation starts as soon as the milk comes out of the cow," says Larsen. "You've got to cool it, process it, and ship it quickly."

And you have to adapt to change, too. To do that, Larsen created a new global structure for the Dairy Board in 1997, with global teams at its center.

For years, New Zealand was the "farm" of the United Kingdom, but the percentage of the country's exports going to the United Kingdom has fallen from 93 percent fifty years ago to less than 7 percent today. "It forced us to go out and hustle," says Larsen. "We've transitioned from a centralized exporter to a decentralized international sales and marketing organization."

Not only that, it competes directly with the big boys: Procter & Gamble, Nestlé, and Kraft. And it was the Dairy Board, a co-op of farmers who are at once the employees, suppliers, marketers, and manufacturers—not a major multinational food conglomerate—that recently sold US$40 million worth of mozzarella to the world's largest pizza chain, Pizza Hut. That's a lot of cheese.

Although it seems monumental to compete on such a grand scale from such a small place, it's a way of life for New Zealanders—they're well positioned for the challenges of working across time, space, and country boundaries. They've been communicating with the world like that for years.

A central ingredient of success is global teams that keep one foot in the region where they're doing business, one foot in the product line they represent, and one foot in the global world. "Members of our teams not only wear a regional hat, they're also responsible for product rollout, profitability, and knowledge transfer in markets around the world," says Larsen. "We're building a global culture of fast-moving consumer goods marketers."

Larsen knows how important collective intelligence is. His new structure leverages this asset and institutionalizes social literacy by making teamwork the central strategy, instituting global team audits, and educating across all levels, functions, and cultures. That's why cooperation and cultural respect define the New Zealand Dairy Board.

Make Teamwork Your Central Strategy

Dairy Board leaders develop three key competencies: leadership, teamwork, and global focus. It's no mistake that teamwork is at the center—it's the glue that holds the other two together.

But it's one thing to say that teams are important; it's another thing altogether to make them your central strategy and have it work. Leveraging the collective intelligence of global teams is a real opportunity, and getting people to communicate across product lines is a real challenge.

"Everything is done in teams," says Larsen. "We create and disassemble teams across the organization all the time. We also build business SWAT teams that focus on solving problems, like the milk powder team we recently sent into Venezuela to tell us what we were doing wrong with that market."

These teams aren't built without forethought, nor do they function well without constant work: "Because we must move our product so quickly around the world, diverse teams must be competent to work cross culturally—the Middle East team has to talk to the North African team, for instance. And we can't let groups form clusters that undermine teamwork. I'll go to any length to ensure that we shift people around."

There's always a New Zealander's face at the table: "Our unofficial rule is that we put at least one New Zealander on the top team of ventures as a reminder that we're all about New Zealand farmers. Having home-country employees sprinkled around the globe is the glue of our company. We recruit, train, mentor, and disperse New Zealand culture carriers—and they're required to learn the local language."

The Dairy Board has to provide an environment where these teams can flourish. "We explain three very basic things to people: First, they have to want to work for us. Second, we make sure they know what their job is and constantly give feedback on how they're doing. And third, we create a work environment where they can succeed. If you do those three things well," he says, "they'll go the extra mile for you."

"We constantly look for team players. I see myself as a quasi–personnel officer moving around the world to see how these teams function."

Farmers have been working on teams for centuries and provide the model for the Dairy Board. "The farmers will go the extra mile as long as you put reasonable propositions in front of them, tell them the truth, and take them with you. Every now and again one of them will say, 'No, I don't want to go down that path.' You've got to stop, put your arm around them, talk to them a bit more, and put the effort in even if it takes you another month or two. Then you move on," Larsen says.

His new global team matrix has meant a philosophical switch for staff. "While your job might still have a regional focus, now you also have global responsibilities," he says. And with new global responsibilities comes a need for new skills, developed and evaluated through new measurement strategies.

Institute Global Team Audits

Global teams work only if there's an understanding of strategy, clarity about roles and responsibilities, and a willingness to discuss differences among team members. The Dairy Board measures teamwork competencies "right up there with financial measures," says Larsen.

Team audits give feedback about the strengths and weaknesses of team members, making it possible for Larsen to build strong complementary teams. "We mix people on teams to make sure we've got gleanings of teamwork, leadership, and global focus skills in all of them. You can't have a whole team that's alike."

Organizationwide cultural audits address two key questions: What is the environment now, and what would you like it to be? "We actually try to measure the culture using a process where descriptors are rearranged to show the current and ideal culture of the organization," explains Larsen. "The gaps become areas for focus, and the 'target culture' is examined against the vision and overall goals of the company."

Not only culture gets audited, but individual performance as well. And the Dairy Board is straightforward about feedback: tell it where it needs work, encourage it to change its approach, and help define who, what, and how to do that. "Financial goals are at the top of our list, but they'll never be reached unless you actually keep developing the human aspects," says Larsen, who does that through education at all levels.

Educate Across Levels, Functions, and Cultures

The Dairy Board educates leaders of all kinds across levels, functions, and cultures. Pairing global marketers with scientists is one example of how Larsen links diverse people to build a culture of innovation. The marriage between the pitchmen and researchers was uneasy at first. Getting marketers to use their flair to educate and excite the scientists was no easy task. But once they did, "innovation has gone up, our time to market is shorter, and we have product launches now that are reaching the frequency and quality that we need."

In matching marketers with scientists, Larsen played the role of catalyst for collaboration: "Research scientists are trained as individuals and tend to work alone, not in teams. Yet in their heads, they've got the key to most of our marketing successes."

By educating people across levels, functions, and cultures, Larsen ensures learning for all: "I want ideas flowing right across this organization."

NEW ZEALAND: "Informal Egalitarians"

National Snapshot

Compared to other executives, New Zealand business leaders say:

- They are more likely to lead by example.
- Their senior executives have more multicultural experiences.
- Focusing on growth is important to building a global company.
- They understand and respect the traditions of others more than their own.
- They focus more on leadership development.
- 84% have customers and suppliers in six or more countries.

THE STORY OF THE DAIRY BOARD mirrors the story of New Zealand itself—a nation in transition from being the "farm" of the United Kingdom to being a world class competitor, leveraging the lush farmland and livestock native to its islands, and linking with a world from which it is so geographically disconnected.

This is a nation recovering from a British colonial history, straddling Asia and the Commonwealth and just now coming to terms with the difference between its psychological market, the United Kingdom, and their geographic one, Asia. This nation, so small and isolated, has realized that its market is truly the world.

An individualistic, informal, and egalitarian people, Kiwis—as New Zealanders are often called—carry the same name as the wingless, nocturnal bird and fuzzy fruit found throughout this country. Their temperate climate and rich pastures are conducive to raising sheep and cattle; their beautiful scenery creates a healthy tourist trade.

Overwhelmingly white Europeans, New Zealanders have only recently had to answer to the demands of the minority Maori, whose 9 percent of the population want compensation for what they believe was the seizure of their lands by the Europeans. As a nation, they're working hard—and effectively—to leverage their diversity and right any wrongs.

New Zealanders have always been socially sensitive. Long before they declared their nation a nuclear-free zone, they were the first members of the British Commonwealth to create old-age pensions, in 1898. They gave women the right to vote in 1893, allowed labor arbitration in 1894, and established widow's pensions in 1911.

The first explorers to reach the islands were Dutch. Captain James Cook landed in 1769, and British colonization continued from then. Britain finally annexed New Zealand in 1838, but only as part of the Australian colony of New South Wales. Though New Zealand became fully independent in 1947, the British queen is and always has been its head of state, and the Union Jack is an integral part of the New Zealand flag.

The country has always relied heavily on the United Kingdom. But when Britain gave up the Commonwealth preference tariffs in the 1980s, this small island nation had to change dramatically. In characteristically resourceful fashion, New Zealanders answered the challenge by reinventing their economy, exporting to survive, and diversifying their customers and

New Zealand: ***At a Glance***
Official name: New Zealand

Economy type: Anglo-Saxon
Trading bloc: APEC (Asia-Pacific Economic Cooperation)

Location: Island nation in the Pacific Ocean, neighbor of Australia
Capital: Wellington **Population:** 3,625,388
Head of state: Queen Elizabeth II, represented by Governor-General Sir Michael Hardie Boys **Official language:** English
Religion: Anglican 24%, Presbyterian 18%, Roman Catholic 15%
Literacy: 100% **World GNP ranking:** 46
GDP (US$ bn): $55.5 **GDP per capita:** $15,470
Unemployment: 6.7% **Inflation:** 1.7%
World export market share: 0.3%

Major industries: Food processing, textiles, machinery, fish, forest products, wool, dairy products
Major crops: Grains, potatoes, fruits
Minerals: Gold, gas, iron, coal
Labor force: 65% Services, 25% industrial, 10% agricultural
Computers per 1,000 inhabitants: 264.8

Assets: World's largest exporter of wool, cheese, meat, and butter. Strong tourist sector. Manufacturing sector is growing. Strong growth in high-tech industries. Very open economy. Expanding trade links with the Pacific Rim. Ease of entry into the banking industry and access to foreign capital markets.

Liabilities: High level of public debt. Reliance on imported manufactured goods. Geography and location are limiting. Volatile exchange rate.

products. They shed their highly regulated economy, cut personal and corporate taxes, and slashed tariffs on imports. Since 1984, New Zealand has changed from being one of the most regulated economies in the world to being one of the most open—and global surveys consistently rank New Zealand as the world's most ethical country.

Its closest neighbor is Australia, with whom it has entered into a trade agreement. Often confused with Australians—much to their chagrin—New Zealanders assert their independence and differences socially, culturally, and economically.

The world's biggest exporters of wool, cheese, butter, and meat, they have also developed rapidly growing manufacturing and high-tech sectors. And according to World Economic Forum survey data, New Zealand companies are some of the most professionally managed in the world.

New Zealanders teach us resourcefulness and change-readiness. They show us what it means to have a truly multicultural and global perspective, shored up by social sensitivity.

UNDERSTANDING THE MIND OF A CHINESE LEADER
Zhu Youlan and China Resources *(China)*

Title: CEO
Headquarters: Hong Kong
Business: "Based in Hong Kong, backed up by Mainland China, geared to the needs of the world." Diversified state-owned conglomerate with 560 subsidiaries, including foodstuffs, banking, insurance, tourism and hotels, manufacturing, retail and department stores, and shipping and warehouse businesses. Returns have doubled every three years, with a tenfold increase in profit since Zhu became CEO.
Employees: 12,000 (10% in mainland China, 90% in Hong Kong)

CHINA IS THE WORLD'S OLDEST CIVILIZATION. *Steeped in stories passed to each generation in a language understood only in context and built on images and subtle differences of tone, the Chinese use history as a mirror and a source of wisdom to guide them into the future. To fully understand Chinese leaders, we must first understand that history, those stories, and their role in teaching principles of life and leadership.*

The *Bing-Fa* of Chinese Leadership

Every Chinese business leader knows the phrase "*Shang chang ru zhan chang*"—"The marketplace is a battlefield." In fact, Sun Tzu's *Bing-Fa*, often translated as *Art of War* and written in the fourth century B.C.E., is a map for business strategy even today. Strategic thinking is an art and formal discipline in China, studied by people from all walks of life. The game of business is the game of war.

The essential components of victory Sun Tzu applied to war are consistently applied to business by Chinese executives: know when and when not to fight; obtain your troops' support by creating a common objective; seize favorable opportunities; free yourself from interference from superiors; and, when the time is right, act swiftly and decisively.

The Chinese love the game. They believe war—and business—is won not by guns or soldiers but by intangibles, by spiritual and psychological elements of battle, and by people totally committing their hearts and minds to the struggle. The highest form of victory is to conquer by strategy, not by fighting—so while Western businesses apply more resources such as people or money to a problem, the Chinese apply more strategy.

Sun Tzu outlines a limited number of tactical principles that can be combined into an infinite number of business strategies, including this one about surveillance: "If you don't use local guides, you won't be able to count on natural advantages." It was a principle true for reconnaissance into enemy territory for soldiers, and it's just as true for business leaders trying to understand the deep-rooted tactical and strategic thinking of the Chinese.

China Resources is one company that provides local guides in the murky terrain of mainland China. Its leader is a woman warrior of Chinese business.

Madame Zhu: A Woman Warrior

Zhu Youlan bridges Chinese government and business—two sectors with a historical chasm between them—just as she bridges companies inside and outside China. Formerly the president of the powerful China National Textiles Import and Export Board, she has woven Chinese history and stories into her leadership of China Resources, a state-owned, regionally focused company that is an intermediary to all national companies in China.

Zhu applies cultural literacy to understand China and its relationship to the West: "Our foundation and ways of thinking are different. I've read books that talk about how to present gifts and present name cards, but this is on the surface. The difference is much more psychological, ideological. There's a long way to go for us to understand each other.

"The culture of Hong Kong is a mixture of the smartness of the Shanghai people, the adventurism of the Cantonese, and the well-calculated thinking of the British." The complexities of the Chinese environment are often underestimated. There are, in fact, fifty different nationalities in China itself, so leaders have to "take care of the different characteristics of different nationalities," Zhu explains.

Not understanding those complexities exacts a high price, says Zhu, describing a British company on the brink of bankruptcy after buying a brewery in China: "They sent more than twenty people to replace the management. They were experts, they knew the industry, they knew the technology, but they couldn't manage in China because we do it a different way."

Doing business successfully with the Chinese requires listening more deeply to the ways they describe business and leadership.

Coats and Sleeves, Boats and Water

Zhu is an image maker herself; her discussions of leadership leave vivid word pictures in her audiences' minds. "The word 'leadership' is based on two Chinese characters that mean 'collar and sleeves,' " she says, evoking the image of a shirt's most important features, the pieces that hold it together.

"And in China," Zhu explains, "the relationship between leader and people is also compared to a boat and water. Water can float the boat, but it can also turn it upside down. A leader must deal carefully with the people he's leading. Sometimes the boat is going with the current, sometimes against it—you have to be very, very careful.."

China's slow-moving economic reforms are one example of the care with which its people pilot the boat: "Not too speedy, not to turn it upside down. That's the Chinese way of thinking."

But leadership isn't just "collars and sleeves" to Zhu. She also talks about it in the new language of technology: the hardware and software of leaders' minds.

"Like a computer," she says, "you must have hardware: intelligence, quickness, the ability to adapt and to manage people." But Zhu also understands the importance of software: "A good leader must listen to their principles and really care about the future of the organization, people, customers, community, and society."

And they must understand the Bing-Fa of leadership.

HONG KONG, CHINA

National Snapshot

Compared to other executives, Hong Kong business leaders say:

- Beating the competition is a strong cultural value.
- They are good at transforming conflict into creative action.
- They strongly value respecting the traditions and practices of others.
- Their leaders engage in many cross-cultural experiences.
- They assess and reward leadership effectiveness.
- Religion has little influence on their personal leadership.
- Their boards of directors are the most international.

SOME SAY THE FORTUNE AND FUTURE OF HONG KONG were symbolically represented in 1982, when Margaret Thatcher literally tumbled down the steps outside Beijing's Great Hall of the People as she left following negotiations with Deng Xiaoping about the reversion of Hong Kong to Chinese rule.

On July 1, 1997, the British Crown Colony of Hong Kong became the Hong Kong Special Administrative Region (HKSAR) of the People's Republic of China—more simply, it became "Hong Kong, China."

It is a city created by the British but largely populated by industrious Overseas Chinese, many of whom came from the mainland. The British started using the natural harbors of Hong Kong in 1821 and in 1898 signed a ninety-nine-year lease on the "New Territories" from China to ensure control of all the surrounding territory. It was that lease that ended in 1997, causing the very public transition of Hong Kong back to China amid speculation and fear of the corruption, cronyism, and authoritarianism of the Communist government in Beijing.

As part of the transition, Chinese leaders pledged to honor two agreements that will govern Hong Kong for the next fifty years. They pledged that Hong Kong's capitalist system will remain unchanged, that China is committed to maintaining Hong Kong's role as an international business and financial center, and that economic autonomy will be allowed. The guiding principle, says China, is Deng Xiaoping's legacy of "one country, two systems."

And while it's clear that China needs Hong Kong's business success, in other areas such as civil service, the media, and education there is at least some concern about Chinese control. Schools have gone from teaching in English to teaching in Cantonese, accelerating Hong Kong's already declining capacity to conduct business in the universal language of commerce.

Hong Kong, with its 6 million inhabitants, is the eighth largest trading economy in the world and has the second largest stock market in Asia. Its economic success came despite daunting constraints: lack of natural resources, waves of immigration of destitute refugees, political uncertainty, and the unavoidable friction of being a colony in a world in which colonies are rapidly disappearing.

Hong Kong is punctuated by Star Ferries traveling across one of the most beautiful harbors in the world; its people are intensely entrepreneurial in big corporations and smaller family firms. Skyscrapers are juxtaposed with small wooden junks of boat people; packed into three sections—Hong Kong Island, the New Territories, and Kowloon—these people are living out a unique history in one of the world's great international cities. Hong Kongers see themselves as Chinese, with all the Confucian and Buddhist values that implies, but they also see themselves as different. Market-driven, they live and die for trading.

CHAPTER TEN

TOOLS

What Resources Do We Need?

ONCE OUR PURPOSE, plan, and networks are set, how do we create the tools and resources necessary for people to excel?

Leaders must build a globally literate workforce whose mindsets and capabilities can thrive in the borderless, multicultural marketplace. To do that, they must develop and educate globally literate leaders at all levels of the business.

What are these new twenty-first-century tools? They are challenging jobs, learning opportunities, knowledge and information, growth potential, cross-cultural experiences, healthy work environments, portable pensions and benefits, a balance between work and family, and a share in the business.

The globally literate leader makes use of these tools by teaching others. By developing a companywide global literacy program that assesses, develops, coaches, and rewards leaders, the globally literate leader creates other globally literate leaders. Together they strengthen their organization's capabilities.

This requires creating learning environments. By helping people gain the skills and self-reliance they need to excel in the global world and by helping them become proficient in the four global literacies, leaders build those learning environments.

The challenge is to develop globally literate leaders in different national cultures. We must create global communications with local language. We must develop global tools tailored to local environments. And we must create global human resource systems that are sensitive to local customs and cultures. Using the four global literacies as a guide will help address these challenges.

Here we'll meet six leaders who are creating tools in their own culturally unique ways: Motorola chairman Robert Galvin from the United States teaches us how to build a global learning culture and Société du Louvre CEO

HOW COMPANIES DEVELOP LEADERS

When asked how their organization engages in leadership development, the global executives as a group gave the following ranking. Each country, however, identified a different area most in need of improvement (in parentheses).

1. Reward leaders (Singapore, Sweden)
2. Assess leaders (Canada, Germany, Netherlands, United Kingdom, Brazil)
3. Train leaders (United States, China, Philippines, Mexico)
4. Coach leaders (Australia, Hong Kong)
5. Rotate leaders (Japan, New Zealand)
6. Provide cross-cultural experiences for leaders (South Korea, France)

Anne-Marie Taittinger-Bonnemaison from France demonstrates how to develop global brands with national identities. Others creating tools for success include San Miguel Corporation's former CEO Andres Soriano, who formed alliances to link his company to the world; Sundstrand Corporation CEO Robert Jenkins, from the United States, and his focus on making vision an action verb; Schock Holdings CEO Friedrich Schock and Blanco CEO Frank Straub, both of Germany and both of whom live quality to make quality.

BUILD A GLOBAL LEARNING CULTURE
Robert W. Galvin and Motorola, Inc. *(U.S.A.)*

Title: Chairman of the Executive Committee
Headquarters: Schaumburg, Illinois
Business: Founded in 1928 by brothers Paul and Joseph Galvin. In 1930 the brothers produced the first affordable car radio, prompting Paul Galvin to coin the name "Motorola," suggesting the idea of sound in motion. A leading provider of wireless communications, semiconductors, and advanced electronic systems, the company has been involved in the creation of all the major industries in which it competes today. It is a $30 billion business operating in more than 45 countries; 58% of its sales are from outside the United States, with fastest growth in Latin America.
Employees: More than 150,000 people on six continents

It must run in the family. The Galvins—founder Paul, his son Robert, and now his grandson Chris—have built a business founded on restless curiosity. Over the past forty years, Robert Galvin has built a connective learning culture, spearheading Motorola's global growth. Today, he is one of the world's great corporate statesmen.

As a business-literate leader living principles of personal and organizational renewal, Galvin's learning mandate shook corporate training in the 1980s: "All employees will receive a minimum of forty hours of job-related training every year."

Motorola is founded on the concept of leadership renewal. It manages for long-term growth and profitability by striving to be best in class, whether in terms of people, technology, marketing, products, manufacturing, or service. Its universal values spring from the American culture in which it was founded: respect for the dignity of the individual, uncompromising integrity, teamwork, and continuous improvement.

"My father was surprised by television," says Robert Galvin of Motorola's founder, Paul. Together the two of them built a family business that institutionalized their openness to technological surprises, such as TV.

To continue to do so, Motorola demands and cultivates personally literate leaders who have great self-confidence and a willingness to speak up. It seeks creative leaders who are able to see things a little differently. And it constantly translates personal renewal into business strategy, to "live the learning process every day inside the company."

By being open to surprises and crafting a global learning strategy, three generations of Galvins have created a company that continually renews itself—and creates its own surprises. It is this ability that helped Motorola weather its most recent surprise—betting on analog products when the world began craving all things digital. By constantly learning, the company is recasting itself from a manufacturer of technology hardware to a software maker. Like their founder, they're still constantly looking for breakaway opportunities as they create this "new Motorola."

Live Principles of Personal Renewal

As we enter the twenty-first century, change is the ultimate business driver. With renewal as its secret weapon, Motorola is ready.

"Renewal means reconfirming our dedication to proven values and roots, cherishing the basics, and embracing the future," says Galvin. "Renewing leaders take us elsewhere, teach us about today and tomorrow, build on past successes, and anticipate the future." Businesses must be built inductively, with the leader as the orchestral conductor.

Renewal takes work. "It is a pointedly personal privilege and duty," he continues. "My father would want the torch I hold high in his image to fire each of our spirits to emblazon our business with constant glowing and growing achievements by ever abler, ever smarter peers who spark our renewal."

Galvin knows firsthand what happens when companies do too well and when leaders act selfishly and don't invest in the future. In the late 1990s,

Motorola faltered: "We're undergoing an unpleasant transitory experience. Our revenues are down because three of our senior guys didn't anticipate the future, didn't invest properly, and didn't allocate the right resources to keep up with our customers. The press picked up on it, and although these reports are an irritation, the press is sufficiently accurate. You've got to be honest with yourself when you screw up. Let's admit our mistakes, correct them, and move on. The press will come around and realize we're back in control of the situation after a few good quarters."

The company's problems came down to allocating resources to build capacity for the company. "When you're doing well and have leadership momentum, comments Galvin, "it's possible for senior leaders to shave expenses to make things look even better for the short term. That's what we were doing until we discovered that our competitors were investing while we weren't—and our customers turned away when we didn't have the capacity they needed.

"The fascinating mathematics of our business is that you never lose just the increment you couldn't have supplied, but you always lose more. If I can only serve ninety percent of your needs now, you still need the other ten percent. But you can't go to someone else and ask them just to provide ten percent; you ask them for thirty percent or fifty percent, which means I've lost a third or half of the business. You better have enough capacity, or you'll lose half your business with that customer."

Out of these mistakes emerged some fundamental questions: "Are we investing enough, and what's our spirit of hope about the future? We must take reasonable risks and always ask the tough questions. We must not be blinded by our own arrogance and hubris. And we must anticipate surprises.

"Many companies since my father's time, like RCA, Philco, and Zenith, have gone away. We didn't run them out of business, they just didn't renew themselves. They weren't able to navigate through the surprises."

Be Open to Surprises

Galvin can count off sixteen surprises in his life—inventions such as television, satellites, transistors, and the computer. He's seen enough to know that the world is full of surprises and he can't anticipate them all—but he can know that new ones are coming.

Galvin is a historical futurist, building on past successes and anticipating the future. Each week, "Motorola Yesterday Today and Tomorrow" delivers a story to employees on their desktop computers that recounts milestones in the company's history, challenging situations, and lessons learned that make up Motorola's rich heritage. "Our goal is to create a common culture that reinforces long-term values," Galvin says.

Even after all that learning, sometimes leaders just have to leap: "From time to time, leaders have to engage in acts of faith and believe things are doable although not necessarily provable. The surprise comes along and you say, 'Hmm, that must be important, we ought to do something about it.' My father used to talk about being in motion for motion's sake. It's like walking through fields where your pants leg picks up a seed and drops it someplace else. We have to do that sometimes." Motorola's business is built on that principle of derivation and evolution: the small radio evolved into something more complex, and the seeds just keep dropping and changing. "That's how literacy improves," says Galvin, "by being in motion."

And when the time is right to move, the company must know how to do that, too. For years Galvin told his people, "Hands off, we're not doing anything with China." Motorola's "scouts" went ahead of the wagon train to learn about the people and culture, finally convincing Galvin to go to China in the mid-1980s. In Hong Kong on the first day of his two-week trip, Galvin read in the newspaper the twenty-two points of liberalization by Deng Xiaoping. "It was like a Magna Carta of free enterprise. On the spot, I created Motorola's strategy for China."

After selling a small number of radios to the minister of transportation later in the trip, Galvin asked the minister what they wanted to be. When he responded, "World class," Galvin warned that the Chinese could never be world class with only joint ventures. They would have to create completely private ownership—at which point he offered to make a $100 million investment to open two factories in China.

As a CEO moving into global markets such as China, Galvin knew what he was willing and not willing to do. For example, in Malaysia it's okay for factory workers to burn evil spirits at the entrance of the factory to ward off illness, but it's not okay for the company to pay bribes to the mayor of the town.

"We aim to respect people and their social cultures, but if their rules aren't in the best interest of the customer, we have to change that." What guides Bob Galvin are Motorola's uncompromising universals: integrity, customer satisfaction, striving to be best of class, and respect for people's dignity.

Craft a Global Learning Strategy

"Training costs nothing," says the large plaque in the entrance to Motorola University's main campus. It's a philosophy that sets Motorola apart.

Its learning strategy is linked directly to the corporation's critical business issues: leadership development in a global market; systems solutions for the customer; growth through organization renewal; global brand equity management; and knowledge management. Motorola's employees learn from one another, from the company's past, from its customers and suppliers, and from the world. This focus on learning also allows it to readily admit mistakes, seek mentors, and ask tough questions about whether it's investing enough in the development of its people.

Motorola University's mission is simple: to be a catalyst for change and continuous improvement in support of the company's business objectives. The university helps create the corporate culture; delivers education to the right people at the right time in the right environment; prepares executives and managers; and ensures a qualified workforce for the future. It's a strategy that has worked for three generations.

This sophisticated learning machine is a tangible example of Galvin's commitment to personal renewal. Motorola University manages facilities around the world, developing culturally literate leaders who understand the world's markets and the people who live in them. By translating and customizing programs to meet specific cultural needs, it is able to respond to local customers. "We need to know how external political, social, and ecological factors influence a society's culture in order to assess the right timing and conditions to go into that country," says Galvin. "And when we get there, we conduct an assessment to really get to know the people and markets."

This focus on anthropology is increasingly important to Motorola: "In the 1970s, we realized the Japanese culture respects power. Once we extracted that piece of cultural knowledge, we changed our strategy and brought in the big guns to show them power. We've been getting orders ever since."

Motorola is transferring that kind of knowledge to other places in the world. "We're now learning the anthropology of the world east of the Caspian Sea: Kazakhstan, Turkestan, and Azerbaijan. That's going to be one of the richest parts of the world in the next hundred years because of their natural resources—that's what I mean by anticipation."

Galvin personally kept Motorola out of South America between 1950 and 1990. Though Catholic himself, he realized that the Catholic Church in South America was corrupt and fostered a society that held people down, undermining success in the private sector. NAFTA started changing that in Mexico, opening the door for Motorola finally to enter what is now its greatest growth market. Galvin has no regrets about the delay: "We would have wasted our time there over the past thirty years—the culture was absolutely impervious to wealth creation by the private sector."

As chairman, his job is now to increase the company's size of the pie, to look at world populations and markets. "Markets," Galvin says, "are an algorithm of population. And because only five percent of people live in the U.S., we really have to think of ninety-five percent of our business being outside the U.S. We simply can't penetrate these markets without understanding their people."

UNITED STATES: "Optimistic Entrepreneurs"

Compared to other executives, American business leaders say:

- They are motivated by strongly held principles and lead by example.
- They attribute leadership to religious and spiritual beliefs.
- Listening and communicating effectively is important.
- Multicultural experiences are not a priority, and there is little need to change.
- They speak the fewest languages.
- They reward people for effective leadership.
- 90% are U.S. natives and they have fewer international boards.
- The U.S. market is highly domestic (32%) and highly global (21%).

Americans are independent, self-sufficient dreamers. Their optimism and can-do spirit shape a diverse nation of entrepreneurs and big business. Cultural exporters, they are impervious to the influence of others.

IN 1515, AMERICA'S FIRST HISTORIAN described the country as a barrier between Europe and Asia. People have long sought routes across this frontier land, becoming explorers and entrepreneurs along their journey. Generous capitalists in a melting pot of cultures that combine but don't blend, the United States of America is a collection of dreamers and doers, where individualism is the uniting factor.

Individualistic by Nature

The home-run hitter is a fitting symbol for a country that glorifies solo performance—along with cowboys, astronauts, and entrepreneurs. A nation that places tremendous value on freedom and individual liberty, the United States is a celebrity-driven culture with a confident personality—some say it's an arrogance of power. And there's some truth to that perception.

Many Americans feel their military, economy, democracy, and ethics are morally superior to the rest of the world's, a feeling of dominion that accelerated after World War I in their attempt to make the world "safe for democracy." In World War II, the United States fought fascism; in the Cold War, it fought the "Evil Empire." Americans see themselves as the good guys.

Paradoxically, the United States suffers from some of the world's worst social ills, including broken families, drugs, homelessness, and violent crime. It's a juxtaposition of good and evil that Americans sometimes just can't see.

Individualism is embedded in the American soul. Children's toys are programmed with songs such as "I'm Proud to Be Me." As kids grow up, this self-absorption is translated into a national obsession with self-development: health, fitness, and psychotherapy.

A largely informal society, Americans are friendly—sometimes superficially so. As a visitor to the United States once remarked, "Americans open their arms to everyone. But rarely do they close them in a genuine embrace." Even on first meeting, many Americans assume they are on a first name basis—in large part because theirs is a mobile society with a fluid class system of "old" and "new" money.

The postsecondary education system graduates some of the best and brightest in the world. Widely considered the creator of the modern business school, the country's graduate schools are recognized the world over. Yet its primary and secondary school system educates some of the lowest-scoring pupils on math and science in all industrial countries. In a recent study, a startlingly high percentage of U.S. high school students couldn't locate Mexico on blank maps of the world. Little wonder that Americans are among the world's least culturally literate.

A strong spirit of consumerism is engrained in the American psyche. Composed of lands taken from Native Americans and removed from British sovereignty, the United States is one of the few nations on earth that has purchased more than half of its occupied area. Louisiana, Alaska, Florida, and other property along the old U.S.-Mexican frontier were purchased for cash. Few other nations can make that claim.

A Land of Immigrants

Most immigrants come to the United States for economic opportunity. Around 40 million immigrants entered before restrictions were passed in 1921, a movement that forever changed the demographic face of America. Since 1970, the number of immigrants has almost tripled to 26.3 million, accounting for nearly one in ten residents, the highest proportion in seven decades.

American workplaces are full of people from these varied backgrounds, presenting opportunities for creativity and misunderstanding across steep barriers of language, racial, sexual orientation, religious, economic, educational, and regional differences.

Once a melting pot in which people shed part of their diverse identity to become Americans, now the differences are seen as being more like a stir-fry, a mixture enhanced and sometimes plagued by the variety. The flavors are also changing, from European to Asian and Latin. But while U.S. businesses spend more than $300 million a year on diversity training, the country doesn't manage this diversity as well as it thinks. Instead of true dialogue and respect, political correctness and tiptoeing around sensitive issues is the tendency. From the glass ceiling to overt racism, there is more work to be done.

One segment of the population that has not shared in the American dream is African Americans. Initially brought to the United States as slaves hundreds of years ago, even today wide disparities exist between black and white America. In health care, for example, African Americans are 34 percent more likely to die of cancer and twice as likely to die of heart disease; African-American babies are two and a half times more likely to die before their first birthday than Caucasian babies are.

Dreamers and Doers

This is a country with rich beauty and natural resources, as well as money for investment and innovation. While elsewhere, people are born into immutable hierarchical classes, the prevailing idea in the United States is that you can become what you want. With economic opportunity for all, it's a land where "anyone can make it"—at least in theory. If you do succeed, it's because of your efforts, and you are applauded for it. If you don't, it's your fault—underscoring principles of social Darwinism that cast everyone as master of their own fate.

The Protestant work ethic permeates U.S. culture, though its religious underpinnings—the belief that hard work glorifies God—has been expanded to more than 1,500 different religious organizations. Since 1900, church membership has increased sevenfold while the nation's population has increased only three and a half times. Faith is still a strong national value—but now America's individualism and immigration have diversified this commitment.

In a verbal culture of direct and friendly communication, Americans demand transparency in relationships and institutions. Their legal system boasts a Freedom of Information Act. Fairness is a national pastime, and whole industries are built around protecting the underdog.

This is a land of talkers and doers, optimistic dreamers who love to market and sell. As major cultural exporters, the Voice of America reaches 128 nations, *Reader's Digest* is distributed in 110 countries, and TV shows such as *Baywatch* are shown in multiple languages and countries worldwide. Shows imported from the United States account for 84 percent of Guatemalan, 71 percent of Malaysian, and 64 percent of Egyptian television programming, while foreign imports into the United States make up less than 2 percent of total programming.

Every year the world tunes in to watch Hollywood's Oscars. Kids around the world wear Levi's jeans, eat in McDonald's restaurants, and listen to the Smashing Pumpkins. Americans consider themselves so much the center of the universe that their national baseball championship is called the World Series.

The United States is a land of immense variety of place, people, and natural resources—ranging from arctic to subtropical, from rain forest to desert, from rugged mountains to some of the flattest plains on earth. Made up of geographic areas with distinct histories and intellectual legacies, the country has significant regional differences in lifestyle and personality.

New England is the oldest and most urban, industrialized area. The South, though changing rapidly, is the most protective of its ways; the Middle Atlantic states are old, prosperous, highly industrialized, and multiethnic. The Midwest is largely viewed as the country's breadbasket and national yardstick for what is "normal." The West is one of the most diverse areas, from the mountains of Montana to the technology-drenched Silicon Valley of California.

A Business Culture Emerges

Americans are results-oriented people focused on time, money, and solving problems. Impatient, change-oriented entrepreneurs who value achievement, they have a short-term time horizon, a surprising blend of materialism and spirituality, and a large—and widening—gap between the salaries of top executives and average workers.

With more than 270 million people in the American domestic market, U.S. companies have a natural advantage over companies in other parts of the world. Their economies of scale help them build large businesses before going overseas. There's also a downside to not having to look outside their borders: a parochial mindset, few multilingual Americans, and a GDP that is heavily dependent on national rather than global trade. But this is changing quickly as international customers, suppliers, employees, and competitors arrive.

U.S. companies deliver the world's highest returns on invested capital in one of the world's most sophisticated and transparent capital markets. With the dollar being the chief international means of exchange, the United States is obsessed with wealth creation, shaping a shareholder capitalism whose unfettered free market is emulated by many.

With a political philosophy that the government that governs least is best, regulation, not ownership, has been the mode of operation. Since the 1970s, deregulation has become the mainstay of the American economy.

The American labor union movement started in the late part of the nineteenth century to protect workers against increasingly powerful corporations. But with the downturn in the American economy in the late 1970s

United States: ***At a Glance***
Official name: United States of America

Economy type: Anglo-Saxon
Trading bloc: NAFTA (North American Free Trade Association)

Location: Occupies the heartland of North America from the Atlantic to the Pacific, plus Alaska and Hawaii **Capital:** Washington, D.C.
Population: 270,311,758 **Head of state:** President William Clinton
Official language: English **Religion:** Protestant 56%, Roman Catholic 28%, Jewish 2%, other 14% **Literacy:** 99%
World GNP ranking: 1 **GDP (US$ bn):** $8,108.2
GDP per capita: $30,260 **Unemployment:** 4.5%
Inflation: 2.6% **World export market share:** 16.5%

Major industries: Entertainment, computers, electronics, chemicals, software, oil and gas, chemicals, film, food processing, defense, banking and finance, autos, aerospace, agriculture, biotechnology
Major crops: Grains, corn, soybeans, fruits, vegetables, rice, cotton
Minerals: Coal, copper, lead, molybdenum, phosphates, uranium, bauxite, gold, iron, mercury, nickel, potash, silver, tungsten, zinc
Labor force: 36% services, 20.7% wholesale and retail trade, 15.8% manufacturing, 7.1% transportation and utilities, 6.5% finance, insurance, and real estate, 6.5% construction, 4.5% government, 2.6% agriculture, 0.5% mining
Computers per 1,000 people: 360.5

Assets: The world's largest and most competitive economy. Vast natural resources. Highly educated, skilled workforce. Traditional strong work ethic. Strong high-tech sector with significant private and governmental investment in R and D. Global brand names. Low acceptance of corruption in business. Overall stability of government and financial institutions is high. The huge supply of venture capital is an exceptional advantage. High risk taking. High customer service. Leaders in management and marketing capabilities. Maximizes use of high technology to increase global competitiveness.

Liabilities: Perceived as arrogant and naive by older cultures and nations. Lack of managers with international experience and foreign language skills. Low level of gross national savings. Shortage of qualified high-tech employees. Racial and ethnic tensions remain. Disparity between rich and poor continues to grow.

and '80s, labor unions lost much of the power and influence they gained in the 1930s and '40s. Today, only 14 percent of American workers are unionized, though the unions are trying to rekindle interest in membership by appealing to people's consumer orientation—including providing low-interest credit cards and special incentives for young people to join.

The business of America is business. While lacking in cultural literacy, Americans have a keen sense of business literacy. The nation is filled with consultants and specialists whose businesses thrive on risk, mistakes, resiliency, and bouncing back. As Lester Thurow, former dean of MIT's Sloan School of Management, has said, "The U.S. is very good at opening up the new—science, technology, engineering, creativity—and shutting down the old that doesn't work anymore through downsizing and restructuring. It's not as good with marginal improvements in mature industries that require patience and training."

Today, formerly hierarchical organizations are giving way to more egalitarian, team-based work cultures. And with over 75 percent of worldwide Internet users in North America, the country leads the world in major technological revolutions in microelectronics, computers, robotics, biotechnology, and telecommunications.

Americans offer the world a model of irrepressible change. The dynamism of American culture celebrates optimism, social mobility, and entrepreneurial energy. Americans' managerial techniques and love of business teach us how to execute our dreams.

FORM ALLIANCES THAT LINK THE WORLD
Andres Soriano III and San Miguel Corporation *(Philippines)*

Title: Former Chairman and CEO
Headquarters: Manila
Business: Largest publicly traded company in the Philippines. Established more than 100 years ago as a brewery; beer now accounts for only 35% of company sales. The Philippines' number one beverage, food, and packing company and its largest private employer. Soriano's grandfather joined San Miguel in 1918, establishing the first non-U.S. national Coca-Cola bottling and distribution franchise in 1927.
Employees: 29,500

Born in Spain, educated in the United States, and working in his family's home, the Philippines, Andres Soriano III, or ASIII as he is sometimes called, was born with a global mindset, a human merger of lineage and experience. He embodies the European, American, and Asian history that has shaped the Philippines.

He is an alliance builder—in his personal life, management style, and corporate strategy. "To be international, you don't have to go offshore," he says. "But you have to be constantly inventive, get to market quickly, be open to global opportunities, and know how to connect with others."

Soriano operates in a nation of paradox and contradiction. The Philippines is at once a democracy with a martial history and persistent political instability and a Catholic nation in the heartland of Eastern religions. Its daunting geography, low per capita income, and uneven distribution of wealth make it a challenging operating environment.

"For me," Soriano says, "paradox is strength. You have to harness the good, like our young employee pool and incredible inventiveness, and you have to let go of the baggage, like our poor infrastructure and tax base."

Whether walking down city streets or watching people talk in a restaurant, Soriano is constantly observing, weighing, and employing the most useful parts of what he sees. "Global is a mindset, not a geography," he says. "Our top people should learn the culture by walking around. You see how places work and what people are buying if you walk. You get a sense of what local people do, not the guy you meet at the head table of a Rotary lunch."

His greatest challenge is finding people with that inquisitiveness: "I always feel we're short on curiosity."

San Miguel develops connections around the world to reach its vision: "It would be nice to be Coca-Cola, but we're not. We can't do it ourselves." San Miguel's merger with Coca-Cola Amatil provided it with an eighteen-country market and a consumer base of 450 million—way up from the single market of 70 million consumers it had had before.

Even in joint ventures, Soriano seeks paradox. For example, China, regarded as the brewing industry's brightest hope, is also its most treacherous market. After achieving quick success with its Guangzhou Brewery, San Miguel hit severe distribution problems. To respond, Soriano created a management team in Hong Kong to target specific markets and established a strong ethnic Chinese management cadre. He saw the problem, and he fixed it.

In the late 1980s, San Miguel's long-term partnership with Nestlé was almost toppled by their conflicting mutual interests. "When Nestlé decided to go into the ice cream business, we were also active in dairy products," Soriano explains. "Rather than come to blows, we realized they were better positioned to make the move from bulk to single-serve ice cream and spun off our dairy business into a joint venture with theirs. We bridged the gap between us."

Soriano has learned many things from those experiences: Don't feel pressured to get started; take time to develop a long-term relationship. Marry the skills of your partner with your own corporate personality. Conduct an honest assessment of your strengths and weaknesses—and determine where you can shore up your weaknesses by partnering. Where practical, lead the charge and have the advantage of making the first move. Numbers and projections can't be the only things you consider; you've got to feel something. Seek out complementary businesses, and know what's expected of each partner. Build a strong, diversified team of good advisers. Develop the ability not only to learn but also to coach. Take risks to solve problems.

After our interview, in July 1998, Soriano was forced out of his position by Eduardo Conjuangco, a former business associate of the late dictator Ferdinand Marcos whose San Miguel shares had been seized by the government after Marcos was toppled in 1986 but were returned to him by the courts soon after current president Joseph Estrada was elected in 1998. Since Soriano and his family are still major shareholders, this battle for control continues to hamper San Miguel's performance.

Despite one's best efforts, external forces can undermine success. In Soriano's case, those forces are clearly a function of the political and historical environment of the Philippines itself.

PHILIPPINES: "Inventive Sociables"

National Snapshot

Compared to other executives, Filipino business leaders say:

- They lead by example and inspire others to excellence.
- They need to improve facing change with confidence.
- They need to improve leadership talent at all levels.
- They offer less autonomy to their international operations.
- They have a domestically oriented economy, with international suppliers.

Mix together more than three hundred years of Spanish Catholic mores and colonization, fifty years of American free enterprise, 70 million people, and a set of Asian values and behaviors—and you've got the Philippines. Like many Asians, Filipinos stress public harmony and overt conviviality—but more often than their Asian neighbors, they do so in Western

Philippines: ***At a Glance***
Official name: Republic of the Philippines

Economy type: Asian manufacturing
Trading bloc: APEC (Asia-Pacific Economic Cooperation)

Location: The world's second largest archipelago, located in the western Pacific Ocean **Capital:** Manila **Population:** 77,725,862
Head of state: President Joseph Ejercito Estrada
Official languages: Filipino, English **Religion:** Roman Catholic 83%, Protestant 9%, Muslim 5% **Literacy:** 95%
World GNP ranking: 40 **GDP (US$ bn):** $61.3
GDP per capita: $806 **Unemployment:** 8.7%
Inflation: 8.4% **World export market share:** 0.6%

Major industries: Food processing, textiles, chemicals, pharmaceuticals, wood products
Major crops: Sugar, rice, corn, pineapples, coconuts
Minerals: Cobalt, copper, gold, nickel, silver, oil
Labor force: 43% agricultural, 23% services, 18% government services, 16% industrial and commercial
Computers per 1,000 people: 8.8

Assets: Openness to foreign investment. Political stability has returned. Low wages. Large labor force.

Liabilities: Poor infrastructure. Frequent power failures hinder economic development. High unemployment and underemployment. Financial institutions underdeveloped and shaky. High interest rates. Poor ports and roads. Little use of high technology for leveraging global competitiveness.

dress. While other Asians see Filipinos as very "Westernized," Americans and Europeans tend to see them as very Asian.

This confluence of Asian, Spanish, and American influences has created the only Asian country to have been both a Spanish and American colony and the only predominantly Catholic country in Asia.

Seven thousand islands make up the Philippines. With its tropical climate, abundant natural resources, rich soil, and strong agricultural economy, the Philippines was expected in the mid-1950s to become one of the "hot" Asian economies. Everything pointed in that direction: a well-educated, English-speaking population with a high standard of living and a stable, democratic government.

But the Philippines never became one of the "Asian Tigers" like South Korea, Taiwan, Hong Kong, and Singapore. It didn't even become one of the "baby tigers" like Malaysia, Thailand, and Indonesia. Instead, President Ferdinand Marcos ruled with corruption and the imposition of martial law in 1972, undermining democracy. Corazon Aquino's "people's power" nonviolent revolution led to Marcos's downfall in 1986; she was succeeded in 1992 by someone more savvy in government administration and free-market economics: General Fidel Ramos.

With a revision of tax law and increased investment-friendly policies, combined with foreign investments and political stability, the Philippines has started to boom. Foreign investment more than tripled between 1992 and 1996, and direct foreign investment rose fivefold.

Like the Asians from which one part of their heritage arises, Filipinos stress harmony and conviviality above all. They value smooth personal relations, togetherness, and conflict avoidance. This cultural mindset compels them to smile no matter what the situation, and to use humor and teasing a great deal in interpersonal relationships at work and at home.

Intricate interplays of social and personal debts form a backdrop for reciprocity and interdependence that binds people together in long business relationships of mutual trust. Choosing carefully the circle of people to whom they will become indebted is vital, so they seek to create *suki,* relationships of long-standing duration. Within those relationships, they are flexible, accommodating, and ingenious in solving difficult dilemmas by doing whatever it takes to solve a problem, whatever solution is required.

In a country that is itself trying to rebuild its own self-esteem after years of internalized self-doubt, *hiya,* or loss of self-esteem, is a powerful force. People work hard to avoid doubting or publicly challenging others, both in social life and in business.

Influenced by several cultures and mindsets, Filipinos model values of togetherness and affability for the rest of the world. Their ability to adapt teaches the world about building alliances with reciprocity and gratitude.

MAKE YOUR VISION A VERB

Robert H. Jenkins and Sundstrand Corporation (U.S.A.)

Title: CEO and Chairman
Headquarters: Rockford, Illinois
Business: The company was begun in 1926 as a machine-tool shop. The modern-day Sundstrand's subsidiaries make aerospace and industrial products for military and commercial customers. Aerospace products account for nearly 60% of sales and include electrical, mechanical, and power systems included in every aircraft made by Boeing and Airbus Industrie.
Employees: 10,400

BOB JENKINS DRIVES AN EXTRA MILE *to shop at Nordstrom, a popular American-based retailer—and it's not because he enjoys shopping or driving. He seeks out Nordstrom because of its exemplary service. That's the kind of "sought-after" company he wants Sundstrand to be; he knows outstanding companies trigger something special in people.*

As CEO, he's in a position to make that happen. He creates tools to support his vision and facilitates global conversations about how to become a "sought-after" leader.

But being sought after isn't just a corporate slogan—it's an aspiration people relate to because we all experience it ourselves. "Whether in religion, relationships, or retail," Jenkins notes, "we all understand the concept of seeking something in our lives."

Sundstrand needed a beacon, a rallying point. It needed a concept to be its signature—and it needed to be global. "Companies use a lot of 'vision words,' " says Jenkins, "but we wanted something with substance. I wanted it to be personal; I wanted to believe it myself at a deep level. And it needed to be condensed to a shorthand that would evoke understanding." Being "sought-after" was the company's answer.

Jenkins wants four groups to seek out Sundstrand: "Employees should take pride in working here. Customers should say, 'Boy, I wish Sundstrand would enter this business because they do everything so well.' Suppliers should know that we'll reward them for their ideas and be loyal to them. And investors should know we'll emphasize the quality of the earnings."

Sundstrand created common principles and tools to help people live the "sought-after" values. The foundation was Sundstrand's three operating principles: simplify, focus, and trust. "These are not options but requirements," Jenkins says emphatically. "They're meant to be verbs—words of action and process." In Sundstrand's lexicon, to simplify, focus, and trust is to figure out what really matters, apply resources and concentration, and build healthy relationships.

But principles such as these have no meaning if they aren't applied and put to good use. Sundstrand's learning tools make that happen: a corporate video of employees talking about how they are Sundstrand leaders, tools and questions to build awareness, and small-group discussions around the world help facilitate this learning.

Jenkins personifies Sundstrand's principles: "I always ask people on the factory floor, 'What has to be right to get your job done? What problems and obstacles get in your way? What irritates you most in performing your job? And what could we do to make your job easier?"

And Jenkins is still learning how to apply them himself: "What I try to do as CEO is articulate a view of something that matters. I want people with great pride and loyalty to say, 'I work for Sundstrand, and I make a difference.' "

DEVELOP GLOBAL BRANDS WITH NATIONAL IDENTITIES

Anne-Marie Taittinger-Bonnemaison, Société du Louvre *(France)*

Title: Chairman and CEO
Headquarters: Paris
Business: Established in 1855, the Société du Louvre is diversified into six sectors: luxury hotels, including the Concorde Hotels Group of 70 hotels; budget hotels, with more than 550 properties; luxury goods such as Baccarat crystal and the Taittinger family champagne house; light industry, including manufacturing and printing companies; banking with the Banque du Louvre; and real estate.
Employees: 6,830

AS THE ELDEST CHILD *in a family of old French money, Anne-Marie Taittinger-Bonnemaison took her father's place as head of this world-renowned business group in 1997. Managing global "landmarks" such as Baccarat crystal, Concorde hotels, Annick Goutal perfumes, and Taittinger champagnes, she is the most recent heir to this dynamic, entrepreneurial French family business.*

As her father did, Taittinger leverages the company's French heritage around the world, capitalizing on the family's reputation. Yet, in a departure from old management styles, she leads with quiet strength and confident humility, doubling the group's profits since taking over as Société du Louvre's chairman of the board.

Life doesn't get any better than this—drinking Taittinger champagne from a Baccarat flute. And few are as acutely aware of how important it is to leverage this perception than the Taittinger family. In France, luxury goods and champagne go hand in hand as global symbols of quality and chic.

Taittinger capitalizes on what is good about France: the grandeur of French culture, the sense of pageantry, and the emphasis on civility and quality of life. At a time when many French are concerned that the global marketplace is eroding French culture, Taittinger operates globally while retaining the essence and personality of France itself.

When she joined Baccarat in 1992, sales were down to 85 million, their lowest point in five years; earnings were just over 1 million, half of what they had been in 1988. "When French consumers think of Baccarat, they see 'art' and respond positively," she says, "but only one fourth of our customers are French. Our overseas clients consider Baccarat as a French luxury"—and at a price many are unable or unwilling to pay.

With more than 30 percent of its sales in the United States, Baccarat broadened its product line to include less expensive items, including a new jewelry line that now accounts for 10 percent of sales. Taittinger augmented the $800 champagne flutes with $80 versions, putting them back on many bridal registries. She gave Baccarat a bigger personality, amplified the brand, and changed the distribution system to include boutiques in department stores. She protected the image by instituting the first authorized dealer agreements requiring retailers to use Baccarat-approved advertisements and displays. Doing so caused Baccarat to lose 20 percent of its U.S. distributors, but it was "an acceptable price," she says, "for protecting our all-important image."

She has cause to be a protective "parent"—Baccarat is the only brand name of crystal recognized worldwide. In Japan for more than a hundred years, Baccarat used to be well known in Russia and India. With Taittinger at the helm, it's returning to those countries—and to other countries, such as Brazil—and reinstating its name and products.

Lead with Quiet Strength

Taittinger's own strong identity is one of quiet strength, a departure from the old management styles of French businesses that depended on more command-and-control approaches.

She uses urgent listening skills to hear the changing needs and buying patterns of global consumers. A proud ancestor, she is respectful of her

French heritage while building bridges with millions of non-French firms around the world.

One of only a few high ranking woman business leaders in France, Taittinger has reframed the traditional power distance and hierarchical structures of French organizations in a quiet, collaborative manner. Though soft-spoken, she has real power as she manages her share of complex family dynamics.

Don't try to second-guess Mme. Taittinger; she used that strength and self-control when fighting off potential raider American Asher Edelman. A Wall Street investor who owns 12 percent of the company, Edelman complained about the pay family members were receiving, taking the company to court to expose their salaries. He lost his suit, vindicating Taittinger and her family.

Capitalize on Reputation and Personality

Though a world symbol of quality and success, Baccarat remains a family business. "Family businesses have the ability to take risks faster than other groups," says Taittinger. "They have intuitive management structures and think in the long term. People identify with family image and know they're getting more for their money. Our reputation in the luxury hotel industry shows that you don't have to be gigantic; rather, it's the personality of your establishment that counts."

Constantly reinventing itself for future generations of Taittingers and consumers, one of Baccarat's new ads shows a wooden boat with crew members sunning themselves on the deck. The caption: "Life is worth Baccarat."

This isn't your grandmother's Baccarat.

FRANCE: "Conceptual Strategists"

National Snapshot

Compared to other executives, French business leaders say:

- Communicating global vision is key to business success.
- "Beating the competition" is a cultural value.
- They face change with confidence, yet know their strengths and shortcomings.
- They give employees decision-making authority.
- They understand their own roots and are least likely to respect the traditions of others.
- Their organizations are more likely to engage in job rotations and cross-cultural experiences.
- 56% of revenues are derived from outside France.

The French are civilized thinkers with a passion for beauty and fullness of experience. They are proud, erudite people, logical and strategic in their thinking. Relishing the finer things in life, they take great pride in their history and culture.

In the early twentieth century, France drew thousands of brilliant thinkers, writers, and artists such as James Joyce, Ernest Hemingway, and Pablo Picasso to its capital city, Paris. It was the intellectual climate that attracted them; it was the French love of debate and beauty that kept them coming back for more.

As one of the chief engenderers of the Western intellectual tradition, France has provided the world's laboratory for advanced thinking. Karl Marx first published his *Communist Manifesto* there in 1848, and Gertrude Stein and Samuel Beckett also published their first works there. Paris—the provocative "city of light"—was simply "the place to be." This heritage has persisted for generations.

Historical Tensions in Europe

Although considered among the world's greatest diplomats—masters of the art of war and alliance—the French have fought with most European countries from the sixteenth to the twentieth centuries. Ninety percent Catholic and long 100 percent French-speaking, this civilized land is now becoming more diverse—with Protestantism and the Muslim faith also represented and languages in some regions ranging from French to Spanish, Portuguese, Arabic, and Polish, among others.

France was a world colonial power whose empire extended far and wide—from North America to India, from Brazil to Southeast Asia and Africa. Many of these regions still retain their French legacy, such as the Louisiana Bayou; Vietnam, many of whose residents still speak French; and Algeria, where the colonial evidence is still evident in Algiers and other cities. But its greatest tensions came from its two primary neighbors, the United Kingdom and Germany.

The fourteenth- to fifteenth-century Hundred Years' War—which actually lasted 116 years—pitted France against the United Kingdom in one of the world's first modern battles. Three centuries after it ended, Louis XV fought three wars with England, losing a great deal of territory, including French Canada and parts of India. Even so, French power reached a pinnacle in the eighteenth and early nineteenth centuries under Louis XVI and later Napoleon. French was the language of international discourse, both commercial and diplomatic, until Napoleon was defeated at Waterloo in 1815, marking the beginning of the new British Empire.

Germany posed a different problem. By the late nineteenth century,

Otto von Bismarck had united Germany, making it almost twice the population and power of France. France has declared war on Germany three times since 1871, admitting defeat twice. By the end of World War II, the French realized Germany could be controlled only by the creation of a united Europe and a strong Franco-German alliance. Since the 1958 formation of the European Economic Community (now the European Union), this relationship of equality between France and Germany has been central to European cooperation and prosperity.

Some French believe that the end of the Cold War and Germany's reunification are creating a more threatening German economy. France's long-standing reservations about outsiders, especially the Germans, coupled with their cautious demeanor, fuel this fear. In fact, many French quietly wonder whether the euro is just a polite name for the deutsche mark.

Grandeur of French Culture

France is a nation of grandeur and pageantry. From Descartes's intellectual reasoning to the earliest Encyclopedists to the nineteenth-century Impressionist artists, the French have shaped our modern understanding and appreciation of the world. Long the home of advanced thought in religious philosophy and economics, France has also given the world many of the major developments in literature, architecture, and the arts.

Theirs is a culture of fine food, drink, and theater. France has been both the bastion of centuries of established national schools of art and the birthplace of many schools challenging the artistic status quo: Paul Gauguin, Auguste Rodin, Henri Matisse, Paul Cézanne, Georges Seurat, and Marcel Duchamp were all leaders of new artistic movements. Because it is an intellectual nation, France simultaneously maintains the classics and creates the modern, both respecting and challenging established ways of thinking and seeing the world.

Not only glamour and historical richness but also erudition and intelligence are born here. With one of the finest and most rigorous educational systems in the world for hundreds of years, learning itself is a seminal event in France. The *grandes écoles* educate the brightest of France, producing the upper echelons of both government and business.

Historically, though too simplistic a schema for today's French society, class culture is divided into three main categories: the *aristocratie,* or aristocrats, the *classes moyennes* or *bourgeoisie* (middle class), and the *classes populaires,* or working class. This highly stratified society gave birth to the 1789 French Revolution, the 1871 Paris Commune, and the 1968 student strike as well as vigorous socialist and communist movements of the twentieth century.

Proud of their language, many French people believe everyone should speak French—and well. For several hundred years, almost every Western diplomat did just that, speaking a language strictly regulated by the French Academy. But with the political and economic convergence of the European Union, open borders, and increased diversity, this emphasis on French is changing.

Seen as formal and private people by outsiders, the French keep a distance around them. They believe that their jobs and incomes are intensely private matters; paradoxically, it is difficult to embarrass them about sex and nudity.

French culture is the height of civilization—and the French want to keep it that way. But as famous businesses and landmarks are bought by foreigners and jobs go to an increasing population of immigrants, some fear globalization will trivialize French culture. Others welcome the chance to be a multicultural nation.

All this is jarring in a country in which friendships matter and life focuses on the civility of relationships. In French society, rituals and social norms are crucial. There is a "French way" of life that is now becoming more international, with pizza, couscous, souvlaki, and corn flakes vying for attention alongside the fine wines and cheeses for which France is known. There is now a tension between leaning toward French culture and language, on the one hand, and toward a European and global identity, on the other.

Cartesian Thinkers

Out of this land of social rank emerge big-picture thinkers and people who love discussion and debate. Independent mavericks, they mistrust the simple and argue and dissect in search of the ultimate truth. Conceptual thinkers, they use their strategic and philosophical minds to understand the world.

As exemplified by their formal *salons*—intellectual clubs for thinkers—these people are proud of their intellectual prowess. Schooled to be formal and logical, argumentative and opinionated, their social and business structures reinforce this way of thinking. With a great appreciation for conversation, they frequently interrupt one another, viewing argument as a form of entertainment.

Always in pursuit of the basic rightness on issues, the French have historically vacillated between their love of authority and their love of democracy.

A Business Culture Emerges

Go to France to do business in August, and your meetings will be extremely short—and lonely. The country virtually shuts down during the last month of summer, a clear indication that quality of life comes first and business careers are a means to an end, not the end itself.

The world's fourth largest economy, France is ranked twenty-second in world competitiveness, primarily because of government intervention, difficult labor relations, and intense bureaucracy—a result of its centuries-old tradition of government economic control. Because the *grandes écoles* produce many of their leaders in both business and government, there's a close relationship between the two sectors, but also an inherent societal distrust of business.

After World War II, the capitalist system in France was changed to a "mixed economy," and certain sectors of the economy, such as banking, electricity, coal, and gas, were nationalized. The "cradle-to-grave" social welfare programs that emerged are viewed as one of Europe's greatest achievements.

However, the creation of "Euroland"—a united economic Europe—has required member nations to reduce budget deficits, cut social welfare programs, and privatize businesses. As a result, socialism itself has changed in France—and other European nations—from "ownership of means of production" to "regulation of free enterprise." This has not been without tension, as French unemployment continues to be high.

The French market is mature, sophisticated, and well served by suppliers around the world. A land with limited natural resources known for its tourism, grapes, and cheese, France must often buy goods and services outside its own borders, and it has a natural predilection to trade with the rest of the European community.

A recent government slogan, "France lacks oil, but not ideas," shows the French focus on minds, not minerals. It was its lack of energy resources, for instance, that led France to develop nuclear power, generating 72 percent of their energy needs at nuclear power stations by the 1990s. At the same time, it is the European Union's leading agricultural producer, second in the world only to the U.S.

Though the French profess gender equality, there are still few women in leadership positions in business and government; women gained the right to vote only after World War II. In this largely patriarchal country, sexual harassment has been illegal only since 1992. Yet Frenchwomen have retained their femininity in business, while in other nations, such as the United States, they have tended to emulate men in their desire to get ahead.

In French business, the person at the top, the *patron,* is all-controlling, creating significant power distance and risk aversion. This hierarchy can create a wide gulf between management and labor, one in which workers feel distrustful and show animosity toward management. Unionism is strong.

Facing global competition, increased opportunities across the European Union, and cross-border mergers, many French companies are reinventing themselves. Other countries increasingly look to France for high-tech inventions and components, such as its high-speed trains. Despite these positive changes, tensions still percolate under the surface. In a blow to its national image, France has been left out of several significant alliances with the United Kingdom and Germany recently, including the proposed merger of the London and Frankfurt stock exchange platforms and the discussions between British Aerospace and Daimler-Benz Aerospace to create a supranational European defense company.

France: ***At a Glance***
Official name: French Republic

Economy type: European Union
Trading bloc: European Union

Location: Straddling western Europe between the Atlantic Ocean and the Mediterranean **Capital:** Paris **Population:** 58,804,944
Head of state: President Jacques Chirac **Official language:** French
Religion: Roman Catholic 90% **Literacy:** 99%
World GNP ranking: 4 **GDP (US$ bn):** $1,360.6
GDP per capita: $23,215 **Unemployment:** 12.5%
Inflation: 1.9% **World export market share:** 6.7%

Major industries: Steel, chemicals, textiles, tourism, wine, perfume, aircraft, machinery, electronic equipment
Major crops: Grains, sugar beets, wine grapes, fruits, vegetables
Minerals: Bauxite, iron, coal
Labor force: 69% services, 26% industrial, 5% agricultural
Computers per 1,000 people: 150.5

Assets: Top graduates continue to enter engineering and technology fields. Strong defense, telecommunications, and automotive sectors. World leader in luxury goods: cosmetics, perfume,wine. Modernized agriculture. Excellent infrastructure.

Liabilities: High unemployment. Many industries failing to compete effectively due to outmoded working practices. High government spending. Difficult to start new businesses. Poor labor-management relations and frequent strikes decrease productivity.

From the French, we learn to see the strategic big picture. Their erudite exploration of ideas reminds us to focus on "thinking" as much as "doing." They teach us to keep work in perspective and to balance business success with personal satisfaction.

LIVE QUALITY TO MAKE QUALITY
Friedrich Schock and Schock Holdings *(Germany)*
Frank Straub and Blanco GmbH *(Germany)*

Schock Holdings

Title: Chairman
Headquarters: Stuttgart
Business: A family business started in 1924 after WWI by Schock's father and his two brothers, Schock Holdings is a medium-sized privately owned group of companies using high performance plastics to manufacture world class kitchen and bath products. They export 25% of their products.
Employees: 1,200

Blanco

Title: President
Headquarters: Stuttgart
Business: Founded in 1925, Blanco is a family business making products of stainless steel and composite materials. Largest company in a family business group, they manufacture parts for ovens, refrigerators, dishwashers, washers and dryers, and export 30% of their products.
Employees: 1,600

"A COLLEAGUE ONCE TOOK A HUNDRED DEUTSCHE MARKS *and drove from country to country in the European Union, just exchanging the money into local currency. He didn't buy a thing, just exchanged money. At the end, he only had ten DM left," says Friedrich Schock, CEO of Schock Holdings. It's a story that tells a lot about the challenges faced by European businesses in search of competitive advantage.*

Germany's advantage is quality. Because of the country's lack of natural resources, German companies have relied on their strengths to build their national economy: workmanship, hard work, multilingual skills, and an export orientation. These are their ingredients for getting higher value out of limited materials—to get more for their money than Schock's colleague was able to do.

The Germans know that quality people make quality products. Their apprenticeship programs are legendary; the high percentage of vocationally trained workers is one of the secrets of Germany's high quality standard. For more than five hundred years, companies have shared in the training of young people—a national commitment to skill development.

Two leaders who gladly share that responsibility are Frank Straub of Blanco and Friedrich Schock of Schock Holdings, family businesses that make up the *Mittelstand*, or middle area, of the German economy.

"Germany's national character strives for perfection, quality, and precision," says Straub. "But there's a tendency to overengineer, to put the quality standard so high that it puts too much cost into the products."

The cost of perfection isn't always financial either, but psychological, and overshadowed by the fear of making mistakes. "In Germany, you are either perfect or imperfect," says Straub. "And imperfect is perceived as failure. The fear of failure and its consequences are strong: if you've failed, you're basically dead. We must change our attitudes about taking risks to be more innovative." Straub illustrates how ingrained this risk aversion is: "In Germany, venture capital is called 'risk capital.' "

Though risk-averse, Germany is a world champion exporter. Proud of Germany's balance of social and market forces, Schock knows the importance of balancing wealth creation with stability, security, and quality-of-life issues. And he knows its practices of codetermination, work councils, and labor-management relations will be an advantage in the long term, but not necessarily today. "In the short term, it binds your hands and you can't move quickly," he says.

Even so, Schock believes that Europe is the up-and-coming continent because of its experience in cross-cultural issues. Schock agrees that "Europe has a painful past and history," Straub explains. "After World War II, we had to cooperate, be open internationally, learn to speak multiple languages, and rebuild our national character." These men are leading the way for a new generation of German managers who are still perfection-oriented, but are building more value- and innovation-driven organizations, pushing leadership to all levels of their companies, and shaping quality people and products—from the inside out.

Remember That Quality Starts with the Customer

The Germans have a natural advantage in delivering quality around the globe, according to Straub: "Our strength is that we learn the world by traveling. That increases our international ability—a 'management by chameleon,' where if we're in a world of green, we can easily change color and become green."

"I visited East Germany before the Wall came down," remembers Schock, "and called on the only manufacturing company making kitchen tops there. They only made white tops, and only after reunification did they expand—to include brown. I showed their CEO our two hundred models in two hundred colors, an expression of our deepest human longing for individuation. In the future, we must see individuals, companies, and cultures as unique. Our total global market will expand, but it will be divided into smaller and smaller segments. The need to customize will require an even greater ability to understand and serve individual and national cultural needs."

In our competitive world, standing up for your national products requires a certain pride. And it's pride that Germany has had to struggle with. "It is easier for Germans to be proud of their company than their country," Straub recognizes. "We aren't nationalistic anymore. We went to the other extreme. You don't see many German flags like in other countries." But they've made their crisis of pride a strategic advantage. "Because of our past, there is a humility and flexibility of Germans working internationally, which is one reason for our success as international exporters," he adds.

Create Quality Symbols for Quality Products

To revitalize that sense of pride, both leaders focus their company's attention on quality of the highest order. Straub has created the "Five Stars of Blanco," a way for Blanco employees to show their dedication to quality. "People like symbols that matter," he explains. "Yet in Germany, pins and flags are often viewed as propaganda from the war. We want to be a five-star company—one that represents very high quality and performance." Today the "five-star" symbol permeates Blanco's corporate culture: "We have a five-year strategy. In 2000, we want to make 500 million marks, with a profit rate of a minimum of five percent. Each person has five targets and should create five proposals for European growth. Everything seems to start and end with 'five.' "

To institutionalize such a mindset, globally literate leaders must personify the symbols themselves by living and working according to the five stars of quality. Straub says he has to manage his time so that it doesn't influence the quality of his leadership. "My interactions must be five-star quality, too, so I have created a principle that I will not talk with somebody about someone else—unless those two people have talked first."

Develop Quality People from the Inside Out

For Schock, quality products and people go hand in hand. His unflinching values center around his Christian faith. A former politician, he has cultivated his business character from the inside out, building on his political past. "Business and politics have many similarities," he says. "You have to make a profit, and you have to be elected—and you can only do that by listening to customers and constituents. In both, you must exchange ideas with people and have a longer-term motivation than just making a profit or getting to the top. Those are partial motives, but you must appeal to people's higher purpose in both business and politics."

Out of that learning, Schock has built a transparent company, sharing all the numbers and standing firm on principle. "Credibility and authentic living are not an obstacle to flexibility," he says. Honest and forthcoming as a person, Schock is highly flexible in business, seeing each individual as unique. He is very clear about his moral principles but flexible with people, markets, methods, and manufacturing.

By appealing to that higher purpose, he finds that quality is the outcome. "You must listen to your conscience; there is no motivation without morality. The word 'success,' means 'it follows' in Latin," he explains. "Success is something that follows, the natural result of behaving right—not the number one target in your life, but an outcome."

CHAPTER ELEVEN

RESULTS

How Do We Measure Success?

AT THE END OF THE DAY, it's results that matter. Yet in a world where our assets are people, not objects; relationships, not status; and culture, not passports, even our measures of success are changing.

Globally literate leaders are committed to building a value-creating organization. To do so, they must learn to think differently about success and how to measure it. As knowledge, relationships, culture, and the ability to learn become paramount factors of productivity and wealth creation, new ways of measuring and accounting for intangible, "soft" assets are needed. The globally literate leader understands that our twenty-first-century organization has new kinds of capital:

- *Financial capital:* The money, investments, property, and equipment of the organization
- *Human capital:* The people in the organization and their abilities, knowledge, skills, experience, capabilities, and relationships
- *Customer capital:* The predisposition of customers to continue doing business with the organization
- *Organization capital:* The systems, structures, and processes that make up the organization's infrastructure
- *Reputation capital:* The image and reputation of the organization in the various communities in which it does business around the world

By leveraging all this capital, valuing the softer, intangible assets of the business, and measuring the costs of mismanaging them, leaders begin to create metrics for all aspects of the business. Showing the real values of these diverse assets on the balance sheets is complicated. There are huge disparities these days between the market capitalization and book value of certain companies, especially high-technology firms such as Microsoft, because we don't know how to express the full value of their intangible assets.

Complicating matters further, the costs of mismanagement are equally difficult to measure. Consider the economic impact of uninformed employees, limited ideas, underdeveloped markets, negative public image, employee sabotage, and alienated customers on the bottom line.

To minimize these problems, globally literate leaders must first build companies with strong values and performance goals. Globally literate leaders start with a picture of what success looks like, craft a social contract that shares the risks and responsibilities between employees and the company, develop a workforce of outcome thinkers, and build a culture of results. By aligning their vision and goals to strategies and success metrics, these leaders create alignment and value inside the business.

Ultimately, globally literate leaders are not successful unless they give something back to society. They are economic and social leaders who value creating and distributing wealth. They are socially conscious and environmentally responsible—critically important in a world where multinational corporations play such a predominant role. The citizens of the world will be watching closely to see whether these global businesses act responsibly with their newfound wealth and power in the twenty-first century.

In a multicultural world, leaders will differ in how they express this social responsibility. In the United States, this is typically done through individual philanthropy; in Europe, through government investment; in Latin America, through families and the Catholic Church; and in Asia, through powerful family networks and a commitment to the society at large.

Though the expression of measurement can be determined by national psychology, leaders all over the world are focused on it: Dana Mead, CEO of Tenneco in the United States, wants to instill a bias for action; Lars-Eric Petersson, CEO of Skandia in Sweden, charts new navigation systems that measure intangible assets; James Stanford, CEO of Petro-Canada, is creating personal best-performance environments; Muhammad Yunus, CEO of Grameen Bank in Bangladesh, shows us how to build a culture of accountability; Eric Molobi, CEO of Kagiso Trust in South Africa, talks about what it means to be a socially responsible leader; and Ray Anderson of Interface in the United States shows how he's building a sustainable enterprise around the world.

DEMAND A BIAS FOR ACTION
Dana G. Mead and Tenneco, Inc. *(U.S.A.)*

Title: Chairman and CEO
Headquarters: Greenwich, Connecticut
Business: *Industry Week* magazine has named Tenneco one of the world's 100 best-managed companies. With revenues of $7 billion, this automotive and packing product maker produces Walker exhaust systems (number one in the world), Monroe shocks, and Hefty and Baggies plastic bags. It is the number one U.S. maker of single-use food containers and supplies virtually every vehicle manufacturer in the world—serving customers in more than 100 countries.
Employees: 49,335 in 32 countries

DANA MEAD MARCHES INTO BUSINESS *battle like the West Point graduate and Vietnam veteran he is. In his twenty-one years in the military, Mead rose to the rank of colonel. With as many years in industry, he has risen to the position of chairman and CEO of Tenneco, one of the thirty-five largest industrial companies in the United States. Mead combines a military mindset with the keen intellect that earned him a doctorate at MIT. His motto is from none other than General Patton: "Plan deliberately; execute violently."*

Under Mead's leadership, Tenneco has made the transition from a large conglomerate with eight major businesses to a world-class industrial growth company with two global manufacturing businesses: automotive parts and packaging.

A leader with a strong bias for action, Mead is confident and achievement-oriented. He has created a fast, aggressive, and results-oriented company. Tenneco is a company of relationships that lives on achieved status; heroes are created here every day by what they produce and the results they achieve. It is a doing culture, personifying the values of America.

Dana Mead's doctoral dissertation at the Massachusetts Institute of Technology (MIT) focused on the creation of military strategy in peacetime. To write it, he also had to know a lot about military strategy in times of war. And it's war that faced him when he joined the late Mike Walsh at the helm of Tenneco in the early 1990s.

He knew the company was in trouble and needed to achieve results, not congratulate itself on best efforts. A leadership bias for action needed to be institutionalized if the company were to measure up against world-class competitors. Mead was prepared to take Tenneco into battle.

Achieve Results, Not Best Efforts

"Eventually, you've either got to shoot or get shot at."

Dana Mead doesn't mince words. He has a bias for action, and demands that the people around him share that proclivity. From the moment he joined Tenneco, he got people focused on outcomes. "Results, not best efforts; output, not process" is his battle cry: "A leader needs to lead. You can study and debate issues to death, but eventually you must take action."

And not just at the top. Mead believes that people at all levels want and need to see action and results. "Employees don't like to sit around and not see tangible activity and results," he says. "You can't warm up on the sidelines all the time, you've got to play occasionally. And when you play you've got to score."

When Mead started at Tenneco, it needed measurable results—and quickly. "There were huge embedded costs in all our companies," he says, "the cost of not taking action was the cost of quality. In a company with $13 billion in revenues, we found $2.3 billion in unnecessary costs.

"At first, everyone just gave excuses, saying, 'We worked our asses off, but the wood wasn't good or the chips weren't the right size.' And we basically said, 'That's just a bunch of crap. Tell us what you're going to do to get us to our goals—how are we going to fix the problem?' "

Mead knew company employees could build confidence in themselves by achieving something. But first they would have to fail at a few things to learn their limits: "Sometimes you hit it, and sometimes you don't. That's part of knowing yourself."

Mead is fond of telling how he learned his greatest leadership lesson. Assigned to a tough Army general as an aide-de-camp, one day Mead endured a lecture outlining every stupid thing he had ever done. The tirade ended with the assessment that Mead was the best aide the general had ever had. Why? "For just one reason: you never make the same mistake twice." That lesson has accompanied Mead throughout his career. "The people you don't want around you are the ones who can't learn by their mistakes," he says. "That's very expensive learning." Mead makes the lesson even clearer: "if you don't learn from your mistakes, you've got to go."

Mead is a physical leader. He's visible, sets the tone, and is comfortable with his own power. Having high expectations of himself and others, he's not a big fan of throwaway empowerment. He believes that a leader must take risks and be out front. But he knows that when you play, sometimes you lose. What he doesn't want is excuses—and his people know there's absolutely no excuse for not hitting their numbers. To underscore this, Mead instituted a reality check: every month for two years, division presidents made presentations before Mead and the top management team to report their performance.

This is a leader who wants less conversation about philosophy and process and more attention on accountabilities and results. He knows that action doesn't just build self-esteem or produce results; it also puts the competition on the defensive and creates unimaginable new opportunities.

Institutionalize Your Bias for Action

Character counts for a lot with Mead. When he was teaching at West Point, a cheating scandal threatened the honor code of the institution. Chosen to lead the Special Study Group on Honor, Mead found that individual values were stronger than institutional values. And it's individuals—lots of individuals—that change an institution.

Mead knows that his bias for action has to be embedded deep in both individuals and the fabric of the organization to have any impact: "We've tried to impress on our managers that they have the power to change the company."

When Mead arrived on the scene, people were unwilling to stand up, to be accountable, and to make decisions. Mead changed the culture in short time by telling his executives he was basing 50 percent of their bonuses on leading change: "The guys went berserk, screaming, 'How can you do this? Tell me what a leader is!' So I put together a list of leadership behaviors for Tenneco. It was like the Supreme Court definition of pornography: it's hard to define, but you know when you see it."

Today, biannual reviews of the top thirty people in each business reveal what they're doing, where they're going, and how they're developing. Mead also began to change people's job assignments, replacing nonleaders with aggressive, take-charge leaders. "Real leaders," he notes, "are often recalcitrants, troublemakers, or gadflies." One of those talented and aggressive leaders was sent to Mobile, Alabama, to be a manager in one of the company's paper mills. A bit of a maverick, he threatened action if the employees didn't take safety issues more seriously.

"One day a guy got a serious cut," Mead relates, "and the manager went out to the mill floor and personally shut down the paper machines. He marched the entire mill out into the parking lot—'Your pay is stopped until I finish'—and proceeded to give a two-hour lecture on safety. He let them know the next time there was an injury, he was going to give another no-expenses-paid lecture out in the middle of the parking lot."

Tenneco needed more people like him. To get them, Mead developed an intensive leadership development program, using company case studies of successful leadership practices. Using 360-degree feedback, the program is revealing and disconcerting, but develops leaders: "We also took twenty-eight of our top guys to Gettysburg for two days and walked the battlefield with Army generals to learn about leadership decision making, both strategic, tactical, and interpersonal."

It's hard to get action in a culture with bureaucratic inertia. Passive, non-action-oriented people are products of their culture, but Mead knows that most people have the capacity to change. To make that happen, he is painfully honest with people about performance but is so privately so leaders don't lose their credibility with the troops.

Mead has zero tolerance for people who can't distinguish what's important and what isn't: "A manager in a world-class business doesn't have the luxury of deciding priorities among things that are essential—you have to do all of them." World-class managers must see the big picture and have big responsibilities. They must develop unique ways of solving problems and constantly push the envelope.

"It's not brain surgery," Mead says. "We're just trying to develop people who look and act and think like we do. We want to change expectations of success." What Mead is after is world-class success. It has been an almost-ten-year journey, starting in 1991.

Measure Yourself Against Your World-Class Competitors

"You don't get any credit for being the tallest midget in the circus."

This comment may not be politically correct, but the image works. It's an image Mead uses to illustrate his need to be world class. In the old Tenneco, top managers set up measures to ensure that they would look good. Mead changed all that.

He started by articulating thirteen challenges for operating in the global marketplace and quickly bumped up against the old culture. At a meeting of four hundred top managers, Mead asked how many had projected less revenue in their annual plan than they thought they could achieve. About 90 percent admitted they had sandbagged their budgets and, on average, had said they could achieve 23 percent less than they actually thought possible. "And I said, 'Why are you surprised that I always kick your plans up a few notches?'

"They had to start measuring themselves against world-class competitors. Of course, they cried foul. For once, they were asked to have measurable results and keep score against the very best. To put this company on its feet quickly, we had to eliminate a lot of failures. But traditional quality programs take years. We had trained two thousand team leaders without results before we started asking, 'Why are we doing all this? It's all process, it's all best efforts, but no value.' We weren't seeing better products, better margins, or happier customers."

Mead took a billion dollars of failure costs out in a year: "We carved up costs across the various businesses and put those costs in their budgets. So if

WHO LINKS PAY AND PERFORMANCE?

(Percentage of executives responding positively)

- North America: 40%
- Asia: 40%
- Australia/New Zealand: 39%
- Latin America: 36%
- Europe : 29%

they didn't get those costs out, they couldn't even get close to their budgets. Suddenly there were changes in infrastructures. They muscled their way through and found ways to do it."

As you enter the global arena, a new set of challenges appears. As chairman of the TransAtlantic Business Dialogue, a group of CEOs from North America and Europe, Mead knows being a global player brings its own lessons. "Every foreign business activity is more politically complex than any of us realize. "We're on our third government in Romania," he says.

"And the sociocultural issues are much more difficult to understand than we ever imagined. We couldn't get anyone in India to wear safety boots because it's too hot there, so we designed lighter boots and provided an incentive to wear them. And people habitually came late to work there until we started feeding them free breakfasts." Sometimes, doing good produces the unexpected: "In Romania, we employ women and pay them well, causing problems when they go home to unemployed husbands, who take out their personal frustrations by physically abusing their wives."

Today, Tenneco is truly world class in a lot of arenas: leadership, management, quality, purpose, and value. But it's the next generation of leaders with a bias for action that will determine its success.

That's Mead's battle plan.

MEASURE YOUR PERSONAL SUCCESS
Amy DiGeso and Mary Kay Cosmetics *(U.S.A.)*

Title: Former President and CEO
Headquarters: Dallas, Texas
Business: Founded by Mary Kay Ash in 1963, the company is the United States' number two direct-sales beauty products company and number one in sales of overall facial skin care and color cosmetics. Annual retail sales are $2 billion.
Employees: 500,000 in 25 countries (70% female)

AMY DIGESO ALWAYS MEASURES HERSELF on the kind of person she is. She uses psychological insight to create positive visions, challenging people to be more than they think they can be. Ultimately, DiGeso teaches benevolence and courage: "I'm a strong believer in leading by example."

A woman with simple roots, she was raised by parents who gave her wonderful things money can't buy: "They taught me never to look down on anyone. My mother believed you could 'praise people to success.' I don't need to abuse power to feel good."

DeGiso works hard to balance optimism with realism: "I'm known as the iron fist in the velvet glove—extraordinarily tough on issues but extraordinarily kind to people. I never ask employees to do anything I wouldn't do myself." Company founder Mary Kay Ash is one of DiGeso's role models: "She used to tell people to imagine the person they're talking with has a sign around their neck that says, 'Make me feel important.' "

DiGeso is happy with her own life, which accounts for part of her success: "Feeling good about what you're doing creates a deeper level of commitment in those around you. When I see women whose lives are changed by working for Mary Kay—how can I not feel great about what I'm doing?" She shares that enthusiasm with others: "I send out a thousand letters a month, telling people what an incredible job they're doing."

Mary Kay is a company of teachers: "We give people the opportunity to maximize their own potential, teaching all five hundred thousand employees to do something they might not otherwise be able to do. Many of our salespeople wouldn't be naturally drawn to a corporate role, or perhaps they wouldn't have the work experience to get one."

By creating networks of global entrepreneurs, Mary Kay is learning firsthand how cultural norms affect business: "Standing in front of a group is new to some cultures, especially parts of Asia." She fondly remembers a saleswoman in Taiwan: "In the first photograph at a sales meeting, she's standing with her eyes to the ground. Today, she's making fifty thousand dollars a month with Mary Kay."

After reaching the $2 billion sales mark, the company created a "thanks-a-billion card" for everyone who had contributed to the company's success. "Sure, we're only making lipstick, but wow, that lipstick has changed people's lives."

BUILD A CULTURE OF ACCOUNTABILITY AND MUTUAL RESPONSIBILITY
Muhammad Yunus and Grameen Bank *(Bangladesh)*

Title: Founder and Managing Director
Headquarters: Dhaka
Business: Launched in 1976 by Muhammad Yunus with a personal loan of $26 to a group of 42 workers—62 cents per person. Established as a bank in 1983. Eight million people in 43 countries are now getting microcredit. In 1998, Grameen Bank lent more than half a billion dollars in increments of an average of $100.
Employees: 14,000 in 35,000 villages

In a small village in Bangladesh, a woman who literally had nothing was able to buy a cow with a loan from Grameen Bank. She repaid the loan by selling the cow's milk and was able to buy a calf, too. Having a cow—much less two—had previously been beyond her wildest dreams.

Her success encouraged her to do the impossible: she took a loan to build a house with a tin roof. Her next goal is to buy a cell phone.

Who made this possible? Muhammad Yunus, father of the microcredit movement, founder of Grameen Bank, and breaker of all the rules of traditional finance. He is driving social change one rupee at a time, building mutually interdependent communities, enhancing people's self-esteem by ensuring that systems are in place to allow them to succeed, and applying those lessons in other cultures to build whole nations of doers. "I'm not a businessman," says Yunus, "I'm just using business to achieve a social objective."

Despite overwhelming odds, employees and recipients of loans from the Grameen Bank, begun in the poorest of nations, produce striking results, including a 98 percent repayment rate. In a world where having committed people and achieving results is vital to business success, we can learn from a country with a traditionally impoverished, unempowered population that has successfully—if somewhat nontraditionally—applied basic principles of empowerment, accountability, and teams.

Expect a Lot

"We're all capable of doing much more," notes Yunus. "It's institutions and concepts that limit us and keep us down. We're almost like a bonsai tree, a tiny plant kept tiny because of the way we're planted. If we had a better place, we would be tall and moving toward the sky. Institutional arrangements and concepts like collateral are real obstructions to the blooming of people, especially poor people.

"We can remove poverty only if we redesign our institutions, policies, and concepts. Poverty isn't created by the poor, nor sustained by them. If we're looking for one single action that will enable the poor to overcome their poverty, I would focus on credit. Credit is a fundamental human right," he says.

"All human beings are basically entrepreneurs," he continues. "People want to solve problems, take on challenges, discover their talents. It's just a matter of opening up the environment and giving them opportunity." Yunus sees capability in even the poorest and most disenfranchised of people. Coming from one of the world's poorest nations, he's still an inveterate optimist who knows that if this great success has occurred in Bangladesh, it can happen anywhere.

"Poverty," he says, "is simply a lack of options. Credit unlocks those doors." He's tested his theory in the most difficult of environments, where paying back loans is essentially counterculture. "And in Bangladesh," he notes, "giving money to women is unheard of." Even in a culture where the deck is stacked against him, Yunus's innovative approach succeeds: "We wanted to lend to the poorest first; that's why our borrowers are more than ninety-four percent women. When they succeed, their families benefit. The wealth trickles down."

Internalize and Socialize the Pressure

Grameen Bank takes the idea of a high-performance team seriously. It requires its borrowers to organize into groups of five. Instead of providing collateral, the borrowers guarantee one another's loans. In effect, they become human collateral for one another. All are cut off if one defaults, so they meet weekly to make payments and critique business plans to make sure that doesn't happen.

Yunus and bank managers don't put pressure on borrowers. Rather, and much more effectively, they've embedded that accountability inside the heads of borrowers and in the spaces between people on these collateral teams. As a result, borrowers motivate themselves, accounting for the phenomenal success of the program.

Remember That Success Breeds Success

"We have started believing the unbelievable—that the elimination of poverty is feasible. There is no reason anyone should remain poor on this planet," says Yunus. He builds systems to make sure that happens sooner rather than later.

Grameen borrowers repay their loans monthly, receiving incremental reinforcement that creates even more momentum and develops their self-confidence: "Success breeds success. We make sure people can succeed and repay their loan so their group doesn't suffer."

This success is being replicated in more than fifty nations. How can Bangladesh, a country of abject poverty, provide a viable model for the rest of the world? "Sometimes we take an idea across borders by making it like TV dinners," acknowledges Yunus, "just open and serve. But you lose the spirit, because Grameen grew out of the necessity of Bangladesh. We weren't even thinking of replicating it elsewhere.

"But even as it grew from local necessity, we knew that it had global application because financial institutions the world over had created a caste of 'untouchables' that they deemed uncreditworthy.

"Our borrowers subscribe to the Sixteen Decisions of Grameen, tenets that we ask them to live by that are very specific to the Bangladeshi condition. If you're doing this in the U.S. and just copy those tenets, people will laugh. That's why each location must adapt those principles, like they've done in Chicago, where they have something called the Fifteen Guiding Principles. Each culture has to find out what the 'sacred cow' is in their context."

Yunus isn't content with cows. GrameenPhone was launched in 1997 to build a cell phone network in Bangladesh. He wants the woman with the cow to have a "village phone," purchased with a loan from the Grameen Bank, so that she can sell phone service to villagers and use the income to repay the loan. "I want every rickshaw driver in Dhaka to have a cell phone in his back seat so passengers can rent the phone while they're riding to their next meeting. When you combine access to credit with access to information," Yunus says, "you change the game for the rural poor."

Yunus is a globally literate leader. He understands his roots and his role of giving something back. He knows that people from New York investment bankers to farmers in Bangladeshi villages are seeking self-esteem, creating a deep social literacy. He realizes that institutions shackle people and works to remove obstacles that keep people from doing their best. And he shows his cultural literacy in the way he creates Grameen principles that fit the different cultures around the world where microcredit flourishes.

The Bengali word *grameen* means "village," a small unit of human life. In English, a gram is a small unit of weight. "When tiny, tiny things start happening a million times, it lays the foundation of a strong economic base," says Yunus.

Since its beginnings, Grameen has given out nearly 16 million tiny loans. "These millions of small people," says Yunus, "with their millions of small pursuits can add up to the biggest development wonder in the world."

Bangladesh: ***At a Glance***
Official name: People's Republic of Bangladesh

Economy type: Emerging
Trading bloc: SAARC (South Asian Association for Regional Cooperation)

Location: Between India and Burma in the north of the Bay of Bengal
Capital: Dhaka **Population:** 127,567,002
Head of state: Prime Minister Hasina Wazed
Official languages: Bangla (official), English
Religion: Muslim 88%, Hindu 11% **Literacy:** 38%
World GNP ranking: N/A **GDP (US$ bn):** $155.1
GDP per Capita: $1,260 **Unemployment:** 1.9%
Inflation: 3.6% **World export market share:** N/A

Major industries: Food processing, jute, textiles, fertilizers, steel
Major crops: Jute, rice, tea
Minerals: Natural gas
Labor force: 64% agricultural, 21% services, 14% industry and mining
Computers per 1,000 people: Limited to a small elite

Assets: Bangladesh supplies 80% of the world's jute fiber supply. Low wages. Expanding textile industry.

Liabilities: A total of 64% of the population is engaged in agricultural work, which is vulnerable to unpredictable and disastrous weather conditions.

CHART A NAVIGATION SYSTEM THAT MEASURES HIDDEN VALUE

Lars-Eric Petersson and Skandia Insurance *(Sweden)*

Title: President and CEO
Headquarters: Stockholm
Business: An international financial services and insurance group with operations in 23 countries. Organized in three strategic business units: Long-Term Savings, Asset Management, and Property and Casualty Insurance.
Employees: 10,200

ALBERT EINSTEIN ONCE REMARKED, "*Not everything that's important can be counted, and not everything that can be counted is important." In a world where the bottom line is king, Einstein would have been considered something of a heretic—until recently. Organizations are quickly realizing he was onto something, that their spreadsheets have been missing something all these years: the seemingly uncountable brainpower of people.*

Lars-Eric Petersson is doing something about that. Skandia Insurance values many kinds of capital—customer, innovation, and process capital among them—and it has created a new balance sheet to show the value of those diverse assets.

It has also changed how it accounts for the value of the business: rather than measure trailing indicators, as most companies do, Skandia has created what it calls "future accounting," in which knowledge is more valuable than physical objects, and intangible assets are the leading indicators of future success.

The hidden value of Skandia comes into focus in what it calls the Skandia Navigator, an image close to Sweden's Viking roots. "Navigation," says Skandia's annual report, "requires balance, location, and direction."

In 1991, at Swedish financial services giant Skandia, Leif Edvinsson became the world's first director of intellectual capital, a job that Thomas Stewart, author of *Intellectual Capital: The New Wealth of Organizations*, has called "part librarian, part intellectual entrepreneur, and part cruise-ship social director." By 1994, Skandia published an intellectual capital supplement to its annual report, setting off shock waves that led Stewart to devote a *Fortune* cover story to it in 1996 and prompting a Securities and Exchange Commission conference on the issue that same year.

A large number of growth companies are valued well beyond their book value. What makes up the difference is the intellectual power of the company, which is usually not found on balance sheets. And because neither human capital nor structural capital is represented in traditional accounting systems, Skandia developed its own method of capturing the true value potential of its organization with the help of two models, the Skandia Value Scheme and the Skandia Navigator.

It has designed a "value-creating" organization and developed a new balance sheet—and, to make sure the concept "sticks," it has developed user-friendly tools for measuring results.

Design a Value-Creating Organization

No longer can we measure a company's worth by bricks, mortar, and machinery. More important than cash and real estate is its ability to generate ideas and devise products and services that keep it on the cutting edge. It's these hidden values that Petersson has focused on bringing to the surface. "It's really change, complexity, technology, globalization, and the pace of knowledge acquisition that's driving Skandia to focus on cultivating intellectual capital," he says. "What you have to do is stretch the organization into the unknown, which means you have to have another kind of leadership, culture, management system, mapping, and structure—all to unleash people, rather than lock them up."

When Skandia started focusing on hidden values, it took stock of all its valuable assets that weren't disclosed in traditional accounting systems, such as trademarks, information technology systems, core competencies, key persons, partners, and alliances. The list became so unwieldy that they reduced it to this simplified definition: Human capital plus structural capital equals intellectual capital.

Structural capital, says Petersson, is what's left at the office when the employees go home for the day. Human capital is employees' competence and capabilities. Now, he says, Skandia needed a new way to account for those hidden values.

Create a New Balance Sheet

Skandia created a new balance sheet to do just that. It became the world's first company to make its measurements of intellectual capital publicly available in an annual "Intellectual Capital Report" that complements the company's conventional report and accounts.

Skandia has identified five key areas in which it must excel and which it must measure: customers, processes, renewal and development, human factors, and finance. Imagine a house with finance as the roof, customer focus and process focus as the walls, human factors as the hearth, and renewal and development as the structure's foundation.

The company's new balance sheet provides a framework for reporting on all five areas, making it easier for managers to ensure they're on track and for Petersson to adjust the course of the whole company. It also allows him to have a broader perspective on the value potential of the organization. Skandia doesn't have "controllers," it has "knowledge engineers," he says.

This is a company that's always looking for new ideas and new concepts to put onto the balance sheet. It does that by keeping a focus on the future, its intangible tomorrow. By understanding tomorrow before it happens, it's able to create new ways of thinking about it and measuring it. Its intellectual capital guru, Edvinsson, has moved from revolutionizing corporate accounting to developing "accounting for the future." His new unit, Skandia Futures Centers (SFC), and his handpicked team of thirty people form an elite squad of what the company calls "Future Teams."

The teams' goal is to understand the archaeology of the future. For instance, the Future Teams discovered that the age group usually targeted for leadership development and training—thirty-five- to forty-five-year-olds—is least open to new ideas and creative thinking. Focus on the under thirty-five-year-olds and the over-forty-five-year-olds, they say, and you'll find the best groups for leadership training.

"We don't talk about the future and what's going to happen," says Petersson. "Instead, we talk about the questions we'll have to deal with in the future."

Create User-Friendly Tools for Measuring Results

Small wonder, in this land of Viking explorers, that Skandia's tool for measuring results is called "The Navigator." Like the Vikings of old, it views the Navigator as an instrument to help it find its way through the uncharted waters of measuring intellectual capital.

The Navigator is a CD-ROM tool that Skandia managers around the world use to plan, strategize, budget, execute, and measure in the same way, using those same five company compasses: customers, processes, renewal and development, human factors, and finance. The Navigator helps Skandia develop an accounting language for the sustainability of the organization—and because it's a numerical language and technology-based, it's globally accessible.

"The Navigator is a tool that talks to people, teaches people, and gets them to understand they're working in a lot of different intangible areas," says Petersson.

"Knowledge intensity on a global scale is growing by one hundred percent every eighteen months. But the availability of people to read the new map is decreasing because complexity is increasing and we're not trained for that."

Skandia has tapped into fundamental laws of the new economy: "While the industrial economy is based on the law of diminishing return, this new knowledge economy is based on the opposite, the law of increasing utility by knowledge sharing.

"If you take a piece of paper and fold it into six pieces, it becomes smaller. But if you have an idea that's shared, it doesn't decrease in value. If you have software and millions use it, it increases in value. If you have a cellular phone system and you have millions of users, it's more valuable than if there's only one user."

These new tools can work only in a culture of high trust and deep relationships. When you're traveling into the unknown, sharing information globally, and asking your people to learn on the job in real time, you need the best of the Swedish collaborative nature.

"To nourish this new economic law of knowledge, you need a culture based on trust," Petersson notes. "You have to move from the head office to the heart office. You have to respect the depth and integrity of relationships and be able to come to the table with a dispassionate, analytic mind.

"The bottom line of our Navigator is renewal and development. If that becomes clear, you change your behavior, your navigation system, and your rewards scheme from rewarding past behavior to rewarding future behavior."

"Books contain capital," wrote Thomas Jefferson to James Madison in 1821. It took more than 175 years, but we're beginning to see what he meant. The focus on knowledge and intellectual capital at Skandia works. The effects on their bottom line became visible immediately: 50 percent of premium income and a significant share of earnings come from operations that didn't exist ten years ago; Skandia has doubled its customer base in three years; and the company has reduced by tenfold the time needed to open an office in a new country.

CREATE A PERSONAL BEST-PERFORMANCE ENVIRONMENT
James Stanford and Petro-Canada *(Canada)*

Title: President and CEO
Headquarters: Calgary
Business: Established in 1975, when many of the Canadian government's energy assets were transferred to Petro-Canada. Now touted as a privatization model, Petro-Canada operates in two business segments: upstream activities (exploration, production, and transportation of crude oil, natural gas, and propane) and downstream activities (purchase, sale, and refinement of crude oil products). Following privatization in late 1990, the government of Canada now holds only 18% of shares.
Employees: More than 5,000.

JIM STANFORD GOT A STRONG TASTE of the extraordinary when Petro-Canada sponsored the Olympic Torch Relay in 1988. It was an event that stands out in the collective mind of its workforce as a time when they were all focused on achieving a nearly impossible goal: carrying the torch through every Canadian province and territory in the middle of winter. The clarity of the goal and the deep personal commitment forged an emotional compact that people did not want to end.

Several years later, the bottom fell out of the company. Debt-heavy and inefficient, Petro-Canada was unable to compete. Stanford sold off businesses and reengineered his company back to health, becoming a model of state oil-company privatization in the process. But there were still major morale problems to contend with.

Stanford needed to replicate the energy and focus the company had experienced with the Olympic Torch Relay. His answer: to create a personal best-performance environment for everyone.

When the dust from the financial turnaround settled, Stanford quickly realized that its own internal environment was keeping its employees from working at their personal best. During the massive change of privatization and cost cutting, they had become disengaged, cynical, and burned out.

To change that, the company began examining what athletes do to operate at their personal best and what companies do to create high-performance environments. Employees offered some free advice: don't engage with us by videoconference, come out and really listen to us. Stanford did just that. He helped his executives become emotionally intelligent leaders, challenged them to develop adult relationships, and jointly created a personal best performance environment for everyone.

Make Developing Emotional Leadership a Priority

"Leadership is real work."

Jim Stanford knows what he's talking about. Coming in as president of a company whose share price had gone from $13 to $8 in one year, with a billion-dollar write-off and a debt-to-cash-flow ratio of greater than 6 to 1, "it's clear what you have to do," he says. "If you're in twenty-five businesses and only eight of them can generate returns, you have to get rid of the others even though some people have their heart and soul in them. That's where the pain comes in, because you have an impact on a lot of people, on company culture, and on individual and corporate self-esteem."

It was those tough but necessary decisions that had created accumulated cynicism, a sense of betrayal as a result of the downsizing, and broken relationships with employees. "In retrospect," Stanford says, "we should have paid more attention to the mental health of employees during reengineering. We were left with some bitter, disenfranchised people."

Stanford realized that leaders in the company—at all levels—would have to behave differently. But first they would have to clarify what values and behaviors would be critical to future success, using employee surveys and 360 appraisals to give honest feedback to executives. "A lot of warts came out. Self-awareness is so important—you must be aware of how other people perceive you."

Then the company put teeth into the success factors it had identified: "By linking compensation to leadership behavior, it showed we were serious. Some team members didn't have the emotional intelligence for it. Some leaders talked a good game at the executive table but were different in the field. At some point as CEO, you say, 'This is my view, and this is where we're going.'

"You must also live these values every day and in every communication to let people know you're serious about change. Leaders can make lots of mistakes if people understand where the organization is going."

The executive team worked hard to create this model of success. First it reestablished the company's business philosophy and direction. Then it linked its leadership messages (vision, values, behaviors, and goals) to the people processes (tools for guiding direction and shaping effectiveness). And finally, it created the right performance environment that linked everything to operating results (reliability, volume, margins, costs, share of market).

"If I could change anything about the process we went through," Stanford says, "I would not tolerate counterproductive behavior for as long as I did."

Engage in Adult Relationships

Creating this kind of healthy, high-performance environment required maintaining adult relationships across the board. This meant that Petro-Canada had to fundamentally change the employment contract, establishing a clear understanding of the new kinds of responsibilities that the company and employees had toward each other. It needed to forge a partnership of shared commitment and mutual benefit.

Today, Stanford and his team are clear about the new relationship: "To excel in the changing marketplace, people must be skilled, experienced, and take responsibility for their own learning and development. The company is responsible for clear direction and leadership, career and learning opportunities, and setting clear expectations for performance.

"Maximizing business success requires personal and economic success for all—and we actively pursue this common goal. Today, there are sacred principles in the way we treat our employees, consistently applied across all parts of the organization."

This mutual meeting of adults is clear in the unscripted meetings Stanford holds with employees. They can ask any question, and he'll answer them, one by one. Shortly after many of the service functions had been outsourced, the first question in one of these sessions produced an audible gasp from the audience: "Why not outsource the executive leadership team instead?" Unshaken by the question, Stanford welcomed it: "I couldn't have had a better first question than that."

Build a Personal Best-Performance Culture

Performing well is not rocket science. If you create a culture where people are treated like adults and where the vision is clear, the leadership team is on board, and all are doing their best work, your company will do well. That's Stanford's business logic.

"Personal best is having informed employees who know what the corporation is trying to do and understand their role in it," he says. "It means having well-educated people who feel a sense of ownership. And it means having an employee population that really respects the corporation.

"In brief, it's somebody who knows what to do—the vision, values, and standards—and why it has to be done—the expectations. It's somebody who has the tools—like authority, information, and time—and the capabilities—personal attributes, skills, and experience—to work effectively. And it's somebody who feels good about doing their part, with the personal motivation and reward systems to sustain the effort."

Stanford integrated the soft and hard sides of business—the finances and the performance conversations—a skill he says is "inside of everyone," even linear, measurement-oriented engineers such as himself.

Today, Stanford enjoys his own personal best-performance environment. "I'm getting e-mails from employees deep in the bowels of the organization who make reference to the personal best-performance environment—they feel it's really working."

His national roots also play a role in his leadership philosophy: "We take the best of British culture in terms of astuteness and perseverance, coupled with the best of American innovation and business drive, and combine it with our Canadian sense of social responsibility and good values—all that is embedded in Petro-Canada's new culture."

CANADA: "Ethical Statesmen"

National Snapshot

Compared to other executives, Canadian business leaders say:

- Knowing their strengths and shortcomings is important.
- They are motivated by strongly held principles and beliefs.
- They are less inclined to make "competition" a cultural value.
- Recruiting efforts are key to creating a high-performance global organization.
- 47% of revenues come from sales outside Canada.

Canadians are trustworthy frontiersmen of integrity. Balancing individualism and communitarianism, they reach out to the world as culturally sensitive pragmatists, even as they continue to learn how to manage their own internal multiculturalism.

IN 1813, A COMMEMORATIVE MEDAL WAS ISSUED in Canada, proclaiming the successful defense of "Upper Canada" against the United States during the War of 1812. The small medallion features the Canadian beaver and British lion watching as an American eagle hovers over Niagara Falls. The eagle is biding its time, the lion is half awake, but the beaver is busy, as a beaver would be. The contrast is striking: the lion and the eagle, majestic and serene; the beaver, quietly and methodically at work, an industriousness that marks the nation it represents.

A Vast, Quiet Frontier

The second largest country in the world, Canada is also one of the least populated. France, by comparison, has only one eighteenth as much land but twice the population. Roughly the same size as the United States, Canada contains less than 10 percent of the population of its southern neighbor.

Much of the country is literally empty and frozen. Two thirds of the population live within 125 miles of the 5,550 miles of the U.S. border, and more than three quarters live in urban areas such as Montreal, Toronto, Ottawa, and Vancouver. Each of these four major Canadian cities is, in fact, closer to the American border than they are to each other. A land of vast natural resources, Canada is a leading producer of agricultural products and one of the largest exporters of manufactured equipment.

Although Canada has acted as a fully independent nation since the Confederation formed in 1867, until 1982 it was illegal for Canada to change its Constitution without the approval of the British government. Even now, the queen of England is the official Canadian head of state, a reminder of the complex relationship between the two nations.

When both the French and British were colonizing what is now Canada, there was constant antagonism between them until 1763, when "New France" finally fell to the British. And although the French areas were ruled by Britain, no attempt was made to force English culture on the region. French-speaking Canadians have held on to their language, religion, culture, and resentment toward the British ever since.

Canada's closeness to the United States brings it into close contact with American popular culture, which is exported to Canada—and the rest of the world—in large doses. As early as 1895, the wife of the Canadian governor-general worried about the impact of the cultural invasion from the south, remarking that its influence would need to "be dealt with ruthlessly." Cultural protectionism has resulted, with the government imposing quotas on play time for non-Canadian music on the radio, as well as mandating similar measures in motion pictures and publishing. Regardless of the cultural onslaught of TV, music, and films, Canada retains its own culture—one of multiculturalism.

A Communitarian Tradition

In Canada's confederation, greater power resides in the provinces than in the federal government. The ten provinces and three territories are not just a geographic convenience; they are distinctly different from one another and provide a greater identity for many Canadians than their national one; most

Canadians consider themselves, first and foremost, to be from Alberta, British Columbia, Manitoba, New Brunswick, Newfoundland, Nova Scotia, Ontario, Prince Edward Island, Quebec, Saskatchewan, the Yukon Territory, or the newly divided Northwest Territories. The third and newest province was established on April 1, 1999, with the division of the Northwest Territories. Called "Nunavut," it is an Inuktitut word that means "our land," a visible symbol of the recent national atonement toward and celebration of the indigenous aboriginal peoples of Canada.

Even with their strong regional and multicultural identities, Canadians have more of a collectivist tradition than do their American neighbors. They look to an activist government to unite the people and provinces, agreeing to government control of transportation, broadcasting, and natural resources. Canada is committed to social responsibility and taking care of citizens who can't take care of themselves; almost one half of Canadian GDP is devoted to social welfare programs. Only recently has Canada begun privatizing and reducing those programs to remain competitive.

Canada is also highly committed to national education. Ninety-three percent of its students complete secondary school, and 75 percent go on to higher education—the highest percentage in the world.

A Tolerant Way of Life

Canada is increasingly a multicultural nation. In the year 2000, there will be more Canadians with roots outside North America than within. Acceptance, understanding, and tolerance of cultures have become part of the Canadian way of life.

Immigration was vital in Canada's founding years to provide labor for development. But while European immigration was encouraged, Asian immigration was discouraged, with a 1923 bill that excluded Asians. Those attitudes changed after World War II, and parts of Canada, including British Columbia, now boast the largest Asian populations in the world outside Asia.

Canadians are proud of their nationality. But they also identify with one or more of the many subcultures that exist within the diverse Canadian community. Their multiculturalism is more a mosaic than a melting pot, with diverse populations becoming Canadian but retaining their own cultural roots, traditions, and norms.

In some senses, there are two separate nations in one country, the English and the French. In the province of Quebec, 80 percent of the population use French as their first language, and many prefer not to speak English even if they can. The Quebecois are more formal in dress and speech than their Anglo counterparts. Yet the enigma of Quebec Province is less a mystery for Canadians than for onlookers. For as long as Canada has existed, separatism has been an issue. Canadians realize that this 130-year "conflict" will always be a part of their culture, and they deal with it in a peaceful, nonviolent way.

A Business Culture Emerges

The seventh largest economy in the world, Canada is ranked fifth in overall competitiveness, according to the World Economic Forum. Its infrastructure, education, management, and finance keep it in high esteem but are counterbalanced by the high number of days lost to labor disputes and high corporate taxes.

Fifty percent of trade is foreign due to the country's limited domestic market, compared to 10 to 20 percent for other OECD countries. And it trades mostly with its nearest neighbor: approximately 80 percent of its exports, 70 percent of imports, and 70 percent of foreign investment are with the United States. Three of the ten largest corporations in Canada are subsidiaries of GM, DaimlerChrysler, and Ford, respectively. The Free Trade Agreement between Canada and the United States in 1989 and the subsequent North American Free Trade Agreement of 1994 are working: trade between Canada and the United States rose by 35 percent between 1989 and 1994, and Canadian trade with Mexico rose from $1 billion to $6 billion (USD).

Government-owned, or "Crown," corporations control large portions of the telecommunications, energy, transportation, oil, banking, finance, and agricultural sectors. In the mid-1980s, Canada began privatization, but many of these sectors still remain in government hands. Trade union membership is fairly high and growing; almost a third of all workers are unionized.

Major Canadian cities have taken on their own personalities and specialties. Ottawa, the nation's capital and head of the federal government, is emerging as Canada's high-tech center. Toronto supports Canada's financial and heavy manufacturing sectors, while French-speaking Montreal is the center of Canada's art and culture community and British Columbia's Vancouver has become the hub of Asian entrepreneurialism.

Canadians tend to be less conservative and reserved than the British, but more so than Americans. Directness, or "getting to the point," is a quality admired by Canadian businesspeople. Canadians themselves perceive their management style as kinder, gentler, less aggressive, and lower key than their American counterparts.

In a recent study of corporate culture comparing Canadian, U.S., and European firms, Canadian companies were considered socially responsible and trustworthy, though conservative, bureaucratic, and less driven. Still, they were overwhelmingly seen to foster higher standards of business ethics and to project a positive corporate image around the world.

Bob Atkinson, executive chairman of Lumonics, the world's largest laser production company, is one of the leaders creating that positive perception of Canadian business. Atkinson helped turn Lumonics around after a string of losses in the late 1980s. By involving people in the problem-solving process, Atkinson created what is known as "the people's plan." Now nine of Lumonics' top twelve product lines are either first or second in its global market niche. It got to this position by "catching people doing something right."

Atkinson is demanding to a fault—first with himself, then with others. But his persuasive manner makes his subordinates so committed and pas-

Canada: ***At a Glance***
Official name: Canada

Economy type: Anglo-Saxon
Trading bloc: NAFTA (North American Free Trade Association)

Location: The world's second largest nation, stretching from the Pacific to the Atlantic above the United States **Capital:** Ottawa
Population: 30,675,398 **Head of state:** Queen Elizabeth II, represented by Governor-General Roméo A. LeBlanc
Official languages: English, French
Religion: Roman Catholic 45%, United Church 12%, Anglican 8%
Literacy: 96%
World GNP ranking: 8 **GDP (US$ bn):** $604.3
GDP per capita: $19,919 **Unemployment:** 9.2%
Inflation: 2.4% **World export market share:** 5.1%

Major industries: Mining, wood and food products, transport equipment, chemicals, oil, gas
Major crops: Grains, corn, fruits, potatoes, grapes
Minerals: Nickel, zinc, copper, gold, lead, molybdenum, potash, silver
Labor force: 74% services, 15% manufacturing, 3% agriculture
Computers per 1,000 people: 295.4

Assets: Broad and plentiful natural resource supply. Extensive cheap hydroelectric energy. Significant oil and gas reserves. Free access to the U.S. and Mexican markets via NAFTA. Solid financial institutions. Good international relations. Good management and marketing skills. Well-managed infrastructure.

Liabilities: Future of the confederacy remains in doubt, which impacts business confidence. High corporate tax rate. Strikes and days lost to labor disputes remain a concern. Many bureaucratic regulations.

sionate, they often surprise themselves with their achievements. He delegates completely and constantly coaches from the sidelines; he trusts his leaders implicitly and in return generates trust; and he is forthright in his communications—he has no hidden agendas. "I always call it as I see it," he says.

Atkinson is a Canadian leader with a lot of heart; the most junior person in the company can get his attention. Unpretentious and personable, Atkinson has a unique skill for dealing with people one-on-one and making people feel special as individuals. He abhors rhetoric, opting for a simple, conservative approach that engages people at all levels. Many Lumonics employees have achieved success beyond their wildest dreams because Atkinson has made them feel he's counting on them to do extraordinary things.

Canadians teach the world to be simultaneously socially responsible and competitive. While their multicultural environment creates political problems, Canadians teach the world a tolerance of differences.

BE AN ECONOMIC AND SOCIAL LEADER
Eric Molobi and Kagiso Investment Trust
(South Africa)

Title: CEO
Headquarters: Johannesburg
Business: Largest national, black-led, nongovernmental, nonprofit development agency in South Africa. Formed in 1986 to achieve a society that offers liberty, justice, and freedom from poverty. Manages and finances charitable, educational, and developmental projects in under-resourced communities.

PRISON IS A GOOD PLACE *to get to know yourself. Eric Molobi learned that first-hand by spending six years on South Africa's Robben Island, a place made famous by one of his prison mates, Nelson Mandela.*

Molobi is a political activist turned media mogul and businessman. His heart is still in the same place—the continuing social, economic, and personal struggles of the new South Africa. He is bridging business and government to create wealth and *social infrastructure in South Africa.*

From humble beginnings in a country brutalized by injustice and in an environment made worse by emergency rule, Kagiso Investment Trust today attracts more foreign funding for development than any other organization in South Africa. During international sanctions, the trust was the single most important investor in the South African economy.

Though funded primarily from abroad, it is an indigenous organization; more than 60 percent of its leadership is black South African, making it a black-led organization, not a white structure that employs blacks—a rarity in South Africa. It has big goals: to promote projects that enable communities to achieve self-sufficiency, build integrated grassroots development programs that can be sustained and replicated, promote gender sensitivity, entrench environmental sensitivity as an integral part of the development process, and provide those disadvantaged by apartheid with access to skills and resources. It is helping to rebuild South Africa.

Lead from Your Principles

Eric Molobi is a personally literate leader. He understands and values himself, balances confidence and humility, and is optimistic and realistic. Above all, he—and the organization he leads—is driven by principles and integrity.

Molobi's leadership philosophy flows from those principles. He advocates an open, collegial environment with joint leadership responsibility; he believes strongly in the power of trust, collaboration, and empowerment.

Molobi uses self-knowledge and self-esteem to manage through his pain, disappointment, and anger about racial injustice. Passionate about success and giving something back to society, he is achieving social commitment with financial success, not in spite of it.

Change Systems, Not People

When Molobi emerged from prison, he entered a white world—and has made it his own by changing the systems, not the people.

"One of the biggest lessons I learned in prison," he says, "is tolerance. When I was arrested, I was impatient and angry—and that sustained me until I met Nelson Mandela at Robben Island. If you judge people on skin color, he said, you'll invariably make a mistake. You must judge them on the systems they create. If they set up incorrect systems, you must help create better ones." That's what Molobi has dedicated his life to ever since.

"Because South Africa is opening up to the global market, black businesses aren't just competing locally, they've been thrust onto the world stage, ready or not," Molobi recognizes. His staff are well positioned to take on the challenges: they have strong roots in the communities they serve and literally and figuratively speak the language of the people: "Our company has more black technical and highly skilled people than most. I have to make sure they feel at home here. I also have white managers—and I have to make sure they feel accepted." Molobi is doing internally what he knows must be done across the South African business sector.

But keeping a company profitable while meeting the needs of your people is a great challenge for any leader. Molobi dreams big, yet he remains pragmatic and realistic about how to achieve those dreams.

It's easy to let business interests overwhelm social interests. "We want to build business with respect, tolerance, and social responsibility," he says. "We need to be a role model in the black community. This openness, this sense of 'Let me hold your hand, you hold mine' is necessitated by our historical situation. The key to the potential growth is the formation of independent businesses run by blacks and partnerships with established businesses.

"Our history, staff, and methods of operation are our greatest assets in successfully embracing the future."

BUILD A SUSTAINABLE ENTERPRISE
Ray Anderson and Interface, Inc. *(U.S.A.)*

Title: Chairman and CEO
Headquarters: Atlanta, Georgia
Business: World's largest commercial carpet manufacturer, making and selling 40% of the free-lay carpet tiles and interior fabrics used in office, health care, commercial, and institutional facilities worldwide. With more than $1 billion in sales in 110 countries and 20 manufacturing facilities in 6 countries, Interface was named one of *Fortune* magazine's 100 best companies to work for in 1997.
Employees: 7,300

IN 1973, RAY ANDERSON started a company called Interface on the premise that corporations exist to create wealth in accordance with the law. For over twenty years, he turned oil into nylon carpet tiles, revolutionizing the industry and becoming a worldwide leader. By 1994, Interface was experiencing growing pains and the business was going south. That all changed the day Anderson read ecoentrepreneur Paul Hawken's book The Ecology of Commerce.

"It was like a spear in my chest," Anderson recalls. And the spear spurred him to start a revolution at Interface, one focused on the environment. In the process, he proved you can earn a good return and do good at the same time: Interface's stock price has quadrupled and profits have doubled since his epiphany five years ago. His message is simple: "Take an in-depth look at what you take, what you make, and what you waste."

Interface is a global company headquartered in the United States, a country perceived as the ultimate materialist and exploiter of the world. But Anderson insists, "We're not America, we're Interface, and we're going to be different from the rest."

It was a simple enough request. In 1994, Interface CEO Ray Anderson was asked to give a kickoff speech to an internal environmental task force. He struggled with drafting his comments, realizing Interface didn't have a worldwide position on the environment. By coincidence, an employee's daughter had just read Paul Hawken's *The Ecology of Commerce* and asked her mom to pass it on to Anderson. The rest, as they say, is history.

"It changed my life," Anderson says bluntly. And it changed the life of the company. His epiphany and resulting commitment became a galvanizing force in the company. He challenged employees to "put back more than we take, and do good rather than harm to the earth." Simply put, he wants Interface to function like a forest ecosystem.

It was a tall order for a company that is 100 percent dependent on petrochemicals derived from oil and natural gas for its raw materials and the energy to drive its processes—and doubly hard for a company that every year produces tons of solid waste, toxic gas, and carbon dioxide. Not to mention its share of the 920-million-square-yard heap of worn-out carpet that goes into the nation's landfills every year.

Anderson is a global capitalist who combines his roles as industrialist and environmental steward. His journey began by discovering the environmentalist in himself, building a sustainable enterprise, and creating an environmental annual report. He knows that the path to sustainability is "a mountain higher than Mount Everest."

Discover the Environmentalist in You

"I am a self-proclaimed plunderer of the earth," says Anderson. "And I am resolved to do what I can to repair the damage this company has done and set an example for other companies. The first industrial revolution turned out wrong; all wealth is coming at the expense of the Earth."

It took some convincing to bring others on board: "The epiphany came in my own heart first; I spent the first year trying to convince people. I knew everyone had to make their own decision about it." Every chance he got, he talked about the plight of the Earth and Interface's responsibilities.

"The European management team was the most skeptical. They looked at America and saw extravagance and waste. And they said, 'This can't be serious—this is just the program of the week.' " But after a speech in Scotland, Anderson noticed a member of his management team in the audience crying. When Anderson spoke with him, he explained, "I had read this before, but now I've heard you and I get it." It was a turning point for the company's efforts outside the United States.

Anderson also began rethinking his role in the company. Recognizing he had become far too controlling, he radically reoriented Interface, turning the operational management over to a more caring, empowering management team. "I emerged with a new mission," he says. "It was a complementary role: I let the operating people run the business, allowing me to disengage and to think further beyond the horizon. I brought in new people, new blood, new energy, and a new understanding of the game, and I let go and got out of the way."

Today, Anderson sees himself as a role model and a proselytizer: "I'm trying to take people beyond denial. The only institution powerful, pervasive, and wealthy enough to make a difference is business."

Build a Sustainable Enterprise

But talk wasn't enough; Interface needed to reinvent itself at all levels to become a prototypical twenty-first-century company, a "restorative, sustainable enterprise." Once committed to the concept of cyclic capitalism, it would transform the way carpets are made and sold and create new systems of industrial production.

First, it reinvented its Interface Research Corporation to provide guiding intelligence for its sustainability efforts. Cross-cultural, interdisciplinary teams came together to share best practices. Today, there are more than four hundred sustainability initiatives active in Interface.

Anderson also invested in experiential learning and teamwork, teaching a whole new approach to people and business around the world: "When you get the barriers out of the way, people accept their differences and embrace diversity. The national lands disappear. There's no nationalistic way anymore, there's the Interface way. We're a global company. And everyone feels part of something bigger than themselves." Today, the company's employees are very proud of its purpose, one reason it landed on *Fortune* magazine's "100 Best Companies to Work for in America" list for 1997.

All this helps Interface stand out from the crowd. "Our customers can't help but notice us," says Anderson. "By developing strong relationships with architects and interior designers, they are predisposed to trade with us. And when people are predisposed to trade because they like what you're doing, that's good business. I set out to try to do the right thing because it was the right thing, and we found out that it was truly the smart thing. The financial community is so numbers-oriented and left-brain-driven. There's a soft side completely missing. In our own business we know how important the soft side is."

Today, Interface has a triple bottom line: "Sustainable development is a platform standing on three legs: financial progress, social equity, and environmental sustainability. We haven't put human and natural capital at the same level as financial capital."

Create an Annual Environmental Report

They call themselves the "Big Chihuahuas"—a dream team of outside experts commissioned by Interface whose mission is to "annoy the whole Earth."

Their first corporate "Sustainability Report" set a new standard. "It detailed the raw resources, waste, and pollution associated with the manufacture of industrial products—in our case, carpet, fabrics, architectural flooring, and chemicals. It was a full disclosure," Anderson says of that groundbreaking report. "It said, 'Here's what we're doing, warts and all. Here's what we take, here's what we make, here's what we waste.' It was a gigantic confession intended to raise the bar to challenge other corporations."

In the report, which is at once an educational tool, a benchmark, and an econometric instrument, Interface defined the problems of industrialism not just for its own company but for all companies. "We're a huge waste-making machine, and we needed to outline our part of the problem—what we call the seven faces of the mountain," says Anderson.

Anderson knows the company still has a large mountain to scale. "The real test," he says, "is going to come when some huge customer says, 'If you want our business, you'll get off this shit,' and we're going to have to tell them in a nice way, 'No, we're staying on this shit.' "

PART FOUR

BECOMING A GLOBALLY LITERATE LEADER

CHAPTER TWELVE

YOUR PATH TO GLOBAL LITERACIES

OUR JOURNEY AROUND THE WORLD is coming to a close.

Along the way, we've met extraordinary global leaders and companies from twenty-eight countries. They've taught us a lot about becoming globally literate ourselves. They've shown us how to see global challenges, think with an international mindset, create fresh leadership behaviors, and mobilize people in culturally mindful ways.

These men and women have leveraged their global assets, solved their business questions, and hardwired their companies with a new way of working, making unique contributions in the world as they navigate through the borderless, multicultural marketplace.

Now change must begin with you. How can you become more globally literate? As Chairman Lee of Samsung teaches us, "Only you have the power to change."

Becoming globally literate is a lifelong process, during which we may travel many roads. Some of us are natural leaders; our mothers and fathers taught us well how to relate in the world. Others of us learn on our own through self-exploration and psychological insight. Religion and spirituality can be a source of inspiration; so can cross-cultural experiences and formal leadership education. Positive and negative role models teach us what works and doesn't work. But probably the greatest teacher of all is learning by doing.

The challenge for all of us is to learn how to learn. So often we sabotage learning through our own arrogance and prejudice. Our ethnocentrism and outdated thinking blind us, keeping us from becoming globally literate ourselves. The first step is to make a commitment to learning by doing.

Globally literate people know how to ask the right questions. Here are six to get you started.

> **THE PATHS TO LEADERSHIP**
>
> When asked to what they attribute their personal leadership skill, global executives said:
>
> 1. Work experience
> 2. Natural ability
> 3. Role models
> 4. Formal training
> 5. Age
> 6. Religion

Are You Unlearning and Relearning the Rules of Business?

We must create new rules in new minds. By unlearning our past assumptions about people and business, we learn new ways of thinking and acting in the world. But it's not easy to venture into uncharted territory. Forced into our discomfort zone, we must manage our learning anxiety—the distress and uncertainty of not knowing. We must throw away past assumptions that don't work and embrace new ones that are untested. But if we are clear about our values and willing to learn with others, the process will unlock our creativity and potential.

Are You Developing a Flexible Way of Thinking and Acting?

The globally literate mind is a flexible mind. It remains agile and nimble as we learn to travel across boundaries and borders. Comfortable with chaos and change, it is able to contain conflicting and often opposing forces while creating cohesion and harmony from disparate parts. It's a mind that tolerates ambiguity and difference as it builds bridges across language, politics, and religions. And it's a mind that thinks and acts at the same time, all with a sense of tolerance and balance. By combining linear, logical reasoning with circular, systemic thinking, the global mind prepares us for the twenty-first-century world.

Are You Using Culture as a Tool for Business Success?

If there is one lesson in this book, it is the power of culture in our lives. There are many layers and levels of culture, and we must learn from all of them. Culture becomes a tool when we understand the similarities and differences among people, companies, and countries. It becomes a tool when we learn how history and psychology influence our worldview. Culture influences which leaders we value, which institutions we build, and which strategies we execute. When we learn these lessons from around the world, we can then leverage culture as a tool for competitive advantage.

Are You Using the Literacies as an Integrated System?

The global literacies are an integrated system of learning, each dependent on the others. We start with personal literacy. Through developing insight, humility, and a sense of optimism, we set the stage for social literacy. By engaging and challenging people, we learn how to tap collective intelligence and learn about ourselves in the process. Business literacy then teaches us how to apply the new rules of business; by building twenty-first-century organizations, we practice the literacies in our daily work. Cultural literacy teaches us how to work with diverse customers, employees, and countries, enabling us to reevaluate our assumptions about people and the world.

Are You Teaching Others About the Global Literacies?

Great leaders are great teachers. Our mandate is to develop globally literate people around us. The process starts by putting a stake in the ground and showing how the global literacies lead to business success. By assessing people on their global literacy performance, we can identify their strengths and shortcomings and design learning plans tailored to their needs. Global literacy education, coaching, and cross-cultural experiences help deepen people's understanding. Ultimately, companies must reward and compensate their employees for exhibiting these new behaviors. Otherwise, they will resist change and remain stuck in their old, unproductive ways of leading and working.

Is Your Business Success Enough?

In the twenty-first century we are all global traders, creating a lot of opportunities for growth and success. But these benefits also bring serious responsibilities. At a time when business is prosperous and powerful, we must build a healthier, sustainable planet for all our citizens. We must be global citizens, working hard to close the gap between the haves and have-nots and dedicating ourselves to raising standards of health, education, safety, and wealth for the world's citizens. We must promote sustainable development and play a leading role in preserving the earth's resources. And we must respect human rights, our democratic institutions, and the integrity of our local cultures. We must all play our small part.

Global Literacies is the twenty-first-century leadership competency. It is the fresh lens, new language, agile software, and set of tools required for tomorrow's leaders to be world-class at home and abroad.

What emerged from the stories of these world-class CEOs is a new set of attitudes, behaviors, and competencies to help leaders at all levels of business be more personally aware, socially skilled, economically enlightened, and culturally wise. As leaders, we must now be realistic optimists, urgent listeners, chaos navigators, and global capitalists all in one. We must understand our national strengths and be aware of our national flaws, preserving what is best in our country while learning from others around the world. And we must think locally, regionally, and globally simultaneously—and constantly.

To thrive, we must lead by example and forge multicultural teams. People must be able to read our road maps for success and understand the global context of our business. As globally literate leaders, we must build productive alliances with customers, suppliers, and even competitors. We must more wisely manage the collection and use of knowledge and recognize the difference between information and wisdom. We must make sound technology investments; build fast, flexible systems; and deploy value creating resources. By creating shared visions and values and building cultures of learning and innovation, globally literate leaders can achieve world-class excellence.

We are truly living on a precipice. Time is of the essence. The choice is yours. You can choose to become globally literate, or be left behind.

Welcome to the new leadership language of the twenty-first century.

APPENDIX: RESEARCH STRATEGY

THE GOAL of this three-year research effort was to create a fresh, practical approach to global leadership that could be used by business leaders around the world. We set out to (1) define the characteristics most common to successful global leaders and their companies; (2) identify the leadership factors most likely to predict global success in the twenty-first century; and (3) identify the unique national contributions to leadership around the world.

We had a three-part research strategy:

- We conducted face-to-face interviews with CEOs of leading multinational corporations in twenty-eight countries.
- We made a quantitative survey of CEOs in eighteen countries.
- We did background research on companies and countries around the world.

The Interviews

We identified 1,000 CEOs from twenty-eight countries by getting recommendations from international and national business organizations, surveys, government representatives, embassies, magazines, and national opinion leaders. We used the Internet extensively throughout the project.

Through our research we identified two hundred target companies. The selection criteria were: the business must operate internationally and have multiple global operations; it must be a large employer with more than 10,000 employees; it must be involved in multiple industries; it must operate in diverse regions of the world; it must have a good reputation and well-known product brands; its leaders must have people-oriented philosophies; and it must have a successful financial bottom line.

We began the project with a conceptual framework including hypotheses about global leadership and world-class companies. We designed a semi-structured interview guide that was revised over time. Each executive interview was conducted face-to-face; each was ninety minutes in length; each was tape-recorded, transcribed, and analyzed for common themes and unique philosophies and practices. After approximately twenty interviews, we began to see the four global literacies and five business strategies emerging consistently in the interviews.

The Survey

The 1999 Global CEO survey "Leading Global Organizations in a Global Economy" was conducted between January and April 1999 by Watson Wyatt Worldwide. The survey was sent to top executives in large firms in eighteen countries. Because of differences in corporate structure and naming conventions around the world, the survey sample includes responses from CEOs, managing directors, presidents, and chairmen of boards of directors. The survey was translated into Japanese, Korean, Spanish, German, Chinese, and French (two versions). Responses were received from more than 1,000 companies.

The written survey was based on the project's conceptual framework. It was designed to explore the origins, character, and effectiveness of business leadership and identify how different national cultures influence leadership and corporate competitiveness.

Once the survey data were collected, we developed a "global success" index. The purpose of this index was to quantify the degree to which the companies represented in the database have been financially successful in their global pursuits. The index represents the multiplicative product of two components: a financial success score and a global activity score.

The financial success score was developed from respondents' assessments of their companies' financial performance over the past two years with regard to return on shareholder value, growth in market share, growth in net income, and return on sales. These responses were standardized, averaged, and then converted into percentile rankings.

The global activity score was developed based on participants' responses to questions involving the number of countries in which their firm had customers, suppliers, and employees; the percentage of revenues derived from sales outside their home country; the nature and character of their international activities; the degree to which their global operations have expanded over the past two years; and global activities planned during the next five years. These responses were standardized, averaged, and converted into percentile rankings.

Finally, the financial and global components were then multiplied by each other to derive a final ranking. Multiplication was used rather than addition to reflect the necessity of both globalness and good financial performance in achieving a high score. In other words, by using multiplication, firms that were highly successful financially but have little or no global involvement would not be able to offset their lack of global activity with a high degree of financial success. This approach ensures that high scoring firms are both global and financially successful.

Simple Spearman correlation analyses were then performed to identify significant correlation between companies' global success scores and various leadership practices, philosophies, and activities. All analyses were conducted by country and region.

The Background Research

Background research was conducted on all leaders and companies interviewed for the project. This included the use of annual reports, CEO speeches, review of business strategies and policies, magazine articles, newspaper reviews, Internet searches, and so forth.

Extensive research was also conducted on each of the countries. A series of country profiles was prepared that examined the impact of history, geography, politics, and culture on the people and businesses of each country.

It is important to note that Mexico was included in the original project design. A prominent CEO of a large Mexican multinational corporation was interviewed, survey data was collected, and a Mexican country profile was written, but the CEO decided not to participate at the last minute. Unfortunately, we were unable to obtain another interview given our publication deadline.

The Analysis

The research team consisted of Bob Rosen, Patti Digh, Marshall Singer, and Carl Phillips. Aaron Wunder was project manager. The team formally met once a month for eighteen months with many additional conference calls and face-to-face meetings. Watson Wyatt Worldwide coordinated the survey analysis. Dan Carpenter was the Watson Wyatt survey project manager. Readers from around the world reviewed the country research and profiles.

SELECTED REFERENCES

The following is a list of selected general references used for writing *Global Literacies.* Because our complete list of references, country by country, is quite extensive, we chose to include only general references here. For the complete list of references, see our Web site at www.globalliteracies.com.

Adler, Nancy J. *International Dimensions of Organizational Behavior.* 3d ed., Cincinnati: South-Western, 1998.

Barber, Benjamin R. *Jihad versus McWorld: How Globalization and Tribalism Are Reshaping the World.* New York: Ballantine, 1996.

Barlett, Christopher A., and Ghoshal Sumantra. "Changing the Role of Top Management: Beyond Systems to People." *Harvard Business Review,* May/June 1995, pp. 132–42.

Barsoux, Jean-Louis, and Peter Lawrence. "The Nature of Work Relations." In David J. Hickson, ed., *Exploring Management Across the World.* London: Penguin Books, 1997.

Beamer, Linda. "Toasts: Rhetoric and Ritual Business Negotiation in Confucian Cultures." *Business Forum,* 18(4) (Fall 1993), pp. 26–31.

Becket, Michael. "How to Feel at Home with Business Abroad." *The Daily Telegraph.*

Bennis, Warren, and Patricia Ward Biederman. *Organizing Genius: The Secrets of Creative Collaboration.* Reading, Penn.: Addison-Wesley, 1997.

Berger, Brigitte, ed. *The Culture of Entrepreneurship.* San Francisco: ICS Press, 1991.

Brake, Terence. *The Global Leader: Critical Factors for Creating the World Class Organization.* Chicago: Irwin Press, 1997.

Brake, Terence, Danielle Medina Walker, and Thomas (Tim) Walker. *Doing Business Internationally: The Guide to Cross-Cultural Success.* New York: McGraw-Hill, 1995.

Brislin, Richard. *Understanding Culture's Influence on Behavior.* Fort Worth: Harcourt, 1993.

Central Intelligence Agency. *The World Factbook.* Washington, D.C.: U.S. Government Printing Office, 1995.

Chakraborty, S. K. *Management by Values: Towards Cultural Congruence.* Delhi: Oxford University Press, 1992.

Chu, Chin-Ning. *The Asian Mind Game.* New York: Rawson Associates, 1991.

Copeland, Lennie, and Lewis Griggs. *Going International: How to Make Friends and Deal Effectively in the Global Marketplace.* New York: Random House, 1985.

Coy, Peter. "Fast-Forward for Finance." *Business Week.* August. 24/31, 1998, pp. 72–79.

Crawford, W. Rex. *A Century of Latin-American Thought.* Cambridge, Mass.: Harvard University Press, 1961.

Csoka, Louis S. *Bridging the Leadership Gap.* New York: Conference Board, 1997.

Dauphinais, G. William, and Colin Price, eds. *Straight from the CEO: The World's Top Business Leaders Reveal Ideas That Every Manager Can Use.* New York: Simon & Schuster, 1998.

Delia-Loyle, Donna. "Going South: Revealing the Realities." *Global Trade,* 111(6) (June 1991), pp. 30–33.

Doremus, Paul N., William W. Keller, Louis W. Pauly, and Simon Reich. *The Myth of the Global Corporation.* Princeton, N.J.: Princeton University Press, 1998.

Dorling Kindersley World Reference Atlas. London: Dorling Kindersley, 1996.

Dununj, Sanjyot P. *Doing Business in Asia.* New York: Lexington Books, 1995.

Economist in cooperation with Korn/Ferry International. *Developing Leadership for the Twenty-First Century.* New York: The Economist Intelligence Unit, 1996.

Edvinsson, Leif, and Michale S. Malone. *Intellectual Capital: Realizing Your Company's True Value by Finding Its Hidden Brainpower.* New York: HarperCollins, 1997.

Egon Zehnder International. "Global Corporate Governance Advisory Board, Inaugural Meeting: Issues and Challenge." London, March 1998.

European Commission. *The European Union and World Trade.* Brussels: European Commission, 1995.

European Commission. *The European Union: Key Figures.* Brussels: European Commission, 1997.

Fernandes, Lorna. "No End in Sight for Internet Use." *The Business Journal,* September 8, 1997, pp. 18–21.

Fishamn, Jashua. "The Fight Over Capital Flows." *Foreign Policy,* Winter 1998/99, pp. 41–54.

Galagan, Patricia A. "Peter Drucker." *Training & Development,* September 1998, pp. 22–27.

Geary, James. "Sowing the Seeds of Speech." *Time International* (Europe) July 7, 1997.

Gertz, Dwight L., and Joao P. A. Baptista. *Grow to be Great: Breaking the Downsizing Cycle.* New York: Free Press, 1995.

Goleman, Daniel. *Emotional Intelligence: Why It Can Matter More Than IQ.* New York: Bantam, 1995.

Gore, Al, et al. "The Global Forum on Reinventing Government." Speech at the Global Economic Forum, January 14/15, 1999, Washington, D.C.

Grolier, et. al. *Grolier Multimedia Encyclopedia.* Danbury, Conn.: Grolier Interactive, 1998.

Hall, Edward T., and Mildred Reed Hall. "The Americans." In Hall, Edward T., and Mildred Reed Hall, eds. *Understanding Cultural Differences.* Yarmouth, Maine: Intercultural Press, 1990.

Hampden-Turner, Charles. *Creating Corporate Culture: From Discord to Harmony.* Reading, Penn.: Addison-Wesley, 1990.

Hampden-Turner, Charles, and Fons Trompenaars. *Mastering the Infinite Game: How East Asian Values Are Transforming Business Practices.* Oxford: Capstone Publishing, 1997.

Hampden-Turner, Charles, and Fons Trompenaars. *The Seven Cultures of Capitalism.* London: Judy Piatkus, 1993.

Heifetz, Ronald A., and Donald L. Laurie. "The Work of Leadership." *Harvard Business Review,* January/February 1997, pp. 124–34.

Heller, Robert. *In Search of European Excellence: The 10 Key Strategies of Europe's Top Companies.* London: HarperCollins Business, 1997.

Hesselbein, Frances, Marshall Goldsmith, and Richard Beckhard. *The Leader of the Future.* San Francisco: Jossey-Bass, 1996.

Hesselbein, Frances, Marshall Goldsmith, and Richard Beckhard. *The Organization of the Future.* San Francisco: Jossey-Bass, 1997.

Hickson, David J., ed. *Exploring Management Across the World: Selected Readings.* London: Penguin Books, 1997.

Hill, Richard. *We Europeans.* Brussels: Europublications, 1993.

Hinnels, John R., ed. *Dictionary of Religions.* New York: Facts on File, 1984.

Hock, Dee W. *Birth of the Chaordic Age.* San Francisco: Berrett-Koehler, 1999.

Hof, Robert, Gary McWilliams, & Gabrielle Saveri. "The 'Click Here' Economy." *Business Week,* June 22, 1998, pp. 121–29.

Hofstede, Geert. *Cultures and Organizations: Software of the Mind.* London: McGraw-Hill, 1991.

Hofstede, Geert. *Culture's Consequences: International Differences in Work-Related Values.* Abridged ed. Newbury Park, Calif.: Sage, 1991.

Kanter, Rosabeth Moss. *World Class: Thriving Locally in the Global Economy.* New York: Simon & Schuster, 1995.

Lane, Henry W., and Joseph J. DiStefano. *International Management Behavior: From Policy to Practice.* 2d edition. Boston: PWS-Kent, 1992.

Leaptrott, Nan. *Rules of the Game: Global Business Protocol.* Cincinnati: Thompson Executive Press, 1996.

Lewis, Richard D. *When Cultures Collide: Managing Successfully Across Cultures.* London: Nicholas Brealey, 1996.

Lipnack Jessica, and Jeffrey Stamps. *Virtual Teams: Reaching Across Space, Time, and Organizations with Technology.* New York: John Wiley & Sons, 1997.

Maccoby, Michael, ed. *Sweden at the Edge: Lessons for American and Swedish Managers.* Philadelphia: University of Pennsylvania Press, 1991.

Mole, John. *When in Rome: A Business Guide to Cultures or Customs in 12 European Nations.* New York: American Management Association, 1991.

Moran, Robert T., and John R. Riesenberger. *The Global Challenge: Building the New Worldwide Enterprise.* London: McGraw-Hill, 1994.

Morrison, Terri, Wayne A. Conaway, and George A. Borden. *Kiss, Bow, or Shake Hands: How to do Business in Sixty Countries.* Holbrook, Mass.: Adams Media, 1994.

Morrison, Terri, Wayne A. Conaway, and Joseph J. Douress. *Dun & Bradstreet's Guide to Doing Business Around the World.* Paramus, N.J.: Prentice Hall, 1997.

Naisbitt, John. *Megatrends: Eight Asian Megatrends That Are Reshaping Our World.* New York: Simon & Schuster, 1997.

Nankivell, Nevin. "Don't Blame Globalization When a Crisis Erupts." Special Report: FP Survey: A Special Report Series on the Global Knowledge Economy, *Financial Post* from *National Post*. February 8, 1999, p. C14.

Parrinder, Geoffrey, ed. *World Religions: From Ancient History to the Present*. New York: Facts on File, 1983.

Pavett, Cynthia M., and Gary Whitney, "Quality Values, Attitudes, and Behavioral Predispositions of Employees in Mexico, Australia, and the United States." *Thunderbird International Business Review*, 40(6), November/December 1998, pp. 42–56.

Porter, Michael E. *The Competitive Advantage of Nations*. New York: Free Press, 1990.

Price, Pritchett. *The Employee Handbook of New Work Habits for a Radically Changing World*. Dallas: Pritchett, 1994.

Pucik, Vladimir, Noel M. Tichy, and Carole K. Barnett, eds. *Globalizing Management: Creating and Leading the Competitive Organization*. New York: John Wiley & Sons, 1992.

Quigley, Carroll. *The Evolution of Civilizations: An Introduction to Historical Analysis*. New York: Macmillan, 1961.

Quinn, James Brian. *Global Growth Leaders*. New York: the Conference Board, 1998.

Randlesome, Collin, and William Brierly. *Business Cultures in Europe*. Oxford: Butterworth-Heinemann, 1993.

Rhinesmith, Stephen H. *A Manager's Guide to Globalization: Six Skills for Success in a Changing World*. 2d edition. Chicago: American Society for Training & Development, 1996.

Rosen, Robert H., with Lisa Berger. *The Healthy Company: Eight Strategies to Develop People, Productivity, and Profits*. Los Angeles: Tarcher, 1991.

Rosen, Robert H., with Paul Brown. *Leading People: Transforming Business from the Inside Out*. New York: Viking, 1996.

Seagrave, Sterling. *Lords of the Rim*. London: Corgi Books, 1995.

Singer, Marshall R. *Perception & Identity in Intercultural Communication*. 2d rev. ed. Yarmouth, Maine: Intercultural Press, 1987.

Singer, Marshall R. *Intercultural Communication: A Perceptual Approach*. Yarmouth, Maine: Intercultural Press, 1997.

Slater, Jim, and Roger Strange, eds. *Business Relationships with East Asia: The European Experience*. London: Routledge, 1997.

Smadja, Claude. "The End of Complacency." *Foreign Policy*, Winter 1998/99, pp. 67–71.

Smith, Hendrick. *Rethinking America: Innovative Strategies and Partnerships in Business and Education*. New York: Avon, 1995.

Smith, Huston. *The World's Religions*. San Francisco: HarperSanFrancisco, 1991.

Stoessinger, John G. *Nations at Dawn: China, Russia, and America*. New York: McGraw-Hill, 1994.

Stopford, John. "Multinational Corporations." *Foreign Policy*, Winter 1998/99, pp. 12–25.

Tayeb, Monir H. *The Global Business Environment: An Introduction*. Newbury Park, Calif.: Sage Publications, 1992.

Taylor, William. "The Logic of Global Business: An Interview with ABB's Percy Barnevik," *Harvard Business Review*, March/April 1991, pp. 90–105.

Thomas, Frank. *The Conquest of Cool: Business Culture, Counterculture, and the Rise of Hip Consumerism*. Chicago: University of Chicago Press, 1997.

Thurow, Lester C. *The Future of Capitalism: How Today's Economic Forces Shape Tomorrow's World.* New York: Penguin,1996.

Tichy, Noel M., and Eli Cohen. *The Leadership Engine: How Winning Companies Build Leaders at Every Level.* New York: HarperBusiness, 1997.

Trompenaars, Fons. *Riding the Waves of Culture: Understanding Diversity in Global Business.* London: Irwin, 1994.

Tuller, Lawrence W. *Doing Business in Latin America and the Caribbean.* New York: American Management Association, 1993.

"The 21st Century Economy." *Business Week,* August 31, 1998, pp. 58–59.

21st Century Learning Initiative (www.21learn.org/cats/ST/fhkhm.html).

Urresta, Lixandra. "Peter Drucker: Long V." *Fortune,* September 28, 1998, pp. 34–39.

U.S. Department of Commerce. *The Emerging Digital Economy: Building Out the Internet.* Washington, D.C.: U.S. Government Printing Office, pp. A2–4.

Van Schendelen, M. P. C. M., and R. J. Jackson, eds. *The Politicization of Business in Western Europe.* London: Croon Helm, 1987.

Viney, John. *The Culture Wars: How American and Japanese Businesses Have Outperformed Europe's and Why the Future Will Be Different.* Oxford: Capstone Publishing, 1997.

Vision 2010: Designing Tomorrow's Organization. New York: The Economist Intelligence Unit in cooperation with Andersen Consulting, 1997.

Wade, Robert. "Capitalism's Last Chance." *Foreign Policy,* Winter 1998/99, pp. 55–66.

Wallace, William, and Jan Zielonka. "Misunderstanding Europe." *Foreign Affairs,* November/December 1998, pp. 65–79.

Watson Wyatt, et al. "The People Factor: A Global Study of Human Resource Issues and Management Strategies," 1995.

Watson Wyatt Worldwide. "Competencies & The Competitive Edge: Corporate Strategies for Creating Competitive Advantages Through People" (research study), 1998.

Watson Wyatt Worldwide. "Competing in a Global Economy. Executive Summary, A Watson Wyatt Study of Senior Executives Across the Globe," 1997.

Wei-ming, Tu, ed. *Confucian Traditions in East Asian Modernity: Moral Education and Economic Culture in Japan and the Four Mini-Dragons.* Cambridge, Mass.: Harvard University Press, 1996.

The World Almanac and Book of Facts 1999. Mahwah, N.J.: World Almanac Books, 1998.

World Economic Forum. *The Global Competitiveness Report 1998.* London: BAS Printers, 1998.

World Economic Forum in Partnership with Deloitte Touche Tohmatsu. *Innovative Leaders in Globalization.* Geneva: World Economic Forum, 1999.

Yergin, Daniel, and Joseph Stanislaw. *The Commanding Heights: The Battle Between Government and the Marketplace That Is Remaking the Modern World.* New York: Simon & Schuster, 1998.

Yoshimura, Noboru, and Paul Anderson. *Inside the Kaisha: Demystifying Japanese Business Behavior.* Boston: Harvard Business School Press, 1997.

ACKNOWLEDGMENTS

GLOBAL LITERACIES is truly a work of collective wisdom. We are deeply grateful to all the people around the world who contributed their ideas, inspiration, advice, and assistance to make this project a success.

Special thanks go to our families for their love and support: Jay, Snapper, Barbara, Rich, Dick, Randi, John, Emma, Melvin, Frances, Boyce, Paul, Molly, Shep, Orna, Juma Attid, Saleha, Maureen, Alison, Eric, Shane, Margot, Jerry, Rick, Chris, Ryan, Devon, Mark, Lynne, Erin, Amanda, and Michael.

To Aaron Wunder, the project maestro, Jim Mathews, Sherri Council, Maureen Mineham, and David Rippey of Healthy Companies International, Gail Ross and Howard Yoon of the Gail Ross Literary Agency, and Bill Rosen and Sharon Gibbons of Simon and Schuster.

To the team at Watson Wyatt: Bob Ellis, Dan Carpenter, Heather Worozbyt, Sue Cameron, John Parkington, Marcia Marsh, Deborah Wallace, John Menefee, Rich Luss, Regina Holmes, Jon Robinson, Mike Button, Grahame Stott, Paula DeLisle, Andrew Dillon, Graham Childs, Graeme Field, Richard Deville, Giovani di Gesu, J. P. Orbeta, Brian Kennedy, Noni Loewenstein, Lisa Swatland, Pete Smith, and Paul Daoust.

To John Ptak, Marilyn Manalo, Natalie Fitz-Gerald, Michael Olsen, Kathy Blumgarden, Keizo Tannawa, David Evans, Randy Donaldson, Judy Rosenbloom, Ted Graham, Moncef and Jacqueline Hicheri, Tom Frank, David and Janine Burns, Dieter Feddersen, Sally Painter, Bob Witeck, Ng Pock To, Sammy Hoi, Lars and Lena Ulenstram, Mei Zie, Deepak Bhattasali, Joe Loughran, Andy Gay, Linda Scott, Tom Mader, Amy Cunningham, Andy Novins, Ellsen Wessel, Elizabeth Goeke, Polly Agee, Barney Lee, Marco Cardamone, Barney Blee, Clay Kisker, John Geare, Bill Brubeck, Stephan-Gotz Richter, Betty Richardson, Randy Dauber, Virginia Littlejohn, Bob White, John Burnim, Helen Mills, Susan Spriggs, Bill Oyler, Bob Jerome, Nancy Adler, Claude Smadja, and Chris Dorval.

To L. Ronald Sheman, Robert O'Donovan, Charles Blunt, Akihiro Tanaka, Steven Muraski, Robert House, Joan Gallagher, John Edwin Mroz, Geoff Davis, Veronique Fornes, Marion Loveland, Unsugh Kenneth Park, Transatlantic Business Dialogue, French-American Chamber of Commerce, Australia Investment 2000, American Chamber of Commerce in Australia,

World Economic Forum, Institute for East West Studies, World Bank, and International Monetary Fund.

To Tony Frost, Eliav Zakay, Geoff Armstrong, Richard Rudman, Kerry Stackpole, Geoff DeLacy, Mike Losey, Luiz Ciocchi, Rosemary Lauth, Gay Clyburn, Lee Gardenswartz, Anita Rowe, Martin and Rita Bennett, J. F. Guder, Alberto Fuster, Lloyd Lewan, Janet and Milton Bennett, Eddie Ng, Armand Mella, Hilde Regnier, Sheridan Simon, Mary Rockett, Maricel Quintana Baker, and Louise Smith.

To Stephen Henning Sieverts, Alex Weilenmann, Peter Kirsch, Robert Whiteman, Nitan Madhav, Stephen Telkins, Richard Saccone, Phil Goin, Paul Kengor, Shawn Bates, Amit Dabla, students at the Graduate School of Public and International Affairs of the University of Pittsburgh, and students at the School of International Studies at American University.

To all the leaders and their staffs around the world for their wisdom and hospitality.

We thank you.

HEALTHY COMPANIES INTERNATIONAL

Healthy Companies International (HCI) is a Washington, D.C.–based knowledge, education, and consulting company specializing in global leadership, national cultures, and world-class organizations. Founded by Dr. Robert Rosen in 1988, Healthy Companies works with clients directly and in alliance with other major firms around the world, providing consulting services and educational products to strengthen the leadership competencies of executives, managers, and their employees.

Consulting services include:

- CEO coaching and executive team development
- Leadership assessment and development planning
- Human capital strategies for world-class success
- Executive learning programs

Learning products include:

- Electronic newsletter on leadership, world-class companies, and national cultures.
- Leadership learning products delivered in multiple formats (facilitated, video, computer)
- Books *(The Healthy Company, Leading People, Global Literacies)* and publications on leadership and high-performance organizations
- Audio and video leadership learning products to teach the fundamentals of leadership

Conference products include:

- Keynote speeches and seminars
- Television, executive forums, and videoconference events
- Leadership learning networks

For more information:

HEALTHY COMPANIES INTERNATIONAL
1420 16th Street, N.W.
Washington DC 20036
USA
Tel.: (202) 234-9288
Fax: (202) 234-9289
E-mail: info@healthycompanies.com
Internet site: www.healthycompanies.com

WATSON WYATT WORLDWIDE

Watson Wyatt Worldwide is an international consulting firm that brings together two disciplines—people management and financial management—to help organizations improve their business results.

The firm specializes in designing compensation and benefits programs to help clients attract, motivate, and retain a talented workforce; in helping clients achieve competitive advantage by aligning their workforce with their business strategies; and in helping clients use technology to reduce costs and improve employee service.

Watson Wyatt has over 5,000 associates in 36 countries across the globe. Corporate offices are in Reigate, England, and Bethesda, Maryland. For more information, visit them at www.watsonwyatt.com.

Dear Friend:

In Global Literacies, we describe the principles and practices that have helped us and countless others succeed in the global business world. I am writing to ask you to join me, and potentially millions of others worldwide, in the Global Literacies Network.

Participation in the Network is open to anyone who chooses to practice the Global Literacies in their business and personal lives. Groups of colleagues around the world have already begun to focus on these practices for global business success.

What literacy behaviors do you excel in? What business practices have worked for you? What unique contributions does your country bring to the global literacies? We'll explore these and other questions as the global network grows.

To join the Global Literacies Network, all you need to do is send your name, address, phone number, and e-mail address. Our Web address is: www.globalliteracies.com, and our e-mail is info@globalliteracies.com.

I look forward to exploring together how the global literacies can transform our business and personal lives in the twenty-first century.

Best,
Bob Rosen

INDEX

ABOUT THE AUTHORS

ROBERT ROSEN

Robert Rosen is an internationally acclaimed author, speaker, and business adviser in the area of leadership and world-class organizations. Combining the fields of psychology and business, his work has been in the forefront in understanding the mind-sets and actions required of executives in the twenty-first century.

As chairman and CEO of Healthy Companies International, based in Washington, D.C., Rosen has consulted with numerous companies around the world. His clients include AT&T, Motorola, Intel, Herman Miller, Citibank, Petro-Canada, UNUM, and Discovery Communications, among others. He is a popular keynote speaker to companies and associations, and his inspiring message is heard by thousands of people each year worldwide.

After receiving his Ph.D. in clinical psychology from the University of Pittsburgh, he has spent his life's career defining superior leadership in high-performance organizations. Rosen's first book, *The Healthy Company*, was published in 1992 by Tarcher/Putnam. Warren Bennis called it "One of the best business books of the decade."

In 1993, the John D. and Catherine T. MacArthur Foundation awarded him a six-year multimillion-dollar grant to study leadership and organization performance. This project led to his second book, *Leading People* (Viking, 1996), which presented eight leadership principles told through the stories of thirty-six American leaders in business, government, and not-for-profit organizations. *Leading People* appeared on the most-recommended list of *The Wall Street Journal* in 1996.

In the area of global leadership, Rosen directs the Global Leadership Forum, a study of CEOs and world-class companies from thirty countries, designed to identify the universal competencies and practices required of global business leaders.

Rosen is assistant clinical professor of psychiatry at the George Washington School of Medicine, is active on numerous boards and commissions, and volunteers with several not-for-profit organizations. A frequent contributor to books and magazines, his writings have appeared in *The Washington Post*, *The New York Times*, and *The Wall Street Journal*; he has also appeared on numerous radio and television broadcasts around the world.

PATRICIA DIGH

Patricia Digh is a business analyst and writer whose Washington, D.C.–based firm, RealWork, focuses on emerging workplace issues. Her comments and articles have appeared in *Fortune, The Wall Street Journal, The New York Times,* and the *Financial Times,* among other publications. A frequent speaker on global business and diversity issues in the United States and abroad, Digh is a co-founder of the Global Diversity Roundtable, a consortium of senior executives from multinational corporations exploring strategies and methodologies in global diversity.

Digh was formerly vice president of International and Diversity Programs for the Society for Human Resource Management (SHRM), representing more than 120,000 human resources professionals worldwide. While there, Digh established the Institute for International Human Resources and the SHRM Diversity Initiative. Active in the nonprofit community, Digh is chair of the American Society of Association Executives' Diversity Committee. Her current research project, "Remaining Relevant," focuses on the ability of nonprofit organizations to cope with globalization and demographic and societal change.

MARSHALL SINGER

Marshall Singer is professor emeritus of international and intercultural affairs at the University of Pittsburgh. One of the world's leading experts on intercultural management, Dr. Singer is the author of *Weak States in a World of Powers: The Dynamics of International Relationships* (Free Press) and *Intercultural Communication: A Perceptual Approach* (Prentice Hall).

Singer's government clients have included the Agency for International Development, the U.S. Customs Service, the U.S. Departments of State and Commerce, and the Peace Corps. His private and not-for-profit clients include the Bayer Corporation, Westinghouse, the Brookings Institution, and the Institute for International Exchange. His foreign clients include the government of Sri Lanka, the University of Malaya (Kuala Lumpur), the National Institute of Planning (Egypt), and the Centre d'Échanges Technologiques Internationaux (Paris).

Singer's current research focuses on the impact of culture on different styles of leadership. He has received numerous honors, including Fulbright and Woodrow Wilson Scholarships and a Ford Foundation Grant.

CARL PHILLIPS, M.A., C.M.C.

Carl Phillips is one of the leading consultants in executive development and formerly head of global development of Watson Wyatt's Executive Consulting Services. Phillips has worked with a cross section of industries, such as financial services, utilities, natural resources, manufacturing and service firms, and high-technology companies. His clients have included York International, Canadian Pacific, Noranda, Grupo Ultra, and ABB Canada.

Phillips is the author of several proprietary instruments, such as the Universal Management Dimensions Model, the Strategic Implementation Process, ChangeLeaders, and Executive Succession and Leadership Development. His work has centered around the dynamics of mind-set change models at the executive level. While the bulk of his consulting has been in North America, he also works with CEOs and boards of directors in Europe and the Pacific Rim.